I0819145

AN ILLUSTRATED ENCYCLOPEDIA OF

UNIFORMS OF THE AMERICAN WAR OF INDEPENDENCE

1775–1783

AN ILLUSTRATED ENCYCLOPEDIA OF

UNIFORMS OF THE AMERICAN WAR OF INDEPENDENCE 1775–1783

An expert guide to the uniforms of the American militias and Continental Army, the armies and navies of Great Britain and France, German and Spanish units, and American Indian allies

DIGBY SMITH • KEVIN F. KILEY • CONSULTANT: JEREMY BLACK MBE

LORENZ BOOKS

This edition is published by Lorenz Books
an imprint of Anness Publishing Ltd
info@anness.com
www.lorenz books.com
www.annesspublishing.com

Publisher: Joanna Lorenz
Editorial Director: Helen Sudell
Executive Editor: Joanne Rippin
Illustrations: Rob McCaig, Jim Mitchell, Carlo Molinari, Giuseppe Rava, Simon Smith, Tony Sanchez, Nick Spender; map and plans: Peter Bull Studio
Designer: Nigel Partridge
Production Controller: Ben Worley

Frontispiece: George Washington leads his troops.

CONTENTS

INTRODUCTION 6

THE FORGING OF A NATION 8

THE FOUNDING OF AMERICA 10
COLONIZATION AND EMIGRATION 12
THE FRENCH AND INDIAN WAR 14
TENSIONS IN THE COLONIES 16
THE BALANCE OF POWER IN EUROPE 18
AMERICA'S FIRST STEPS TO NATIONHOOD 20
THE AMERICAN ARMY 22
THE BRITISH ARMY 24
THE FRENCH ARMY 26
OTHER COMBATANTS IN THE WAR 28
BATTLES AND CAMPAIGNS 30
THE NAVAL WAR 44

MILITIAS, EARLY CONTINENTAL UNITS AND STATE TROOPS 46

MILITIA AND STATE TROOPS 48
PRE-WAR MILITIA UNITS 50
THE MINUTEMEN 52
MILITIA INFANTRY 54
THE FIRST CONTINENTALS 58
THE CANADIAN REGIMENTS 62
THE MASSACHUSETTS AND NEW YORK CONTINENTALS 64
MILITIA CAVALRY AND ARTILLERY 66
THE PHILADELPHIA CITY TROOP OF LIGHT HORSE 68
REGIMENTS ON THE FRONTIER 70
CONTINENTAL REGIMENTS: 1776 72
ADDITIONAL CONTINENTAL REGIMENTS: 1777 76
THE PHILADELPHIA ASSOCIATORS 80
RIFLEMEN AND THE STOCKBRIDGE INDIANS 82
STATE TROOPS 84
STATE ARTILLERY UNITS 86

THE CONTINENTAL ARMY 88

THOSE RAGGED CONTINENTALS 90
COMMANDERS AND STAFF 92
HEADQUARTERS TROOPS 94
CONTINENTAL INFANTRY 96
COLOURS AND STANDARDS 102
LIGHT INFANTRY 104
UNIFORM REGULATIONS OF 1779 106
LEGIONS AND PARTISANS 112
CONTINENTAL CAVALRY 114
CONTINENTAL ARTILLERY 118
SPECIALIST TROOPS 122

SOLDIERS OF THE KING 124

THE ARMY OF THE BRITISH EMPIRE 126
COMMANDERS AND STAFF 128
INFANTRY 130
FOOT GUARDS 132
ROYAL REGIMENTS 134
FUSILIERS 136
HIGHLAND REGIMENTS 138
IRISH REGIMENTS 140
ENGLISH REGIMENTS 142
COLOURS AND STANDARDS 144
GRENADIERS 147
LIGHT INFANTRY 148
CAVALRY 150
ARTILLERY 152
SPECIALIST TROOPS 154
AMERICAN LOYALIST INFANTRY 156
LOYALIST CAVALRY 160
RANGERS 162
LOYALIST MILITIA 164
AMERICAN INDIANS 166

THE FRENCH, GERMANS AND SPANISH 168

ALLIES AND MERCENARIES 170
FRENCH COMMANDERS AND STAFF 172
FRENCH INFANTRY 174
COLOURS AND STANDARDS 176
ROCHAMBEAU'S EXPEDITIONARY FORCE AND COLONIAL TROOPS 178
FRENCH CAVALRY AND LEGIONS 182
FRENCH ARTILLERY 184
THE GRIBEAUVAL ARTILLERY SYSTEM 186
HESSE-CASSEL INFANTRY 188
HESSE-CASSEL ARTILLERY 190
BRUNSWICK INFANTRY 192
BRUNSWICK CAVALRY 194
ANSPACH-BAYREUTH, ANHALT-ZERBST AND WALDECK 196
HESSE-HANAU 200
GERMAN *JÄGERS* 202
SPAIN 204

THE NAVAL FORCES OF THE WAR 208

THE WAR AT SEA 210
SHIPS OF THE LINE AND FRIGATES 212
SLOOPS, CORVETTES, BRIGS, SCHOONERS AND PRIVATEERS 216
GUNBOATS, GUNDALOWS AND GALLEYS 218
ROYAL NAVY OFFICERS 220
ROYAL NAVY SEAMEN 222
BRITISH MARINES 224
FRENCH ROYAL NAVY 226
FRENCH SEAMEN 228
FRENCH NAVAL ARTILLERY AND NAVAL INFANTRY 230
NAVAL GARRISONS 232
CONTINENTAL NAVY OFFICERS 234
PETTY OFFICERS AND SEAMEN 236
CONTINENTAL MARINES 238
GUN CREWS 240
AMERICAN STATE NAVIES 242
NAVAL ORDNANCE 246
LANDING PARTIES 248

GLOSSARY 250
INDEX 252
ACKNOWLEDGEMENTS 256

INTRODUCTION

The period after 1763 should have been one of peace and prosperity in the English colonies of North America. The ancient enemy, France, had been thoroughly defeated in the long war of 1754–63 in both Europe and North America, and the British were dominant on the sea, the ubiquitous Royal Navy reigning supreme over a colonial empire that extended around the globe. Internally, the American Indians had largely been suppressed, except for a brief, intense resurgence in 1763, and English colonists, now calling themselves Americans, cheered and toasted the British troops that had helped them against both the French and the Indians.

Trouble, however, was just over the horizon. The American colonies had been largely left to govern themselves by the British Crown and Parliament during their development from 1608, and only in the recent war were large numbers of British troops committed to garrisoning the country. Also, Great Britain had a very large financial deficit following the war, and Parliament believed that the North American colonies should share in paying off the debt as a quid pro quo act of responsibility. Without consulting any of the colonial governments, Parliament imposed taxes and restrictions on the colonies that Americans interpreted as a restriction of their independence and liberty and provoked many to think of breaking away from the mother country.

▼ The surrender of General John Burgoyne, to Horatio Gates at the Battle of Saratoga, was the turning point of the war.

A Social Contract

This was also the Age of Enlightenment and the Age of Reason, in which men started to think and write about their rights as individuals, and the responsibilities of governments and kings to those they governed. This idea of a social contract threatened the age-old doctrine of the divine right of kings. Colonialists started to believe in self-rule and in government that was not based on a monarchy.

The Second Continental Congress, a body of representatives from all walks of life appointed by the legislatures of 13 British North American colonies, was set up on 10 May 1775. This body acted as the de facto national government of the United States by raising armies, directing strategy, appointing diplomats, and making formal treaties.

▲ Thomas Jefferson drafting America's declaration of independence from Britain, one of the first steps to nationhood.

Rebellion or Revolution?

The whisper of insurgency began to be heard across America, first in taverns, homes and churches; then in the state legislatures and among the gentry. Secret societies were formed, and colonial governments, as well as local governments, formed more militia units to defend themselves from what they saw as English tyranny. Rioting broke out in Massachusetts against the king's troops, and revolutionaries preached open rebellion. British troops were once again sent to the colonies, landing in Boston and becoming a de facto garrison of this revolutionary hotbed. Most of the other colonies were either apathetic to the situation or still loyal to the Crown, but there was enough support for open rebellion to make the situation critical.

Some members of the English Parliament who supported the Americans and their grievances were partially successful in repealing some of the more resented acts of taxation, but it was too little, too late. New England was arming clandestinely, and sometimes openly, and support from the other colonies was mounting.

▲ *The early English colonies of North America had matured into the first 13 states by the time the War of Independence began.*

The Armed Forces

There was no standing army in the colonies when the fighting started. The colonies had myriad militia units of varying worth and expertise, but there were no regular units to put into the field. There were, however, men with hard-won fighting experience against the French and Indians, and this was a basis around which an army could be built. Congress' wisest act was to appoint George Washington as the commander of the newly-named Continental Army, a man equal to the Herculean task given to him. He and Benjamin Franklin were truly the indispensable men of the struggle.

Washington's nascent Continentals and the local militias were indifferently clothed, equipped, and disciplined. Washington, however, knew what was necessary, and laboured long and hard to achieve it, with the assistance of European professionals and home-grown soldiers. Washington's subordinates strived to provide clothing and equipment from diverse sources and to put uniformity into the ranks, even producing the one American contribution to uniformology, the hunting shirt. The army they forged faced the hardened British and German professionals on the battlefield and fought a bitter conflict that eventually resulted in an American victory.

The British had their own problems. Without the manpower needed to fight a war of this type, they were forced to hire substantial numbers of mercenaries from the German states of central Europe, thereby deploying the largest expeditionary force ever to leave their shores.

Alliance and Independence

The war spread far beyond the shores of North America. Fighting took place there and in Europe, and in the East and West Indies, and progressed from the suppression of a rebellion into a fight for the survival of the British Empire. It was a bitter struggle, taking on the aspects of civil war in parts of the new United States, and was the first time colonies separated successfully from a mother country in history. The resulting loss to Great Britain of what could have been the jewel in its crown was immense in both revenue and prestige, and it would not go unnoticed around the world.

Further, the initially impudent and generally impotent Declaration of Independence became a beacon around the world of how the people could control their destiny. Written as a founding document for a new nation, it would later spawn the Declaration of the Rights of Man that swept across Europe during 23 years of almost continuous warfare, changing the world forever. America's independence in 1783 gave birth to an autonomous nation that would change the scope, shape, and destiny of world history. What also happened, however, was that Britain and her former colonies would eventually forge an alliance that would stand the test of time.

▼ *Washington's military and political skills were vital for America's success in the war.*

THE FORGING OF A NATION

The year 1763 was a momentous one for Great Britain. The ancient enemy, France, had been utterly defeated, its navy destroyed and its army in tatters. British colonies and holdings in India had been expanded, and in North America the French had been expelled from Canada. While protecting the 13 North American colonies from the French and their American Indian allies, British Regulars had overcome a skilled and deadly enemy that had harassed the British colonists for over 100 years. Great Britain reigned over an American empire that ranged from the Atlantic to the Mississippi River and from Florida to the northern reaches of Canada. This was all about to change.

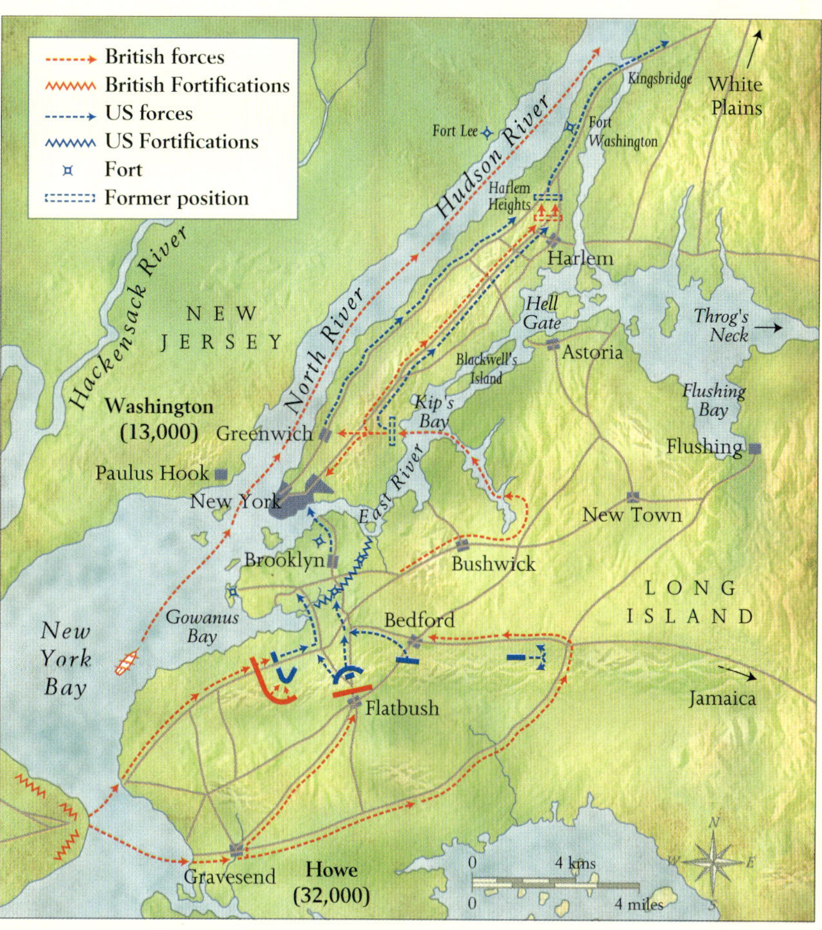

▲ *The Battle of Long Island was a disaster for Washington and the Continental Army. It was Washington's worst defeat, and one from which most armies would not have recovered.*

◀ *This heroic portrayal of Washington crossing the Delaware to attack the Hessian post at Trenton, New Jersey, typifies the attitude among the Continentals to conquer or die trying.*

THE FOUNDING OF AMERICA

The European discovery of the Americas was a seminal event in world history. Christopher Columbus was on his way from Spain to find a new, westward route to Asia and the East Indies. He had little idea that a huge landmass was to curtail his voyage, and he mistakenly named the natives he found 'Indians'.

The Conquest of America

While Columbus' discovery of the New World was accidental, Spain, Portugal and other seagoing European powers were quick to exploit the windfall. In the course of the following centuries, Great Britain, France, Sweden and the United Provinces (more often known by contemporaries as Holland) would also join in the race for territory and riches in the 'new land', and this quickly became yet another bone of contention for the powers of Europe, both great and not-so-great.

Spain and Portugal had a head start and quickly established colonies in Central and South America. To avoid war between the two powers, an appeal was made to the Pope, who, with the aid of extremely inaccurate maps, declared a 'line of demarcation' through South America. Both parties considered it fair at the time of the Treaty of Tordesillas (1494), which confirmed the division, but, as mapping became more of an exact science, it was later discovered by the two antagonists that Spain had received the lion's share of the disputed territories, Portugal receiving only what is now Brazil.

▼ *Columbus' 1492 landing on the island of Hispaniola marked the European discovery of America and the misnaming of its natives.*

▲ *Jamestown was the first English settlement in North America. The site of the fort, seen here being built, was rediscovered in 1994.*

A stream of explorers, soldiers of fortune, adventurers and merchants was let loose upon the Americas to search for land to conquer and exploit for the benefit of the crowned heads of Europe and the countries they ruled.

It was Spain, soon to be the most powerful European empire, newly purged of the Moorish menace and more than ready for new conquests, that despatched the most expeditions to the New World looking for treasure, lands to conquer and fame. Hernando Cortes invaded and destroyed the powerful and feared Aztec Empire with 500 men and willing Indian allies who had been mistreated by the Aztecs. Francisco Pizarro entered Peru and conquered the Incas, discovering the potato in the process. Vasco Nunez de Balboa reached the Pacific, naming that "peaceful" sea. Juan Ponce de Leon ventured into Florida, where the first permanent European settlement in North America would be established at St Augustine. Francisco Vasquez de Coronado went north from Mexico into what is now the south-west United States looking for the Seven Cities of Cibola, stories of which the American Indians swore were true.

Portugal also played the game of conquest. Prince Henry of Portugal, dubbed 'the Navigator', sent forth captains intent on discovery. Ferdinand Magellan circumnavigated the globe at his prince's behest, dying on the way but being brought home by his depleted crews.

Later Britain and France cautiously sent privateers westward both to keep an eye on Spanish adventures and to return home with news, and spoils, from the New World. The Dutch also carefully despatched their fine ships and competent captains to North America, one of them charting a large river that runs through what is now New York State and which bears the name of its discoverer, Henry Hudson.

Ultimately, it would be down to three major European powers to divide the Americas among them. Spain, France and Britain colonized their respective territories in different ways. The Spanish and French both sought to exploit what they had either claimed or conquered, while the English built permanent settlements that began to absorb immigrants from Europe. Not only English, but Scots and Irish, Germans and French migrated to the British colonies and settled there. These colonies, eventually 13 in number, also absorbed what the Dutch and Swedes had tried to build. They were elbowed out of North America by the English, forcing those northern European powers elsewhere.

The Spanish were direct and to the point. They wanted immense wealth, gold specifically, which they needed to finance their aggressive policies in Europe. They exploited the indigenous peoples they conquered, destroying what had been and enslaving the populations, many of the captives dying from disease and ill-treatment. Fleets of treasure ships launched from New World ports for Spain, sometimes being ambushed by pirates or privateers, acting with official government licence.

France sent some colonists to Canada following the founding of Quebec in 1608. Those that went, while having an interest in the same areas along North America's eastern coastline, eventually moved northward and settled in what is now Canada, dubbing it 'New France' and claiming the territory for their king. These *voyageurs* ranged far and wide through New France, and also explored Ohio, the Great Lakes and down the Mississippi Valley, claiming all they saw for their sovereign. By accident or design, they effectively hemmed in the budding English colonies along the coastline, which would later be a strategic advantage in the wars that would begin in earnest with the advent of the reign of the 'Sun King', Louis XIV. The French colonists sided early with the native Algonquins, who made steadfast and deadly allies. France, however, was a European sea power, and so the colonies were under the Ministère de la Marine, and deemed a naval concern. The French Navy, which had been carefully built by able ministers, was neglected by Louis, who was more interested in European conquests, and barely enough was done by officers and administrators to establish an effective administration and military organization.

▼ *The European settlers in North America fought many bloody wars with the Indians, with little quarter given on either side.*

Britain's Colonies

The British were the most interested, and most enterprising of the European colonial powers. There were more than enough prospective colonists to send to North America. England was crowded and people wanted land. This was an available commodity in the colonies in America – the idea that the native Indians were there first barely caused a pause for thought. The plethora of religions that existed in Europe because of the Protestant Reformation, and the religious wars and persecutions that followed, also swelled the ranks of those willing to leave their familiar surroundings in Britain and Ireland, and the Continent, and venture forth to what for them must have been akin to stepping off the edge of the world.

▲ *William Penn, a Quaker for whom Pennsylvania is named, established a colony that allowed religious freedom, and laboured long and hard to develop and sustain good relations with the Indian tribes.*

Elizabeth of England, involved in a life and death struggle with Philip II of Spain, and soon to face the huge Armada that the Spanish finally sent against her, began the process by establishing colonies on the eastern coast of North America. The first, at what was called Roanoke, disappeared without a trace, but others clung on, such as Jamestown in Virginia in 1607, named after James I, Elizabeth's successor. The Massachusetts Bay colony was founded by Puritans from England in 1630 and with these settlements began a long struggle with the North American Indians, which would not be settled until more than a century after independence.

COLONIZATION AND EMIGRATION

The colonists came by ship across the Atlantic, weathering storms, seasickness and disease. Three small ships anchored off Jamestown, in Virginia, an area named after Elizabeth, the Virgin Queen. Further north, along the stark, dreary coast of what later became New England, the Puritans landed in the *Mayflower* in 1620.

▲ *The 1620 landing in Massachusetts was a mistake but resulted in a successful colony.*

The Thirteen Colonies

Life was hard in these fledgling settlements. Many people died of disease, neglect and the harsh elements, but, helped by their own innate toughness and the aid of some of the American Indians, many survived. More settlers followed to expand the fledgling colonies. At first, the colonies were proprietary in nature, with individuals in the Crown's favour given colonies to rule and run for profit. This system, however, was open to corruption, and the Crown began to appoint royal governors to rule instead.

Virginia, the first colony, grew into the richest and looked down on the others, especially her southern neighbours in the Carolinas. There, the claimed territory began as one colony, but later split into two. Georgia was founded by the able James Oglethorpe, who led convicts and adventurers into the wilderness and stayed there. His first settlement, Savannah, resembled a military camp when first built.

▼ *The Dutch ship* Half Moon, *sailing down the river in New York State that now bears her captain Henry Hudson's name, in 1609.*

Tiny Rhode Island was founded by religious refugees from Massachusetts. Ironically, the original settlers from the larger colony, who had sought religious freedom, were adamant about not giving it to others. New Hampshire would also break away from Massachusetts by 1691. Connecticut was wrested from the Dutch in the 1630s. Quaker William Penn founded Pennsylvania and allowed religious freedom, even to the hated Catholics, and Cecilius Calvert, later Lord Baltimore, founded Maryland and allowed religious freedom for all, a measure that pleased Catholics who had been shunned and persecuted in other colonies.

Other colonies were founded and grew or changed allegiance. New York was originally established by the Dutch and named New Amsterdam but was finally taken and held by the stronger British. The New Amsterdam colony was renamed New York in honour of the Duke of York. New Jersey was also taken from the Dutch in 1664, as was the colony of Delaware.

These "English" colonies were populated by more than just English settlers, however. Those heading to the New World were predominantly northern Europeans and included people from Scotland, Ireland, Germany and Switzerland, who had been displaced by war or intolerance. Each group brought its traditions and customs with it, and each developed ruling legislatures, subject to the Royal Governor – modelled on the English Parliament – and court systems in which English common law held sway.

Slavery was also brought to the colonies. The introduction of African slaves to North America occurred at Jamestown shortly after the settlement was established. A Spanish ship with a small number of slaves on board for sale or trade stopped there en route to the West Indies. The Spanish captain ended up selling or trading the slaves

▲ *The first African slaves in North America were sold by Spanish traders docking at Jamestown, Virginia, in the early 1600s.*

he held to the colonists, so without any political decision the 'peculiar institution' became part of the economics of the English colonies.

Along with social and legal structures, the British also brought their military systems to the colonies. From the beginning, militia companies, charged with the defence of the colony, were formed by the fledgling governments. The colonists faced a hostile environment but also faced a potentially hostile native population, and their ability to handle their relationship with the American Indians would be key both to their survival and to the future of the colonies singularly and as a whole.

Colonies at War

The colonists quickly found that European tactics, armour and attitudes were not suited to the woodland environment in which they found themselves. In addition, the American Indians used tactics that were unfamiliar to the colonists, who had to adapt their own methods of fighting or lose. The Indians were skilled hunters, warriors and scouts; they were also expert woodsmen who could make the terrain fight for them and seemingly enhance their numbers by the use of the dense wilderness. The colonists suffered many disasters and embarrassments at the hands of the Indians before acquiring the necessary skills to meet the Indian on equal terms. Raiding, ambushing and skirmishing in the woods were skills that had to be learned, and the American Indian was the best teacher, even as an opponent. More often than not the greatest fear of the farmer on the edge of the wilderness, or the townsman in a stockaded settlement on the frontier, was the war whoop out of the night and the sound of Indian hatchets at the door, backed up by the ubiquitous Frenchmen who came stealthily across iced-over lakes and across snow drifts to kill and burn.

The Indian Wars were sanguinary, brutal on both sides, and frequently without quarter. The Carolinas were ravaged by the Yamassee in 1715 and 1716. There were frequent massacres of settlers in New England as the colonists encroached on Indian lands. Deerfield was attacked by the French and Indians in 1704 in a winter assault that was accomplished by troops getting over the walls of the town by clambering up the snow banks that had been allowed to build up against the wooden palisade.

No less deadly were the Europeans fighting each other. The French Fort Caroline in Florida (near present-day Jacksonville) was attacked and taken by the Spanish in 1565, its garrison massacred, and turned into a Spanish colony. In 1568 the French took the fort, burned it, and hanged captured Spaniards for "robbery and murder".

In spite of these conflicts and reverses of fortune, the new settlers kept arriving in enough numbers to survive war, hardship, disease and starvation. Eventually, all 13 colonies not only maintained themselves, but thrived, prospered and became one of the most important territories in a nascent British empire.

▲ *Roger Williams founded the city of Providence in what would become Rhode Island. While in Massachusetts, he acted as mediator with the Indian tribes, specifically the Pequots, Mohicans, and Narragansets.*

▼ *By the 1660s, the early colonies were well established and thriving, as seen in this depiction of Boston, Massachusetts.*

THE FRENCH AND INDIAN WAR

Wars fought in America usually echoed the succession of wars in Europe in the 17th and 18th centuries. The War of the Grand Alliance (also known as the War of the League of Augsburg) was dubbed King William's War in America (1689–97). The War of the Spanish Succession (1701–13) became Queen Anne's War in America and the War of the Austrian Succession 1740–8 was known as King George's War by the Americans who fought in and lived through it.

Conflicts in the Americas were fought by the colonists with relatively little assistance from Britain. Britain viewed its colonies as valuable assets yet, paradoxically, established a system sometimes referred to as 'benign neglect'. As long as the colonies produced what the mother country needed or dictated, she left their internal affairs alone. Small numbers of British troops were sometimes sent to the colonies to help, but most of the fighting was done by provincial troops raised by the colonies.

The number of British regiments in North America was increased dramatically during the French and Indian War, a clash that began in 1754, in which a young Virginian militia officer, George Washington, fought. Starting as a small, backwoods clash, the conflict escalated into a full-scale war that raged across two continents and beyond until 1763. Britain and Prussia faced France, Russia and Austria in Europe while France and Great Britain also fought each other in North America, Africa and India.

French and British Interests

The objectives of the two main belligerents were diametrically opposed. Great Britain was fighting for an empire and dedicated most of her assets to that aim. France, on the other hand, was mainly a European power, and her overseas colonies took second place. The French did despatch some regular regiments to Canada to support the effort there, but it was insufficient compared to the resources the British government of William Pitt the Elder dedicated to North America.

For the first time, large numbers of British regulars were sent to North America to aid the colonists in their fight against the French and Indians. Although it could not be foreseen at the time, and though the Americans rejoiced in the help they received from Britain, it was also the beginning of a decline in the relationship between the two countries, and the start of what was to be perceived later as British interference in American affairs.

▼ *General Braddock's force marches on Fort Duquesne, Pennsylvania, an expedition that ended in disaster for the British.*

▲ *The young Colonel Washington almost single-handedly began the French and Indian War by ambushing a party of French soldiers and American Indians.*

Early Campaigns

The early part of the war in North America was disastrous for the British. The French and their Indian allies rampaged across the northern frontier in New England and New York, burning and scalping their way from farms to settlements and terrorizing the frontier settlers. French forts in the Ohio Valley ringed the colonies and provided bases from which damaging raids could be staged. The first British expedition against Fort Duquesne (near what is now Pittsburgh), commanded by General Edward Braddock, was met by a force of the French and Indians in an engagement that was disastrous for the British, and in which Braddock was mortally wounded. His aide-de-camp, George Washington, was distinguished by his coolness under fire, but the move against the Ohio Valley was defeated.

▲ *Both the French and British had Indian allies that fought long and hard for them.*

The British forces were obviously disorganized, led by commanders who did not understand woodland warfare, contemptuous of the American Provincial units that were sent to fight beside them, and ineffectual against the French and American Indians, who appeared to be able to strike when and where they pleased.

The French had sent one of their most talented commanders to North America, the Marquis Louis-Joseph de Montcalm-Grozon, who listened both to his Indian allies (within reason) and to officers who had been in North America for years. He destroyed Fort William Henry on Lake George and held strongholds at Ticonderoga and Crown Point on Lake Champlain.

The Tables Turn

By this time William Pitt had assumed leadership of the British government and was determined to win decisively in North America. He chose a trio of competent British generals – James Wolfe, John Forbes and Jeffrey Amherst – to take command of the British army in America, under the overall direction of Amherst. Wolfe was sent against Louisburg and Quebec. Forbes undertook the expedition into the Ohio Valley, and Amherst took command of the main theatre in upper New York State.

Wolfe took Louisburg and immediately set out against Quebec, the capital of New France. The campaign was not initially successful and proved frustrating for all involved. However, Wolfe was determined to succeed, and his British light infantry and American rangers cleared a way up the heights, overwhelming the French outposts before they could raise the alarm. Morning saw the 5,000-man British army formed for battle on the Plains of Abraham to the west of Quebec. Montcalm, commanding the French, attacked. Holding their fire until the last possible moment, the tightly disciplined British fired at close range, ruining the French attack and mortally wounding Montcalm. The British followed this up with a bayonet attack, routing the French, although Wolfe expired on the battlefield.

Forbes, mortally ill, advanced his campaign against Fort Duquesne. More cautious and a better tactician than his predecessor, Forbes pressed on into the Ohio Valley and took Duquesne without firing a shot. The French abandoned and destroyed the works before the British arrival.

Amherst pressed his offensives from the British base at Crown Point. Robert Rogers and his rangers were sent against the Abenaki stronghold of St Francis in an epic raid, destroying the Indian town that had raided into New England for years. Amherst's forces inched up Lake Champlain, and by 1760, Montreal had been taken and the French hold on Canada and the Ohio Valley was broken. Great Britain had won itself an overseas empire, while the fall of Quebec signalled the death knell of the French North American empire. Only two powers remained in North America with holdings of any consequence: Great Britain and Spain. The Americans were ecstatic. The French threat was gone, and all looked forward to peace and prosperity under the British Crown.

▼ *In 1759, General James Wolfe laid siege to and took Quebec, defeating the French. But both he and the French commander, General Montcalm, were mortally wounded.*

TENSIONS IN THE COLONIES

Following the victory over France, Great Britain was financially exhausted from her contribution to Prussia's war chest and the huge effort she had expended in North America. Believing, rightly, that the American colonies should help shoulder the burden of national debt, Parliament, with the wholehearted agreement of the new king, George III, planned taxes for the Americans that would offset the debt.

Tensions and Strains

The prospering American colonies were rich in natural resources, especially those resources that a mercantilist power such as Britain required. American merchants and shipbuilders had become both rich and famous. American ports such as New York, Boston, Savannah and Charleston were centres of the 'triangular trade' in which American slavers departed from colonial ports, picked up African slaves in western Africa, sailed to the West Indies and traded some slaves for rum and other goods, and brought their cargoes to American ports.

There were restrictions such as the Navigation Acts, periodically enacted by Parliament, which both restricted American trade with powers other than Britain and hindered the development of manufacturing in the colonies in order to keep them dependent on the mother country for finished goods. These were usually ignored by the entrepreneurial Americans, and not only was illicit trade conducted with other powers, but budding manufacturing industries blossomed, especially in the north.

The southern colonies formed an agrarian society. Large plantations, owned by the gentry, grew immensely rich from keeping their labour costs down by using slaves. From the first small group of African slaves that had landed at Jamestown at its shaky beginnings, slavery had now become an industry, and flourished across the Atlantic until it was outlawed in 1807.

▼ *After the successful conclusion of the French and Indian War, England's Parliament was faced with the bill, which was immense.*

▲ *The successful suppression of Pontiac's uprising led to the Proclamation of 1763, which further alienated the Americans.*

American Indian Unrest

Other strains on the colonies came from their relationship with the native Indians. The end of the French and Indian war and the subsequent Treaty of Paris had ignored the situation of the North American Indian tribes. The main problem the Indians had was that they were not nations or states in the European sense, but were tribes who changed allegiance and fought each other. Seldom in their history was there a leader who could unite the tribes in a common goal. One such was Pontiac, who, dissatisfied with the new status quo, and unhappy with the incursion of the English colonists across the Allegheny Mountains, united a significant number of Indian tribes to fight the British.

The uprising was carefully planned and skilfully conducted. Seemingly peaceful Indians playing lacrosse outside the gates of British forts suddenly rushed the opened gates and slaughtered the garrison. Several British outposts were taken by Pontiac's men in this way, and only a few, such as the former French stronghold at newly named Pittsburgh, held out. However, Pontiac's initial success was short-lived. Troops, both British and Provincial, were mustered and sent to put down the insurgency. Under skilled officers such as Henry Bouquet, the Indians were defeated in the field and the rebellion suppressed.

Pontiac did accomplish one unintended objective. The British government passed the Proclamation of 1763, which forbade any colonial expansion past the Appalachians, sowing the seeds for a larger and ultimately successful rebellion that became colonial revolution.

This Act of Parliament was followed by a series of taxes put on goods, requiring stamps on official documents, all of which required that the Americans pay a fee, largely nominal though it was, on many of their activities and on goods that they consumed from Britain. What this led to was furious and active contempt for the king, his Parliament, ministers and representatives, including the royal governors, that would eventually culminate in open warfare.

English Attitude

King George's government felt fully within its rights to levy what it saw as reasonable taxes on its colonies. Huge sums had been expended sending both an army and a fleet to aid the colonists in this last, victorious war with the French. The Americans had been rescued from the attacks of the French and American Indians and, it was thought, needed to repay the mother country for the privilege of being defended.

Ministers in England proposed courses of action to generate revenue, which Parliament duly passed, with no one thinking to explain to the Americans what it was for and that it was expected of all subjects of the Crown.

Another tension between England and America was the contempt some Britons in high positions seemed to feel for Americans, a sense of superiority that was exacerbated by dealings with them late in the war. The English almost always ignored American effort and losses in the war, even though British regular regiments had recruited during the war from among the American populace and those recruits served just as well and gallantly as those recruited in England, Ireland, Scotland and Wales.

Discontent Turns to Rebellion

Another problem was that the royal governors did not work through their respective colony's legislatures to ease the transition of an increase in taxes with influential citizens. The king, Parliament and the governors believed that if a law was passed it had to be imposed and, therefore, obeyed. Protest or disgruntlement was to be treated as treason.

The trouble began with a trickle of discontent in New England, and the tension built a momentum all of its own. Unchecked, the discontent turned to rebellion. Disgruntled colonists met in town meeting halls and churches to air their complaints. Committees were formed to protest against the taxes and representatives in the colonial legislatures brought the issues up for debate. Shortly afterwards, some Americans began thinking of independence, and began to seriously contemplate a war of liberation.

▼ *Tobacco was a valuable cash crop, and fortunes were made on the backs of African slaves who first came ashore at Jamestown.*

▼ *British tax collectors were not popular with the Americans. Here, one has been tarred and feathered, and is being force fed tea. After being refreshed, this unfortunate would be ridden out of town.*

THE BALANCE OF POWER IN EUROPE

Meanwhile, back in Europe there was a new balance of power. Great Britain, now the leading colonial power in the world, Spain notwithstanding, was not a major land power and had no desire to be. Her ambition for the European continent and its almost constantly warring powers was that there should be a balance of power in Europe. Britain's foreign policy was, and was to remain for almost the next two centuries, that no one European power should be dominant on the continent.

France had been knocked into almost total military impotence. Easily the nation with the largest population, save Russia, France was also an ambitious nation that had, until recently, terrified the crowned heads of Europe. The wars of Louis XIV had ravaged Europe for decades, and France had developed the most modern and dominant army on the continent. Its defeat in the Seven Years' War had changed all that, at least for the time being. Its army was badly in need of reform, and the navy had to be completely rebuilt. Inevitably there were generals and admirals who were ready to do just that and wait for an opportune moment for revenge.

▼ *Frederick the Great at the Battle of Kolin 1757. The Prussian king was Great Britain's ally during the Seven Years' War.*

Prussia, Russia and Austria

In 1763, at the close of hostilities, emergent Prussia had become Europe's dominant military power. It had outlasted its enemies, and enhanced the brilliance and reputation of Frederick the Great. Russia had pulled out of the war with Prussia when the Empress Elizabeth died. The new Tsar was an admirer of Frederick and would not consent to keep Russia in the field against him.

Russia was a puzzling nation to most Europeans. Russian armies were a combination of green-clad regulars with plenty of artillery, and a horde of irregulars (Cossacks, Kalmucks, Bashkirs) controlled, or not, by Russian commanders who had little idea as to how many such irregulars were with any field army. More Asian than European, Russia had been modernized by Peter the Great, and his ruthless manner of despotic rule. Russia was always a wild card when it came to European politics and power. It didn't have the best troops in Europe, but they were plentiful and Russian commanders expended them to further the Tsar's aims.

With Russia neutralized and France ruined, Austria had no choice but to seek peace in 1763, leaving Frederick with the gains he had made in both the War of the Austrian Succession and the Seven Years' War. Prussia's former enemies had also left it with an invincible military reputation that would last until Napoleon destroyed Prussia and its army in 1806.

The Hapsburgs of Austria had undertaken certain military reforms after the War of the Austrian Succession, notably in the army's artillery arm, which became the best in Europe by 1763 and had given Frederick some nasty surprises. Though technically defeated in the Seven Years' War, Austria remained a strong and dominant power in Europe, and, always land-hungry, the Hapsburgs eyed territory in Poland and Bavaria with envy. They also had to face and deal with the Turks, against whom they would be the aggressor under Maria-Theresa's successor, Joseph II.

France Recovers

The reform-minded generals and admirals in France would have been powerless to rebuild the army and fleet without an alliance with certain powerful ministers who came to power after the shooting stopped. With revenge definitely in mind, and lessons thoroughly learned, the army was overhauled, new tactics in manoeuvres were experimented with, particularly in Normandy in the 1770s, and the French artillery arm was completely reformed. Under the remarkable artilleryman, Jean-Baptiste de Gribeauval, who had seen and studied both the Prussian and the Austrian artillery, new, well-balanced and light field artillery pieces were cast and tested, and new tactics were practised, emphasizing infantry/artillery co-operation on the battlefield.

The French Navy was entirely reformed and rebuilt, French naval designs being the best in the world at the time. Beautiful frigates and ships of the line came off the slipways that were better designed and faster than the comparable British classes. French naval bases and arsenals were rebuilt and reorganized to support the new fleet, and by the mid-1770s, both the French Army and Navy were ready to take the fight to the British once again. These reforms would bear fruit for France and the new United States with the coming of the Alliance in 1778.

▲ *This portrait of Teodoro de Croix, Viceroy of Peru and Chile, illustrates Spain's proud presence in South America.*

Spain and Holland

The Spanish and Dutch were no longer major players in the European power game. Spain still had a respectable army, but the ships in its navy were outdated and under-resourced. However, British military leaders believed that Spain could be a force to be reckoned with if allied with a major power. One of Britain's worst fears was the threat that would be posed by a combined Franco-Spanish fleet.

Spanish holdings in North America were still considerable and Spain still had its empire in Central and South America. The troops stationed in its colonies were well-organized and led, and would prove to be a threat to the British in Florida when war broke out. Both the Spanish and the Dutch would enter the war on the side of France, but unlike France would not conclude an alliance with the United States. The contributions of these two powers to the war would be in drawing off valuable British resources that could have been used to quell the rebellion and in making the war a world war. Their struggle with Britain would be to settle old scores and to conquer or reconquer overseas colonies that swelled the coffers of the nations that owned them. For Spain, war was a chance to retake Gibraltar, which had been lost to Britain in 1704, and overturn an affront to Spanish pride.

The Dutch opted to make their main colonial effort against the British in the East Indies. No Dutch soldier set foot in North America during the war, and no Dutch warship sailed in support of the Americans against the British. While their French and Spanish allies were hardly selfless in their support of the Americans, the policy of the Dutch resembled a vulture going after carrion.

▼ *The new, reformed French Navy had newly built ships that were better designed and faster than those of the British Navy, and its fleet took to the seas with revenge in mind.*

AMERICA'S FIRST STEPS TO NATIONHOOD

The 13 separate colonies that made up part of British North America in 1775 spoke the same language and were similar in traditions, local and colonial government, religion and origin. Yet there were many important differences. The colonies were not united in purpose, and each administration proceeded down a separate path to achieve its particular goal. Since their separate founding and establishment, the colonies had more or less depended on themselves to implement policy and to govern trade with the mother country. For the colonists to begin to consider themselves Americans was a slow and gradual process. Most still considered themselves English and were loyal to the Crown.

Colonial Expansion

Geographically and economically, the colonies were divided into three groups: New England in the north-east (Massachusetts, Rhode Island, Connecticut and New Hampshire); the Middle Colonies (New York, Pennsylvania, New Jersey, Delaware and Maryland); and the South (Virginia, North and South Carolina and Georgia). Seven of them were Crown colonies with a royal governor (New Hampshire, New Jersey, New York, Virginia, Georgia and the Carolinas); three were still proprietary colonies (Pennsylvania, Delaware and Maryland); and the three remaining (Massachusetts, Connecticut and Rhode Island) were corporate colonies.

▼ *The Americans' desire to claim new lands to the west bought them into direct conflict with England's anti-expansion laws.*

▲ *Fur trading with the tribes was very lucrative for the colonists; the Indians received a very poor deal for their valuable pelts.*

New England had a thriving shipping industry, with many Americans going to sea to earn a living, and sometimes make a fortune, while others profited from all the maritime activity (one merchant from Salem, Massachusetts, became the colonies' first millionaire before 1770). Farming was not a profitable business in New England, with short summers and long winters, and the land itself being rocky and not as fertile as the south.

The Middle Colonies were probably the most profitable, the land being suitable to make a profit from farming, supported by a lively merchant class. There was also a manufacturing base, though it was largely forbidden by the mother country. Those who wished to go into the forbidden manufacturing trades did so anyway, regardless of regulation or punishment. By the time of the battles of Lexington and Concord, the colonies had industries sprouting like spring crops.

The Southern Colonies, even though they used slave labour on a vast scale, were probably the poorest. They were a perfect fit into the mercantilist system that Britain wanted, raising crops it needed (tobacco, rice and cotton, as well as indigo for dyes). London merchants set the prices for everything the southern planters grew, and this nearly bankrupted many of them, who had to buy manufactured goods from Great Britain.

The colonies were also land hungry and ready to expand across the frontiers. There were always eager, adventurous settlers who dared to go into the wilderness to the west, braving hardship and the constant Indian threat, to carve out a new home for themselves and their families. Between 1765 and 1768, over 30,000 colonists crossed the Appalachians to seek new homes and land, confronting the unknown and the many dangers contained in the dark forests.

These expansionist tendencies brought colonial administrations into conflict with King and country. The colonies were there to support the mother country. That was the essence of the mercantilist system, and acceptance and tolerance of the system was required for it to work. Now, with economic and population growth, many colonists, rich and poor alike, chafed at the imposition of a distant Parliament's decrees and taxes from 1763 onward. The hated Proclamation of 1763, largely ignored by the colonists who were looking for free land, the Stamp Act, Navigation Acts and Townsend Act, all created a decisive rift between Great Britain and its valuable possessions.

▲ *American militia units formed minutemen companies, specially designated units to form at a minute's notice in an emergency.*

Rebellion

By the time of open rebellion, as John Adams later characterized the situation, perhaps only one-third of the population supported revolt, one-third remained loyal to the Crown and the remaining third were apathetic. However, it is not essential to achieve majority support to stage a revolution. Grumbling led to debate, debate to open protest, protest led to violence, violence to open rebellion, focused on the British garrison in Boston, Massachusetts.

The open flame of revolt flickered across the land, spreading from Boston southward. Massachusetts soon had its patriot clubs (such as the Sons of Liberty), liberty poles and the oratory of the fanatical Sam Adams, preaching open rebellion against the Crown.

▼ *At what became known as the Boston Tea Party, Americans boarded British ships and dumped their cargo of tea into the harbour.*

Such developments were echoed in the Virginia House of Burgesses by another red-hot orator, Patrick Henry, who famously shouted 'Give me Liberty or Give me Death' at his colleagues. He had enough opponents to make his second request entirely feasible.

Debate soon burst into open defiance and revolution. The representatives of the Crown were tarred and feathered or run out of towns and villages by infuriated colonists. Statues of King George were pulled down and melted down for musket balls or round-shot. Lonely British sentries were assaulted with snowballs loaded with rocks. A Boston mob was fired on by a frustrated British officer and his guard. The soldiers were later defended in court by John Adams; all but two were acquitted, and the two convicted were given light sentences. British revenue cutters were taken and burned, and colonial militias were forming units of minutemen, so called because they were required to turn out at a moment's notice to face an emergency.

The situation in Massachusetts, especially Boston, became so bad that large numbers of troops had to be brought in and billeted on the inhabitants, adding to the complaints of the insurgents, and feeding their propaganda. The leaders of this rebellion-in-the-making were hoarding weapons and ammunition throughout the colonies, and one such cache would be the objective of an abortive raid from Boston that would begin the armed struggle in April 1775.

Divided as the colonies were, the 13 united to face the threat that they perceived Britain posed after 1763. Their first unified action would be the establishment of a 'Continental Congress' (which first met in 1774) giving them a de facto national government. Legally, they had no international status, except as colonies of the mother country. That would change with the Declaration of Independence in July 1776.

THE AMERICAN ARMY

When hostilities opened between the American colonists and the British Army after the fighting at Lexington Green and Concord, there was no American army. For some time, there had been militia companies, modelled on the English 'trained bands' and organized, trained and led by able officers, but these disparate bodies were intended to keep the peace and act in self-defence, so could not play the part of a cohesive national force.

A Nation in Arms

After Lexington and Concord a New England Army of a kind was organized under the command of stalwart citizen Artemus Ward, who laid siege to the British in Boston. He was later relieved by George Washington, who was sent by Congress in Philadelphia to command the newly christened Continental Army that had been formed in June 1775. Initially, however, Congress would rely on a collection of individuals and individualists haphazardly assembled, slackly commanded, untrained and led by officers who were as inexperienced as their men.

American Veterans

There was a nucleus of experienced men in the colonies who were familiar with military matters and who set about organizing armies with a will. These hard-bitten former soldiers had seen active service in the French wars. Washington was one, and there were also such men as Israel Putnam and John Stark. They had served with the British and saw the efficiency of well-trained regiments and what could be accomplished by steady troops under capable non-commissioned officers led by professionals.

Washington needed a large, well-trained army that could meet the British and their German allies on even terms on the battlefield. In pursuing this goal he had to stand up to Congress, which had developed a mistrust of a standing professional army; deal with infighting among the generals of the army, who sometimes upset his carefully laid plans on the field and off; and cope with a lack of trained officers. The Continental Army suffered reverse after reverse, and its successes were few and far between. That it persevered through hardship, combat, boredom and disease to ultimate victory against what was considered to be the best army in the world is worthy of note. No American army has endured so much to accomplish so much – the Continentals won independence for their nation and continent.

Infantry Organization

The Continental Army infantry went through three main reorganizations: those of 1776, 1778 and 1781. The regiments were modelled on the British system, but usually did not have a grenadier company, although light infantry companies were raised early on and were in the tables of organization for every infantry regiment by the time of the 1778 re-organization. Regiments were fielded as either one or two battalions and fought in two ranks. Periodically, the light infantry companies were pulled from their parent regiments to form the Continental Corps of Light Infantry, which was considered to be the elite of the Continental Army. These men were employed for special missions. In its final form, the Continental infantry regiment would have nine companies, one of them being the light infantry company.

▼ This 19th-century painting gives a good general impression of what the early American soldier wore, but is inaccurate in small details.

Continental artillery was also organized in regiments, but this had an administrative and not a tactical purpose. The main tactical unit of the artillery was the company, which had any number of guns from two to six, depending on the strength of the company and the availability of guns and of horse teams to pull them. The chief of artillery was a former bookseller from Boston, Henry Knox. He was competent, forceful and loyal, and he served as Washington's artillery chief. During this period the term 'battery' for American and French artillery meant any number of guns in position, and should not be confused with modern use denoting a company-sized artillery unit.

The small Continental cavalry arm served with growing efficiency throughout the war. First formed in 1776–7, it had the usual growing pains of an expensive arm. There were not enough horses or equipment to allow it to reach its authorized strength. In addition the commanders who led it had to learn their profession, as did their NCOs and troopers. Four regiments of light dragoons were eventually formed. Each had six companies, numbered consecutively one to six. Because of a shortage of suitable horses and equipment these were reorganized later in the war as legionary corps each of three mounted and three dismounted troops.

In May 1777, Washington formed the army into permanent brigades and divisions. Four or five regiments formed an American brigade, and two brigades formed a division. This gave the army permanence and flexibility. By then commanders knew their subordinates and units were working together, with cohesion and flexibility.

Foreign Volunteers

The Continental Army was reinforced by European volunteers, mainly through the auspices of the American Minister to France, Dr Benjamin Franklin. Some were worthless, more adventurer than professional soldier, but many of them were vital to the Continental Army and provided much needed expertise and manpower.

The most valuable of the volunteers was probably the Baron von Steuben. Presented by Franklin as a former Prussian general, von Steuben was in fact a retired Prussian captain with extensive staff and Free Corps service. He was also an expert drill master. Arriving at Valley Forge just when Washington needed him, he expertly trained the Continentals so they knew their manual of arms and could manoeuvre easily on the field of battle. He also emphasized marksmanship, and the firing commands were changed so that the troops should 'take aim' instead of the British command of 'present'. He codified his drill into the 'Blue Book', the first drill manual of the United States Army.

▲ *American ministers to France recruited European officers for the Continentals. Here, Baron de Kalb (centre), one of the recruits, introduces Lafayette to the American delegation, of which Silas Deane was part.*

Other foreign officers also contributed to the professionalism and success of the Continental Army. Duportail, the French engineer, became the father of the US Army's Corps of Engineers and was responsible for the siege works at Yorktown in 1781. Other French officers became battalion commanders in the Continental Corps of Artillery. Huge, competent Baron de Kalb, a Bavarian in the French service, commanded the famous Maryland Division of Maryland and Delaware Continentals in 1780. Polish artilleryman Tadeuz Kosciuzko built the defences at West Point.

The Continentals were ostensibly controlled by Congress, but as the war progressed they deferred to Washington, whose influence and stature cannot be over-emphasized. In spite of the severe initial defeats that he incurred, it was Washington's skill and authority as a national leader and commander that led him and his army to victory. That, with the political skill shown by Benjamin Franklin and other Americans who enabled the French Alliance, together with British errors, made victory certain.

▼ *Washington took command of the newly named Continental Army shortly after Bunker Hill. He wore his old militia regimentals, but his troops were not uniformed anywhere near as well as this idealized picture suggests.*

THE BRITISH ARMY

In 1763 the British Army had recently been triumphant in North America, and had won honours from fighting in Europe. The army that had fought and won in North America was an excellent force that had adapted to fighting in difficult circumstances. It was experienced, tough and well trained, but the British themselves proceeded to ruin it.

▲ *The 17th Light Dragoons served throughout the war in North America, providing yeoman service to the British forces.*

Britain's Armed Forces

All line infantry regiments above the number 70 were disbanded without regard to service, battle honours, or experience. The light infantry, an elite arm that was vital to defeating the French in North America, disappeared. Cavalry regiments above the number 18 disappeared, and the always small British regular army became even smaller, with an end strength of only 31,300 to guard the enlarged empire.

By 1775 when hostilities started once more in North America, the British had a strength of 48,647 regulars. Of that total, 39,294 were infantry, 6,869 were cavalry and the remaining 2,484 were artillerymen. Some 19 infantry regiments and 16 cavalry regiments were in England, with another infantry regiment in Scotland. Twenty-one infantry regiments and 12 cavalry regiments were on the Irish station, with a further 18 infantry regiments in America.

At the time of the conflict the British Army was small, well trained and largely uniformed according to the 1768 clothing warrant. However, many of the skills honed in the French and Indian wars had been forgotten, even though each regiment was given a permanent light infantry company in the early 1770s. Further, in terms of organization, the army was a collection of regiments with no permanent higher units such as the brigade or division. The higher tactical units were formed on an ad hoc basis and commanded either by a brigadier general or the senior regimental commander. Still, as the French had found, it was a formidable force on the battlefield: well-trained, generally competently led, and accustomed to hardship and campaigning.

Officers and Commanders

The general weakness of the British Army of the period was the myriad levels of bureaucracy that controlled, fed, and paid it. The cumbersome hierarchy was also responsible for directing it in wartime. At times effort was duplicated, a tangle of influence and squabbling ministers and officials tried to seem responsible for any particular task. Managing a war 3,000 miles from home, as well as clothing, paying, and feeding the army, was a fraught and near impossible task. Yet there was just enough influence to make it seem to the commanders in the field that there was much unwelcome meddling going on.

The British senior commanders in America were a mixed lot. General Thomas Gage, who commanded when the war broke out, had been an excellent light infantry commander during the French and Indian War, as had General William Howe. Gage's failure in either containing or suppressing the rebellion in Boston caused him to be removed and replaced by Howe, who was competent, courageous and generally efficient. A superb combat leader, he had demonstrated his skills in the French and Indian War and in engagements such as Bunker Hill, but he was also opposed to the war in America and hoped for reconciliation. Although defeating General Washington at the battles of Long Island and Brandywine, and commanding the huge expeditionary force in 1776–8, he failed to destroy Washington's Continental Army, an accomplishment that would have brought the war to a conclusion.

Howe was replaced by Henry Clinton in 1778, a competent but unpopular officer. His management of the remainder of the war was weak, and several opportunities for success were missed, but it was his relationship with General Charles Cornwallis, perhaps the best British general of the war, which spelled ultimate failure for the British cause. Where Cornwallis sensed success, Clinton saw danger and possible failure. When Cornwallis' campaigns in the south were gaining repeated successes for the British, he was not supported in his efforts by Clinton, safely ensconced in New York. This undoubtedly was a major cause of British failure in the south.

General John Burgoyne was an average soldier, but popular with the rank and file because he took good care of them. His well-planned invasion of New York state in 1777 was hamstrung by a lack of drive and common sense on Burgoyne's part, a lack of support from Howe and then Clinton, and poor co-ordination from London. A concerted effort might very well have succeeded, but Burgoyne's errors coupled with an aggressive response from the Americans doomed his expedition to failure.

Regimental Organization

A British regiment was organized in ten companies: eight battalion companies and two elite companies, the grenadier company, which held the post of honour on 'the right of the line', and the light infantry company, which held the 'left of the line'. These two flank companies were the elite of each

▲ *Lieutenant Colonel Banastre Tarleton, wearing the uniform of the British Legion, which he led in the Southern campaign.*

particular infantry regiment. The grenadiers were chosen from the biggest, bravest and most experienced men in the unit. The light infantry were chosen from the most agile and experienced not tall enough to be grenadiers. The light infantry excelled in scouting and skirmishing, and were adept at fighting in open order and as advance, flank and rearguards.

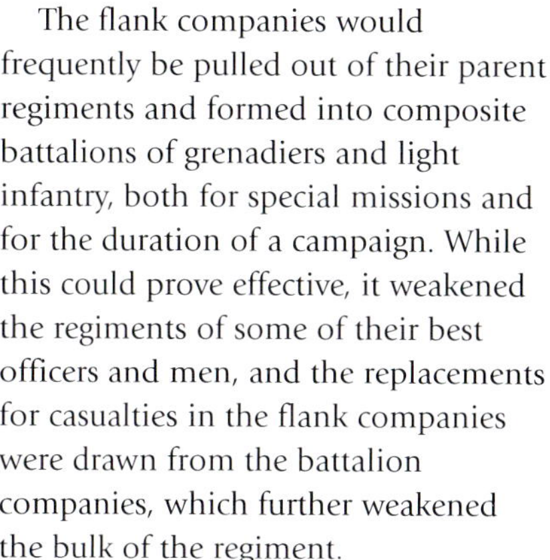

The flank companies would frequently be pulled out of their parent regiments and formed into composite battalions of grenadiers and light infantry, both for special missions and for the duration of a campaign. While this could prove effective, it weakened the regiments of some of their best officers and men, and the replacements for casualties in the flank companies were drawn from the battalion companies, which further weakened the bulk of the regiment.

After the entry of France into the war in 1778, 29 new infantry regiments and four cavalry regiments were raised for overseas service. This put a massive strain on recruiting, but the objective was achieved between 1778 and 1781. To these units were added the myriad Loyalist regiments raised in America, some of which were highly effective and did good service, and the hired German mercenaries who were sent to America.

British cavalry and artillery were excellent. British artillery served in every theatre and on nearly every battlefield of the period. Only two regular British cavalry regiments were sent to North America.

The British army was desperately stretched during this period, needing to maintain units at home and in Ireland, India, and the Caribbean. From 1778 recruiting, always a problem, had become critical.

The British in America

The 30,000-man expeditionary force sent to fight the Americans in 1776 was the largest the British had ever sent anywhere. Jails were emptied of men to meet the recruiting needs of the army, and additional mercenaries were hired from German states.

The Loyalist units raised were of uneven quality and had as many problems meeting their recruiting goals as the British regulars. The Queen's Rangers and Tarleton's British Legion were two outstanding Loyalist units created during the war to serve in any theatre, the Queen's Rangers in particular achieving an outstanding reputation under John Graves Simcoe.

▼ *The British Army at the Battle of Bunker Hill assaulted the American positions three times before being successful.*

THE FRENCH ARMY

By the time of the conflict in North America the French Army had undergone rebirth and reform after the disasters of the Seven Years' War. Reforms were masterminded by general officers such as Victor-François, Duke de Broglie, and the artilleryman Jean-Baptiste de Gribeauval. These officers were backed by a War Minister of rare skill and vision, the Duke de Choiseul. He had an uncanny eye for talent, knew what had to be done, and applied himself to the task at hand.

French Officers

De Broglie was one of the few French general officers to achieve success on the Continent against the British and Prussians. In the early 1760s, as the Seven Years' War was coming to a close, he organized his troops into provisional divisions that would later become commonplace and permanent organizations within the French Army.

▼ *The Marquis de Montcalm celebrates his successful battle near Fort Ticonderoga, against the largest British force ever assembled in North America up to that time.*

In addition, in the 1770s, he held tactical manoeuvres in Normandy to experiment with new tactics and to co-ordinate the operations and training of the different arms (cavalry, infantry and artillery) so that they might work together on the battlefield as a co-ordinated whole.

Gribeauval had been seconded to the Austrian Army as an artillery officer, the Austrians being short of experienced senior artillerymen. He not only fought well, but considerably improved the Austrians' engineering arm, which had been poor. He served so well that Frederick the Great asked him to enter the Prussian service. Gribeauval, who was dissatisfied with the French artillery arm, and had developed ideas from his experience of both the Prussian and Austrian field artillery, went home and began work on his excellent artillery system. This became the leading artillery system in Europe by 1789. His guns and system were brought to the United States by Rochambeau and were tested in combat. Later, the United States would partially adopt this system.

▲ *Jean-Baptiste Waquette de Gribeauval, the man who developed the new artillery system that helped reform the French Army.*

While the French reformers had mixed results and there were evident setbacks, the French Army which embarked for America was well-trained, had new uniform regulations, a new light artillery system superior to any in Europe and was backed up by a military education system that was second to none.

French Regiments

The far-reaching reforms after 1763 resulted in a standardization that made both the French infantry and artillery more efficient. In the spring of 1776, regimental organization for the infantry, with the exception of the Régiment du Roi and the Guards regiments, was set at two battalions per regiment. The most senior (*vieux corps*) of the infantry regiments each had four battalions, and these were ordered to have their 2nd and 4th battalions removed and formed as new regiments in the line. While the regiments were new, the battalions had already been in existence for many years and had been fighting in the same regiment, a fact which greatly aided cohesion.

Infantry battalions were reduced from nine companies to six, and the number of officers was reduced per company while the enlisted strength was increased. The six companies comprised one grenadier, one chasseur (light infantry) and four fusilier companies. Chasseur and fusilier companies consisted of six officers, one cadet, 17 non-commissioned officers (NCOs), one surgeon's assistant, two drummers and 144 privates. The grenadier companies consisted of six officers, one cadet, 14 NCOs, one surgeon's assistant, two drummers and 84 privates.

The authorized strength of an infantry battalion was 963 all ranks, plus 26 all ranks that were assigned to an auxiliary recruitment company. The total regimental strength for each regiment was 1,990 all ranks, which included the regimental staff of 12 officers and men.

The seven artillery regiments, all of which fell under their regimental number of 64 in the French line, also acted as the French artillery schools.

▼ *Lauzan's Lancers served with Rochambeau's expeditionary force. About half of the 300 light cavalrymen were armed with lances.*

▲ *By the time Rochambeau set sail in 1780, the French Army's uniforms had benefited from a thorough reform programme.*

These were of excellent calibre and were probably the best in Europe. The seven regiments were known by the names of the towns in which the unit was stationed: La Fère, Metz, Grenoble, Auxonne, Strasbourg, Toul and Besançon. Each consisted of 20 companies, which were further subdivided into two battalions of ten companies each. All of the companies were organized in the same manner with four officers and 71 other ranks. Included in the 10 companies per battalion were four bombardier (specialist artillerymen) companies and two sapper companies. The other four companies were gunners. The sappers were part of the artillery during this period, as the French engineer arm had no enlisted troops. There were also six companies of miners and nine companies of labourers (*ouvriers*) which belonged to the artillery. The total strength of the French artillery arm in 1776 was 909 officers and 11,805 other ranks.

The cavalry arm would see no action in North America. Instead mounted troops belonging to volunteer legions (*Légions Volontaires Etrangères*) were raised, and these belonged to the French Navy as they were officially colonial troops and not part of the regular army.

The colonial regiments had no standard organization during the period. This would be enacted after the war was over.

The French in America

France did not enter the war on the side of the Americans out of altruism but in the quest for revenge for their defeats in the Seven Years' War and with the aim of regaining some of their colonial holdings lost to the British. Much of the French war effort would be directed towards the West Indies and the valuable islands there. Some of the French plans were unsuccessful, such as the Siege of Savannah in 1779, but the despatch of Rochambeau's expeditionary force to North America can be considered a turning point in America's revolution.

This 5,000-man force was a well-trained and organized expedition that greatly enhanced Washington's chances of a decisive strategic victory over the British on land. The two men liked and respected each other, which made working together easy, and the ensuing military partnership made the victory at Yorktown possible.

Attached to Rochambeau's army was the Legion of the Duc de Lauzan, a force of both infantry and cavalry that was actually raised by the navy for service overseas. The hussars of the legion were dressed in hussar style and would perform well in North America. They later became the 5th Hussars of the French Army.

OTHER COMBATANTS IN THE WAR

A number of other countries were involved in the war either directly, as active participants, or by sending men as mercenaries.

The Germans

German mercenaries were hired out in considerable numbers by their sovereign princes, and were engaged in many of the war's principal actions. Casualties were high: of the 29,875 men that were enlisted for the duration of the conflict, 12,562 did not return home. Others deserted and remained as new citizens of the emerging United States. Six separate treaties were initially signed with the governments and sovereigns of those German states willing to provide men.

The great majority of these troops were infantry. Brunswick sent one dragoon regiment, which, however, served on foot. There were artillery contingents with the Hessian troops, as well as detachments of elite light infantry (*Jägers*). The Germans fought under their own commanders but were also brigaded with British troops. Some units never saw combat, such as those that remained in Canada on garrison duty, but those who came into action fought exceptionally well.

▼ *The Spanish Army of the 18th century was a respectable force that would inflict humiliating defeats on the British in Florida.*

The Spanish

Spain had a respectable 18th-century force in its colonies, with units scattered across the continent and in the West Indies. Inevitably these were small units, but they were to enjoy some success against the British forces on land.

At this time the Spanish Army consisted of 41 infantry regiments, each of two battalions. Each battalion had nine companies of fusiliers and one of grenadiers. Some regiments had an additional company of light infantry (*cazadores*). Fusilier companies had a paper strength of three officers and 66 other ranks. Grenadier companies had three officers and 52 other ranks. Provisional grenadier battalions were formed when deemed necessary, concentrating together the grenadier companies of the available regiments. Light infantry battalions had six companies.

The Spanish artillery regiment had four battalions of seven companies each. Artillery companies consisted of four officers and 96 other ranks. Additionally, there were 12 battalions of naval infantry of six companies each, as well as 14 brigades of the Royal Corps of Naval Artillery for service afloat and on shore.

The Spaniards fought well and achieved substantial gains for their government back in Madrid. When Bernardo de Gálvez, governor of Louisiana, was informed that Spain was at war with Great Britain in July 1779, he immediately mounted an expedition against the British holdings on the lower Mississippi, taking all of them. He also took Mobile from the British in March 1780. Spanish troops under de Gálvez also successfully besieged the British in Pensacola in the Florida panhandle, the British capitulating on 10 May 1781. Esteban Miro, who commanded the Spanish Regiment Fijo de la Louisiana, succeeded de Gálvez in 1782 and successfully defended his territory from the British until the end of the war.

▲ *Cornplanter, chief of the Seneca tribe, wears a mixture of American Indian and European dress. The gorget was undoubtedly a gift from the British, while the gauntlets are probably a product of the artist's imagination.*

Spanish units in North America

- Infantry Regiment Hibernia
- Infantry Regiment Soria
- Infantry Regiment Fijo de la Louisiana
- Infantry Regiment Rey
- Infantry Regiment Espana
- Infantry Regiment Principe
- Infantry Regiment Fijo de la Habana
- Fusilier Company Montana
- Royal Naval Infantry
- Dragoon Regiment America
- Dragoon Regiment Mexico
- Coloured Militia of New Orleans
- Free Battalion of Havana
- Carabiniers of New Orleans
- Royal Corps of Artillery
- Royal Naval Artillery
- Royal Corps of Engineers

▲ *A Mohawk village in central New York State about 1780.*

The Indian Contingents

The American Indians are often the forgotten participants in the war. While most of the tribes, especially those of the Iroquois Confederation, sided with the British, a few, such as the Oneida and Stockbridge Indians, took the part of the Americans. The Indians were skilled in fighting, scouting and hunting (for man or beast) in the American wilderness, and the British used these skills to the utmost in border fighting along the frontier. Tories (Loyalists) worked hand in hand with the Indians, especially Butler's Rangers, and inflicted some defeats on the Americans, such as the Wyoming Massacre, and fought hard actions such as Oriskany in 1777. Frequently worthless in a standup fight, the Indians were useful and valuable in raids, ambushes and forays into enemy territory. They were also a useful terror weapon.

Frequently, though, as when they accompanied Brigadier General Barrimore St Leger and General John Burgoyne in 1777, the American Indians proved to be unreliable allies, staying loyal as long as things went the British way. When the situation turned or it looked as if the British were going to lose, they melted away, appearing later if prospects for loot and easy victory improved. Joseph Brant was an important Iroquois leader who was fanatically loyal to the British and stayed the course, which in itself was unusual. Even so, the tribes did provide invaluable assistance and could survive where a British or German regular might perish. They were tough opponents, and good for damaging enemy morale, even if they were unreliable on the battlefield.

When the war along the frontier was not going well for the Americans in February 1779 a decision was made to deal with the Iroquois. An expedition commanded by General John Sullivan was launched into the land of the Iroquois, numbering 4,400 Continentals and volunteers. The Iroquois could not muster the manpower to oppose this, although there was scattered fighting during the expedition. The Iroquois abandoned their towns, withdrawing before the American juggernaut.

Iroquois villages, towns, crops and livelihoods were methodically destroyed by the Americans, hurting the Iroquois severely. The Indians were forced to depend more on the British for their livelihood. If they hated the Americans before the Sullivan expedition, they hated them even more after seeing their homeland devastated. In many ways, the cohesion of the Iroquois Confederacy was destroyed by Sullivan's operations, and the military power of the tribes was ruined.

The one true Indian ally the American forces had was the Stockbridge Indians from New York State. They had fought with Rogers' Rangers in the French and Indian War and stayed loyal against the British.

▼ *The Wyoming Massacre in July 1778 was a good example of fighting along the frontier. If you lost, you died, and little quarter was given, especially when Indians were involved.*

BATTLES AND CAMPAIGNS

The American Revolution was a political, social and military event that ran from the end of the French and Indian War to the adoption of the United States Constitution by the 13 states in 1789. The Revolution was a struggle that was to deprive the British of their most valuable colonies and inflict on Great Britain one of the worst defeats it had ever suffered.

Boston 1775

Blood had already been spilled before shots were fired in anger on Lexington Green on that fateful early spring day in 1775. The king's tax collectors had been tarred and feathered by angry subjects. His Majesty's revenue cutters had been waylaid, and in at least one case attacked at sea, boarded, run aground and burned. Colonists had been fired on in Boston in 1770 in what became known, thanks to American propaganda, as the Boston Massacre. In reality it had been provoked by a gang hired by radicals, led by Sam Adams, who desired an incident in Boston. The group of men, later joined by other civilians, taunted British troops, who fired into the crowd, hitting 11 men, 5 of whom died. The Boston rebels learned not to confront armed troops with snowballs, but did achieve the withdrawal of the garrison from the centre of town. The British soldiers were later acquitted in a Boston court, defended by two American lawyers, John Adams and John Otis.

The real fighting began in April 1775 with a British raid from Boston to capture the American arms and ammunition store at Concord, and snatch some of the leaders of the incipient rebellion supposedly staying in the village. All the raid did was infuriate the populace and bring the militia out in force. It almost destroyed the British raiding party and started what eventually developed into a war involving France, Spain and Holland joining the newly declared United States against Great Britain.

After the Massachusetts militia had chased the British raiders back into Boston, the newly formed New England Army laid siege to the British, occupying a peninsula that jutted into Boston harbour next to the prosperous hamlet of Charlestown. British general Thomas Gage despatched a force of 2,000 regulars to dislodge them. Surprisingly, the Americans held firm, and bloodily repulsed two assaults by the British, inflicting crippling losses. Rallying his decimated troops for one last try at the hill, the British field commander, General Sir William Howe, led his men forward one last time. The Americans fired until they ran out of ammunition, and this last British assault gained the redoubt and took it, the Americans withdrawing to across the Boston Neck. The Americans had lost, but only just, and they grimly settled down to continue the siege.

In the summer of 1775, George Washington arrived at Cambridge, near Boston, to take up his appointment as commander of the grandly named Continental Army. What he found was a shambles, an armed mob rather than an army. Still, there was talent to be had and hard-working, dedicated officers established at least the hint of order and a semblance of discipline. Henry Knox was despatched to newly captured Fort Ticonderoga to bring the captured artillery there to Boston and the army. His expedition, conducted in the dead of winter, was a masterpiece of military engineering, endurance and fortitude, and forced General Howe, now replacing Gage as the British commander in North America, to evacuate Boston and retire to Halifax.

▼ *The so-called Boston Massacre, provoked by waterfront thugs, left five Americans dead and a propaganda opportunity for the Americans.*

Canada 1775

America's fascination with Canada was undoubtedly a hangover from the terrifying days when French and Indian raiding parties swooped on American settlements, killing settlers and burning their homes. In 1775, American plans were more ambitious than mere retaliatory raids; the Continental Congress wanted to take Canada from the British and add it to the colonies, an ambition that was never fulfilled.

The American invasion of Canada was to be a two-pronged assault by General Richard Montgomery, a former British officer, and Benedict Arnold, a man of talent who would become a driving, aggressive combat leader and turn traitor to his cause. Montgomery took the traditional invasion route up

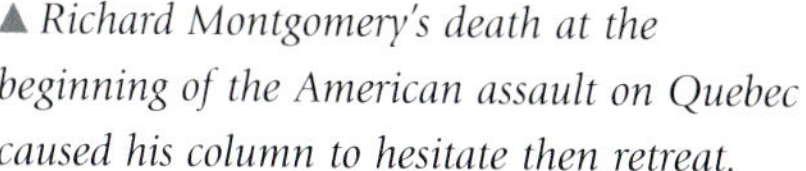

▲ *Richard Montgomery's death at the beginning of the American assault on Quebec caused his column to hesitate then retreat.*

Lake Champlain into Canada, while Arnold boldly went through the Maine wilderness in an epic march, an achievement that is usually overlooked. Both commanders were generally successful and joined at Quebec, determined to take the city or die in the attempt. The assault went in from two directions in the dead of a Canadian winter, through a blinding snowstorm and determined British resistance. Montgomery was killed while reconnoitring, and Arnold was badly wounded leading his men through Quebec's lower town. Both assaults failed, and the expected Canadian assistance did not materialize. Reinforced American units barely held on in Canada until spring, and a determined British offensive flushed the Americans southwards.

The British commander in Canada, Sir Guy Carleton, headed south while Benedict Arnold rallied what troops he could to face the oncoming British threat. Carleton had a fleet suitable for service on the lakes manned by competent personnel. Arnold, ever the intriguer, improvised a fleet on Lake Champlain to meet him, manned by seven-thumbed landsmen, and fought Carleton to a standstill. However, the American ships were largely destroyed or captured. While he was the tactical victor at the Battle of Valcour Island, Carleton withdrew into Canada after the battle, leaving Arnold the strategic victor in a campaign of attrition.

▼ *The battle of Trenton, in the dead of winter, though small in scale, was an excellent tactical victory over a Hessian outpost, which had an immense impact on American morale.*

New York and Princeton 1776

Although difficult, if not impossible, to defend without a functioning navy, Washington believed that he had to defend New York. It was not a wise decision and it turned into a disaster.

Howe arrived off New York with an army of 30,000 British and German regulars, while Washington was greatly outnumbered, chose poor positions and was fielding untried, unreliable militias. Supported by the Royal Navy, Howe defeated the Americans at the Battle of Long Island, 23–30 August 1776, nearly capturing Washington together with his entire army. There was a successful counter-attack by the Americans that saw British troops turn tail and run at Harlem Heights, more commonly referred to as the Hollow Way, but that was a minor action and the defeat and retreat of the army continued unabated. Washington was driven from New York, losing again at White Plains, and the British took Fort Washington on the Hudson by direct assault, the Americans losing men and material they could ill afford. To cap it all, Fort Lee across the Hudson River was abandoned.

On the other side of the Delaware River, with winter approaching, Washington and his key subordinates marshalled the remnants of their men. Losses, desertions and expired enlistments had left Washington with an army of just 5,000 men that now looked as if it were dying on its feet.

Washington, however, planned a bold river crossing of the ice-choked Delaware on Christmas Day 1776 and took the Hessian garrison of Trenton. The British, who had thought Washington all but finished, sent General Charles Cornwallis after him. Washington held before Trenton, fooled the British with a night march and scattered the British rearguard at nearby Princeton, before going into winter quarters at Morristown.

Charleston 1776

The British had also moved against the south in the summer of 1776 in an effort to take another strategic seaport, Charleston, in South Carolina. With numbers of troops ready to land and take the city, the attack on the forts that protected the place was defeated by a tenacious American defence and by British tactical errors. The plan was to attack from the sea as a prelude to an amphibious operation. The initial naval attack was botched, with three warships running aground. Strongly fortified in and around Charleston harbour, the Americans waited for the British to navigate the channel and come within range.

When the fleet eventually drew near, American artillery inside the forts opened fire and maintained a vigorous cannonade against the British ships, outshooting and outfighting the Royal Navy. British counter-fire from the fleet did little damage to the palmetto-logged forts, and the Americans sustained few casualties. Surprised by the American resistance and unable to land an army without first silencing the American fortifications or at least rendering them ineffective, the British, sulking, withdrew. Licking their wounds and with their professional pride damaged, the British went northwards to New York to join William Howe in his invasion of the middle colonies and his effort to take and occupy New York City and its great natural harbour.

▼ *Lafayette became a friend of Washington and fought with him at Brandywine.*

▲ *At the battle of Brandywine, Howe feinted along the American front, conducting a turn around the right flank, defeating Washington and winning Philadelphia for the British.*

Brandywine 1777

The two campaigns of 1777 would prove to be the turning point of the war. The main American army under Washington would fail, again, to defeat General Howe.

Howe moved to take the American capital at Philadelphia and defeated Washington at Brandywine on 11 September 1777. Washington had taken up a strong position to face Howe, but Howe, a consummate tactician, feinted and outflanked the Continental Army, Washington and his subordinates carelessly leaving their flanks in the air and unprotected. Once again, Washington had been defeated in a major battle against the British, and once again Howe had failed to pursue effectively and destroy the Continental Army. As long as that army existed, the revolution lived.

Philadelphia 1777

The victorious British Army occupied Philadelphia in September 1777, parading through the streets to cheering citizens as had Washington's army earlier in the year. Later that same month, American General Anthony Wayne's command was taken by surprise in a night attack at Paoli.

The British troops under General 'no flint' Grey (so called because of his preference for the bayonet) caught the Americans sleeping. Their outposts were silenced, and the Americans were being slaughtered as the alarm was sounded. Driven from their encampment with heavy losses, the Americans learned a valuable lesson in both night assaults and the use of the bayonet. It would be put to profitable use later in the war.

▲ *Washington's attempt to take Chew House wasted time and men, and helped turn the tide of the battle into an American defeat.*

Germantown 1777

Undeterred by these repeated defeats and unwilling to give up Philadelphia without a determined final effort to regain the city, Washington planned a bold attack against the British Army outside Philadelphia. The British were encamped in and around the small village of Germantown five miles north of Philadelphia. Washington planned to attack them with a concentric effort involving an intricate timetable and four attacking columns that began their march out of mutual supporting distance. Errors and delays plagued the American movement, with some units becoming lost, but the attack eventually went in with ferocity on 4 October 1777, and hit the unsuspecting British, sending their best units hastily to the rear.

However, the American attack was held up by British troops barricaded in a large mansion, Chew House. Some of the attacking units were detailed to take the house instead of bypassing it and continuing the successful attack. This, plus the late arrival of Greene's column and its launching of a fire-fight with friendly troops, slowed the momentum of the assault, allowing Howe to rally his shaken troops and counter attack. The Americans withdrew, again losing, but gaining confidence in their abilities.

The progress the Americans were making with their new army had not gone unnoticed. The French had been clandestinely supplying the Americans with arms and ammunition for some time through a front company run by the shadowy Monsieur Beaumarchais. American prowess on the battlefield against France's traditional enemy was growing, slowly but surely, and the French were impressed with both the planning and the execution of the Germantown operation. There was pressure in France to come in openly on the American side.

▼ *General Wayne, a driving, relentless commander, was dubbed 'Mad Anthony' by his troops because of his behaviour in combat.*

▼ *After Brandywine, Washington planned a counter-attack against Howe at Germantown. His plan was too complicated, and although initially he drove the British before him, his supports were late, and the British recovered.*

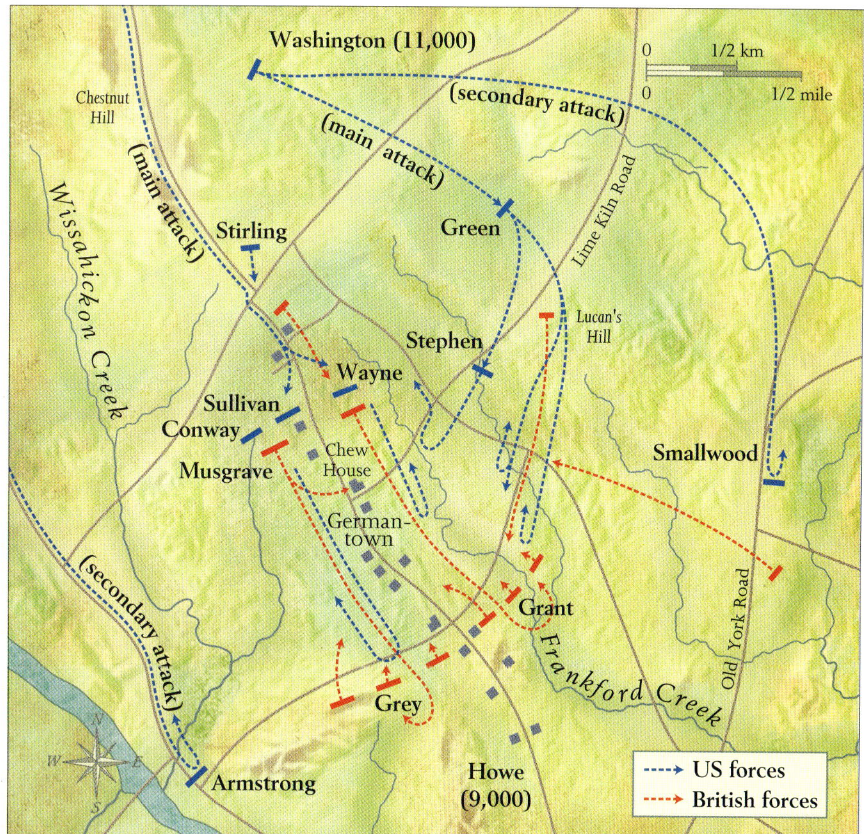

Burgoyne Attacks Albany 1777

The Americans would now face trouble from the north as the British gathered their strength in Canada. A British force was being organized under General John Burgoyne for an invasion of the colonies, aiming to separate New England from the rest of the rebel colonies. Burgoyne planned a three-pronged invasion, commanding the largest force himself to descend from Canada along the traditional invasion route of Lake Champlain, Lake George and the Hudson River. Colonel Barry St Leger would take a force of British regulars, Loyalists ('Tories') and Indians and threaten the Mohawk Valley in upper New York state. Howe would simultaneously strike up the Hudson River. The three offensives would meet in Albany. The plan was brilliant, and with proper co-operation and vigorous execution it might well have succeeded. However, operations were hamstrung from the beginning. St Leger was not strong enough to successfully complete his part in the enterprise. He moved into the Mohawk Valley by way of Lake Ontario and Oswego, and besieged old Fort Stanwyx, which refused to be reduced.

▲ *Horatio Gates reviews his British prisoners after the surrender of General Burgoyne.*

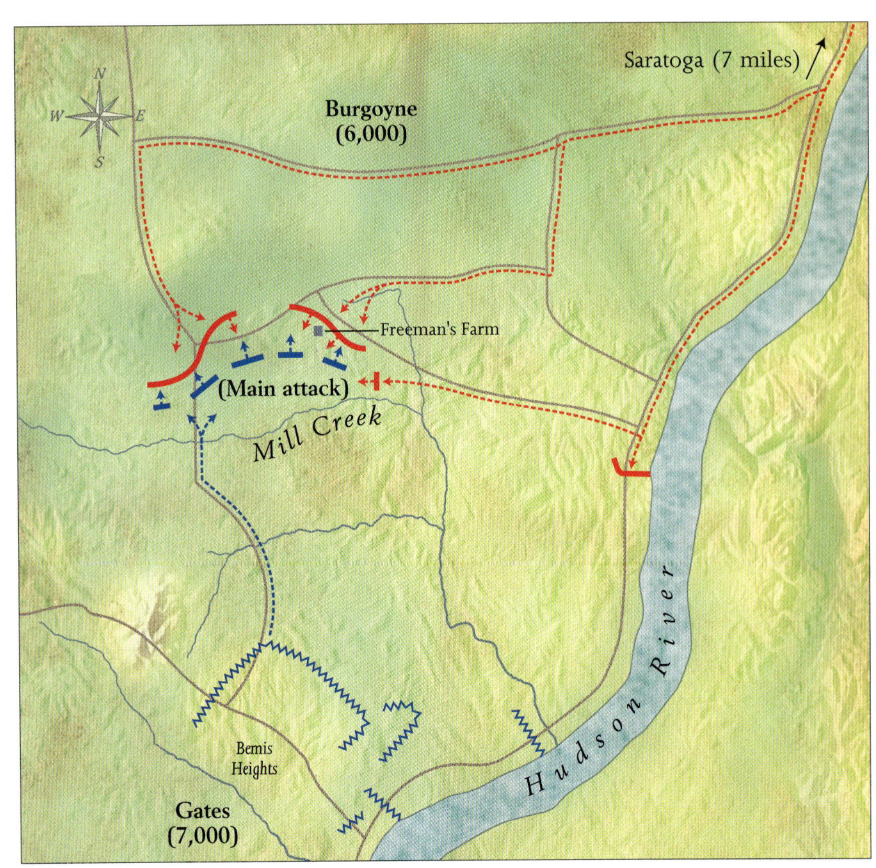

▼ *The British offensive at Freeman's Farm was hit head on by the Americans, causing heavy losses, but the arrival of Riedesel's troops prevented a catastrophic British loss.*

The American militia was called out to relieve the fort but was ambushed by St Leger's Tories and American Indians at Oriskany. It was a bloody, no-quarter fight, and both sides were mauled. The militia turned back, but Arnold was near to hand with a force of Continentals. He sent rumours of an overwhelming American force coming to relieve Fort Stanwyx and wipe out the Indians, and St Leger's allies evaporated into the forest. With the remnants of his small army, the colonel had to return to Canada.

The attack up the Hudson from New York barely materialized. Howe went after Washington and Philadelphia, and the only assistance Burgoyne received from New York was a limited attack up the Hudson late in the campaign by General Sir Henry Clinton, who commanded a force of 7,000 British and Tories. Clinton did not have the combat power to reach Albany. He did attack upriver, however, and took Stony Point and Verplanck's Point, key positions on the Hudson below West Point. Further north the British took Forts Montgomery and Clinton and started operations around West Point. By this time, however, Burgoyne himself was in dire straits, and Clinton could not get any support to him in time. Burgoyne and his army would find themselves isolated in an increasingly hostile countryside.

Burgoyne's idea had been fine in strategic terms. He would probably have had enough men at his disposal to carry it out without support from either St Leger or Howe, but he burdened his army with too much baggage and artillery and his movement southward was a slow crawl. Ably supported by his second in command, General William Phillips, Fort Ticonderoga was taken and a successful action fought at Hubbardton. A Brunswick detachment was sent to Bennington in nearby Vermont to find provisions, but was caught and largely destroyed by a local militia under the command of the formidable John Stark, who had been an officer in Rogers' Rangers in the Seven Years' War and who had fought stoutly at Bunker Hill in 1775. Vowing to win or his wife would be widowed, Stark launched a furious attack that overwhelmed the largely German force and robbed Burgoyne of a considerable portion of his combat power.

Surrender at Saratoga 1777

As Burgoyne crawled south with his army, the Americans were massing a force of Continentals and militia to face him. The original American commander, General Phillip Schuyler, was replaced by General Horatio Gates, nicknamed 'Granny Gates' by less than respectful subordinates. Seconded by the capable Benedict Arnold, the British were brought to action twice, at Freeman's Farm and at Bemis Heights. The fighting was conducted in the woods and in the open, and generally speaking the Continentals gave better than they got. American Colonel Daniel Morgan and his corps of riflemen were in the front rank of the heavy fighting, and one of them brought down the popular and competent British General Simon Fraser, which was a grave loss to Burgoyne and his army.

Finally, with his southward progress stopped, cut off and having lost a considerable part of his army to enemy action, and now without hope of any help from Howe, Clinton or St Leger, Burgoyne surrendered his beaten army at Saratoga in October. This event triggered the formal French alliance, which was the decisive event of the war. Without French intervention on the side of the United States, it is highly doubtful that the Americans could have won.

▼ *Bemis Heights, the second of the Saratoga battles, left the British with heavy losses, including General Simon Fraser, who can be seen here being carried off the field.*

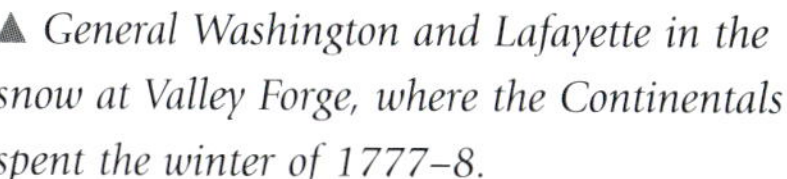

▲ *General Washington and Lafayette in the snow at Valley Forge, where the Continentals spent the winter of 1777–8.*

Valley Forge 1777–8

After Germantown, Washington took the Continental Army to Valley Forge in Pennsylvania for winter quarters. The winter was bitterly cold, and the Continentals were short of food, clothing and the barest essentials for survival. They did endure, however, despite hunger and disease, and Washington's officers worked hard to supply and feed the army. In the middle of the winter, one of Benjamin Franklin's recruited foreign military experts marched into the encampment, presenting himself as a former Prussian general and confidant of Frederick the Great. Friedrich Wilhelm von Steuben was in fact a retired Prussian captain, but he had seen active service in Europe in both combat and staff posts, and was an expert drill master.

Convincing Washington to let him begin the training of the Continentals in the regimen of uniform drill, von Steuben set out to create a disciplined force out of the excellent raw material he said was available. Not speaking any English, and talking through two interpreters, one French and one American, von Steuben created a new drill system that was simple, effective and easy to teach. Von Steuben took the best from the Prussian, French and British drill regulations, with which he was intimately familiar, and created his new system.

The troops liked and respected von Steuben, the ragged scarecrows admiring of and amused by his quickly learned range of English profanities. The troops worked and drilled hard, and the new expertise grew from company to regiment, and later to brigade and division. By the time the Continentals took to the field in June 1778, they were the best trained army that Washington had led, equal on the battlefield to the best of the European professionals they now had to face.

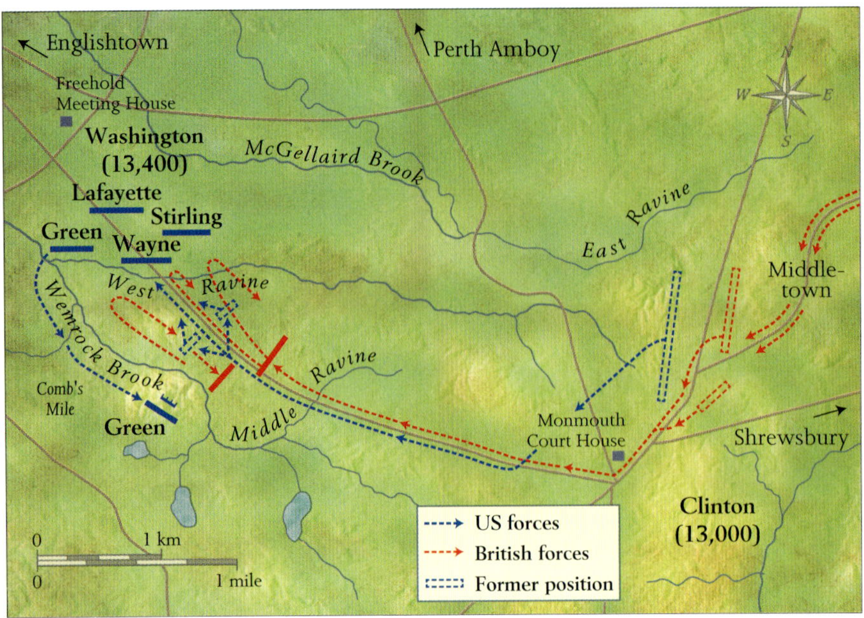

▲ *The battle of Monmouth was the last major action in the northern theatre. The main armies did not meet in battle again.*

Monmouth 1778

Sir William Howe had been replaced as the British commander in North America over the winter by Sir Henry Clinton. Clinton planned to evacuate Philadelphia and withdraw to New York, as the possession of the American capital had not had any noticeable effect of dampening the American war effort. He withdrew the army with a lumbering baggage train that Washington's scouts soon spotted. A plan was undertaken to attack the British, and command of the American advance guard finally devolved upon General Charles Lee, the former British professional who exuded much confidence but whose competence and loyalty were questionable.

Lee moved out to intercept the British, and Washington followed. Blundering into contact with the British column near Monmouth Courthouse, New Jersey, in June 1778, Lee had no coherent plan, nor had he informed his subordinates of his intentions. He wasted time and energy, and after leaving Anthony Wayne exposed to the full force of a British counter-attack, ordered a retreat, with hardly a shot being fired, that had all the makings of a full rout had it gone unchecked.

Washington thundered on to the all but lost battlefield full of righteous wrath, told Lee what he thought of him in no uncertain terms, and relieved him of his command on the spot, in full view of his men. This act may very well have been Washington's finest moment as commander in chief, as he publicly demonstrated fearless, uncompromising leadership at a crucial point in the heat of battle.

Organizing the American counter-attack, Washington and his galvanized subordinates rallied the advance guard under fire. The remainder of the day was a hard fought action with the Americans trying to get their entire army onto the field and engaged, while the British fought furiously to keep the resurgent Continentals from capturing their baggage train and overrunning the British army. Both sides fought magnificently. The Continentals clearly demonstrated their mastery of the intricacies of drill and minor tactics, and fought the British to a standstill. The heat was punishing on the field that day, and casualties were incurred by both sides from heat exhaustion as well as from battle wounds.

In the end, it was a bitter draw. The Americans had had an excellent opportunity to catch the British overextended on the march and inflict a serious reverse on them. Lee's bungling, which might have been intentional, wasted that opportunity. The British saved their huge baggage train, and disengaged expertly, the Americans being too exhausted to pursue effectively. The British successfully withdrew to New York and held that strategic city until the end of the war. This was the last major engagement of the main armies for the remainder of the war. Subsequent operations would be undertaken by either subordinate armies or smaller commands detached from them.

▼ *Monmouth could have been a decisive victory if not for the incompetence of Charles Lee, seen here being relieved of his command.*

▲ *General John Sullivan led the unsuccessful Battle of Rhode Island but is more famous for the campaign against the Iroquois a year later.*

Newport, Rhode Island 1778 and Penobscot Bay 1779

The French alliance now brought French troops and a fleet into action to support the Americans. The first operations, however, were fraught with difficulties and, on the whole, were not successful. Operations at Newport and Savannah ended in defeat. It was not until more competent commanders, such as Admiral François Joseph Paul de Grasse for the navy and Jean Baptiste Rochambeau for the army, gained prominence and command, that allied success was assured.

The allied operation against Newport, Rhode Island, took place in August 1778. John Sullivan was the American commander, and the French fleet was commanded by Admiral Charles Hector d'Estaing, not the best choice to work with the Americans. Operations were met by an aggressive British defence, and little active co-operation between the French and American allies. D'Estaing suddenly withdrew because of threatening weather, and with him went most of the American militia.

Sensing weakness, the British commander, General Robert Pigot (who had fought at Bunker Hill) sortied out of his defences and defeated the Americans. The American operation had to be abandoned, which was a bitter pill for Sullivan, who had begun the campaign with high hopes but saw opportunities slip away one by one. He was not a lucky commander.

The Americans also failed miserably in the Penobscot Bay operation in July and August 1779. The British had occupied the bay on the Maine coastline, which was then part of Massachusetts. A decision was made to mount an expedition to eject the British, and the American naval officer chosen to lead it, Captain Dudley Saltonstall, was not only incompetent, but untrustworthy and cowardly.

The core of the naval expedition consisted of Continental Navy ships, but the British proved too hard to beat. Saltonstall dallied with councils of war instead of prompt action, and a Royal Navy squadron showed up in his rear, and chased the American ships up the bay, where they all were taken or burned to prevent capture. Saltonstall was court-martialled and dismissed from the service. Taking that factor into account, it might be said that some good emerged from this disaster; yet it did not make up for the heavy losses in men, material and money.

▼ *Henry 'Light Horse Harry' Lee, an outstanding American cavalry commander, led the assault at Paulus Hook in 1779.*

▲ *Anthony Wayne commanded and led the Continental Corps of Light Infantry in a night bayonets-only assault against Stony Point.*

Stony Point and Paulus Hook 1779

Two small operations, both on land and mounted by the Americans, brightened 1779. Anthony Wayne mounted a night assault on the British fortifications at Stony Point, leading his Continental Corps of Light Infantry into its first action. Attacking with unloaded muskets and bayonets only, the Americans performed superbly and killed, wounded or captured the entire British garrison. British casualties were 63 killed, 70 wounded and over 500 captured. It was suitable revenge for the Battle of Paoli.

Not to be outdone, Henry Lee mounted a similar assault against the British garrison at Paulus Hook, withdrawing after inflicting over 200 casualties. The Americans were learning the profession of arms.

Neither of the actions gained anything in terms of land, fortifications, or new positions for the Continental Army, but both definitely demonstrated that the Continentals were coming of age as a military force. Outstanding leadership, more than adequate training, discipline, tactical ability and flexibility were now possessed by the Continentals.

Loyalist and Rebel Clashes 1780–1

The war was, in many cases, a civil war among the American population of the British colonies. Whether Whig or Tory, Loyalist or Rebel, Americans fought each other as bitterly and fiercely as the British fought the Continental Army and militia.

There were two areas in the United States (designated as such on 4 July 1776) where the contest between Americans with divided loyalties became bitter and prolonged. The first was regional and contained in the Hudson Valley above New York City. There the supporters of the Crown, nicknamed Cowboys, and the supporters of an independent United States, fought a hit-and-run war with little quarter granted on either side. The fighting was bitter and prolonged, prompted as much by old family quarrels as by divided loyalties.

It was in the south, however, that the most bitter fighting between Americans was conducted. Partisan units under such commanders as Francis Marion (the famous 'Swamp Fox'), Andrew Pickens and Thomas Sumter fought a hit-and-run war against the British and their Loyalist supporters. These three partisan commanders co-operated more or less (Marion especially) with the field army under Nathaniel Greene, but there were others who organized themselves to fight against their neighbours, be they Loyalist or Rebel. Farms were burned, crops ruined, families murdered and old scores settled.

Between June and September 1780 there were at least two dozen actions between Loyalists and Rebels, the end result being that there was no large rising of Loyalists to support the British effort in the Carolinas. The fighting between Americans displayed a level of brutality that was rarely seen in other theatres of the war. Prisoners were sometimes executed after an action, usually by hanging, and often to settle personal scores. A shocked British general remarked "these people are beyond every curb of religion and humanity". At times regulars from both sides became involved. Colonel Henry Lee's Legion surprised and defeated a Loyalist unit at the Haw River in February 1781, and joined with Marion in several successful operations that helped capture British outposts in the interior of South Carolina, including forts Motte, Granby and Watson. Not to be outdone, the British Legion, under Banastre Tarleton, destroyed Buford's command at the Waxhaws, slaughtering the Americans after they had surrendered, giving rise to the term 'Tarleton's Quarter'.

Charleston 1780

Monmouth was the last time that the two main armies would meet on the battlefield during the war. Because of the American and French alliance in 1778, and the subsequent involvement of the Spanish in 1779 and Dutch in 1780 against Great Britain, the conflict took on a global scope. North America was now one theatre of many. British troops who had originally been deployed to North America were sent elsewhere, such as the West Indies, where French and British interests clashed.

The British made a strong effort to occupy and pacify the southern colonies of Georgia, North Carolina and South Carolina, and also launched effective raids into Virginia. Savannah was taken in 1779, and withstood a combined Franco-American siege later that year. General Phillips, seconded by Benedict Arnold, now a British brigadier general, raided deeply and devastatingly into Virginia, which was

▼ *During the British attack on Charleston in 1776, the American colours were cut down by British naval gunfire. Sergeant Jasper climbed the parapet and put them back in place.*

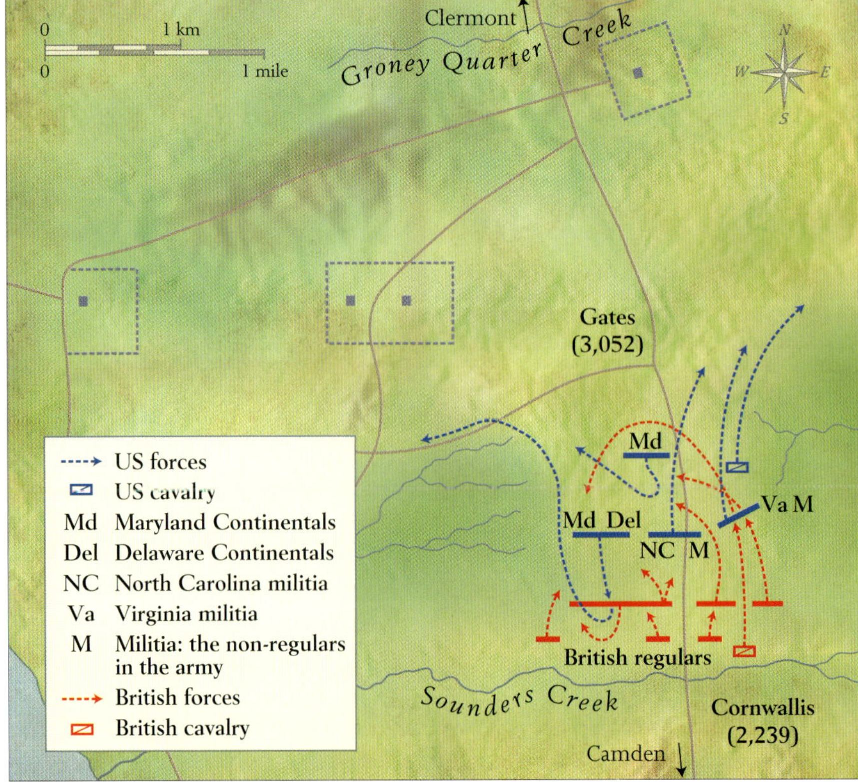

▼ *Camden was an American defeat, but demonstrated the discipline, expertise and spirit of the Continental regiments.*

▲ *Green arrives in Charlotte to take over command of the Southern army from Horatio Gates, following Gates' defeat at Camden.*

woefully unprepared to defend itself, because of the general incompetence of its governor, Thomas Jefferson.

The most devastating blow, however, was the siege and capture of Charleston, South Carolina, in 1780. Not only was this important seaport taken, but over 5,000 troops were surrendered by their commander, Benjamin Lincoln. The Continental lines of Virginia, North and South Carolinas, and Georgia were all taken in the surrender. It was a disaster for the Americans and it would take them a long time to recover.

A small Continental force had been despatched from the main army to reinforce Charleston under General Baron Johann de Kalb. It was a relatively weak body of men numerically, but it contained some of the best troops in the Continental Army. The Maryland Division, consisting of the Maryland Continental Line and the Delaware Regiment, had been commanded by the competent de Kalb for some time. There was mutual respect between the troops and their commander, and that devotion would soon be proven. De Kalb commanded the only Continental force south of Virginia after the fall of Charleston. Congress considered that being commanded by a foreigner was a bad idea, and asked Washington for a replacement for de Kalb. Washington immediately suggested Nathaniel Greene, who was probably the ablest of his subordinates, but Congress overruled him, choosing Horatio Gates, the victor of Saratoga, instead. It was a terrible choice.

In spite of his ambition, 'Granny Gates' was mildly incompetent, and a chancy comrade-in-arms. He wanted to supplant Washington as commander in chief of the Continental Army, and had a considerable following among the officers. A terrible tactician and no strategist, he assumed command in the south, was reinforced with militia and a few other reliable units, and was determined to fight and defeat the British no matter what the situation or the odds were. He ignored the advice of able subordinates such as de Kalb, Mordecai Gist, Otho Holland Williams and John Eager Howard, and went about his duties without employing all the resources he had to hand. Completely ignoring the military potential of such partisan units as those of Francis Marion, Major General Gates marched headlong into disaster at the Battle of Camden, where he was routed by the British, and fled.

Battle of Camden 1780

At Camden, under Gates, the militia, with the exception of one regiment, "ran like a torrent" taking Gates along with them for good measure. The steady Maryland and Delaware Continentals maintained their position on the battlefield as the militia headed for the rear, and fought in line of battle under the revered de Kalb, executing furious bayonet charges and bringing the British regulars to a standstill. Cornwallis turned his entire army against the stubborn Continentals until they were finally overcome, their commander captured, dying from his wounds. Finally, the survivors headed to the rear and safety after incurring heavy losses.

▲ *Close combat at the conclusion of the Battle of Cowpens, the only battle of annihilation during the war.*

▼ *An excellent commander, Daniel Morgan led the American light forces to victory against Tarleton at the Battle of Cowpens.*

Greene's Southern Campaign 1781

Washington again nominated Greene for the southern command, and this time, almost too late, Congress fawningly approved. Sent south, Greene met his new command in North Carolina, fewer than 1,000 men short of arms, ammunition, uniforms and equipment.

However, the Continentals who had survived the Camden disaster were iron men that nothing could discourage or defeat. Greene also inherited excellent subordinates, a group of lieutenant colonels, who would inspire and lead the backbone of the southern army. Mordecai Gist was sent north to recruit the Maryland line back up to strength, but there was also Otho Holland Williams and John Eager Howard of the Maryland Line, and Robert Kirkwood of the Delawares. In addition Greene had the cavalryman William Washington (a cousin of the commander in chief and arguably the most able cavalry commander on either side during the war), the artilleryman Edward Carrington, and Henry Lee who came with his green-coated legion of infantry and cavalry. This was one of the most talented groups of subordinates any American commander has had the privilege to lead.

Even so Greene was not in an enviable position. The war chest was empty, the troops' clothing was in tatters and supplies were nonexistent. He nevertheless decided on a bold course of action. He would divide his small army in two, giving command of the smaller half to veteran Daniel Morgan, who had arrived to offer his services. Giving Morgan the pick of the Continentals, he despatched him into the interior of North Carolina, seeing what Cornwallis would do. Taking the bulk of the army, and most of the militia, Greene headed north, hoping to eventually reunite with Morgan.

Cornwallis, instead of concentrating against one of the American detachments, also divided his force, giving the pick of his light troops to Tarleton, who was ordered to pursue and destroy Morgan. Morgan stopped to fight at a place called Hannah's Cowpens, which the locals used to graze their cattle.

Battle of Cowpens 1781

With his back to the Broad River, a ploy which was done to ensure his militia stayed and fought, Morgan organized his army for combat. He placed it in three lines. The first was the most unreliable of his militia, and all he requested of them was two shots apiece, and then they could retire to the rear to rally.

In his second line he placed the more reliable militia under Pickens, the partisan commander who joined Morgan for this fight, and the third line was reserved for his reliable Maryland and Delaware Continentals under the indefatigable and very competent Lieutenant Colonel John Eager Howard of Maryland. He placed Washington's Continental Light Dragoons and mounted militia in reserve to be ready to support the Continental infantry. Tarleton came on the battlefield and immediately attacked. The militia in the first two lines did as Morgan had instructed. Instead of a planned withdrawal, Tarleton saw what he wanted to see, and drove on until he ran into the solid line of Continentals. They gave the now disorganized British infantry a volley at close range, then executed a devastating bayonet charge, driving the British infantry before them. William Washington's cavalry charged, the rallied militia counter attacked, and Tarleton's army fell apart. Many were killed, wounded or captured. Tarleton's force was completely destroyed.

The Race to the Dan 1781

After his total victory at Cowpens Morgan did not tarry in the area. Informing Greene of his victory he immediately headed for the Virginia border with his prisoners, grimly aware that he had considerably provoked Cornwallis. General Greene, when informed of victory, headed north to meet Morgan, and shortly after the two forces rejoined, although Morgan went home because of illness. Knowing that Cornwallis would be hot on his trail, Greene gave command of the rearguard to Otho Holland Williams of Maryland and headed north to the Dan River and Virginia.

▲ *Cornwallis was undoubtedly the best British field commander of the war. Demanding, able and tough, he also took good care of his men.*

Cornwallis was infuriated over Tarleton's disaster. This was the second American battlefield victory since Camden, and it had resulted in the annihilation of the British force. The other one had been in October 1780, when Patrick Ferguson had been surrounded and trapped on King's Mountain by a force of American 'over the mountain men' and annihilated, Ferguson himself being shot out of the saddle and killed.

Cornwallis was determined to catch and destroy Greene. To make his army more mobile, he ordered the army's baggage burned, including his own. That done, and the troops carrying what they would need, he set off after Greene in what would come to be known as the "Race to the Dan".

The campaign, in the dead of a North Carolina winter, was cold and wet. Troops marched and fought, the American rearguard barely staying ahead of Cornwallis' advance guard at times, but never drawn into a general engagement. Williams demonstrated skill and leadership in the handling of his troops, and he was always between Greene and the British. Rivers were crossed, bogs and swamps bypassed, and finally the Americans, Lee's Legion being the last over, crossed the Dan into Virginia. As Greene had confiscated everything that would float and carry man or horse over the river, Cornwallis was stuck on the south bank. The British had lost the race.

After having destroyed his baggage and now far away from his own supply depots in South Carolina, Cornwallis had no choice but to withdraw from the Dan River line to feed and resupply his worn-out army. This encouraged Loyalist militia to take to the field in support of Greene. Partisan bands under Marion, Pickens, and Sumter were alive and well and prepared to do damage both to Cornwallis' frayed line of communication and any Loyalist stirrings in the Carolinas. Unlike his predecessor, Gates, Greene understood the value of the partisans and did not hesitate to send Continentals to support them whenever necessary.

▼ *Greene never won a battle, but did win every campaign, with operations reminiscent of those of French Marshal Turenne.*

Battle of Guilford Courthouse 1781

Cornwallis was now out of supplies and his troops were worn out. They had done their best, but had failed. They withdrew back into North Carolina to regroup and refit. Greene crossed back into North Carolina in February. By March, he had 4,400 men under arms, almost 1,700 of them Continentals. He met Cornwallis in battle at Guilford Courthouse that month, and while not being able to defeat Cornwallis tactically, he mauled the British army, inflicting 21 per cent casualties on Cornwallis' army of 1,900. Some of Cornwallis' most able subordinates had been wounded or killed, and he had failed in his objective of destroying Greene's army. He would eventually withdraw into Virginia to a little town on the James River called Yorktown.

Greene now embarked on a campaign to rid the Carolinas of the British. He never won a battle, but never lost a campaign. He lost tactical brawls at Hobkirk's Hill and Eutaw Springs in 1781, where he again inflicted crippling losses on his British opponents. His siege of the key British fortification at Ninety-Six was a failure, but after he lifted the siege, the British destroyed the works and withdrew. By mid-1782 in a masterful campaign, reminiscent of the campaigns of the great French Marshal Turenne in the 17th century, Greene had driven the British into Savannah and Charleston, two ports that the British would hold until the end of the war, thanks to the Royal Navy. The war was all but over.

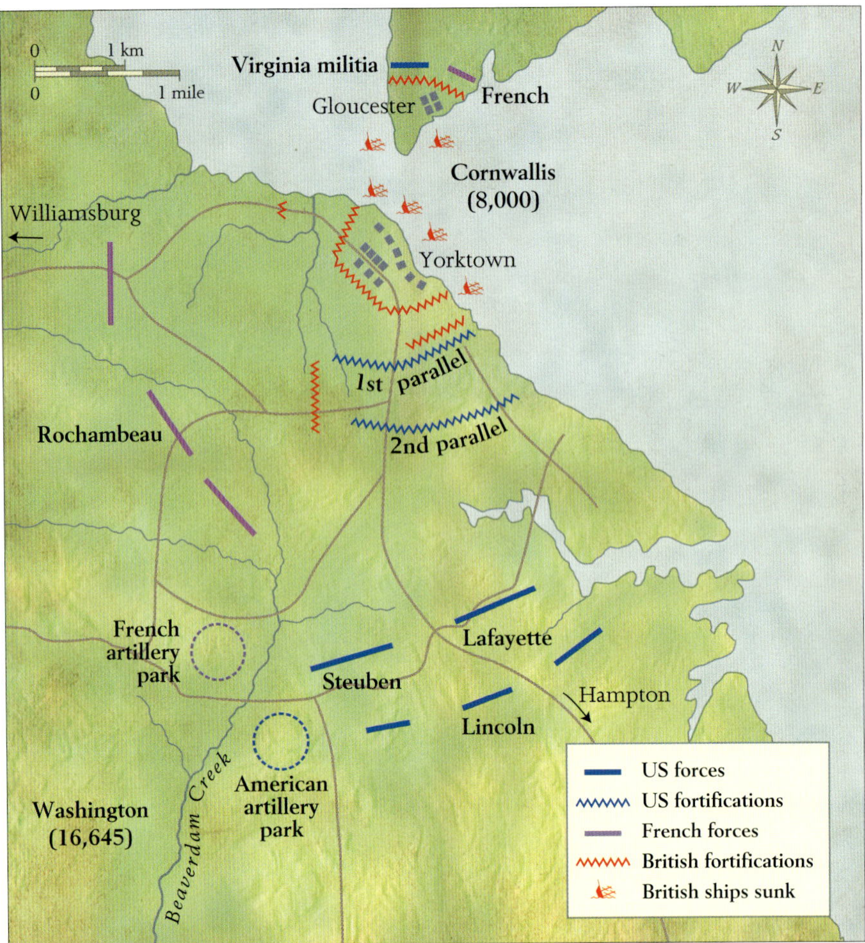

▲ *The Siege of Yorktown saw the combined Franco-American army, supported by a French fleet, force the surrender of the British Army.*

▼ *The veteran 1st Maryland Regiment, in line of battle with William Washington's 3rd Light Dragoons, charge at Guilford Courthouse.*

The Siege of Yorktown 1771

After the mauling that Cornwallis took at Guilford Courthouse, he withdrew to Wilmington, North Carolina, to refit and rest his troops. They had campaigned over difficult terrain, had lost most of their baggage, and had incurred heavy losses with nothing to show for it. Eventually, Cornwallis made the decision to withdraw into Virginia; campaigning in the Carolinas against Greene would be left to others.

He rested his troops in Virginia and built up the strength of his army. He manoeuvred expertly against the new American field army that had been sent south into Virginia under the

French general Marquis de Lafayette. The two armies skirmished and fenced, but no decisive actions were fought. Still, Lafayette's force was present as Cornwallis withdrew to the coast, eventually taking and fortifying positions at Yorktown and Cape Gloucestershire across the river. There, supplied and protected by the ubiquitous Royal Navy, all seemed secure for the British.

The French had despatched an expeditionary force to North America to work with Washington in 1780. Landing in Rhode Island, Rochambeau, its commander, and Washington became friends and comrades, and the French commander readily subordinated himself to the tall Virginian. The French Army was excellent: well trained and equipped, and liberally supplied with artillery of the new Gribeauval design. Washington wanted to attack New York and finally retake the city and harbour. Rochambeau had a better idea. In conjunction with de Grasse's French fleet, which could be off the Virginia Capes in October, why not concentrate against Cornwallis in Virginia and take that objective?

Convincing Washington of the idea, the armies marched south. Massing against Yorktown, and reinforced with troops and a siege train from the West Indies, the allies opened siege operations against Cornwallis. Allied artillery pounded the British defences, and also sank ships in the British anchorage in the river. Two redoubts were taken by storm in night bayonet attacks, and although the British sortied against the allied siege works, the siege lines tightened. Allied artillery, well served by both French and American gunners, maintained the bombardment of the British lines. De Grasse's fleet kept the Royal Navy out of the Chesapeake, and Cornwallis was forced to ask for terms. For the second time in the war, a British army marched into captivity.

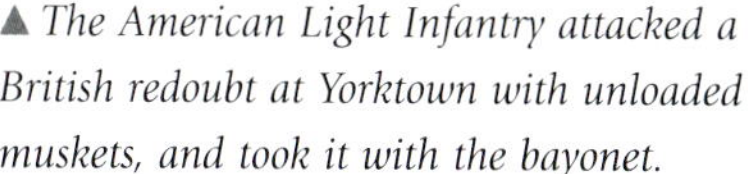

▲ *The American Light Infantry attacked a British redoubt at Yorktown with unloaded muskets, and took it with the bayonet.*

▼ *The British admit defeat, and surrender to General Washington, after the Americans' victory at the battle of Yorktown, Virginia.*

The End of the War

Although there were still engagements, especially in the south where Greene's army slowly herded the remaining British troops into the protection of the Royal Navy in Savannah and Charleston, Yorktown was the last major engagement of the war. The Treaty of Paris in 1783 signalled the end of the conflict, with the United States emerging victorious, humiliating Great Britain and depriving it of its most valuable colonies.

THE NAVAL WAR

After victory against France in the Seven Years' War, Great Britain became the dominant naval power in the world. Royal Navy ships protected its commerce and kept open its sea lanes; overseas trade, especially with its colonies, was Britain's lifeblood. When the war with America broke out, the colonies did not have a navy. They did, however, have valuable access to naval stores, upon which the British depended, and they had their own capacity to build ships. Recognizing the need for a fleet, the Continental Navy was created in October 1775, with the Continental Marines created shortly afterwards on 10 November.

▲ *Single ship actions were usually won by the ship with the best crew. The British generally fired into their enemy's hulls to disable their opponent, while the French fired into the masts and rigging, as here.*

The Continental Navy

A deep-water navy is not built and trained overnight, and although plans were ambitious and some successful operations were carried out, the overall achievement of the Continental and State navies was second-rate. Good solid frigates were built – ships that were captured by the British were good enough to be put into service by the Royal Navy. Some American captains, such as John Barry, Joshua Barney and the ex-slaver John Paul Jones, performed noble deeds with their ships. American privateers also harried British merchant ships, but the Continental Navy was never large enough or solid enough to present a challenge to the Royal Navy at sea.

▼ *The* Hannah, *the first warship of Washington's navy, proof that Washington realized the importance of naval power.*

The French Navy

France's naval threat, on the other hand, was a different matter. Bitter over the myriad defeats and humiliations of the Seven Years' War, on both land and sea, various reform-minded officers and ministers wanted to rebuild France's army and navy with vengeance very much in mind. Once they had constructed their beautiful, powerful warships, which could out-sail anything afloat, they only needed an excuse to prove that they were as good as their British counterparts.

Naval Battles

After the French–American Alliance and France's entry into the war (to be followed by the Spanish and Dutch and their navies), most of the naval war was carried on in the West Indies as the British and French struggled to control the colonies in the valuable Sugar Islands. Amphibious operations took and retook islands in the Caribbean, Dominica falling to the French and

▲ *The massed French ships in Comte de Grasse's action at Frigate Bay, St Kitts, 26 January 1782, against Sir Samuel Hood.*

St Lucia and St Kitts being taken by the British. The French also attacked and seized Grenada in 1779. There was also an important naval war between Britain and France in the Bay of Bengal. Fleet actions of note took place, including the Moonlight Battle in 1780, Dogger Bank in 1781 and the Saintes in 1782. Gibraltar underwent and withstood a Spanish siege from 1779 to 1782, but the combined weight of fighting three navies, plus the annoyance of the Continental Navy, stretched the assets of the Royal Navy to the breaking point.

Battle of the Chesapeake

Undoubtedly the most decisive naval action of the war, at least from the American viewpoint, is the Battle of the Chesapeake, also known as the battle of Virginia Capes. No Americans were present, and the fighting was less than decisive tactically, but as a strategic success, it was overwhelming. The French and British fleets met off the Chesapeake Bay and had a running fight. Ships were damaged and men killed and wounded. There were no dramatic or desperate actions, as would occur at the Battle of the Saintes the next year, where Admiral George Rodney broke the French line. But de Grasse kept the Royal Navy out of the Chesapeake and prevented Cornwallis, undergoing a siege at Yorktown, from being relieved. The British were defeated, and Cornwallis surrendered, ensuring American independence.

With two armies on the North American continent having surrendered to the Americans and French, British chances for recovering the American colonies were nonexistent. After considerable delay, in which the British delegation sulked over a lost war and refused to sit for the portrait of the negotiators of the peace, a Treaty was signed in Paris in 1783. The United States was a sovereign nation.

▼ *The successful action of the Battle of the Saintes captured the French Admiral de Grasse, and allowed Britain some bargaining power at the peace table.*

MILITIAS, EARLY CONTINENTAL UNITS AND STATE TROOPS

In April 1775 there was no American regular army. Each colony maintained local and sometimes state militia units, but there was no military force for the defence of the colonies as a whole. There were experienced fighting men who had served against the French and American Indians in the old Provincial forces or as part of the British Army, and knew how to organize, equip, and lead soldiers. Eventually, with the guidance of George Washington, the motley collection of militiamen in that summer of 1775 would evolve into a professional military force that would win independence for a new nation.

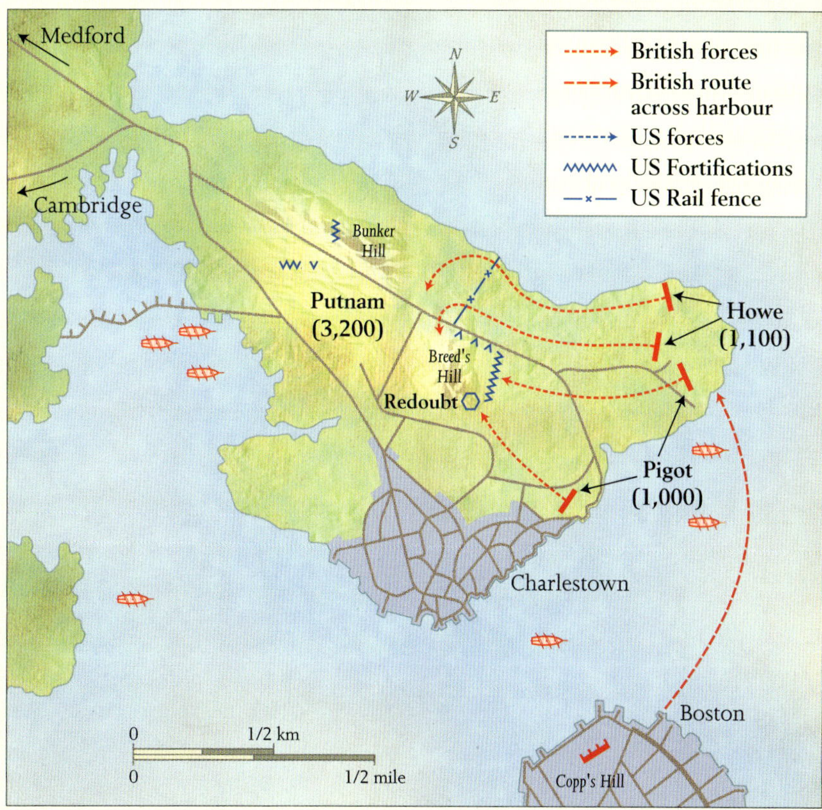

▲ *The Battle of Bunker Hill was a disaster for the British, who held the Americans in contempt and believed they would sweep them from the field. This was a costly error.*

◄ *At the Battle of Freeman's Farm, 19 September 1777, the Americans inflicted heavy losses on Burgoyne's British troops, and stopped their advance, but eventually gave up the field.*

MILITIA AND STATE TROOPS

The armed forces of the American colonies had steadily evolved as the colonial empire had grown. Rooted firmly in tradition, American military culture would initially rely on militias and volunteers to field manpower to fight the British.

Beginnings

There had been locally organized, as well as colony-sponsored, militia units in the British colonies since the first settlements had been established at Jamestown, Virginia, in 1607. The British colonists brought their institutions and traditions with them, and their military system was one such institution. The men organized to defend the new settlements were the successors of the Trained Bands of England, bodies of men that were called to fight for king and country according to the Assize of Arms of 1181. In North America the colonial militias were the only means of defence from the American Indians and from those Europeans in the New World looking for land and wealth.

The first Virginians established a martial law in 1611, requiring that all who were soldiers were to be drilled daily and had to come armed and uniformed, completely equipped and armoured. The southern colonies organized their militia by counties, as the settlements were more spread out, with a plantation system evolving as the basis of the economy for the region. In Massachusetts and the other northern colonies, which were more densely populated, the militia companies were organized by the towns. The southern militia officers were appointed by provincial governors, while in the north they were elected.

The militias were necessary, and partly evolved from the traditional British distrust of a standing army, a feeling that was reinforced by the experience of Cromwell's dictatorship. The North American units fought the French and Spanish, who were also vying for colonies in North America, and, inevitably, the various American Indian tribes. This was a new kind of warfare and was usually brutal and merciless. The militiamen also fought the pirates whose ships swarmed up from the Caribbean, targeting coastal townships or settlements.

Originally using arms and armour brought over from Europe and of the kind being used in European warfare, they learned how to fight against a diverse range of enemies in varied terrain. Pikes and armour were gradually discarded for more comfortable clothing, and the preferred arms were soon the musket, knife, bayonet and hatchet. Equipment was reduced to a minimum, only consisting of what was necessary to fight and survive against more skilful enemies in the field.

The American militia evolved from these crude beginnings into what passed for regular soldiers in America in 1775. Militia units had served well in the past. It was largely militias, led by amateur officers, that besieged and took Louisburg in King George's War. Tough, independent minded "ranger" units were formed to fight the American Indians in the 18th century, some of them becoming quasi-regulars and on the king's payroll. Those units that were commanded by the Gorham brothers and by Robert Rogers (who went on to achieve legendary status) performed good service against the French and Indians.

▲ *African slaves were bought to Jamestown by Dutch traders as early as 1619.*

▼ *The settlers of Jamestown, the first permanent British settlement in America, fighting American Indians in 1607.*

Conflict with Britain

Militiamen were expected to arm and equip themselves, but they frequently came in under-equipped, sometimes on purpose, and had to be armed and equipped at state expense, "forgetting" to hand in their issued accoutrements when they returned home.

While there were smartly uniformed colonial militia units in 1775, most wore a mixture of civilian clothing and military items, and the hunting shirt, a purely American item, was very popular with units formed on the frontier. Washington would have liked it to become an issue item as it was comfortable, smart-looking and could be dyed in any colour. It could also camouflage whether or not a unit was militia or regular, state or Continental, to the confusion of the British.

Militiamen were armed with an assortment of weapons. The Brown Bess, fowling pieces, rifles, and whatever else could be procured might appear in the same unit. This made resupply difficult, but if the troops made their own bullets and had their own bullet moulds, all that had to be provided was the lead.

Training for the units was varied and, more often than not, nonexistent. Militias on the whole could not engage in a stand-up fight with British and German professionals. Washington damned them as a "broken reed". Militia and state units usually had a higher bounty or higher pay than the Continental units, drawing off valuable manpower where it was actually needed. If a campaign was long and arduous, militias might just drift off and go home. Long marches resulted in shorter columns of militia as the less robust fell out and quit. Worse, the militias often ran when they came into contact with the enemy, discarding their arms and equipment so they could move faster. Standing up to a British bayonet charge could be terrifying, and it required properly trained and well-led troops that would stand and fight. Generally speaking, the militias were neither trained for this type of warfare nor did they usually have the leadership to stand up to it.

▲ *The militia can be seen here fighting behind the Continental Army at Saratoga in the attack on a Hessian redoubt.*

The Militia System

By the time of the great French wars, the militia were no longer used on campaign. As the militia system in the British colonies evolved, volunteers were taken, and if these were insufficient, pressed or conscripted men were used to form provincial units to go on campaign. The quality of such Provincials during the French and Indian War was usually dismal. British commanders damned and criticized Americans as soldiers, but the raw material was not the problem. Of the British regular regiments in North America during that period, at least half of the privates were Americans, the British actively recruiting among the colonial population throughout the period. The problem with the provincial units was their leadership and training, the greatest shortcoming being experienced NCOs to train and hold the troops to their duty.

The militiamen who opened fire on the British in 1775 were the inheritors of this system. Volunteers were again called for and sent. Men hired substitutes to fight in their stead, and slaves were at times sent instead of their owners with the promise that they might be freed if they survived.

When called out by a state, the militia would usually only serve for three months. The Continentals' names for them, "long faces" and the "locusts of Egypt", correctly labelled a great many that showed up reluctantly, ate hard-found rations, used up stores of clothing and supplies, and often just disappeared and went home before their service was up.

However, the militia did have one advantage over the Continentals: there were a lot of them. If competently led by intelligent commanders, such as Morgan, they could operate effectively. They could also occupy ground abandoned by the British, establishing an American presence that was hard to dislodge. Wherever they stayed, the territory was no longer under British control, and so it was that the British never controlled much beyond the coast, which they held thanks to the support of the Royal Navy.

In the final analysis, however, and contrary to American myth and legend, it was the Continentals and not the militiamen that won the war. The militia system was flawed and insufficient, a fact that would again be proven during the War of 1812. Indeed, this would be the last war in which the United States would rely on militias to take to the field.

PRE-WAR MILITIA UNITS

Some militia units had considerable pedigree, while others were hastily raised in the heat of the moment. All units were unregulated by any central authority; some colonies provided arms and equipment for their men, others left it to the individuals who were called up.

Units in the Field

Some of the militia units in existence in the different colonies prior to the war were organized on a regular and permanent basis. These units varied in quality as all militia units did, but some were quite well trained and uniformed. They presented a neat, military appearance when mustered on parade, and formed the basis of the military organizations that were later to be combined into the Continental Army. Red or dark blue was the preferred colour for uniforms, following the general pattern of the British Army, and the men were armed and equipped along the lines of their British brethren. The overwhelming majority of the units were infantry, which was not only the arm that was the basis for any armed force, but was that which had hitherto been most utilized in the wars in North America.

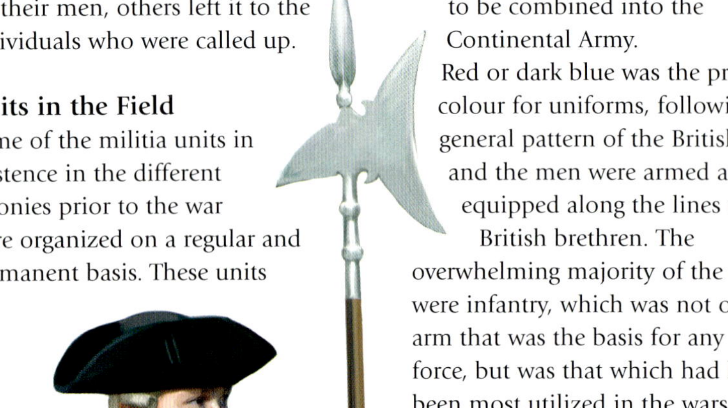

Colonial Uniforms

No colony had a set of uniform regulations for its militia units, and there was no national standard for uniforms until the Continental Regulations of 1779. Many militia units had no standard uniform at all, and mustered in civilian clothes with their equipment, their own personal effects and weapon, or that issued by the respective colony. Many simply wore a piece of regulation clothing on top of whatever civilian clothing they chose to wear on a given day. Typical examples of American units in the colonies prior to the opening of hostilities are the following:

2ND BATTALION OF NEW YORK PROVINCIAL FORCES. This unit was uniformed in a light tan coat with dark blue facings. The coat was cut short, and white, light tan or dark blue waistcoats were worn. Officers wore the traditional red sash, and

◀ **SERGEANT, FAIRFAX (VIRGINIA) INDEPENDENT COMPANY OF VOLUNTEERS, 1774–5** *Independent companies were English military units in the colonies in North America. From them developed the militia units, but independent companies were still in existence at the beginning of the Revolution.*

▶ **OFFICER, LIGHT INFANTRY COMPANY, CHARLESTON REGIMENT, SOUTH CAROLINA MILITIA, 1773–6** *One of the colours favoured by American militia units was red or scarlet, as for the British Army. This smartly turned-out unit was quite British in appearance and must have looked striking on parade. Units of this type provided officers and men for newly formed Continental regiments when fighting began in 1775.*

NCOs had a red sash with a dark blue stripe through it. The tricorne was worn, that of the officers and NCOs being bound in white tape. Drummers did not wear the usual reversed colours but had the buttonholes bound in white tape. Breeches, stockings and shoes were worn, mounted officers wearing riding boots and spurs.

GRENADIER COMPANY OF THE NEW YORK CITY INDEPENDENT MILITIA. This body was an example of an unusual unit in the American military. British infantry regiments all had grenadier companies composed of the strongest, tallest, most experienced troops in the regiment. This militia company was modelled on European lines and had a mixture of uniforms from the French and Indian War period and more recent innovations. The old grenadier cap was used, as was a coat of older, fuller cut. Waistcoat, breeches, stockings, and half gaiters over shoes gave the unit a more modern appearance, but the hair remained long, braided and powdered. The coat was dark blue, and had a stand-up collar. Facings were red with gold button lace. Waistcoat, breeches and stockings were white, and black half gaiters were worn.

FAIRFAX INDEPENDENT COMPANY OF VOLUNTEERS. In 1774 and 1775 this company was simply uniformed in dark blue and buff. Officers and sergeants wore regulation uniforms, and the privates wore a hunting shirt of the same colour. The tricorne was worn. Officers carried a sword as a sidearm, and might also carry a cane. Sergeants had swords and halberds, used as a badge of rank but now on the way out as a combat weapon. The rank and file was armed with rifles.

CHARLESTON REGIMENT OF THE SOUTH CAROLINA MILITIA. This had a light infantry company that was initially uniformed in scarlet and dark blue. All ranks wore a light infantry cap with the South Carolina crescent badge on the front. Bayonets were worn by the privates on a shoulderbelt over their right shoulder, and their cartridge box was worn on a belt around the waist, located at the front, over the stomach, hence the term "belly box". The officers were armed with a sword or hanger, and the NCOs with a sword and halberd.

These units either went into the field or provided cadres for units that were raised for the Continental Army. One such unit was the Independent Company of Cadets, formed in 1741. In the early 1770s the unit's lieutenant commandant was John Hancock, who was president of the 2nd Continental Congress when it drafted the Declaration of Independence. His signature is the first on that document.

◀ **PRIVATE, GRENADIER COMPANY, NEW YORK CITY INDEPENDENT MILITIA, 1775–6** *Few American units actually had uniformed grenadier units, and this one took the older uniform of the British grenadier companies during the French and Indian War. Uniforms like this didn't last long once the war started.*

▶ **PRIVATE, 2ND BATTALION, NEW YORK PROVINCIAL FORCES, 1775** *"Provincial" for American regiments was a term left over from the French and Indian War, and was usually a derogatory term used by the British, not without cause. Many of the American units were poorly led and disciplined, but eventually improved enough to become the basis of the Continental Army.*

THE MINUTEMEN

Units of Minutemen were formed and organized in 1774 and were supposed to be a form of militia that could be called out at a minute's notice, and rushed to where they were needed.

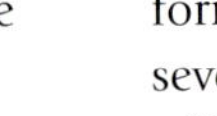

▼ **Officer, Taliaferro's Company, The Minute Battalion of Culpeper County, Virginia, 1775–6** *This officer shows a different type of hunting shirt with matching legging trousers. More flamboyant than that of enlisted men, it was still functional and comfortable in the field.*

A Patriotic Militia

When the Massachusetts militia re-formed itself from three regiments to seven, in 1774, it purged itself of officers that were loyal to the Crown. The militia alarm companies, as well as the Minutemen, were formed from one-third of each town's militia company. Officers were elected, and the youngest and most active of the militia companies were chosen to make up the new companies, which were then organized into regiments. These units were provisional and often only lasted for six months.

The reputation of the Minutemen as units that were on permanent stand-by, ready and able to respond to any emergency or call-out at a minute's notice, is the stuff of myth and legend. They have often been presented in history books as the tough, gallant and intelligent American farmer who stood up to and defeated the British regular. Such is not actually the case.

Generally speaking, they were not uniformed in any manner and wore civilian clothes on duty, although their officers sometimes wore a uniform. Fortunately for them, there were enough veterans of the French Wars that were still able to take the field and give them a stiffening of men who had actually heard a shot fired in anger. Expected to arm themselves, Minute companies were formed throughout the colonies, although those in Massachusetts are the ones that are usually the most remembered because of their involvement in the battles of Lexington and Concord.

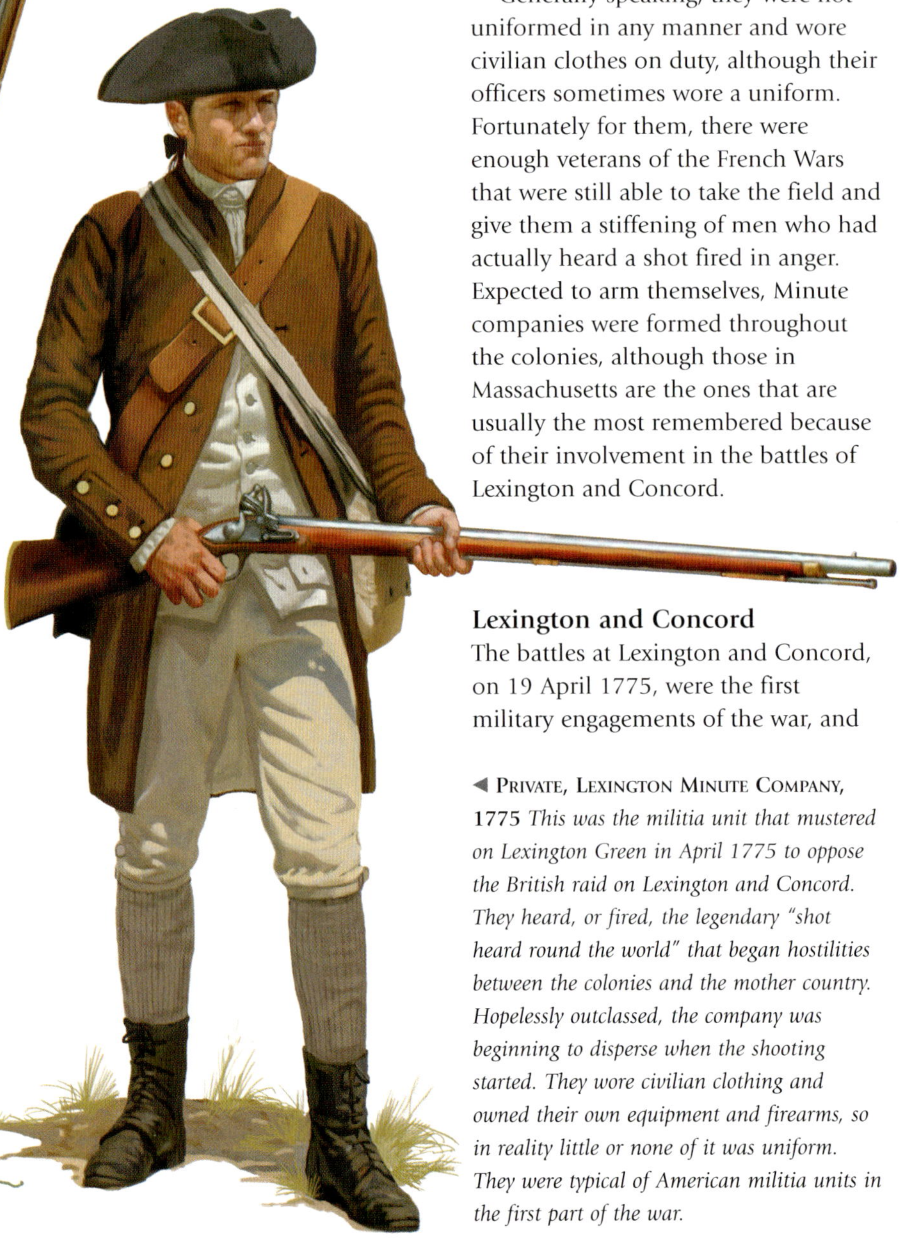

Lexington and Concord

The battles at Lexington and Concord, on 19 April 1775, were the first military engagements of the war, and

◄ **Private, Lexington Minute Company, 1775** *This was the militia unit that mustered on Lexington Green in April 1775 to oppose the British raid on Lexington and Concord. They heard, or fired, the legendary "shot heard round the world" that began hostilities between the colonies and the mother country. Hopelessly outclassed, the company was beginning to disperse when the shooting started. They wore civilian clothing and owned their own equipment and firearms, so in reality little or none of it was uniform. They were typical of American militia units in the first part of the war.*

◀ **Private, The Minute Battalion of Culpeper County, Virginia, 1775–6** *This militia unit, which was a Virginia "regular" unit, was uniformed in hunting shirts and leggings, probably of the uniform colours shown here. The motto "Liberty or Death" was derived from firebrand Patrick Henry's speech before the House of Burgesses, which helped foment rebellion in the colonies. The uniform is quite handsome and very functional, and is unique to the American colonies.*

are interesting in that many Minute companies really did turn out at the first and subsequent alarms. This in itself must have been something of a shock to the British, and therefore a tactical advantage for the Americans.

There was no overall American commander, and undoubtedly many of the militia that showed up to fight may have fired a few rounds, quickly thought their duty done, and started to head for home. As the militia fell back, the Minutemen swarmed into the fight and blazed away at the British column, inflicting casualties and taking them in turn. What is not generally known is that the British light infantry companies flanking the British column were ordered to flush the Americans into the open. Many militiamen were surprised from the rear and attacked with a bayonet, a weapon that few, if any, of the Americans possessed at this time, or knew how to use properly.

However, the British broke ranks under the onslaught and fled, and there were so many militiamen fighting on that long road back to Boston that the British would probably have been overwhelmed if a relief column had not been sent from Boston to support them.

Other Minute Companies

Minute companies were formed in many colonies and not just New England, although the New England companies were probably the model for the others. One outstanding example was a Minute battalion that was raised in Culpeper County, Virginia, in 1775. Known as the Culpeper Minute Battalion, it was raised in York and James City counties and was well organized and equipped, with a uniform of hunting shirts and leggings. It was armed with rifles, and the men wore roundhats with a buck's tail in them. One of the officers was destined to be a famous chief justice of the Supreme Court, John Marshall. He was a lieutenant in Captain William Taliaferro's company and wore a uniform of either a purple or a pale blue hunting shirt, with leggings of the same colour and with the hat as described. Officers bore rifles.

Apparently, the Culpeper Minute Battalion had a stand of colours, as well as a drum and two fifes. In addition, material was purchased to be made into "camp colours" that were probably temporary marker flags for the unit while encamped. These marked the limits of the unit's bivouac.

▶ **Officer of Pickett's Company, The Minute Battalion of Culpeper County, Virginia, 1775–6** *This uniform, of an officer in William Pickett's company of the same battalion, would be the regulation dress of the unit. The distinctive features are the aiguillettes on the right shoulder, the high, or grande gaiters, and the full cut of the coat, which is of an earlier style than the period of the Revolution. It is also a simple, yet very elegant uniform.*

MILITIA INFANTRY

Regional variations and uniform distinctions marked all of the American local militias throughout their history. Uniforms, organization and behaviour all had to take into account local conditions, resources and mentalities. The result was a body of men that included units that ranged from the excellent – disciplined and trained, but badly equipped, to the indifferent – unreliable and badly led, but well equipped.

Northern Militias

A number of militia units served in Canada and were uniformed and equipped locally in a style that took account of the harsher climate and wooded terrain.

The Green Mountain Boys was an atypical unit of militia in the early part of the war. Recruited in the Hampshire Grants (which is now part of Vermont), they were known as an independent group and were treated differently from other regiments that were being recruited in 1775.

The Mountain Boys were allowed to elect their officers, and Ethan Allen, who had organized them, was not elected their commanding officer. Seth Warner was elected, probably because he had been an officer of Rogers' Rangers in the French and Indian War. Known from that point as Warner's Regiment, the unit was taken into the Continental Army under that name.

The regiment was probably uniformed in green coats with red facings, buff breeches and waistcoat, wearing stockings and shoes. Their tricorne hats were bound in black tape and their crossbelts or waist belts were either brown or of American Indian pattern. Warner's Regiment served in Canada and the northern department and was disbanded before the end of the war, in 1781.

Virginia Militia 1780–1

Another militia unit whose uniform took account of local conditions was the Virginia militia, which would play a major role with Generals Gates and Greene in the southern theatre.

◄ **Private, Seth Warner's Green Mountain Boys, 1775–6** *This was actually a Continental Regiment formed as a 500-man battalion. It lost heavily in Canada and the remnants were reformed as Warner's Regiment. This unit later fought in the Saratoga campaign against Burgoyne's invasion from Canada in 1777.*

▲ **Private, Virginia militia, 1780–1** *These troops served at both Camden and Guilford Courthouse in 1780 and 1781. Their performance at Camden was dismal, shaming their commander General Stevens. At Guilford Stevens swore that they would do their duty and stationed 25 picked marksmen in the rear of his position to shoot anyone who ran. Stiffened by Stevens' resolve and a number of former Continentals in their ranks, they engaged the British regulars in a fluctuating tree-to-tree fight and gave as good as they got before retiring.*

The Virginia militia's performance at the Battle of Camden under Gates in August 1781 was dismal. Running "like a torrent" at the first contact with the British, their commander, General Stevens, a man who learned from both success and failure, was so ashamed that he vowed it would not happen again. When they mustered early the next year and joined Greene for the Guilford Courthouse campaign, the militia had an entirely different makeup and attitude, mostly because of Stevens. When positioned in the American second line at Guilford Courthouse on 15 March 1781, there were many former Continentals in their ranks, and Stevens stationed 25 picked men behind his portion of the line to shoot anyone who ran. This fact was advertised to the men in the ranks. Their position was in the woods, and they took advantage of the cover. When the North Carolina militia fell back from their position in the American first line, the Virginians let them through, waited for the British to appear, and stood firm. Because of the terrain, the fighting turned into a large-scale skirmish, with small parties of British and Americans hunting each other in the undergrowth and trees. Stevens' half of the line did not withdraw to the rear until the right side of the line had given up and Stevens had been wounded. The unit's performance made up for Camden.

The Virginians were probably uniformed in a mixture of civilian clothing and uniform items. No doubt many were in hunting shirts, probably presenting a more uniform appearance at Guilford than most units. They were tough, self-reliant and capably led.

◄ **Trumpeter, Richardson's Regiment, South Carolina Regiment of Militia Light Horse, 1781–2** *Cavalry units were crucial for operations in the south as the country was sparsely populated and the territory that had to be covered was vast. Expensive as they were, some states raised them as troops for their own security. Militia cavalry units maintained the tradition of mounting their trumpeters on greys or whites if possible, and their uniforms were at least of a different colour than the rest of the unit.*

North Carolina Militia 1780–1

Called out in support of the Southern army, the North Carolina militia of 1780 and 1781 had some major operational problems, including the continued supply of arms, ammunition and uniforms.

The North Carolina Continentals had been captured by the British, along with the Continental Lines of Virginia and South Carolina, when Charleston had fallen in 1780. New Continental units had to be raised to replace them, and the civil authorities in North Carolina also had to undertake the logistical support of the Southern army. For a colony that was usually considered to be Virginia's poor southern neighbour, it was a burden that was hard to bear.

The North Carolina militia that was turned out to support General Gates in August 1780 turned and ran when the first shots were fired at Camden (along with the Virginia militia already mentioned). There was an exception to this retreat, however. Colonel Dixon's gallant regiment stood firm and fought against overwhelming numbers of British and Loyalists alongside the stalwart Maryland and Delaware Continentals under Baron de Kalb.

In March the next year, the North Carolina militia dutifully turned out again to fight at Guilford Courthouse. Nathaniel Greene realized they were the least reliable of his troops, and he stationed them in his first line. The orders he gave them were that they had to fire twice at the advancing British, after which they could withdraw. They had a two-gun section of Continental artillery to support them as well as Continental units on both flanks to bolster their confidence. However, they did not have a commander of the calibre of General Stevens to hold them to their duty.

When the British advanced, some of the North Carolinians did their duty, especially those closest to the Continental flank units. A considerable number of British troops were hit, a fact remarked upon by some survivors of the action on the British side. The tactic was not entirely successful, however, and

► STANDARD BEARER, BALTIMORE TROOP OF LIGHT DRAGOONS, 1781 *Standards were as necessary as trumpeters in a mounted unit. They were a source of pride and something to be protected in combat. They were also more than useful as a rallying point and could be seen above the smoke and roar of an action, especially a melée.*

◀ **OFFICER, BALTIMORE TROOP OF LIGHT DRAGOONS, MARYLAND VOLUNTEER MILITIA, 1781** *Boots of almost any type were the best footwear for cavalry. They were easier to wear on horseback than shoes, and they protected the legs when mounted, especially in a mounted action where horses would hit against each other and a trooper's legs were in danger of getting smashed. It was also easier to attach the necessary spurs to the heel of boots than shoes.*

▼ **PRIVATE, NORTH CAROLINA MILITIA, 1780–1** *These troops served alongside the Virginia militia at both Camden and Guilford Courthouse. With the exception of one regiment, they broke and fled before the intimidating British bayonets at Camden. Placed in the first line at Guilford Courthouse, they fired one or two volleys, taking a heavy toll, at the advancing British, and then went to the rear in haste, some not stopping until they reached their homes. They were listed in the casualty report after the battle as missing. Their "uniform" was usually civilian clothing, often, and at best, a functional hunting shirt.*

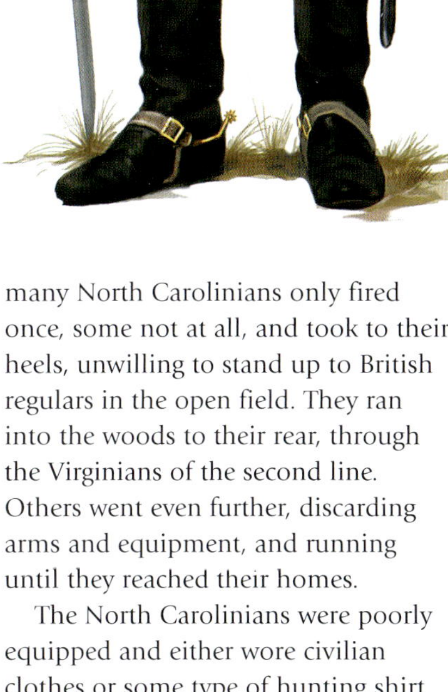

many North Carolinians only fired once, some not at all, and took to their heels, unwilling to stand up to British regulars in the open field. They ran into the woods to their rear, through the Virginians of the second line. Others went even further, discarding arms and equipment, and running until they reached their homes.

The North Carolinians were poorly equipped and either wore civilian clothes or some type of hunting shirt and leggings. They did not have the luxury or advantage of having a high percentage of veterans in their ranks as the Virginians of the second line did, and that definitely showed when they could not be rallied after their "withdrawal" from the field.

Delaware Militia 1775–6

While Delaware would only furnish one Continental regiment, there were militia units uniformed and fielded during the war to support the Continentals.

DOVER LIGHT INFANTRY COMPANY. This was a small unit that was on active service for only a month or so, but in that month it fought at both Trenton and Princeton, and set an excellent record for itself. It was commanded by Thomas Rodney, the brother of Cesar Rodney who had signed the Declaration of Independence. The company was uniformed in green coats faced red with white lining and turnbacks. Brown overalls were worn over shoes, and a light infantry cap of jockey style with a feather on the left side was worn. Ammunition was carried in a black belly box. Apparently they were issued with grey overcoats. If so, they were undoubtedly looked upon with envy by the rest of the army.

CANTWELL'S MIDDLE REGIMENT OF NEW CASTLE, COUNTY DELAWARE. This regiment (there were also Upper and Lower Regiments, all of which were uniformed similarly) was uniformed in sky blue short coats, faced red and lined white with white belts, waistcoats, breeches, stockings and half gaiters. The uniform was completed with a round hat, again with a feather on the left side.

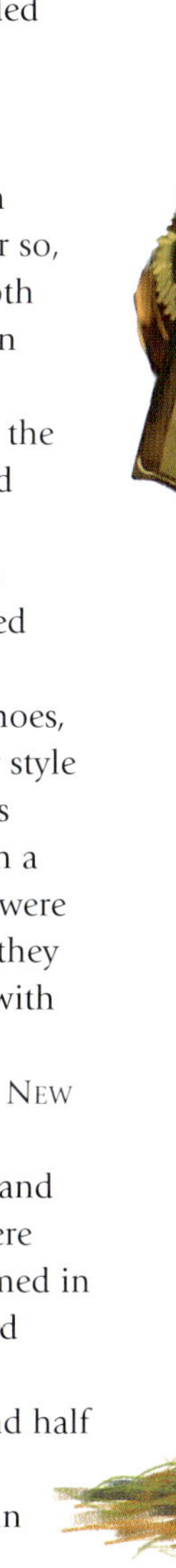

THE FIRST CONTINENTALS

George Washington was the driving force behind the creation of a regular army to supplement, if not replace, the local militia system. This regular force was christened the Continental Army and the troops were invariably known as Continentals.

Washington's Plan

When George Washington took command of the assembly of militia units around Boston in the summer of 1775, there was little organization, no uniformity in either clothing or drill, no staff and very little discipline. Washington immediately began to sort out the major problems that he faced, initially taking all the responsibility himself. With his impetus, the newly formed Continental Army could begin to sort itself out. Men of character and responsibility, as well as enthusiasm for the profession of arms, began to rise to the top, and the desire for units to be in some sort of uniform, as well as being drilled into a semblance of military order and discipline, emerged.

Washington wanted a professional army for the war, one that could meet the British and their German auxiliaries in the field on equal terms. Though he did not achieve all that he wanted to, he escaped complete reliance on a feckless militia, and did fashion an army that was capable, by the spring of 1778, of meeting his enemies on even terms. This was due to Washington's hard work, the development of subordinates who knew their business, the influence of European volunteers, and a growing professionalism that began in 1777 and flourished in 1778.

Development of an Army

The history and development of the Continental Army can be divided into two phases. The first, from 1775 until the winter of 1777 to 1778, was a long, and sometimes agonizing, process where officers and men learned their profession and became, to all intents and purposes, professional soldiers. The second ran from 18 June 1778, the Battle of Monmouth, to the end of the war and it saw a competent army of professionals take the field.

◄ CONTINENTAL RIFLE CORPS, 1778–9 *Washington wanted no more than 1,000 riflemen with the Continental Army at any one time. To be effective, they had to be supported by musket and bayonet-armed regular infantrymen, as the rifles could not be fitted with bayonets and were slow to reload. Properly supported riflemen were deadly in combat, as was shown by Daniel Morgan's rifle corps in the Battle of Saratoga.*

► RIFLEMAN, 1776 *This handsome uniform consists of a long shirt rather than a hunting shirt, along with a light infantry cap, long leggings and gaiters. These skilled light infantry riflemen were armed with the Pennsylvania or Kentucky long rifle. In addition, they carried a scalping knife, a hatchet, powder horn, and bullet pouch, all shown here.*

▲ **Rifleman, 1776** *The large roundhat worn by this figure was a common piece of clothing in the Continental Army, and riflemen wore it often. Sometimes it would be turned up on the side and might have a feather or bucktail tucked into the fold. The hunting shirt this rifleman wears was made of homespun linen, and would have been lighter and thinner than the other type. The shirt might also be a wraparound design which needed a waistbelt to fasten it closed.*

The Continentals matured during the winter of 1777 to 1778 at the camp at Valley Forge and were thoroughly trained and disciplined by Baron von Steuben, who would write the Continental Army's drill regulations and become the Army's inspector general. From then on, it was a different war, with the Continentals having an army-wide discipline and drill system, an excellent artillery commanded by Henry Knox, and competent leadership.

Before the Uniform Regulations of 1779 specified what each state's troops were to wear, and how they were to be faced and coloured, most uniform coats were either blue faced red or brown faced red. Naturally there were variations. Some units wore captured British uniforms, which could lead to confusion on the battlefield. Other states used captured cloth or uniforms and dyed them, the result coming out a brown or purple. Whatever the state or individual regiments did, however, did not prevent regimental commanders from wanting their men uniformed as smartly as possible.

The Rifle Regiment

In late 1775, Continental infantry regiments were numbered by their seniority in the service. The first group of Continental regiments were enlisted to serve until the end of 1776. The 1st Continental Regiment was a rifle regiment and was uniformed in hunting shirts and gaiter trousers. The hunting shirts were usually of a shade of brown or drab, or sometimes white. Hats could be tricornes, roundhats, or even of a light infantry pattern.

The Kentucky or Pennsylvania long rifle acquired a legendary reputation on the American frontier. The reputation is not based on fact, but on the myths that have grown up around the American frontiersman and his marksmanship. The rifle was certainly an excellent weapon of its time. It was accurate and deadly to 200 yards, and was superior to the musket in both range and accuracy. The rifle was also, however, slow to load, not of uniform calibre, and it could not take a bayonet. It was found that while riflemen were useful, they had to be supported by musket-armed infantry who were also equipped with bayonets. Contemporary accounts support the accuracy of the weapon and the skill of the riflemen, but Washington understood the tactical limitations of the long rifle, and never assigned more than 1,000 riflemen to the army at any one time.

▼ **Rifleman, 1776** *This rifleman has a hunting shirt along with the normal clothing and equipment rifle-armed troops would have. Their weapons and equipment were not issue but personal items. It should be noted that the rifle could not be fitted with a bayonet, putting the riflemen at a distinct disadvantage when in a close fight with musket armed infantry. In combat, they were frequently supported by infantry armed as such.*

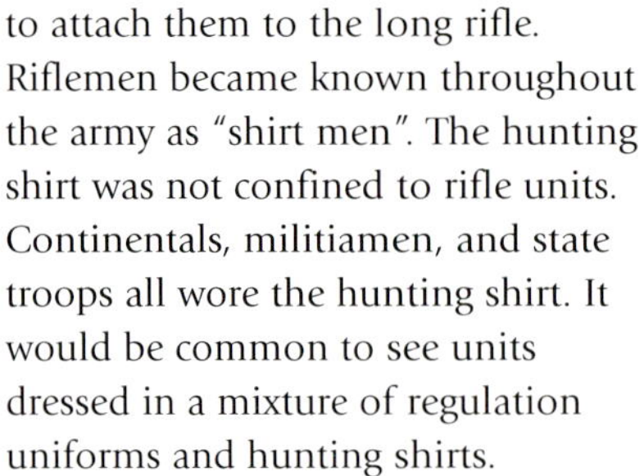

The Hunting Shirt

The riflemen's hunting shirt is the American contribution to the military fashion of the period and was a useful and utilitarian garment. Washington would have liked to have had the entire Continental Army uniformed in hunting shirts, but that never came to pass. The shirt came in more than one style and could either be fastened down the front or worn as a wrap-around, being fastened in place by a leather belt from which the hunting knife and hatchet, or tomahawk, were worn. Both of these weapons were essentially issue items for rifle-armed troops because of the lack of bayonets and any useful way to attach them to the long rifle. Riflemen became known throughout the army as "shirt men". The hunting shirt was not confined to rifle units. Continentals, militiamen, and state troops all wore the hunting shirt. It would be common to see units dressed in a mixture of regulation uniforms and hunting shirts.

Morgan's Rifle Corps

Daniel Morgan was one of the most distinguished and skilled commanders in the Continental Army. In 1777 he formed a provisional rifle corps from Pennsylvania, Virginia and Maryland at Washington's instigation. He led it northward where it was engaged against Burgoyne in the desperate battles of the Saratoga campaign.

Some rifle unit commanders learned through hard experience to co-ordinate Morgan's operations with supporting musket-armed infantry, and in the Saratoga campaign, where his rifle corps did good service, they were supported by Henry Dearborn's Continental Light Infantry, who protected them from British and German infantry.

Evidence concerning the uniform of Morgan's men is not clear. Morgan himself has been pictured in the famous painting of Burgoyne's surrender in an all-white hunting shirt with gaiter trousers. The general appearance of the riflemen was undoubtedly hunting shirts of various light browns and white, along with breeches and leggings or gaiter trousers of various hues. Indeed, some might even have been dark blue. One version of their uniform has them in white hunting shirts and leggings and wearing roundhats turned up on one side, with the usual cockade and bound in white tape. Another has them in white shirts, blue leggings or gaiter trousers, and with a slouch hat.

They were armed with the long rifle and carried the usual accoutrements of shot pouch, powder horn, scalping knife and hatchet, along with haversacks and any other items of personal equipment the men deemed necessary and were acceptable to their officers. All ranks were rifle-armed, and the officers probably wore the red sash

◀ **Officer, Baltimore Independent Cadets, 1776** *This uniform is traditionally seen as the Maryland Regiment's original uniform in 1776. This may be legend or fact, but it is included here as a "reconstruction" in order to illustrate a possible regimental distinction. The Baltimore Independent Cadets did wear this uniform, but whether or not it was officially adopted by Smallwood's regiment is still conjecture.*

▼ **Private, Smallwood's Maryland Regiment, 1776** *Apparently, the Marylanders wore gaiter trousers or leggings and dark blue hunting shirts at the Battle of Long Island. Regular rifle regiments continued to wear the hunting shirt through the War of 1812.*

as a badge of rank. Headgear was probably either roundhats with some type of feather in them or a cut down tricorne as a light infantry cap, or one that was turned up on the side.

Maryland and Delaware

The Continentals benefited greatly from a reputation wrought by two outstanding early units. The Maryland and Delaware Continentals were well uniformed and professional bodies of men, who were equal, if not superior, to the British and German professionals. Smallwood's Maryland and Haslet's Delaware regiments were uniformed, well trained and well led, and were considered the elite of the Southern army. The only fault was that there were not enough of them.

Smallwood's Men

Led by William Smallwood, the traditional view of the Marylanders' uniforms is that they were originally outfitted in scarlet coats with buff facings because one of their companies, the Baltimore Cadets, wore that uniform. Whatever the case, they were seen uniformed in hunting shirts and overalls at the Battle of Long Island. From then on the Maryland Line was uniformed in either dark brown coats faced red, or dark blue coats faced red. Regiments might be distinguished by small items such as coat buttons stamped with an "MD" or the regimental number. Maryland privates had white tape around their tricornes, officers had black.

Haslet's Unit

The Delaware Regiment, when led by John Haslet, was nicknamed the Blue Hen's Chickens (Haslet being the blue hen). Haslet led the Delaware Regiment for a year, but was killed in action at Princeton in early 1777. The Delaware Regiment was reformed under Colonel David Hall for the rest of the war, and was decimated at Camden. The survivors were reformed into a two-company battalion under Captain Robert Kirkwood and served as such for the remainder of the war.

The Delaware Regiment are pictured in coats of dark blue faced red, up to 1780, at which point they were transferred to the southern department and were uniformed in hunting shirts. As there was only one Continental regiment from Delaware for the entire war, they were usually brigaded with the Maryland regiments.

Initially the regiment wore a light infantry cap with the arms of Delaware on the front flap. After Haslet's death the battalion companies wore the tricorne, the light company probably retaining the light infantry cap. Breeches with half gaiters or gaiter trousers were worn. Delaware privates had yellow tape around their tricornes, officers had black tape. Hunting shirts were worn by both regiments when available; for the southern campaigns, Kirkwood's Delawares wore light grey hunting shirts and gaiter trousers made out of blue and white bed ticking.

► **Private, Haslet's Delaware Regiment, 1776** *This is typical kit and uniform for the Delaware Regiment during its first year of existence. When reformed under Colonel Hall (after Haslet was killed in action at Princeton in early 1777), the light infantry caps were no longer worn, except possibly by the regiment's light infantry company.*

▼ **Officer, Haslet's Delaware Regiment, 1776** *After 1776, officers were issued with spontoons instead of light muskets on Washington's instructions.*

THE CANADIAN REGIMENTS

The members of the American Congress, along with many other political bodies at the time, believed that the Canadians were also on the verge of rebellion. Canada had only been part of the British Empire since 1763, and it was believed its citizens would welcome an opportunity to join with their southern comrades and help in the attempt to throw the British out of North America.

The outcome of this mistaken assumption was the American invasion of Canada, an enterprise that was entirely unsuccessful.

The two regiments formed in Canada in 1776 served throughout the war, the 1st Regiment being disbanded in January 1781. Its personnel were then incorporated into the 2nd Regiment, this in turn being disbanded in 1783 at the close of hostilities.

1st Canadian Regiment. The 1st Regiment participated in the invasion of Canada and also the defence of what territory was taken thereafter. It fought at Lake Champlain, in the Mohawk Valley and in the ill-fated Rhode Island Campaign.

The regiment seems to have worn a variety of coats. Some seem to have worn captured British coats, others blue coats faced red. The majority would seem to have been dressed in light brown coats faced white. Personal equipment was as for other Continental infantry regiments, and the troops were armed with muskets and bayonets. Officers were equipped with spontoons and swords.

2nd Canadian Regiment. This unit was one of the best in the Continental Army and maintained high standards for the entire war; they were picked men who performed their duties ably and professionally. It was the only regiment in the service that had a four battalion organization that was maintained for the life of the regiment. The regiment was among the first, if not the first, unit to organize and

◀ **Officer, 2nd Canadian Regiment, 1777–9** *This exceptional regiment was raised, led and commanded by Colonel Moses Hazen, who was later promoted to general officer rank. It was originally recruited among sympathetic Canadians in southern Canada and in northern New York state. Later in the war it became the home for all of the "foreigners" in the Continental Army and still maintained its good reputation for discipline and steadiness in action. It was the only four-battalion regiment in existence in the Continental Army.*

▶ **Drummer, 2nd Canadian Regiment, 1777–9** *The musicians of the 2nd Canadian Regiment maintained the practice of "reversed colours", which was taken from European military tradition. It allowed them to be easily recognized and found in the smoke-filled confusion of a battlefield, which was vital for their purpose: to transmit orders to the men above the din of battle, and as a rallying point for a scattered unit.*

▲ **Infantry Regimental Kit**
1 Wooden canteen, standard issue in both the Continental Army and the British Army. 2 Metal Cartridge box. 3 Leather cartridge box with drilled wooden insert. 4 Metal canteen, superior to the wooden version. 5 Haversack, carried on the right hip by the shoulder strap. Personal articles would be carried in it, and it was standard issue for the Continentals and militia. 6 Shoulder belt with frog for hatchet and bayonet. Hatchets were useful for cutting away underbrush as well as splitting skulls in close combat. 7 & 8 Pack, which would hold items such as blankets and shoes. 9 Tricorne hat, the usual type of headgear worn by the Continentals. 10 Light infantry-style cap. 11 Roundhat.

maintain a permanent light infantry company. Commanded by the able Moses Hazen, the regiment maintained its excellent reputation even though all of the foreigners in the army were assigned to it in 1781, with the exception of Armand's partisan corps. Designated as "Congress' Own", the regiment was recruited from all locations and was not assigned to any state quota or line.

The regiment wore a brown uniform coat throughout its existence, initially having white facings, which were later being authorized red. Waistcoats, breeches and stockings were white, and black half gaiters or gaiter trousers were worn. The regiment wore the tricorne, with the exception of the light infantry company, the men of which wore a simple light infantry cop with COR (standing for "Congress' Own Regiment") as a cap device.

The individual equipment was the usual for a Continental regiment, and the troops were armed with muskets and bayonets. Officers were equipped with spontoons and swords.

The 2nd Regiment was sent north for the defence of the territory held in Canada after the failure to take Quebec. It participated in the fighting in northern New Jersey and in Washington's campaign to defend Philadelphia in 1777. The regiment was stationed in New York and New Jersey in 1780 and 1781, and was moved south in 1781 to take part in the siege of Yorktown.

► **Private, 2nd Canadian Regiment, 1777–9** *The regiment's original uniforms were brown coats faced with white, later changing to brown faced red in 1779. Apparently the regiment didn't reuniform in dark blue as the rest of the army did, or attempted to do, with the 1779 Uniform Regulations. It was one of the first regiments to have a light infantry company.*

THE MASSACHUSETTS AND NEW YORK CONTINENTALS

The first Continental Army units raised for the war against the British suffered from an improvised organization, applied under pressure and without any time for lengthy consideration. They also had to improvise uniforms and equipment. Units that were raised for the campaigns in the northern theatre suffered as badly in this respect as those raised for service in the South. The first five states to recruit troops for Continental regiments included Massachusetts and New York.

The First Regimental Organization

The organization that was in existence in 1775 for the newly christened Continental Army around Boston was not uniform among the states that had troops present. The number of companies authorized for each regiment was ten, but these companies varied in troop numbers so that each regiment had a different authorized strength that the individual states were supposed to maintain. Of those five states that had troops present around Boston in 1775 (Massachusetts, Connecticut, Rhode Island, New Hampshire and New York), the individual organization of regiments showed some regional variations.

Uniforms would vary for the units present, although browns and blues, usually faced with red, were typical.

▶ **Private, 14th Continental Regiment, 1776** *The enlisted dress of the regiment was most probably what is pictured here. Composed of New England seamen, this regiment ferried the army across rivers three times in less than a year – twice during the New York campaign to save it from annihilation, and once for its counter-offensive against the Hessian outpost at Trenton, New Jersey.*

◀ **Officer, 14th Continental Regiment, 1776** *Also known as Glover's Marblehead Regiment, this was another of the one-year regiments of 1776, and one that performed yeoman work for the army. It was well commanded and disciplined, and its commander, John Glover, was another officer who stayed with the army after his regiment was mustered out. Composed largely of sailors and fishermen from Marblehead Massachusetts, it was this regiment that ferried Washington and his army across the Delaware in December 1776 for the surprise attack at Trenton.*

Glover's Marblehead Regiment

This unit, also known as the 14th Continental Regiment, was recruited from sailors in and around Marblehead, Massachusetts. They wore either light or dark brown coats faced with red, and some accounts have them in the sailors' dress of the day. The officers probably wore some kind of early regulation dress.

The "Marbleheaders" turned amphibious if necessary, using their maritime skill in the use of large boats

Organization of Continental Regiments

Total authorized strength:
Massachusetts: 599
Connecticut: 1,046
Rhode Island: 607
New Hampshire: 648
New York: 758

Field Grade Officers per regiment:
Massachusetts: 3
Connecticut: 3
Rhode Island: 3
New Hampshire: 3
New York: 3

Staff Officers per regiment:
Massachusetts: 6
Connecticut: 6
Rhode Island: 4
New Hampshire: 5
New York: 5

Company Grade Officers per company:
Massachusetts: 3
Connecticut: 4
Rhode Island: 3
New Hampshire: 3
New York: 3

Non-commissioned Officers per company:
Massachusetts: 8
Connecticut: 8
Rhode Island: 6
New Hampshire: 6
New York: 6

Musicians per company:
Massachusetts: 2
Connecticut: 2
Rhode Island: 2
New Hampshire: 2
New York: 2

Privates per company:
Massachusetts: 46
Connecticut: 90
Rhode Island: 49
New Hampshire: 53
New York: 64

to evacuate the army twice during the New York campaign in the summer of 1776. The Marbleheaders were the troops that rowed the army across the Delaware in December 1776 to surprise and take the Hessian garrison at Trenton.

The 3rd New York Regiment

This unit wore a grey coat of the usual cut with red facings and a grey lining. Waistcoat, breeches, and stockings were also grey. Crossbelts and leather equipment were black, and the tricorne was edged with black tape.

◀ Private, 3rd New York Regiment, 1776 *The regiments that were formed for active service in 1776 were only enlisted for one year. This regiment was actually formed in 1775 and was commanded by James Clinton. Apparently, it wore this interesting and unusual uniform featuring grey coats, faced with green.*

▶ Private, 14th Continental Regiment, 1776 *Glover's regiment may or may not have actually been dressed in regulation Continental dress on the battlefields, but the uniform it was officially prescribed is pictured here. Tough, well disciplined, and indefatigable, this regiment became legendary after only a year's service.*

MILITIA CAVALRY AND ARTILLERY

Not all militia units were infantry. Some states or volunteers could afford to field cavalry, a very expensive arm to equip and support, and maintain their own quite modest artillery.

Cavalry

Horses were expensive to buy and care for, and the personnel in such units were also the most difficult to train. Not only did a new recruit have to be familiar with his issue weapons of sabre, carbine and pistol, but he had to be a good horseman.

Cavalrymen could be uniformed in a myriad of colours.

THE BALTIMORE LIGHT DRAGOONS. These men were part of the Maryland Volunteer Militia, and like the Philadelphia City Troop of Light Horse were only a company-sized unit. They were uniformed in short light grey coats with medium blue facings, and privates wore either gaiter trousers with spurs buckled over the shoes or breeches, stockings and half gaiters over shoes with spurs.

Trumpeters wore reversed colours, and officers apparently wore riding boots, some of which came above the knee. All ranks were armed with sabres and pistols, and they wore a typical jockey-type light dragoon cap with the monogram "LH" on the upturned flap on the front of the cap.

The war in the south after the fall of Charleston devolved into a civil war between Loyalist and Rebel militias, partisans, and the regular units of both sides that supported them. This featured mounted action and grim fighting, and some of the states raised units to either defend their own state or to support General Greene's army in the field. Though the partisans and other state units were technically militia, the state light horse outfits were usually adequately uniformed and well mounted. Generally, they gave good service, particularly if their leadership was competent.

THE SOUTH CAROLINA LIGHT HORSE. This unit formed more than one regiment and was usually uniformed in light blue, with facings varying by regiment. They wore the usual shortened coat that was typical of light cavalry of the period, and the trumpeters were supposed to wear the traditional reversed colours. Gaiter trousers with spurs were more usual for troopers, but officers wore riding boots. Officers were armed with sabres or

◀ **PRIVATE, DOVER LIGHT INFANTRY COMPANY, 1776–7** *This company of much-needed light infantry was employed in its only active service in the Trenton/Princeton campaign. The jockey cap for an infantry unit is noteworthy, as are the brown gaiter trousers. Also, note the "belly box" cartridge pouches, which were usually issued to cavalrymen.*

▶ **GUNNER, RHODE ISLAND TRAIN OF ARTILLERY, 1775** *Uniformed in brown coats faced red, the unique Rhode Island light infantry-type caps were later worn by some of the Rhode Island infantry units.*

▲ PRIVATE, MIDDLE REGIMENT (CANTWELL'S), NEW CASTLE COUNTY DELAWARE, 1775 *Light blue wore well and usually did not fade. It was not a popular colour, however, and very few units elected to use it as the colour of their uniform coats.*

swords and a brace of pistols; troopers with a sabre. The headgear was a cap of light infantry cut.

Artillery

In European armies it was becoming the norm for artillery officers to be school trained. It was a technical branch, as was engineering, and artillerymen were expected to be intelligent. The study of mathematics, gunnery, drafting, ballistics and mechanical drawing were becoming a prerequisite. Organization varied from state to state. The Massachusetts Artillery Regiment of 1775 was composed of a headquarters of one colonel (commanding officer), two lieutenant colonels, one major and one ordnance shopkeeper, four conductors and two clerks. There were 10 gun companies composed of five officers, six NCOs (three sergeants and three corporals), and 44 privates. There was also an artificer company consisting of one master carpenter, one master blacksmith, one master wheelwright and 47 workmen. This last company maintained the gun carriages and ancillary vehicles such as limbers and battery wagons.

The South Carolina Artillery Regiment was organized with a regimental headquarters of one lieutenant colonel (commanding officer) and one major, supported by a staff of one quartermaster, one adjutant, one paymaster, one surgeon, one surgeon's mate (assistant), one laboratory sergeant, one armourer, one assistant armourer, one sergeant major and one quartermaster sergeant (the last two being added to the table of organization in February 1776). There were three gun companies composed of five officers, eight NCOs, two musicians (a drummer and a fifer) and 96 privates.

The traditional artillery colour was dark blue, although some European artillerymen wore black or dark green. Dark uniform colours were chosen as the large amounts of black powder being used would show up too much on a lighter uniform.

THE RHODE ISLAND TRAIN OF ARTILLERY. This artillery unit was formed in 1774 as the Providence Train of Artillery and was combined in April of the following year with the Providence Fusiliers to form the United Company of the Train of Artillery of the Town of Providence. This mouthful was usually shortened to the United Train of Artillery. The unit was uniformed in brown coats faced red, with white or brown leather equipment, although the officers probably had black leather. Waistcoat, breeches and stockings were white, and the men wore black half gaiters, while the officers wore riding boots. The headgear worn by all ranks was a light infantry-style cap with an elaborate fouled anchor device on the front flap.

▶ MILITIA OFFICER, 1775 *Generally speaking militia officers wore a civilian coat, gaiters, breeches and stockings and adorned this with military accoutrements such as aiguillettes, lace, and gold or silver buttons. Tricorne hats were usually worn.*

THE PHILADELPHIA CITY TROOP OF LIGHT HORSE

Although sometimes comparatively small units, some militia cavalry could demonstrate just what might be achieved within the militia system. There were exemplary units, well equipped and well outfitted.

The famous Philadelphia City Troop of Light Horse unit, also known as Philadelphia Light Horse, was founded in November 1774 and had an initial strength of 28 all ranks. The troop was commanded by a captain, and had an organization of three other officers, a quartermaster, two sergeants and two corporals, as well as a sword master and a riding master, trumpeter and farrier. The remainder of the unit's strength was composed of privates. The uniform was a short brown coat, faced and lined with white, buff leather riding breeches, white waistcoat and white crossbelts that held the sword and carbine for the privates and the sword for the officers. Trumpeters wore reversed colours of white coat and brown facings. There is some contention as to what the headgear of the troops was, but it appears that a combination of dragoon helmets and modified jockey caps was worn. High-topped cavalry boots were the usual footwear.

Horse furniture was "handsome and expensive" according to contemporary accounts, the brown shabraques being embroidered with the legend "LH" for light horse. Brown leather saddles, bridles, stirrup leathers and reins completed their tack. They had bearskin-covered pistol holsters on their saddles.

◀ **Trooper, Philadelphia Light Horse, 1776–7** *The enlisted men of the Philadelphia Light Horse were as socially prominent as their officers, and this unit was handsomely uniformed as shown here, as well as well armed. They were also very well mounted, which gave them an advantage in combat. The uniform coat was of the short design for mounted troops, brown faced white, with white waistcoats and buff riding breeches. The tall boots protected the wearer's legs when mounted.*

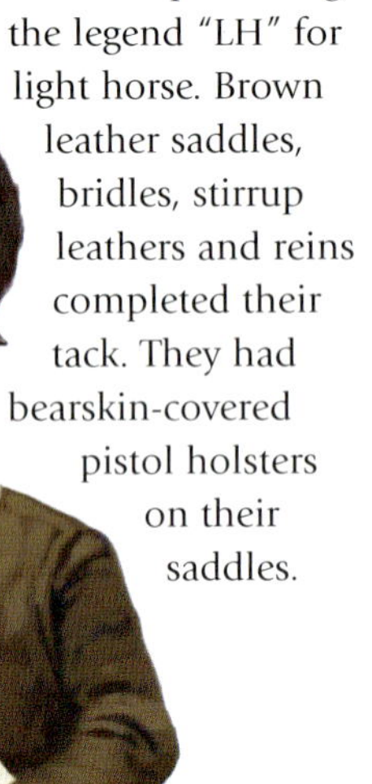

▶ **Officer, Philadelphia Light Horse, 1776–7** *Formed and organized by twenty-eight socially prominent men in 1774, the City Troop of Philadelphia is one of the oldest formed militia units in the United State still in existence. Never more than a company-sized unit during its service in the Revolution, it gave excellent service from late 1776 to the end of 1778 in everything from a courier and escort service for George Washington to charges with their trademark "whoop and a holler".*

This unit was never more than a company in strength and they served with distinction at Trenton and Princeton. They were also called up for service periodically during the war, always serving with efficiency, and were one of the best of the American cavalry units, retaining their reputation as an elite unit for the entire period and beyond. The uniforms of the Philadelphia Light Horse were distinctive. Their colours were also quite distinctive, having a yellow field with the coat of arms of Pennsylvania on them.

As the gentlemen of the troop were responsible for providing their own uniforms and equipment, so were they responsible for providing their own mounts. That being the case, they were well mounted and took good care of their horses. As an interesting aside, American cavalry units were much better mounted than their British and Loyalist opponents. This became very obvious in the southern theatre after 1780, when Continental cavalry was finally employed in a mounted role both on campaign and on the battlefield. Lee's Legion routinely outrode their British counterparts, and it was noted by Lee in his memoirs that in his opinion this was because of the care with which the Legion procured and maintained their mounts.

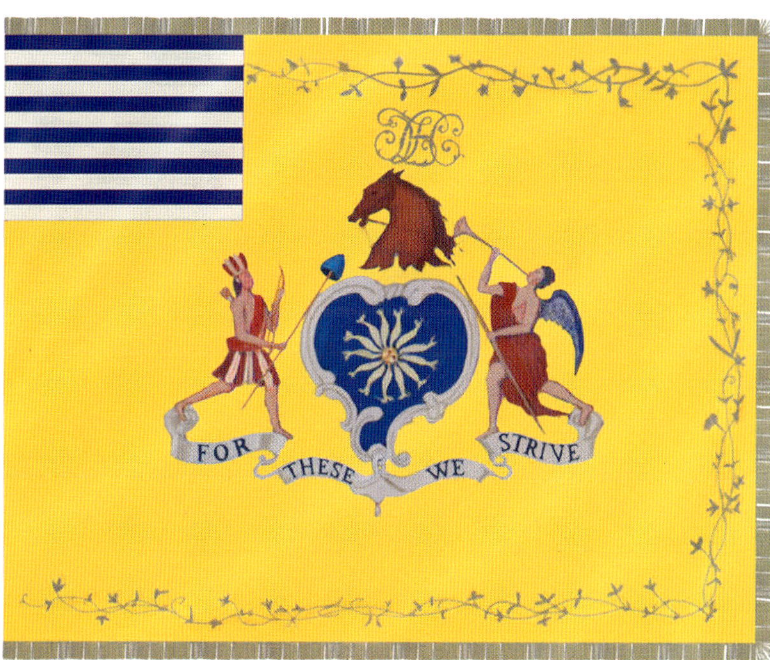

▲ **Trumpeter, Philadelphia Light Horse, 1776–7** *Once again, the troop followed common cavalry practice in uniforming their lone trumpeter in reversed colours. The same was done with the horse that was ridden by the trumpeter; mounting him, whenever practically possible, on a grey or white horse made for easy identification in a melée or when rallying after a charge.*

◀ **Philadelphia Light Horse Standard** *This standard is one of the best known colours of the Revolutionary period as well as being one of the most striking. Originally, it had the Union Jack in the upper left-hand corner, later covered by the stripes motif. Even though the standard was carried in the field, the original flag has survived, and is preserved in the unit's museum.*

REGIMENTS ON THE FRONTIER

A number of volunteer units operated in peripheral theatres where small-scale raids and skirmishes allowed a number of commanders and troops to earn a tremendous reputation for partisan warfare.

Conquest of the Old Northwest

While the field armies clashed in well-known battles and campaigns, there was constant warfare along the frontiers of the states, especially to the west, where huge expanses of territory were fought over by small units that gained or lost immense wealth for their particular side. Much of this campaigning, marching and dying has generally been ignored in most histories of the war.

The most famous campaign in the West during this period is that of George Rogers Clark. He set out with a small force of 200 men and conquered the Old Northwest for the United States. He and his command campaigned in the worst weather, through rain and flood, to take and retake fortified settlements in the Ohio country, cutting British support for the American Indian tribes of the area and denying them vital aid for the remainder of the war.

Some units involved in these actions had definite regimental uniforms of the accustomed style, but many, if not most, of the troops on the frontier simply wore the hunting shirt and leggings. Cavalry uniforms of the different state contingents included short coats of various colours, such as grey and light blue, with either breeches and boots or gaiter trousers covering the shoes. Spurs were then attached over the gaiters. Light infantry-style caps were often used among mounted troops.

◄ **Volunteer, Illinois Troop, Virginia Light Dragoons, 1780–3** *This is an excellent example of frontier dress for volunteers who would augment a state or regular unit in an emergency. Their "uniform" would be everyday wear for them, though they might be issued extra arms and equipment by the state to conform to the unit to which they were attached.*

▲ **Private, Illinois Troop, Virginia Light Dragoons, 1780–3** *Troops who served on the frontier were usually homesteaders, accustomed to defending their claimed land from attack by the American Indians. They were also inured to fending for themselves and living on their own, as their nearest neighbours would often be miles away and they had to be prepared to defend their homes until and if help arrived. Homesteaders hunted for their survival, and were also usually well armed when they signed up. If taken into service, uniforms may not have been provided. Shown here is an example of a well-uniformed and cared-for unit.*

One item of winter wear that was used for both sides was the Canadian blanket coat. Heavy, warm and comfortable, it afforded sufficient warmth against the cold, rainy weather of the Northwest. The use of the garment was uniform in all but name. At the Battle of Vincennes, Clark's entire contingent was wearing them.

Continental units were not generally involved in the North, except for General Sullivan's strategically successful expedition against the Iroquois in 1779. The men and units who fought these wide-ranging campaigns were made up of state troops or volunteers raised specifically for use in one or two campaigns.

The Southern Theatre

The other war that was being fought, especially in the South, was a vicious, no-quarter civil war between Americans, loyalists and rebels. This often degenerated into settling age-old scores between families. Many were settled with little or no mercy, sometimes ending with no quarter or the hanging of prisoners. There were massacres on both sides and fighting continued after the armies had passed.

THE ILLINOIS TROOP OF VIRGINIA LIGHT DRAGOONS. Cavalrymen and dragoons were most useful to General Greene in the South in 1782 and 1783 as the British were gradually driven into their remaining strongholds of Charleston and Savannah. These cavalrymen wore two types of uniform. The first was typical rifle dress but with the difference that these were dragoons and were therefore armed with a long, straight thrusting sword in addition to their rifles. They were expected to fight both mounted and dismounted.

The other uniform worn was a combination of dragoon and frontier dress. Dark blue coats piped in white with grey breeches and waistcoats were worn, along with Indian leggings and moccasins. A light infantry cap was worn. Equipment was buff leather, and rifles or muskets, along with the sword, were used. Firearms were slung on the right side of the saddle. It appears that officers wore dark blue riding cloaks.

◀ PRIVATE, CAPTAIN DE LA PORTE'S FRENCH COMPANY, VIRGINIA STATE FORCES, 1777–8 *This is another example of a uniformed unit that belonged to the state of Virginia and not to the Continental service.*

▶ PRIVATE, VIRGINIA FRONTIER INDEPENDENT COMPANY, 1779 *This ranger-type unit was formed for duty to protect the state against raids by hostile Indians and to range the state border to serve as an early warning to any threat that might develop on the western frontier. Dress and equipment would be practical and individualistic, and those men that commanded such units undoubtedly had their own interpretation of military discipline in their respective companies.*

The Virginia Frontier companies wore a mixture of uniform and frontier dress. They had the appearance of ranger units, wearing brown coats with yellow or buff facings, grey waistcoats and either breeches with Indian leggings of various colours or overalls. Leather equipment was white or buff leather, and Indian multicoloured belts were also worn. They were rifle-armed and carried knives and hatchets. Scottish caps were probably worn.

Captain de la Porte's Company was more regularly uniformed in dark blue coats faced red and lined white. Breeches and vests were light tan or buff, and belts were white. Stockings were white. On campaign they probably wore gaiter trousers or leggings, and their hats were bound in white tape.

CONTINENTAL REGIMENTS: 1776

It was inevitable that the Continental regiments would expand and adjust their organization accordingly as the war progressed. Greater uniformity was also more apparent than it had been when the war commenced. Infantry regiments in 1776 were authorized to have an organization of a regimental headquarters and staff consisting of one colonel (commander), one lieutenant colonel, one major, one surgeon, one surgeon's mate, one adjutant, one quartermaster, one paymaster, one sergeant major, one quartermaster sergeant, one drum major, one fife major and a chaplain (initially one for every two regiments, but this was changed to one per regiment in June 1776). There were eight companies per regiment, each of them composed of four officers, eight NCOs, two musicians, and 76 privates. States that contributed units to the army and did not follow the above organization were Maryland, Pennsylvania, Rhode Island, Virginia, and South Carolina.

▼ PRIVATE, 12TH CONTINENTAL INFANTRY REGIMENT, 1776 *Commanded by Moses Little, this was one of the 27 new 1776 Continental regiments raised. It was noted as being one of the few units to be properly uniformed and equipped.*

States with Their Own Organization

Field Grade Officers per regiment:
Maryland: 4
Maryland State Companies: 0
Pennsylvania State Rifle Regiment: 5
Pennsylvania State Musket Regiment: 3
Rhode Island State Regiment: 3
Virginia: 3
South Carolina Rifle Regiment: 3
Southern Ranger Regiment: 2

Staff Officers per regiment:
Maryland: 5
Maryland State Companies: 0
Pennsylvania State Rifle Regiment: 8
Pennsylvania State Musket Regiment: 5
Rhode Island State Regiment: 4
Virginia: 9
South Carolina Rifle Regiment: 6
Southern Ranger Regiment: 2

Company Grade Officers per company:
Maryland: 4
Maryland State Companies: 4
Pennsylvania State Rifle Regiment: 4
Pennsylvania State Musket Regiment: 3
Rhode Island State Regiment: 3
Virginia: 4
South Carolina Rifle Regiment: 4
Southern Ranger Regiment: 3

NCOs per company:
Maryland: 8
Maryland State Companies: 8
Pennsylvania State Rifle Regiment: 8
Pennsylvania State Musket Regiment: 4
Rhode Island State Regiment: 8
Virginia: 8
South Carolina Rifle Regiment: 8
Southern Ranger Regiment: 2

Musicians per company:
Maryland: 2
Maryland State Companies: 2
Pennsylvania State Rifle Regiment: 2
Pennsylvania State Musket Regiment: 2
Rhode Island State Regiment: 2
Virginia: 2
South Carolina Rifle Regiment: 0
Southern Ranger Regiment: 0

Privates per company:
Maryland: 60
Maryland State Companies: 92
Pennsylvania State Rifle Regiment: 68
Pennsylvania State Musket Regt: 52
Rhode Island State Regiment: 50
Virginia: 64
South Carolina Rifle Regiment: 92
Southern Ranger Regiment: 50

Number of companies:
Maryland: 9
Maryland State Companies: 7
Pennsylvania State Rifle Regiment: 12
Pennsylvania State Musket Regiment: 8
Rhode Island State Regiment: 12
Virginia: 10
South Carolina Rifle Regiment: 7
Southern Ranger Regiment: 10

Total strength:
Maryland: 679
Maryland State Companies: 806
Pennsylvania State Rifle Regt: 1,000
Pennsylvania State Musket Regt: 500
Rhode Island State Regiment: 763
Virginia: 792
South Carolina Rifle Regiment: 737
Southern Ranger Regiment: 554

◀ **PRIVATE, 2ND RHODE ISLAND REGIMENT, 1777** *Uniformed in dark blue and white, this unit was originally a state unit taken into Continental service in 1777.*

▶ **PRIVATE, 7TH PENNSYLVANIA REGIMENT, 1776** *The Pennsylvania Line mutinied because of pay and other issues before going south in 1781, and had to be completely reformed under Anthony Wayne.*

▼ **PRIVATE, 18TH CONTINENTAL INFANTRY REGIMENT, 1776** *One report has this unit wearing uniforms of undyed wool, which would make the clothing easy to wash without colour loss. In reality they wore whatever they could get their hands on.*

Increased Uniformity

Greater efficiency in the supply of military clothing meant increased uniformity among the Continental Army's units.

2ND RHODE ISLAND REGIMENT. This was uniformed similarly to the Rhode Island Train of Artillery in brown coats faced with red. Small clothes (vests, breeches, stockings, etc.), belts and equipment were probably either the same or similar as they had been taken from the same stock that uniformed and equipped the artillerymen. The men may have worn brown breeches instead of white. They wore a tricorne bound in white tape.

12TH CONTINENTAL REGIMENT. The men of this unit wore brown coats faced in red.

18TH CONTINENTAL REGIMENT. These men wore grey coats faced buff, brown waistcoats, buff breeches, stockings and black half gaiters. They were equipped with white or buff leather belts, and wore the tricorne hat without the coloured tape edging.

7TH PENNSYLVANIA REGIMENT. This unit wore blue faced and lined with red. Buff breeches and blue stockings were worn with half gaiters and belts were buff leather. They also wore a tricorne without coloured binding.

Although 1776 proved a testing period for the Continentals, they emerged from their winter quarters as a capable fighting force with individual units becoming much more professional in conduct as well as in appearance.

Attrition on Campaign

The Continental regiments of 1776 had a very hard time. They were repeatedly defeated in the New York area and were unable to hold that strategic city, with its excellent harbour. They suffered heavy casualties and witnessed the militia repeatedly running from the British and German regulars, usually isolating the Continentals. There were excellent regiments among them, and the survivors became "men of iron" whom nothing could discourage. They attacked and routed the British in the small action at the Hollow Way (also called Harlem Heights), and had other small successes before retreating through New Jersey.

Yet, these regiments held the army together and were the nucleus of the counter-attack and victory at Trenton in December. They also attacked and won at Princeton in January 1777. Most of these units had only enlisted for a year and they were disbanded after Princeton, but many re-enlisted in the new Continental regiments formed in 1777. They then stayed to the bitter end, campaigning throughout the war. Some of them were present at Yorktown, or with Greene in the Carolinas, and even saw the British abandon New York, Savannah and Charleston, the last three outposts the British still held when the peace treaty was signed in Paris in 1783.

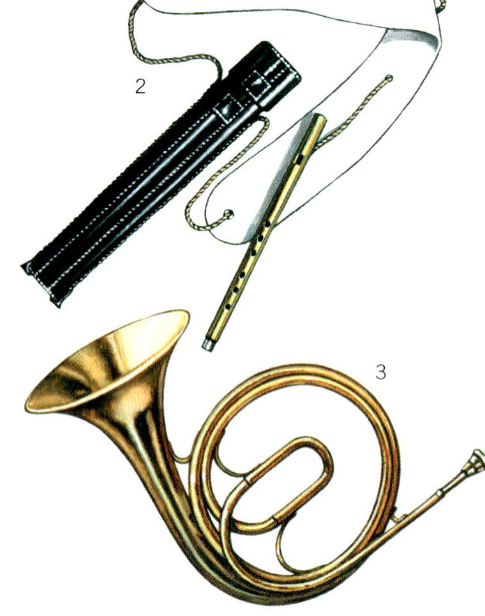

▲ Musicians' Instruments, 1775–83
In the armies of the period not all of the musicians were soldiers. Drummers and fifers normally were, but the other musicians who would make up a regimental band were hired musicians and had a habit of disappearing when the shooting started. 1 Cavalry trumpet. 2 Military fife, with its case. 3 Hunting horn, which at the time was also known as the bugle horn and was similar to the modern-day French horn.

Variations in Uniform Dress

Despite every effort, the Continental Army was still uniformed in a variety of styles. This characteristic individuality was further augmented by the rigours of campaigning.

3rd New Jersey Regiment. This unit was uniformed in a light tan coat with dark blue facings. Breeches were buff leather and belts and leather equipment were either white or buff coloured. The regiment was issued the tricorne, which was bound in white tape. It was a fully equipped regiment of eight companies and the men wore stockings and black half gaiters. Sometimes the New Jersey regiments were termed "Jersey Blues", a term first used for New Jersey provincial troops in the French and Indian War. This regiment did not campaign with the main army and so missed New York, Trenton and Princeton. It was sent into the Mohawk Valley and garrisoned Fort Stanwyx and Fort Ticonderoga.

6th Virginia Regiment. This unit was dressed and equipped in an altogether different manner. It was formally uniformed in grey hunting shirts with

◀ Officer, 6th Virginia Regiment, 1776
This is a simple, elegant, and impressive uniform, from the early years of the war. It was martial in appearance, and was comfortable for wear in the field. American company grade officers at the start of the war carried the same type of firearm as their British opponents did. George Washington later ordered that they were to carry spontoons instead of muskets, as he wanted them to be free to concentrate on commanding their men in combat without having to be concerned about loading and firing muskets. The spontoon was a very effective weapon in close combat.

red facings. Collars, cuffs and "capes" (the large collars of hunting shirts that were fringed) were in red cloth, making the "shirtmen" appear to be a little more uniformed than others of this type. Leather equipment was white and officers wore the customary red sash over the hunting shirt. Breeches of brown buckskin were worn with either European-style high gaiters, coming above the knee, or with stockings and half gaiters. Blue or brown overalls were also worn. Small roundhats jauntily turned up on the left side were also worn, sometimes with a feather or a buck tail on the left side.

All ranks, including company grade officers (ensigns, lieutenants and captains), were armed with a musket and a bayonet. Officers also bore swords, and privates were required to carry hatchets.

◀ **Private, 3rd New Jersey Infantry Regiment, 1776** *This unit was known as the Jersey Blues, a nickname that was a holdover from the French and Indian War. There are two different uniforms reported for this unit. One account states it consisted of a dark blue coat faced red, the other account details a light tan or drab coat, faced in dark blue. The latter, shown here, is probably correct.*

▶ **Drummer, 3rd New Jersey Infantry Regiment, 1776** *While the rather drab coats of the regiment may not have been as handsome on parade as dark blue or even dark brown, the unit was known for its smart appearance and being fully equipped and ready for action. It served with the northern army in the Mohawk Valley, helping to man and rebuild Fort Stanwyx. It was disbanded in March 1777.*

▼ **Continental Army Drums, 1775–83** *During this period the ubiquitous military drums were made of wood, not brass as they would be at the beginning of the 19th century. They were used to communicate in combat and would be massed for training under the regimental drum major, a man of some consequence within his regiment. Neither officer nor enlisted man, the drum major was responsible for training his drummers. Little music notation was written down, instead it was demonstrated and then repeated in training. Those slow to learn might experience a rude awakening from the drum major's demanding disposition and ready hand. The bass drum, below right, during the period was quite different from the modern version.*

ADDITIONAL CONTINENTAL REGIMENTS: 1777

As the war expanded in terms of the territory it was fought within, so too did the number of units Washington required. In late 1776, Washington requested that 16 "additional regiments" be raised. He was granted authorization by the Continental Congress to raise them for field service. Only 14 of the 16 were actually raised, and most of these had teething problems and were amalgamated with other units later in the war. There were exceptions to this, such as Colonel Samuel Webb's Regiment, also known as the 9th Connecticut Regiment, which had an outstanding reputation for order and discipline and fought at Rhode Island. However, of the regiments that were actually raised, or attempted to be raised, only Sherburne's, Jackson's, Gist's, Sheppard's and Spencer's retained their separate identity during the war. These regiments were initially known as Additional Continental Regiments.

SHERBURNE'S ADDITIONAL REGIMENT. This unit wore brown coats with buff facings and had natural buff leather equipment belts. Cocked hats were plain without lace or coloured tape, and the junior officers were equipped, as the men were, with crossbelts and muskets, at least initially. George Washington insisted that the junior officers did not need to be armed with either muskets or fusils and were to be issued with spontoons for hand-to-hand fighting and self-defence, along with their swords.

Waistcoats and breeches were brown, stockings white or grey, and half gaiters were worn over shoes. Undoubtedly gaiter trousers were used and whatever was available was probably the order of the day when uniforms needed to be replaced.

LEE'S REGIMENT. This regiment saw action at the Battle of Monmouth and the Battle of Rhode Island. The unit was uniformed in blue with red facings, as the Pennsylvania, Maryland and Delaware regiments usually were. Roundhats with a feather on the left-hand side were worn, and equipment belts were buff leather or blackened leather. Waistcoats and breeches were

◀ **PRIVATE, SHERBURNE'S ADDITIONAL CONTINENTAL REGIMENT, 1777** *This and the six regiments that followed it were formed in 1777 and were originally known by the names of their commanding officers. Sherburn's Additional Continental Regiment was formed from recruits taken from Connecticut and Maryland, and they served until May 1780.*

▶ **COLONEL, SHERBURNE'S ADDITIONAL CONTINENTAL REGIMENT, 1777** *This is the typical uniform worn by a regimental commander in the Continental Army. Field officers (majors, lieutenant colonels, and colonels) were supposed to be mounted and would therefore have worn riding boots fitted with spurs.*

The Additional Regiments

Webb's: redesignated the 9th Connecticut Regiment on 24 July 1780 and consolidated with the 2nd Connecticut Regiment on 1 January 1780.

Thurston's: consolidated on 22 April 1779 with Gist's Regiment.

Sherburne's: disbanded 1 May 1780.

Spencer's: disbanded 1 January 1781.

Lee's: consolidated with Jackson's Regiment on 9 April 1779.

Forman's: consolidated with Spencer's Regiment on 1 April 1779.

Gist's: captured 12 May 1780 at the capitulation of Charleston.

Jackson's: disbanded 1 January 1781 after being redesignated the 16th Massachusetts Regiment on 24 July 1780.

Henley's: consolidated with Jackson's Regiment on 9 April 1779.

Grayson's: consolidated with Gist's Regiment on 22 April 1779.

Hartley's: consolidated with the 3rd Pennsylvania Regiment on 17 January 1781.

Patton's: consolidated with Hartley's Regiment on 13 January 1779, less one company, Captain MacLane's, assigned to the 2nd Partisan Corps.

Malcolm's: consolidated with Spencer's Regiment on 1 April 1779.

Sheppard's: disbanded 1 June 1778.

buff, as were gaiter trousers when worn. Stockings were blue, and black half gaiters were probably worn over shoes when the men wore breeches. Hartley's Regiment. The men of this regiment were dressed in blue coats with white facings and white waistcoats; they probably wore buff overalls over shoes as a matter of course. Unadorned roundhats were also worn, along with buff leather equipment belts.

The 14 additional regiments of Continentals that were mustered in 1777 filled a definite need. The first Continental regiments of 1776 were only enlisted for one year, and Washington insisted on amending this to three years or the duration of the war, whichever was longer. That being the case, the interim solution was the Additional Regiments, some of which later became permanent, like Webb's, and lasted through Yorktown in 1781.

▼ Private, Hartley's Additional Continental Regiment, 1777 *This regiment was formed from recruits from the states of Pennsylvania and Maryland. In early 1779 it went into the Pennsylvania Line, forming the new 11th Pennsylvania Regiment. Dark blue and white regimentals were mentioned in newspaper accounts of the time as the uniform the regiment had been seen wearing.*

▼ Private, Lee's Additional Continental Regiment, 1777 *Another of the 16 additional regiments, Lee's Regiment was recruited in Massachusetts and lasted until April 1779, when it was finally amalgamated with Jackson's Additional Continental Regiment. The uniform shown may not have been worn by the entire regiment during its service.*

WEBB'S REGIMENT. This was one of the best disciplined and uniformed regiments in the Continental Army. It was dressed in scarlet coats, reputedly captured British items, faced yellow. The regiment maintained its reputation throughout the war and was the best of the additional regiments. Belts were white, as were waistcoats, breeches and stockings. Black half gaiters were worn and the tricornes for privates were bound in white tape. The regiment reportedly also maintained a band.

▼ **OFFICER, WEBB'S ADDITIONAL CONTINENTAL REGIMENT, 1777–81** *Colonel Samuel Webb raised this regiment for service after the expiration of enlistments of the 1776 Continental regiments. He clothed his regiment in captured British uniforms, over which he had considerable trouble and argument, for obvious reasons, finally securing Washington's approval.*

▼ **PRIVATE, WEBB'S ADDITIONAL CONTINENTAL REGIMENT, 1777–81** *Webb's regiment was later redesignated the 9th Connecticut, and it appears that they retained their scarlet uniforms throughout most of the war. They are one of the Continental regiments whose standards are known today, one of them being illustrated in the flag section.*

▲ **PRIVATE, SPENCER'S ADDITIONAL CONTINENTAL REGIMENT, 1777** *This regiment was organized and raised in New Jersey, and it is sometimes referred to as the 5th New Jersey Regiment. It served until disbanded in 1781 and was not amalgamated with any other unit upon being disbanded. Note the type of pack the soldier is carrying. This was a type that was a holdover from the French and Indian War and was known as a tumpline. It was essentially a bedroll with one strap attached, which was later replaced by the more recognizable pack with shoulder and breast straps that was more practical and undoubtedly more comfortable.*

Unit Distribution: The 1776 Infantry Regimental Quotas

New Hampshire: 3
Massachusetts: 15
Rhode Island: 2
Connecticut: 8
New York: 4
New Jersey: 4
Pennsylvania: 12
Delaware: 1
Maryland: 8
Virginia: 15
North Carolina: 9
South Carolina: 6
Georgia: 1

Regiments raised under the 1776 quota:
New Hampshire: 3
Massachusetts: 15
Rhode Island: 2
Connecticut: 8
New York: 5
New Jersey: 4
Pennsylvania: 13
Delaware: 1
Maryland: 7
Virginia: 15
North Carolina: 9
South Carolina: 5
Georgia: 5

Additional regiments:
New Hampshire: 0
Massachusetts: 3
Rhode Island: ½
Connecticut: 1½
New York: ½
New Jersey: 2
Pennsylvania: 2½
Delaware: 0
Maryland: 0
Virginia: 3
North Carolina: 1
South Carolina: 0
Georgia: 0

Extra regiments:
New Hampshire: 0
Massachusetts: 0
Rhode Island: 0
Connecticut: 0
New York: 0
New Jersey: 0
Pennsylvania: ½
Delaware: 0
Maryland: 1
Virginia: 0
North Carolina: 0
South Carolina: 0
Georgia: 0

Artillery regiments:
New Hampshire: 0
Massachusetts: 1
Rhode Island: 0
Connecticut: ½
New York: ½
New Jersey: 0
Pennsylvania: 1
Delaware: 0
Maryland: 0
Virginia: 1
North Carolina: 0
South Carolina: 1
Georgia: 0

Cavalry (light dragoon regiments):
New Hampshire: 0
Massachusetts: 0
Rhode Island: 0
Connecticut: 1
New York: 0
New Jersey: 0
Pennsylvania: 1
Delaware: 0
Maryland: 0
Virginia: 2
North Carolina: 0
South Carolina: 0
Georgia: 0

Note: There were three regiments, the two Canadian regiments and Warner's, that were not assigned to any quota.

▼ PRIVATE, HENLEY'S ADDITIONAL CONTINENTAL REGIMENT, 1777 *The uniform shown, as unusual as it was handsome, was mentioned as being worn by a deserter from the unit. Light infantry caps were common, as they were made from old tricornes. They were also popular among the units and gave the impression to the enemy that they were encountering elite light troops. Washington discouraged the use of red or scarlet uniforms for Continental troops for obvious reasons. Colonel Samuel Webb's experience in getting permission from Washington is a sterling example of the difficulties encountered. However, red was a popular colour with some regiments, and Colonel Henley undoubtedly thought it a good idea, as it set the regiment apart from the rest of the army.*

HENLEY'S REGIMENT. This was also uniformed in scarlet or red coats faced and lined sky blue. Belts were white, as were waistcoats, and the regiment probably wore gaiter trousers during its existence. The overall effect was quite striking. Light infantry caps were worn by at least some of the regiment.

SPENCER'S REGIMENT. This regiment wore the ubiquitous blue coat with red facings and buff leather equipment along with roundhats and white waistcoats. Some sources state that they wore trousers made out of blankets that buttoned up the sides, but undoubtedly they also wore either gaiter trousers or breeches with stockings and half gaiters.

The Additional Continental regiments definitely filled a need in early 1777. The army had almost disintegrated in late 1776 because of the expiration of enlistments of the 1776 Continental regiments. Trenton and Princeton were fought with those regiments, some of them, such as Glover's Marbleheaders, of excellent quality, who stayed in the ranks because of pleas from Washington. The war was being waged on a shoestring, and everyone knew it, except the British.

The fate of the Additional regiments is interesting. Some, such as Webb's, lasted as long as the war, though they were either renamed or amalgamated. A reason for Webb's success was that he was at one time part of the commander in chief's military household.

THE PHILADELPHIA ASSOCIATORS

There were a few militia regiments that stood apart from the rest in terms of organization, ability and effectiveness. Indeed some militia units formed virtual brigades, uniformed and equipped in fine style. One of these was the Philadelphia Associators, a volunteer militia unit.

The Associator battalions served through Valley Forge, freezing and starving with the rest of the army. Initially, food was short and replacement clothing nonexistent, troops sharing clothing and footwear to maintain their posts in the worst weather conditions. One sentry was noted as presenting arms perfectly to a passing officer while standing post in his hat to keep his feet out of the snow and ice. These Philadelphia units also underwent the new training regime instituted by Washington and "Baron" von Steuben, a European professional who was an expert drill master. They were taught how to keep themselves clean, and therefore free of disease, while in the field; how to maintain, or police, their living areas; and what the "sinks" or latrines were for and how and where to construct them. In short, they learned their new profession, and when they emerged from the frozen hell of their winter encampment, they were no longer the raw militiamen who joined the army in 1776. The Continental Army that marched out of Valley Forge in June of 1778 was a new army, honed to a keen edge by hardship and training. By anyone's measure, they were a fine army, ready to cross bayonets with their enemies, the former Philadelphia militiamen among them.

◀ **Rifleman, 5th Battalion, Philadelphia Associators, 1775** *Benjamin Franklin was one of the original founders of this militia unit in 1747. By 1763, however, the Associators had been much reduced in strength and were not an effective unit. There were only two active companies by early 1775. Because of the fighting in Massachusetts in early 1775 the Associators were reactivated, and by August there were five infantry battalions and an artillery battalion for active service. One of the infantry battalions was a rifle battalion; an enlisted man of that unit is shown here.*

▶ **Light Infantryman, Philadelphia Greens (3rd Battalion), Philadelphia Associators, 1775** *Light infantrymen in the 1st through 4th Battalions had shortened coats, and all members wore the roundhat for battalion companies, or the modified jockey cap for the light infantry companies. Facings for the units were red, white, buff or yellow, and the small clothes (breeches, stockings and waistcoats) were white. Hats had different colours of "turbans" around the base of the cap or hat and were usually decorated with feathers of some type stuck into the turned-up side of the hat. Light infantry caps may have had a bucktail attached from the back and over the top.*

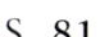

◀ **Private, 3rd Battalion, Philadelphia Associators, 1775** *The Associators saw active service in the Trenton/Princeton campaign. Like any untried troops, after they had been in action and had been "blooded", they settled down and gave good service. They also provided officers and men for the Pennsylvania Continental Line. After 1777 they were reorganized as the Philadelphia Brigade and were commanded by General John Cadwalader, who once commanded the Philadelphia Greens.*

▶ **Private, 2nd Battalion, Philadelphia Associators, 1775** *The uniform coats worn by the Associators were adopted by the Pennsylvania Line during the war before the 1779 Uniform Regulations. These units did present a uniform and smart appearance, but this would be worn down by active service. Roundhats were preferred by many units over the tricorne, as they didn't accumulate rain or snow inside the turned-up brims and they were much cooler in hot weather. They were also much more comfortable to wear.*

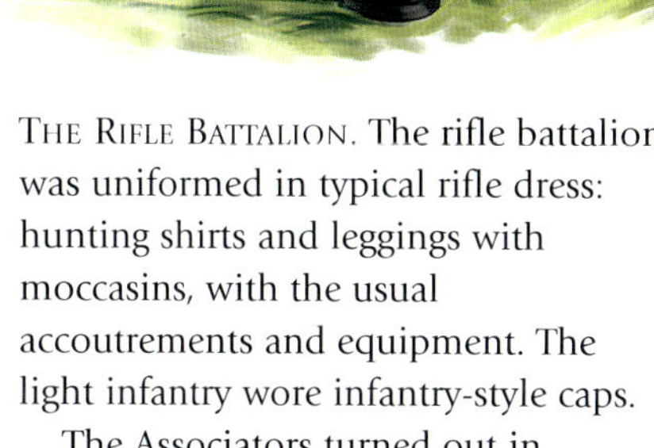

Benjamin Franklin was one of the founders of the Philadelphia Associators in the city of Philadelphia in 1747. Because of the strongly Quaker-influenced administration in Pennsylvania, interest in maintaining this unit after the end of the French and Indian War had been almost nonexistent. By the time war broke out against Britain there were probably only two companies in existence, and these had been greatly mismanaged.

However, the opening of hostilities in Massachusetts in 1775 set the tone for a military response, and by the middle of 1775 there were four "uniformed battalions" in existence plus some independent companies. By the end of the year, four infantry battalions, one rifle battalion and an artillery battalion had been organized, armed, uniformed and equipped. In addition to these troops, there was also a battalion of City Guards, which performed police functions in the city. Before being engaged as formed units, they had supplied individual replacements to the Continental Army.

The Infantry Battalions. The infantry battalions were smartly uniformed in brown coats with different coloured facings among the battalions: the 2nd and 3rd had red facings, the others yellow and either buff or white. The coats seem all to have been lined in white, so the turnbacks for the coats would have been white. The hats were all roundhats, with the brim turned up on one side. All units either wore a feather, the most common decoration, or a short plume in their headgear.

The Rifle Battalion. The rifle battalion was uniformed in typical rifle dress: hunting shirts and leggings with moccasins, with the usual accoutrements and equipment. The light infantry wore infantry-style caps.

The Associators turned out in strength for the Trenton-Princeton campaign and fought well, especially after their first engagement. They were later reorganized as the Philadelphia Brigade with Brigadier General Cadwalader, who had been one of the commanders of the battalion, as their brigade commander.

RIFLEMEN AND THE STOCKBRIDGE INDIANS

Riflemen have always captured the imagination of Americans. There were regiments of riflemen besides Morgan's Rifle Corps, although that unit is probably the most famous. At the Battle of King's Mountain in late 1780, after the disaster at Camden, a victory was won over a Loyalist unit commanded by British Major Patrick Ferguson by troops that were neither Continental nor militia, but were all rifle armed.

Stockbridge Indians

Of Mohican (or Mohegan) heritage, the Stockbridge Indians had moved to northern New York State from New England before the French and Indian War. They had sided with the British in that conflict, working harmoniously with Rogers' Rangers and forming a company in that unit. They were skilled scouts, warriors and light infantry, and their contribution to Rogers' operations was noteworthy.

In the war against the British, the Stockbridge Indians were one of the few tribes that sided with the Americans, probably because of their earlier association with Rogers. They again provided skilled warriors for the Americans and fought gallantly in a war not of their making.

◀ **Stockbridge Indian, 1777** *Captain Johann Ewald, an officer of Hessian Jägers in British service in North America, has a sketch of a Stockbridge Indian in a straw hat in his journal. The moccasins were made out of deerskin, the trousers out of coarse linen. The long shirt or tunic was almost to the knees and was worn outside the trousers or other legwear. The belt held several pouches containing powder and shot and sometimes food. Hatchets and knives were also carried. Besides the musket, bows and arrows were still carried. The straw hat was made of woven basswood bark, and the hatband was a ribbon.*

▶ **Stockbridge Indian, 1777** *This is based on an eyewitness drawing of a Stockbridge Indian serving with the American Army. The Stockbridge Indians were originally Mohican Indians who settled in a Massachusett village called Stockbridge. It is estimated that the Mohican had lost almost half of their male poulation by the time the war ended, and many of their villages had been destroyed.*

The Stockbridge wore leggings, moccasins and shirts. They were armed with either a long rifle or a musket. Most of them wore earrings and other traditional Eastern woodland American Indian clothing and accoutrements.

Over-the-mountain Men

These patriot frontiersmen, or "over-the-mountain men", were incensed by the perfidious Loyalists, and joined up for service of their own accord and

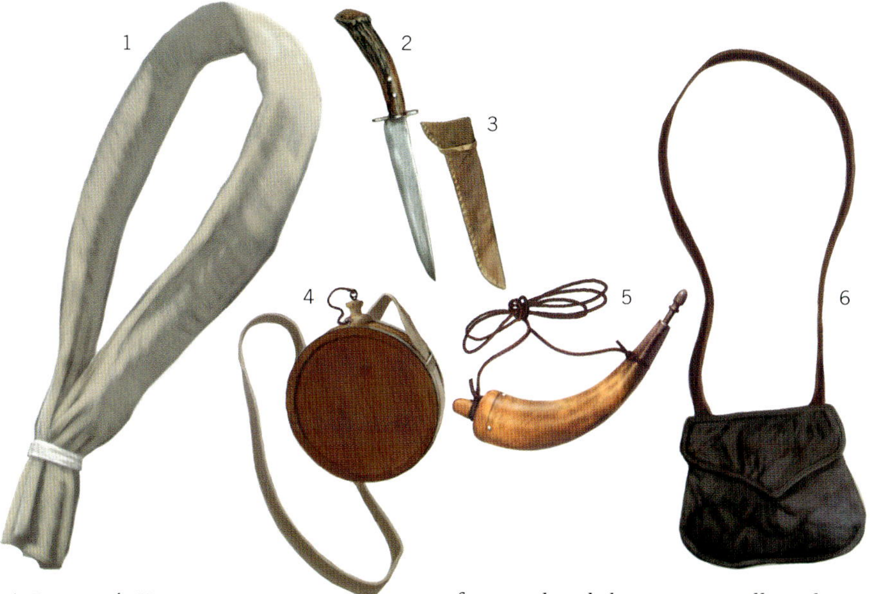

▲ **Rifleman's Kit, 1775–83**
1 Blanket roll, into which some troops would fold their belongings and wear it across the body. 2 & 3 Scalping knife and sheath. Scalping was common on the frontier by Americans, Indians and the British as a way of demonstrating how many enemies had been killed. 4 Canteen. 5 Powder horn. Hollowed out cow horns were used to carry the rifleman's powder and keep it dry in bad weather. 6 Shot bag. Ammunition would be kept in this bag, worn on either hip. It could also be used as a haversack.

under their own officers. They trapped the Loyalists on King's Mountain in South Carolina and, engaging the enemy in a fluctuating fight uphill, annihilated Ferguson's command, shooting Ferguson dead out of the saddle as he was trying to rally his command. They also hanged a number of the Loyalist prisoners they took.

Rifle dress was both comfortable and functional, and retained enough uniformity and smartness to be considered handsome military attire to be worn in combat. The hunting shirt has already been described. It might be of any colour, particularly if a unit dyed its shirts. Both blue and purple are known to have been used as colours, but, more often than not, the hunting shirt was probably a tan colour, although white is a possibility.

Either leggings or gaiter trousers were worn by riflemen, the former with Indian moccasins, the latter with issue shoes. Any type of hat was worn, from a slouch hat to a roundhat, the latter sometimes turned up on the side. A light infantry-type cap is recorded as being worn by some rifle units.

Rifles

The long rifle, known as either a Pennsylvania or Kentucky long rifle, was not of a uniform calibre and was individually made by local gunsmiths. Ammunition was cast by the individual riflemen and was not issued, although the lead for the rounds sometimes was. The rifle took a patched ball, which had to be rammed forcefully down the barrel, the cloth patch covering the bullet and fitting into the rifling in the bore, which gave the ball its spin, accuracy and range. A good rifleman could get a clean hit at 200 yards. The disadvantage to this was that the weapon was slow-loading and it did not take a bayonet.

The rifleman was equipped with a shot pouch or haversack along with a powder horn. There wasn't a cartridge for the weapon, but loose powder was poured into the muzzle when loading the weapon. A knife and hatchet completed the weaponry and the men undoubtedly carried their personal items in a pack or haversack.

Lynch and Campbell and their riflemen were veterans of King's Mountain, and they attached themselves to Greene's army and fought well at Guilford Courthouse. They fought on the flanks of Greene's army, although one company took its place in the third line of Continentals for the hardest fighting of the day.

These hardy frontiersmen wore the usual rifle dress of a hunting shirt, breeches and Indian leggings. They were armed with the long rifle.

▶ **Rifleman, Campbell's Riflemen, 1781**
There were two units of volunteer riflemen at the Battle of Guilford Courthouse in March 1781. They weren't militia, but they weren't regulars either. Most of them, under their own commanders, had been at King's Mountain. They were tough and experienced, and were brigaded with Lee's Legion and William Washington's command.

STATE TROOPS

Not all American soldiers went into a Continental regiment or were called up as a temporary measure by the militia. Some were established as more or less permanent state troop regiments, uniformed and equipped at an individual state's expense. State troops were much better disciplined than the militia but were often resented for taking valuable local resources away from the Continentals.

A Trained Reserve

The individual states, which were tasked with providing troops for the Continental Army after its creation, and were assigned quotas by Congress for doing so, also maintained their own private state armies during the war. These were maintained ostensibly to give the states some reliable troops with which to defend hearth and home. Some also had their own state navies during the period, and some, such as Maryland, had state marines for duty onboard ship. They would and could be a trained replacement pool for a state's Continental units, but their existence could also be a liability to the overall war effort.

On the surface this appeared to be a common-sense approach for states providing for their own defence in times of emergency (such as in 1780 when the British raided into Virginia and routed the governor, Thomas Jefferson, who had not prepared his state to face any external threat), but what this actually did was to deprive the Continental Army of a valuable source of manpower.

The units raised and maintained by the states for their defence, as well as the local militias, had better enlistment bounties than Congress could offer

◀ **Private, 4th Maryland Independent Company, 1776** *This figure is typical of the troops raised by the states for local self defence during the war. They were not Continentals, and were definitely not militia. Again the hunting shirt was the preferred dress for troops in the field. The state units sometimes contained former Continental troops, which would add experience and steadiness to the recruits, but this practice also kept men from Continental service where they were desperately needed.*

▲ **Corporal of Horse, Colonel Dabney's Virginia State Legion, 1782–3** *Legions were a popular organization, because they were a combination of infantry and cavalry, sometimes even having a few light guns attached. The organization was adopted from a European system that was developed in the middle of the 18th century. Both Continental and state forces used the organization, and it was adaptable for use in both partisan and regular warfare.*

for the Continentals, as well as better terms of service. Furthermore, these troops were for state defence, not service across the country wherever they were deemed needed if in Continental service.

Important stocks of clothing and cloth for uniforms were issued to the state troops first at times, depriving the Continentals, who were usually in dire need of resupply of everything from cloth to eating utensils, of material not only to fight the war and maintain themselves in the field, but to keep themselves in one piece both physically and mentally.

A Drain on the Continentals

For many reasons, the maintenance of their state troops and militia being one of them, some state governors were loath or unable to aid Continental troops in the field, even when they were campaigning in their state. In 1780 and 1781, Generals Gates and Greene bitterly complained about the lack of support they received for the Southern army from Governor Thomas Jefferson in the bitter campaigns in North and South Carolina. Many of Greene's men, after he took command from Gates after the disaster at Camden in August 1780, were without proper clothing, food, weapons and ammunition. Jefferson, despite desperate appeals from Greene, did little or nothing, leaving Greene to find his own provisions and supplies.

The militia and state units did form a source of manpower for the Continental Army, but it was not an organized system and was different from state to state, and sometimes within the already formed units of a particular state. The Philadelphia Associators was known not only for its service to the Continental Army, but as a pool of trained manpower that sent officers and men to the Pennsylvania Continental Line. However, the "system" didn't always function properly, and the Continental Army was always short of men. Former Continentals served past their enlistments, but in militia or state regiments, undoubtedly stiffening the new recruits but overall not helping the Continentals who continued to serve through all conditions. After 1779 the only real problem with the Continental Army was that there was never enough of them in the ranks, as the states gave precedence to paying and clothing their own militias first.

▶ **Sergeant, South Carolina State Regiment of Light Dragoons, 1779–80**
Dragoons were originally mounted infantry on inferior horses employed solely as transportation, the dragoons then dismounting for battle, to fight on foot. Dragoons eventually became another branch of cavalry while partially maintaining a capability for dismounted action. Light dragoons were classed as light cavalry, used for scouting, skirmishing, and with the capability for effective mounted action.

STATE ARTILLERY UNITS

The American artillery units that were formed in the early colonies used those of the British as a model. The first units of Continental artillery struggled to get established but soon earned considerable honours in the field.

The Art of Artillery

There were no artillery schools in the 13 colonies, and setting up artillery units from scratch was a particularly difficult challenge. Artillery equipment was expensive to manufacture and transport, artillerymen were expensive to train and equip, and finally, artillery was just plain hard work. Back-up and support systems were also complex. The pieces had to be cleaned and maintained after use, the gun carriages and ancillary vehicles, such as gun limbers and ammunition wagons, had to be kept in good repair. There were no established artillery train troops to haul the guns and maintain the horse teams required for that purpose. This commonsense support organization would not be forthcoming until after the war, when the small, regular United States Army would use properly trained artillerymen for this function.

During the war against Britain the Continental Army used the usual system, as the British did, of contracted civilians, who brought their horses and harness with them. While this was economically attractive to governments during peacetime, it was very unfortunate in combat. Civilians were tempted to depart when things became unpleasant, leaving the gunners and

◀ **Driver-Matross, 4th South Carolina Regiment (Artillery), 1775–80** *Matross was a term that denoted an artilleryman who was akin to being an assistant or apprentice gunner, and was subordinate to a fully qualified enlisted artilleryman. The use of matrosses as artillery drivers was unusual during this period, and was solely an American practice; most armies followed the practice of hiring civilian drivers and horses for that service. The horse's tail was tied up so as not to get caught in the harness. The harness used a combination of leather and chains to take up the weight of the gun limber and field piece it would help to pull. The saddle helped to keep any rookie matross in the saddle. On campaign the harness of these large draft horses would be continually adjusted because of the animal losing weight through exertion.*

▲ **GUNNER, CHARLESTON BATTALION OF ARTILLERY, 1778** *Dark blue was almost the universal colour for all artillerymen. Firing artillery was a dirty business as the black powder used produced clouds of smoke when in drill and action, and the dark colour of the uniforms made them much easier to clean and maintain.*

their pieces on the field to fend for themselves. Nevertheless, artillery units were raised in the colonies and were usually uniformed quite well and equipped with at least the minimum pieces and sidearms to man the guns if things became difficult. So there was a pool of men who were at least familiar with the rudiments of the trade and were able to be properly organized, especially if they went into the Continental service.

Artillery Organization

The artillery regimental organization of 1776 was a headquarters and staff composed of a colonel commanding, two lieutenant colonels and two majors, one chaplain, one surgeon, one surgeon's mate, one adjutant, one quartermaster, one drum major and one fife major. There would also be at least two cadets training to be lieutenants attached to the regimental headquarters. There were 12-gun companies composed of five officers, eight NCOs, two musicians and 48 privates.

Massachusetts, South Carolina and Rhode Island fielded artillery before the war started, Rhode Island's being touted as a train of artillery, as opposed to merely a battalion or a regiment. The beginnings of the artillery arm in combat, at Bunker Hill in 1775, were dismal at best. However, fortunes began to improve immediately after with the accession of the self-taught artilleryman Henry Knox, who was appointed as a colonel of artillery. He brought the large artillery train from newly captured Fort Ticonderoga to Boston in the winter of 1775 to give the American siege of Howe's British forces some teeth. He also brought competence, enthusiasm and a very loud, booming parade ground voice to organize and employ the growing Continental artillery arm in siege and on the battlefield. From that point forward, the state artillery organization gave way to Continental artillery that would grow in both numbers and skill to become a formidable combat arm and presence on the battlefields of the war, where Washington himself would say of it, after the Battle of Monmouth in 1778, that "no artillery was served better than ours".

▶ **OFFICER, VIRGINIA STATE ARTILLERY REGIMENT, 1778–80** *States such as Rhode Island, Virginia, and South Carolina all organized artillery units. These, along with cavalry, were expensive to raise and maintain. Further, they were a technical arm that required substantial training to master. The artillery, which needed horses to pull its guns in the field, had all of the cavalry's problems procuring mounts and harnesses, along with finding drivers to pull the guns and ancillary vehicles that were needed to run an artillery unit in the field.*

THE CONTINENTAL ARMY

When the shooting started between the American colonists and the British, the Americans had no effective army. The Continental Army was formed by Congress in June 1775, and George Washington was named its commander in chief. It was not an easy task, faced with opposition within the army and the Congress, as well an American distrust of a standing military force, but in the end the Continentals were as good as, if not better than, their opponents. No American army since has suffered so much hardship, fought against longer odds, nor gained as much as did the hard-bitten Continentals of Trenton, Valley Forge, Guilford Courthouse, and Yorktown.

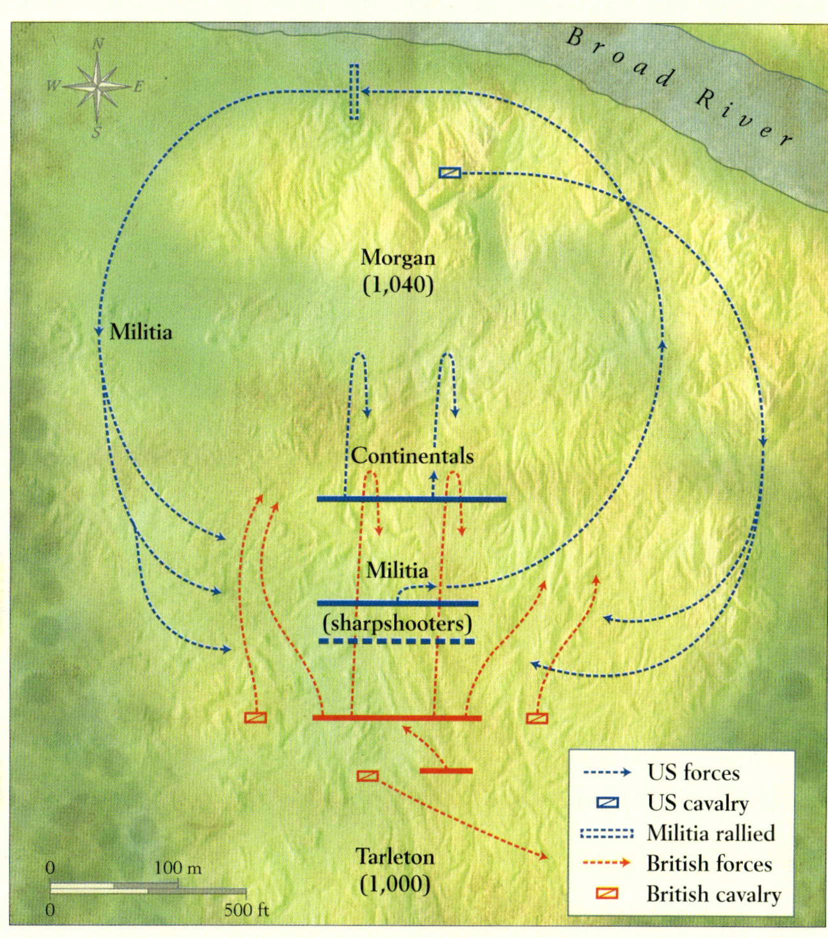

▲ *At Cowpens, General Daniel Morgan met and defeated a British command of equal strength under Colonel Banastre Tarleton, commander of the crack British Legion.*

◀ *The American Army under General Horatio Gates fought superbly near Saratoga in October 1777, and forced Burgoyne's surrender, a victory that led to the French Alliance.*

THOSE RAGGED CONTINENTALS

Regimental Allocations of 1781

Infantry regiments
New Hampshire: 2
Massachusetts: 10
Rhode Island: 1
Connecticut: 5
New York: 2
New Jersey: 2
Pennsylvania: 6
Maryland: 5
Delaware: 1
Virginia: 8
North Carolina: 4
South Carolina: 2
Georgia: 1
Total: 50 (including the 2nd Canadian Regiment, which was not allotted a state)

Artillery regiments
New Hampshire: 0
Massachusetts: 1
Rhode Island: 0
Connecticut: 0
New York: 1
New Jersey: 0
Pennsylvania: 2 (includes the Artificer Regiment)
Maryland: 0
Delaware: 0
Virginia: 1
North Carolina: 0
South Carolina: 0
Georgia: 0
Total: 5

Legionary corps (formerly the light dragoon regiments)
New Hampshire: 0
Massachusetts: 0
Rhode Island: 0
Connecticut: 1
New York: 0
New Jersey: 0
Pennsylvania: 1
Maryland: 0
Delaware: 0
Virginia: 2
North Carolina: 0
South Carolina: 0
Georgia: 0
Total: 4

Partisan corps
Both partisan corps (Lee's and Armand's) were not on any state allocation

Total regiments:
New Hampshire: 2
Massachusetts: 11
Rhode Island: 1
Connecticut: 6
New York: 3
New Jersey: 2
Pennsylvania: 9
Maryland: 5
Delaware: 1
Virginia: 11
North Carolina: 4
South Carolina: 2
Georgia: 1
Not Allocated: 3

The Continental Army's growing pains through the first years of the war caused Washington considerable irritation. Professional armies cannot be developed overnight, and the fits and starts of the Continental Army's creation led to problems and delays. There was promise, however, and stalwart officers saw the army through its darkest days. One positive aspect, which gave cause for hope, was the influence of European professionals who were recruited by American agents from across the Atlantic.

Foreign Professionals

From the beginning of hostilities, European professionals were eagerly sought out by American agents in Europe. These mercenaries, idealists or adventurers from the corners of Europe were a diverse group. Some were untrustworthy and were worse than worthless; others were proven professionals whose expertise and dedication brought great advantage to Washington's efforts and eventually helped the Continental Army develop into a professional fighting force that was the equal, if not the superior, of their British and German enemies. The first group fell by the wayside after arriving in America. The second made an impact on the Continental Army that was profound and invaluable.

The most important of the European professionals were Louis Lebèque Duportail, the highly competent French military engineer who became the father of the US Army's Corps of Engineers; Gimat and Fleury, two quietly efficient French infantry officers who contributed much to the Continental Corps of Light Infantry, leading and commanding component battalions of that corps; the Bavarian baron, Johann de Kalb, an outstanding combat leader whose Maryland and Delaware Continentals would follow him anywhere and a man who would sustain 11 wounds at Camden in 1780; and the Prussian baron, Friedrich von Steuben, undoubtedly the most valuable of them all, who forged the Continental Army into a fighting force.

Raw Material into Soldiers

The advent of Baron von Steuben and his imposition of order and regulation on the Continental Army was a turning point in the war. Arriving at the winter encampment at Valley Forge with an inflated dossier prepared by the American ambassador to France, Benjamin Franklin, von Steuben impressed Washington. The Prussian spoke no English and Washington no German, but von Steuben was fluent in French and through interpreters the two could communicate, eventually

▼ *Friedrich von Steuben drilled the ragged Continental Army into a cohesive force that could effectively challenge the British troops.*

◀ *Washington leads his battered Continental Army to their Valley Forge winter camp.*

Continental Army Strength by Year

1775: 27,443	1780: 21,015
1776: 46,891	1781: 13,292
1777: 34,820	1782: 14,256
1778: 32,899	1783: 13,476
1779: 27,699	

Note: These figures are based on information compiled by Henry Knox, the Continental Army's chief of artillery, assembled for a report to Congress. Knox stated that there were inaccuracies, but they give an idea of approximately how many troops were under arms for the given year.

becoming friends as well as colleagues. Friedrich von Steuben was presented by Franklin as a former Prussian general. In fact he was a retired captain who had extensive staff experience and service with Prussian light troops. The title of baron may or may not have been accurate, but what was proven was von Steuben's professionalism, practical expertise and knowledge of European drill. He was immediately put to work with the starving, freezing Continentals, and the army he wrought at Valley Forge was the greatest single contribution anyone made to the progress of America during the war.

American Drill

Declaring the Continentals to be excellent raw material, von Steuben modified the European drill, using a combination of British, French and Prussian regulations, and the Continentals, for the first time, were introduced to a uniform system of manoeuvre. Von Steuben was a hard taskmaster, demanding perfection (and sometimes getting it) from the Continentals he personally trained. Taking a musket himself, teaching and swearing at his subordinates through two interpreters (which greatly amused the troops), he started at the bottom, carefully instructing his new pupils in the military arts. Companies and battalions became adept in his new system, and the ubiquitous von Steuben taught, guided and supervised the troops as they learned not only drill but also camp and personal hygiene and sanitation.

As conditions improved at Valley Forge, so did the army too as an organization. Soldiers became proud of their abilities. Morale rose, and von Steuben's positive influence was readily apparent. Two things emerged from the experience at Valley Forge: a new Continental Army and the codified Drill Regulations written by von Steuben, the famous "Blue Book" which would be used by the United States Army until 1814.

When the Continental Army marched out of Valley Forge in the spring of 1778, it was an efficient organization ready and willing to take on the professionals of Europe. No longer would they be at a tactical disadvantage on the battlefield. They would meet their enemies in the open in linear formation in the best European tradition.

▼ *The surrender of Cornwallis to General Washington at Yorktown, 1781.*

COMMANDERS AND STAFF

In the late 18th century the concept of having a general staff to assist the commander in chief in his command was still very much in the embryonic stage. A commander's staff is supposed to relieve him of all administrative work and allow him to concentrate on the army. The minutiae are to be delegated to, and executed by, officers in different staff sections that are assigned to a specific area of concern (such as operational planning, logistics, supply and paperwork). The staff would be headed by a chief of staff who would co-ordinate the different sections and be responsible to the commander for these myriad tasks.

General Officers

For the early part of the war, what Washington had was a few trusted aides, and he relied on these to run the army. Both Congress and Washington realized that this arrangement was unsatisfactory. What was developed was a staff that was well on the way to becoming a professional body headed by a de facto chief of staff, and it went a long way into making the Continental Army a real professional fighting force.

Aides-de-camp (ADCs) are junior assistant staff officers whose official function is to assist the commander in his duties. Friedrich von Steuben was assigned the duties of inspector general to the commander in chief. In that function he served as the de facto chief of staff to Washington, taking some of the administrative burden of commanding and running the Continental Army from him. Generals relied upon ADCs to communicate, and an ADC was expected to look after his general, perform routine staff duties, and convey his general's wishes to the general's subordinates, speak in the general's name, and supervise the execution of orders.

George Washington reported for duty in 1775 wearing what was essentially his old militia uniform of a dark blue coat with buff facings. The coat was lined in buff, making the turnbacks, facings and collar, also known as a cape, buff too. His waistcoat and breeches were buff, and he wore fashionable riding boots.

General officers in the Continental Army generally wore a uniform modelled on that of the commander in chief. There were some variations for personal taste. Benedict Arnold wore a variation in which his waistcoat was trimmed in red, the buttonholes of his waistcoat had buttonhole lace, and his dark blue coat was faced red and lined in white. General officers were distinguished by their gold epaulettes on both shoulders and by the coloured sashes they wore. Washington, as commander in chief, had a light blue sash. Brigadier generals wore pink ribbons and major generals purple to distinguish them even on worn-out or shabby uniforms. In 1780 new regulations were issued for the uniforms of general officers. Dark blue and buff was still the standard, but the sashes disappeared. Instead, the gold epaulettes were to have silver stars designating rank. Brigadier generals

◀ **General Washington in his Uniform of Commander in Chief, 1775** *George Washington assumed command of the Continental Army in the summer of 1775 dressed in his old Virginia militia regimentals. His belief that an army should be properly uniformed began with his own immaculately smart appearance.*

were also to be distinguished by a white feather in the hat; major generals by a black and white feather. Small clothes were either buff or white for both grades.

Staff Officers

The staff officers of the Continental Army had no prescribed uniform. They were usually in the uniform of their original unit with the normal rank insignia for their grade. After 1780, however, staff officers were distinguished by coloured feathers in their hats. Aides-de-camp were a little different. If they were taken from their units for ADC duties, they wore the uniform of their original unit. If they were unattached, they would wear the same uniform as their generals, with their own rank distinctions. ADCs to Washington wore a version of the commander in chief's uniform in the same colours, but with the rank distinctions of the ADC's grade. All ADCs wore a green feather in their hat. ADCs to the commander in chief wore a green and white feather. Washington wore a plain black tricorne without lace or feather.

▼ **Aide-de-camp to a General Officer, 1777** *An aide-de-camp (ADC) was part of a general officer's "household". He was the commander's eyes and ears on the battlefield, took care of the general's needs on campaign and in garrison, and was an integral part of the staff.*

▼ **Major General, 1779–81** *Regulation uniforms for the general officers of the Continental Army were modelled on Washington's uniform as commander in chief. Waistcoats and breeches were either buff or white. Buff is a colour that can range from a very bright, light tan to a more subdued light brown, so variations were inevitable, as general officers were responsible for uniforming themselves.*

▼ **Brigadier General in Regulation Uniform, 1779–81** *Brigadier generals had one silver star on each epaulette, while major generals had two. The feathers in their caps helped identify them from a distance, though how long they lasted on campaign is debatable. Washington's staff officers were probably uniformed as they or their general preferred.*

HEADQUARTERS TROOPS

Small bodies of infantry and cavalry were assigned to General Washington's headquarters to protect the commander in chief and for specialist, technical purposes.

Washington's Guard

As commander in chief of the Continental Army, Washington had a small headquarters guard made up of a reinforced infantry company. It was well trained and led from the beginning, and as time went on the selection process became more stringent. The primary duties of the guard were to protect Washington's person and his baggage, as well as to protect headquarters. When deemed necessary, from time to time, detachments from the four Continental light dragoon regiments were assigned as additional headquarters guards, the most frequent being from the 3rd Regiment, or from the 3rd Continental Light Dragoons, also known as Baylor's Horse. In some sources this regiment is referred to as "Lady Washington's Horse". This regiment, along with detachments from the other Continental light dragoon regiments, was commanded by the commander in chief's cousin, William Washington, in the southern army commanded by Nathaniel Greene. He led with skill and dash, proving himself one of the best cavalry officers of the war on either side.

The infantry company was increased to 150 men by von Steuben while at Valley Forge and used as a demonstration company for the new drill regulations. Afterwards, however, its strength was probably around 70 all ranks. Guardsmen were all to be native born Americans, between 5ft 9in and 5ft 10in (1.8m) tall. Prior to 1778 they were all Virginians, but subsequently they were taken from a cross section of the Continental Army. Their commander, Captain Caleb Gibbs, was from the North.

They were uniformed in dark blue and buff, like their commander, with red or scarlet waistcoats and initially wore the tricorne bound in white tape. They either wore breeches, stockings

◀ **Private, von Heer's Provost Company, 1778** *Also referred to as the Marchusée, after the French Army's equivalent, this company was the military police force of the Continental Army. Initially formed of chosen men, it was undoubtedly hated and feared by the average Continental and militiaman. The company was later assigned to the Pennsylvania quota for recruiting and replacement, and was undoubtedly efficient, as it served until the war was over.*

▶ **Officer, Washington's Guard, 1776** *This was a company-sized unit that was charged with the protection of the commander in chief's person and baggage. It was considered a crack outfit and was uniformed in a variation of Washington's general officer's uniform. Throughout the existence of the unit the officers wore the tricorne hat.*

and black half gaiters or were dressed in gaiter trousers. Both breeches and gaiter trousers were supposed to be buff. Later headgear consisted of a light dragoon-type cap with a bearskin strip down the centre of the entire cap, and a blue and white cut-feather plume on the left behind the black cockade, which later had a white centre in honour of the French alliance. Officers, although wearing basically the same uniform, probably wore tricornes throughout the existence of the unit, along with riding boots instead of shoes and gaiters. In the field the company probably wore hunting shirts

◄ PRIVATE, WASHINGTON'S GUARD, 1777 *The new cap with a blue and white cut-feather plume was probably more of an adapted tricorne with the fur along the top sewn to it. What is shown here is how the company was supposed to be uniformed in the last half of the war. The buff gaiter trousers were most suited to the type of terrain that was encountered throughout North America.*

to save wear and tear on their regimentals. This unit was not merely a "guard" unit but was a combat unit that Washington was not reluctant to commit if necessary. It was also one of the last units of the Continental Army to be disbanded in 1783. The uniform cap, with its bearskin strip down the centre, was later copied by General Anthony Wayne for the troops of his Legion of the United States in 1794, for his campaigns against the American Indians of the Old Northwest.

The Provost Company

This company was a mounted unit uniformed and equipped as light dragoons. It was formed in 1778 to assist the judge advocate general in the performance of his duties. Its members were the equivalent of the modern military police and were sometimes termed the Provost Corps or known by the French term *Marchusée*. They rounded up deserters and other miscreants, and on occasion had the unpleasant duty of hanging offenders. By all accounts they were efficient and among the best mounted troops of the Continental Army.

The company, commanded by the provost marshal of the Continental Army, Bartholomew von Heer, consisted of one captain, four lieutenants, two trumpeters, two sergeants, four corporals, one clerk, one quartermaster sergeant, 43 provosts (privates) and four executioners. The uniform of a blue coat with yellow facings was reported by a Hessian prisoner of war who saw them in Reading, Pennsylvania, while on parole. Light dragoon helmets were worn, and the trumpeters probably wore red coats with yellow facings. High-topped cavalry boots were worn, and the horse equipment was standard light dragoon issue.

► PRIVATE, WASHINGTON'S GUARD, 1777 *The first uniform of the enlisted men of the company included the "regulation" tricorne. Red vests were supposed to be worn, but the uniform situation even with this company was probably the same as with the rest of the army, and they were dressed as best they could be under the supply situations.*

CONTINENTAL INFANTRY

The Continental infantry regiments were reorganized on 27 May 1778 and had a headquarters of one colonel, one lieutenant colonel (who would be designated lieutenant colonel commandant if there was no colonel in command) and one major. The regimental staff was composed of one surgeon, one surgeon's mate, one adjutant, one quartermaster, one paymaster, one sergeant major, one quartermaster sergeant, one drum major and one fife major. The adjutant, quartermaster and paymaster were junior officers drawn from the companies to perform these functions as additional duties. The regiment had nine companies: one light infantry, two or three field officer companies, and five or six line companies. All companies contained three officers, six NCOs, a drummer, a fifer and a total of 53 privates.

▼ **Private, 1st New Hampshire Continental Infantry Regiment, 1778** *The light infantry-style cap was popular as it was easily made, and old cocked hats could be cut down and formed into this handy and handsome item. It also had the advantage of giving the impression of more light infantry being present.*

Early Uniform Variations

When dealing with the Continental infantry regiments and their uniforms, it should be noted that the most common uniform worn before the uniform regulations of 1779 were issued was either dark blue coats faced red or brown coats faced red. Maryland, Delaware, Pennsylvania, New York and South Carolina were states that furnished their troops with uniforms of these basic colours. Blue had been common with Provincial units in the French and Indian War, and was still a very popular colour. Some units did wear captured British uniforms, but were encouraged to dye the red to brown or purple so there would not be confusion once the shooting started and smoke obscured the battlefield.

The units described here have been selected for two reasons: first, because it was an unusual uniform out of the mainstream of tradition that is worth noting; or second, because the unit had an outstanding combat reputation, such as the Maryland and Delaware regiments, that should be stressed.

2nd New Hampshire Regiment. This had sky blue coats lined with white and faced with red. Buff small clothes were worn, as were white crossbelts. A black roundhat was issued, as were black half gaiters.

▲ **Drummer, 1st New Hampshire Continental Infantry Regiment, 1778** *This is an example of reversed colours on the musicians' uniforms before the Continental Army's regulations of 1779.*

3rd New York Regiment. Initially this unit had a grey coat faced green and lined with light grey. Black leather equipment was worn, as well as light grey small clothes and a tricorne that was bound with black tape. This regiment later had blue or brown coats, faced green.

2ND MARYLAND REGIMENT. This unit wore a dark blue coat faced red and lined with white, black tricorne bound with black tape, blue breeches, brown waistcoat, white stockings, black half gaiters, and white crossbelts. The survivors of the Battle of Camden went into the reorganized 1st Maryland. The reconstituted 2nd Maryland was brigaded with the 1st Maryland at Guilford Courthouse in March 1781.

4TH NEW YORK REGIMENT. These men wore a handsome uniform of white linen faced with scarlet. White gaiter trousers and black leather equipment, topped off by a simple, elegant light infantry cap completed the uniform.

1ST CONNECTICUT REGIMENT. This unit wore a red coat, faced white (some accounts say red, faced dark blue) with white turnbacks, a roundhat, white crossbelts, green or brown waistcoats and white breeches with black half gaiters.

3RD MASSACHUSETTS REGIMENT. This unit had a simple, elegant uniform of dark blue faced and lined with dark blue with red piping around the cuffs and lapels. Black tricorne hats were bound in black tape. Small clothes were white. Officers wore knee-high boots and the men wore white stockings with black half gaiters.

2ND VIRGINIA REGIMENT. The men had a dark blue coat and facings, with white buttonhole lace on the lapels and cuffs. Small clothes and leather equipment were white, and a black roundhat was worn bound with either white or black tape. The left side of the hat was turned up. Black half gaiters were worn.

The Second Reorganization

The infantry regiments were reorganized again on 1 January 1781 in a better, more efficient manner. The field officer companies were abolished, and there was now one light infantry company and eight line companies. Each had three officers, nine NCOs (one being the all-important bedrock of Western civilization, the first sergeant), one drummer, one fifer and 64 privates. The regimental staff consisted of a colonel, a lieutenant colonel and a major (if the regiment was commanded by the lieutenant colonel, two majors were authorized for that regiment), an adjutant, a quartermaster, a paymaster, a surgeon, a surgeon's mate, a sergeant major, a quartermaster sergeant, a drum major and a fife major. A permanent recruiting party, consisting of a lieutenant, a drummer and a fifer was on the rolls of the regimental staff, and these parties were stationed in their home state. It should be noted that the continuing reorganizations of the Continental infantry regiments were attempts to make the units more efficient fighting organizations. The number of Continental units that were authorized and required from each state during the war changed from time to time, usually coinciding with the major reorganizations. Units that had fallen under-strength were sometimes amalgamated with other units that were under-strength, forming a new regiment that might be renumbered in the state line. (The term "line" is used here to denote how many regiments the state could put in the line of battle. The entire Continental Army was referred to as the "Continental Line".) The issue was further complicated by the fact that the first regiments of 1776 had only been enlisted for one year. Consequently, the states were forced to recruit and organize all over again for 1777.

► PRIVATE, 2ND MARYLAND REGIMENT OF THE CONTINENTAL LINE *This man represents the original 2nd Maryland, which was largely destroyed, with the other Maryland regiments and the Delawares, at Camden, August 1780.*

◄ PRIVATE, 3RD NEW YORK CONTINENTAL INFANTRY REGIMENT, 1776 *This regiment was uniformed in dark blue faced in green. The short gaiters were easier to wear than the long gaiters that were worn by the French.*

◄ **Private, 2nd Virginia Regiment, 1775–8** *This unit was noted for wearing roundhats, which they sometimes turned up on one side, with the usual Virginia uniform coat with blue lapels and cuffs and white turnbacks. The buttonhole lace is unusual for an American unit. The Continental artillery also wore buttonhole lace, but the greater majority of American infantry units didn't wear it.*

▼ **Private, Rhode Island Regiment, 1781** *The 1st and 2nd Rhode Island Regiments were reformed into a consolidated Rhode Island Regiment in early 1781. A good proportion of its men were black, and the regiment was considered to be one of the most efficient.*

In 1775, however, the New England army had 26 Massachusetts infantry regiments, and the three other New England states – New Hampshire, Connecticut and Rhode Island – had three each. For the rest of the war, Massachusetts raised a total of 37 infantry regiments, but only ten were

▼ **Private, 4th New York Regiment of the Continental Line, 1778–9** *This smart uniform was ordered specifically for the regiment, and the entire unit was also issued light infantry-style caps. Interestingly, as white fabric was an undyed material, it was the easiest to keep clean because it could be washed without worrying if the dye would fade. Further, if it became stained, it could be corrected with pipe clay, which, when applied to the stain, covered it effectively.*

Regiments in the Field

The number of regiments actually in the field varied from year to year. The regiments authorized and in the field in 1775 and 1776 had to be re-raised as their enlistments ran out. This causes some confusion for researchers and renders tracing lineages difficult, as they sometimes do not exist. For example, the Delaware Regiment that was re-raised from Haslet's Regiment of 1776 is very easy to trace, as a number of Haslet's veterans were in the new regiment. Also, Delaware only had one Continental regiment through the war. The relatively small Maryland line is also relatively easy to trace from Smallwood's battalion of 1776. The same names appear with the new regiments in 1777.

present when the war ended in 1783. Connecticut raised 20, New Hampshire and Rhode Island five each. By 1783 Connecticut had five remaining, and New Hampshire and Rhode Island each had one. This numerical attrition was due to the strains of the service and losses. Quotas for various states obliging them to raise and maintain a certain number of regiments are shown in the table.

Maryland had four regiments in the field in 1783, while New York had two, New Jersey had two and Pennsylvania had five, respectively. The Pennsylvania line mutinied in 1780, and had to be completely reorganized, which is one reason the number of regiments dropped. Anthony Wayne brought them to Virginia in 1780 to support Lafayette, and they ended up under Greene's command in the Carolinas.

The Southern lines were captured at Charleston in 1780, which wrecked the contributions from those states. By the end of the war in 1783, Virginia and North Carolina had two regiments in the field, South Carolina and Georgia only one each respectively.

Greene's Army in the South

The Southern campaigns, especially after Nathaniel Greene's assumption of command of the Southern army in the autumn of 1780 after the disaster at Camden, are the decisive campaigns of the war. There were enough survivors of Camden to reform one Maryland regiment, and only enough Delawares to organize a small battalion of two companies. Lee's Legion, at Greene's request, was assigned to the Southern army, and with William Washington's surviving veterans of the 3rd Continental Light Dragoons and detachments from the 1st and 4th Continental Light Dragoons formed an excellent cavalry force for Greene. With these sound troops as a hard core, Greene waged a series of campaigns from early 1781 through to 1783 that destroyed the British presence in the Carolinas.

Units that were sent south differed from their Northern fellows because of the unique campaigning conditions. Situated far from major sources of supply, and led by an independent and aggressive commander, it was inevitable that Greene's Southern army took on a character and appearance that was distinctive from Washington's regulars. Unit commanders were given a great deal of freedom in uniform regulations, or forced to compromise and make use of captured British equipment, in a series of campaigns marked by attrition and hard fighting.

◄ **Private, 3rd Massachusetts Regiment, 1776–83** *The uniform of this regiment consisted of a dark blue coat, lined and faced with dark blue, and both officers and men wore white waistcoats and breeches or gaiter trousers. This uniform would have been easily converted by regimental or contracted tailors to conform to the 1779 uniform regulations. Handsome and quite simple, it is typical dress for Continental units early in the war.*

► **Private, 1st Connecticut Regiment of the Continental Line, 1777** *The 1st Connecticut was one of the few American regiments dressed in red, which was usually frowned upon for obvious reasons. Facings are reported as being either white or dark blue, and these undoubtedly had to be captured units. The 1st Connecticut was amalgamated with the 5th when the Connecticut Line was reorganized in 1781.*

Greene's Commanders

Greene was assisted in his campaigns by a talented group of subordinates. Otho Holland Williams and John Eager Howard were veterans of the Maryland line. Williams commanded the Maryland brigade at Guilford Courthouse and was a commander of rare insight. He also commanded the "light corps" of the Southern army after the Battle of Cowpens in January and February 1781. These highly distinguished troops, infantry from Maryland and Delaware, and Washington's cavalry and Henry Lee's Legion, were the rearguard of Greene's army in the famous "Race to the Dan".

As Greene's main body desperately moved north to the Virginia/North Carolina border, Williams' light corps kept Cornwallis at bay, confusing the British commander as to Greene's exact line of march, and fighting desperate delaying actions while not becoming decisively engaged with the British. Run, turn and fight, and run again, was the order of the day, and Williams showed he was a talented officer. That he was successful speaks volumes for his skill, valour and intelligence.

William Washington and Henry Lee were Greene's cavalry commanders. Both were skilled soldiers who led by example, and were fearless in action. Lee excelled at small unit actions (his legion was Williams' rearguard in the "Race to the Dan"), and was equally adept at working with the American partisans against the local Loyalists and the British lines of communication. Washington was a superb combat leader and was one of the few cavalrymen in either army who led successful charges on the battlefield against formed infantry, correctly sensing the exact moment to set his troopers to the charge.

Edward Carrington was an artilleryman who was especially skilled at logistics. It was he who performed the reconnaissance needed to cross the many natural obstacles that Greene's army ran into on the march to the Dan. Finally, Robert Kirkwood, a mere captain, was one of Greene's most trusted subordinates. He was the senior surviving Delaware officer after Camden and assembled infantry companies from the survivors of the Delaware Regiment. He could not be promoted because of the seniority rules of the Continental Army, but he exerted an influence on the Southern army out of proportion to his grade. These were the subordinate commanders who enabled Greene to maintain his army in the field and to fight the British.

▼ **Private, Hall's Delaware Regiment, 1778** *This regiment was the successor to Haslet's Delaware Regiment of 1776. Many of Haslet's veterans enlisted in this regiment and its reputation was second to none in the Continental Army and equal to any British or German regiment.*

▲ **Private, Light Infantry Company, Hall's Delaware Regiment, 1778** *Some of the light infantry company of the Delaware Regiment may have worn the old cap of Haslet's Regiment when it was formed in May 1778 under Captain John Patten. There is some evidence that both the cap and the tricorne were worn.*

Greene's Record

Interestingly, Greene never won a battle. The three he fought, Guilford Courthouse, Hobkirk's Hill and Eutaw Springs, were all held by the British. In each, Greene withdrew because he would not sacrifice his Continentals to gain a tactical success. These British successes were ultimately worthless because of the crippling losses Greene inflicted. His near-victory at Guilford Courthouse in March 1781 ruined Cornwallis' field army, forcing him to withdraw into Yorktown, where he was besieged by Rochambeau and Washington and forced to surrender. Without Greene, the war would not have been won.

▼ **Private, 5th Pennsylvania Regiment, 1777–83** *Enlisted men wore white hunting shirts or dark blue coats, faced white as late as 1779 and probably later. The striking light blue coveralls are noteworthy. Some units also had only one crossbelt, for the cartridge box, and wore the bayonet on a waistbelt in the older manner, with the bayonet attached by a frog. Belly boxes for cartridges were also worn.*

Southern Uniforms

The Maryland and Delaware Continentals, around which Greene built his Southern army, were arguably the toughest troops in the Continental Army. The nucleus of both lines had been with the Continental Army since 1776, and the survivors were hardened marchers and killers.

The Pennsylvania line was a late arrival in the South. Led by General Anthony Wayne, nicknamed "Mad Anthony" by his troops because of his behaviour in combat, it was a solid group of regiments that had been in the thick of the fighting in the north through Monmouth in 1778. Present at Yorktown, their presence in the Southern army was a boost to Greene's army.

Hall's Delaware Regiment. This was the successor to Haslet's Regiment of 1776. It was raised with Haslet's veterans as a cadre. They were uniformed in a dark blue coat with red facings and lining. Waistcoats were white, and the regiment was issued brown gaiter trousers. The light infantry company was similarly dressed but might have worn the old cap from Haslet's Regiment. Their overalls may have been of undyed cloth so would have contrasted with the rest of the regiment. Many Continentals were issued with a tin ammunition box in addition to, or in lieu of, the usual cartridge box. Hats for the battalion companies were tricornes bound in yellow tape. Officers were armed with spontoons, which Washington preferred, and their tricornes were bound in black tape.

Pennsylvania regiments were usually dressed in either dark blue or brown coats faced with red.

1st Pennsylvania Regiment. This unit had brown coats faced green. They probably wore buff small clothes and light coloured stockings with black half gaiters. The tricorne was bound in black tape.

5th Pennsylvania Regiment. These men wore dark blue coats faced and lined with white; light infantry cap, brown breeches, white vests or white gaiter trousers were also worn. They probably wore a belly box instead of the crossbelt carrying the cartridge pouch, as many thought it more convenient and easier to reach. Officers wore white breeches. Light blue overalls were also worn, as were white hunting shirts with white overalls, and light infantry caps.

▲ **Private, 1st Pennsylvania Regiment, 1777–81** *First uniformed in a combination of brown and dark blue, faced with red, the preferred post-1779 regulation uniform was dark blue, faced red. By this point in the war, gaiter trousers were preferred, and they could be in a variety of colours, though the best material for this uniform item was probably that used for bed ticking.*

COLOURS AND STANDARDS

Banners, flags and standards are as old as armies themselves. The ancient Egyptians carried symbols into battle, and the eagle standards of the Roman legions are duly famous. The biblical saying "terrible as an army with banners" is an ancient truism. By the 18th century, colours and standards were vital in the smoky, deafening confusion of battle because of the need for commanders to be able to identify their own troops, and they had also become a symbol of a soldier's unit and a source of pride. If the colours fell, it was a reliable indicator that the unit was in trouble. To lose colours in combat was a disgrace unless there were no more troops left to defend the flag. Devotion to a unit's colours was customary, and it was part of the *esprit de corps* of a unit that the regiment's soldiers would die defending it. It was, therefore, a great honour to capture the colours of an enemy, which together with the capture of the enemy's guns, was a traditional measure of victory.

Precise details on the colours carried by the Continental Army are rare. Few are intact and those represented in art of the period may not be accurate. Some, however, are well known, such as Washington's command flag and the colours of the Philadelphia City Troops of Light Horse.

Infantry

There is no doubt that most, if not all, of the Continental infantry regiments had a standard of some type. Many militia units also had standards; for example, the Bedford Minutemen used a standard modelled on those of the trained bands in England centuries before. The 2nd New Hampshire was known to have had two regimental colours of the same design but of different colours, and Webb's Continentals, the 1st Continentals and the 3rd New York were all known to have had colours of some type.

There were two systems of colours employed by the Continental Army. The first was designed by General Charles Lee, who proposed that every regiment should have one regimental colour and a colour for every two companies in the regiment (two infantry companies were referred to as a "division"). These latter colours were known as "grand division" colours, and they have made any study of the Continental Army's flags problematic. Webb's regiment definitely used this system. The number issued was between two and four per regiment, and the colours used for the flags were

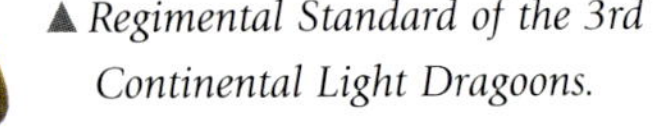

▲ *Regimental Standard of the 3rd Continental Light Dragoons.*

▲ *Rhode Island Train of Artillery 1775.*

▲ *1st Continental Regiment of 1776.*

▲ *Webb's Additional Continental Regiment, 1777.*

▲ *Washington's Headquarters Flag, 1781.*

▲ *2nd Pennsylvania Continental Infantry Regiment.*

green, red, blue and yellow. The second system was proposed by von Steuben and was to revert to the two colours per regiment, as the British had done. Both systems were probably used simultaneously.

Continental flags of many designs were used throughout the war. The slogan "Liberty" was liberally used, as were the mottoes "Join or Die" and "An Appeal to Heaven". Many flags had 13 vertical or horizontal red and white stripes, and a snake, state coats of arms and the Liberty Tree were common motifs.

▼ *Standard Bearer, Rhode Island Continental Infantry Regiment, 1780-1. Amalgamated from the 1st and 2nd Regiments of the Rhode Island Line. The cap's anchor was typical of Rhode Island regiments.*

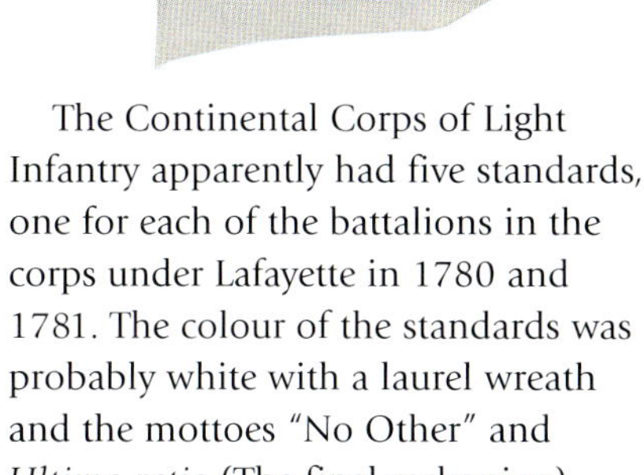

The Continental Corps of Light Infantry apparently had five standards, one for each of the battalions in the corps under Lafayette in 1780 and 1781. The colour of the standards was probably white with a laurel wreath and the mottoes "No Other" and *Ultima ratio* (The final reckoning).

Cavalry

The 2nd Continental Light Dragoons had two standards of the same design, but different colours. Pulaski's Legion had an interesting standard of crimson silk, 18in (45cm) square with silver fringe and a sleeve to mount it on its staff. The obverse of the flag has a circle of 13 eight-pointed stars enclosing the "all-seeing eye" (also used on US dollar bills). The motto *non alius regit* (no other governs) encircles the stars.

▲ *New Hampshire Continental Infantry Regiment, 1777.*

▲ *2nd Continental Light Dragoons.*

▲ *Philadelphia City Troop of Light Horse.*

On the reverse of the standard were the letters "US" with the motto *Unitas virtus forcior* (Union makes valour stronger). There were yellow and white flaming grenades in the corners of the standard. The so-called Eutaw flag was carried by Washington's 3rd Light Dragoons and was reportedly cut from a red damask table cloth.

Artillery

Details of artillery colours are even more elusive. The Rhode Island Train of Artillery had their own colours, however, and the design uses Benjamin Franklin's representation of a rattlesnake to represent the 13 colonies and the motto "Don't Tread on Me".

LIGHT INFANTRY

Light infantry, for scouting and skirmishing, and to break up enemy attacks, was invaluable in the terrain of North America. Both sides had numbers of light infantry at their disposal, and the Continental troops were among the best on either side.

Light Infantry Companies

While the Continental infantry regiments were modelled on those of Great Britain, few American regiments had a grenadier company, and most of those were disbanded early in the war. However, the practice of having a light infantry company in each regiment was one the Continentals readily adopted and developed to a very high degree of professionalism.

4th Massachusetts Regiment. This regiment had a light infantry company with a distinctive light infantry cap that was simple and elegant, and that distinguished a unit otherwise dressed in a regulation uniform adhering to the 1779 regulations. The dark blue coat was faced and lined with white, and white overalls were worn. Deborah Sampson, the first known American woman to impersonate a man, join the army and take part in combat, was a member of this company.

Kirkwood's Delaware company. This company, one of two that remained of the Delaware Regiment after Camden, was issued a drab or light grey hunting shirt (probably made from undyed cloth) for service in the South. The men wore bed-ticking overalls of white or light grey with blue stripes. While perhaps irregular, this cloth was actually excellent material for uniform trousers or overalls. Bed ticking was tough and utilitarian, and therefore ideally suited for making clothes for campaigning in the rugged terrain of North America. The two companies (the other was commanded by Captain Jaquett and attached to the 1st Maryland Regiment) wore the regulation tricorne bound in yellow tape. During this period they wore the alliance cockade of white over black, the black portion being the larger.

◀ **Private, Kirkwood's Delaware Battalion, 1781** *Captain Robert Kirkwood was the senior surviving Delaware officer after the Camden disaster in 1780. He reformed the survivors into two new companies, one commanded by him, the other by Captain Jaquett. The clothing they were issued came from North Carolina stores, and this handsome, practical uniform was the result.*

▶ **Private, 4th Massachusetts, the Light Infantry Company, 1781** *This company was made up of men who were chosen for size, endurance and skill. It had the distinction of having a woman, Deborah Sampson, enlisting and serving in the unit in 1782. Her gender was discovered after she was wounded in action and was treated by a surgeon.*

◀ **Private, Light Infantry Company, 2nd Canadian Regiment, 1776** *Canadians and men from the Northern American colonies made up this regiment, which maintained an excellent reputation throughout the war. It was one of the few Continental infantry regiments that maintained a multi-battalion organization.*

5th Pennsylvania Regiment. The light infantry company of this regiment wore either a dark blue coat with white facings or a white hunting shirt and white overalls with a light infantry cap. Officers and men both wore this smart outfit, and it was distinctive and utilitarian. They were armed with a musket and bayonet and the usual infantry accoutrements.

2nd Canadian Regiment. The light company of this regiment was dressed like the rest of the unit with a brown regimental coat lined with white. The only difference was the simple light infantry cap. The coat initially had white facings, but these were changed to red later in the war. The light infantry cap bore the legend "COR" for Congress' Own Regiment, with the addition of a scroll above it bearing the motto *Pro aris et focis* (For altars and hearths).

Continental Corps of Light Infantry

The practice of detaching the light companies from the regiments serving with the main army during campaign season and forming them into provisional battalions was common. It led to the establishment of the Continental Corps of Light Infantry, which developed into a true elite formation and was the flower of the Continental infantry. In practice, the men not only performed light infantry duties, but also duties that would usually be given to the grenadier companies. The Continental Army's light infantrymen were the pick of their regiments, strong men who were also noted for their intelligence.

The corps consisted of men drawn from light infantry companies, and they retained their existing uniforms. Initially there were no distinguishing features, but when Lafayette was their commander, he reintroduced swords for the men as well as black and red plumes for all ranks. Even the artillery supporting the corps was issued with the new plumes.

The corps is famous for two actions. The first is the bayonets-only night assault on the British fortifications at Stony Point on the Hudson River below West Point. The other, led by Alexander Hamilton, was the night assault against Redoubt Number 10 at Yorktown in October 1781. Once again, the light infantry went in with unloaded muskets and did not wait for the forlorn hope that sappers would clear the way through. The troops went in on the run through the ditch and up the walls, over the palisade of sharpened wooden stakes and into the redoubt. Redoubt 9 was taken at the same time by the French.

▶ **Officer of Light Company, 5th Pennsylvania Regiment 1781** *This regiment began the war in dark blue faced with white. The first issue breeches were of buckskin, and the stockings were a light blue. Coveralls and shortened coats were worn by the light company by the late 1770s, and the light infantry cap was a universal pattern that was quite common among the Northern state regiments. The spontoon was used as a weapon as well as a badge of rank.*

UNIFORM REGULATIONS OF 1779

It took the Continental Army a number of years before it could issue precise, detailed regulations on uniforms and equipment. These regulations defined what the troops were supposed to wear – although, as we shall see, variations persisted.

Professional Uniforms

The study of military uniforms, or uniformology, must take three points into account. First, the uniform regulations that existed for the army, or armies, being studied. Second, what the officers and NCOs of that army wanted the uniforms to look like on parade. Third, what the troops actually wore. This third point is particularly apt when considering the Continental Army's uniform regulations, issued in October 1779.

One of the indicators that the Continental Army was growing into a professional fighting force was the issue of uniform regulations for the entire army in 1779. Washington and his subordinates wanted a smartly uniformed army that would appear to be both competent and professional. It is also a military axiom of long standing that if troops are dressed as professional soldiers, they will think of themselves as such, and a feeling of pride and *esprit de corps* develops in the individual units and the army as a whole.

The 1779 regulations were simple and practical, and ensured that the army was to be elegantly uniformed in accordance with the best European traditions. Cloth and accoutrements were to be brought from France, and there was meant to be enough money to clothe the entire army. What actually occurred was rather different. While Washington and his commanders did their best to issue

◄ **NCO, Massachusetts Regiments, 1779** *Continental NCOs under the new regulations were still armed and equipped like the enlisted men, but all were to wear authorized small epaulettes on their shoulders to denote their rank. This elegant and simple uniform was the ideal that was attempted by Washington in the new uniform regulations, but there is no evidence that it was achieved army-wide. The uniforming of the army depended on funding and material from the states, and the poorer states could not uniform their troops up to standard year after year. What the troops were supposed to look like and what they actually wore were two entirely different things.*

▲ **Officer, Massachusetts Regiments, 1779** *This handsome uniform, simple in concept and facing colours, was prescribed for the New England regiments of the Continental Army. Throughout the war, uniforming the Continentals was a constant battle for its commanders, especially at the regimental level. Always short of funds and other resources, this regulation uniform was probably seldom achieved, though there are examples of its existence in many of the Army's regiments which were smartly uniformed as closely to regulation as possible.*

the material for the prescribed uniforms, and regimental commanders tried hard to keep their troops properly uniformed, the regulations were probably never applied uniformly.

The estimate for the number of uniforms that were needed to clothe and re-uniform the entire Continental Army was 88,480 infantry uniforms, 3,088 for the cavalry, 6,480 for the artillery and 6,000 uniforms for the wagon train. France provided 10,000 uniforms along with 15,000 stands of arms. While this helped, it did not provide for a new uniform to be issued according to the new regulations. Some regiments were lucky and could comply. Others were not and it was up to the regimental commanders to do the best they could.

Usually officers, and perhaps musicians (drummers and fifers) too, were given uniforms as close to the regulation uniform as possible. Most of the regiments either kept their old uniforms, if they were still serviceable, used hunting shirts as the two Delaware companies did, or improvised. The first priority was not uniformity, but being clothed practically and warmly.

Campaigning in North America was hard on uniforms. A unit might be well uniformed or clothed as the campaign season opened. However, by the end of the campaign, and if not re-supplied in a timely and efficient manner, the officers and men would be in rags. Regulations were one thing, and reality was another. Some units were still wearing captured British uniforms after 1779, though these were dyed and came out with a purple hue, which was distinctive but odd. Bed ticking was still used for coveralls, and was sturdy, colourful, and held up well on campaign, but was hardly regulation. Still, the army was uniformed more or less properly, though the hunting shirt was still a popular and functional item.

Infantry Regimental Quotas

New York 7	Virginia 15
New Jersey 4	North Carolina 10
Pennsylvania 13	
Maryland 7	South Carolina 6
Delaware 1	Georgia 4

◀ PRIVATE, MASSACHUSETTS REGIMENTS, 1779 *Even when units were properly and smartly uniformed at the beginning of the campaigning season, they might very well be in rags by the time they went into winter quarters. The generally harsh terrain and conditions in which they marched and fought was hard on uniforms, and this was also true for their enemies. What they were supposed to look like was evidently different from how they actually appeared both on parade and in the field.*

▶ DRUMMER, MASSACHUSETTS REGIMENTS, 1779 *This uniform is another excellent example of reversed colours in a regiment's musicians. Regiments were sometimes judged by the appearance of their musicians, referred to in the French service as the "heads of column", as they usually led the regiment on the march and into combat. Musicians may have been young, but they bore no resemblance to today's teenagers, who would be considered very immature in comparison. They were considered by their commanders to be men and combat soldiers, not children.*

▼ **Officer, Maryland Regiments, 1779** *The Maryland Continental Line was uniformed in these colours, and wearing the tricorne, since at least 1777. There is evidence that some units may have been uniformed in brown coats faced with red, but that changed, at least in the regulations, if not in the field, in 1779. The units that marched south in 1780 would have been uniformed in this manner.*

New England Regiments

The regulations provided for dark blue coats faced and lined with white. Musicians would be in reversed colours (white coats faced with dark blue), and they would wear a light infantry-style cap. Privates and probably the company grade officers would wear gaiter trousers in white, made from different material for winter and summer. Belts would be of white or light buff leather, and the headgear would be the tricorne with the black and white alliance cockade. Privates would have their hats bound in white tape, the officers in black. The regulation light infantry companies would wear the same uniform but with light infantry distinctions such as the ubiquitous cap and wings on their shoulders. The 4th Massachusetts' light company was uniformed in this manner. It also unknowingly included an enlisted woman in its ranks. Deborah Sampson is thought to be the first woman to impersonate a man in order to join the army, and she hid her gender among her comrades until she was wounded in action.

The reality of uniforms after 1779 departed from the vision expressed in the regulations.

1st Connecticut Regiment. This regiment probably kept captured British uniforms at least through 1779, the year the regulations were implemented.

6th Connecticut Regiment. All the men, not just the light infantry company, had leather caps.

7th Connecticut Regiment. This unit followed the new regulations and was uniformed according to them.

8th Connecticut Regiment. In early to mid-1779, the 8th was uniformed in red coats faced white and wore brown waistcoats and leather breeches.

1st New Hampshire Regiment. The men were dressed in hunting shirts and trousers in early 1779.

2nd New Hampshire Regiment. This unit had their officers at least in the regulation dress, and the musicians in reversed colours as prescribed.

3rd New Hampshire Regiment. The regiment was probably uniformed in brown coats faced red, most likely to have been French-made.

2nd Rhode Island Regiment. The unit was in the prescribed uniform in late 1779, but although the coat was blue with white facings, it was lined with

▼ **Drummer, 1st Maryland Regiment, 1781** *The famous 1st Maryland of Guilford Courthouse fame is again represented here by a drummer wearing reversed colours. Good commanders usually took care that at least their drummers were uniformed properly, so that they could be identified readily in combat, and that they were smartly dressed. This eye-catching uniform, however, might have caused some trouble on the battlefield, looking very much like a British uniform.*

yellow instead of white, so the coat's turnbacks were yellow. The combined Rhode Island Regiment of 1781–3 that replaced both the 1st and 2nd Regiments was made up largely of black troops. These were well uniformed and were sketched by a French officer as being in an all-white uniform with red cuffs, brown crossbelts and white overalls. They wore a

▲ *Baron von Steuben drilling American recruits for the new Continental Army at its winter quarters at Valley Forge in 1778. Those that survived the bitter weather, meagre rations and iron discipline were hardy, well-trained troops, ready for battle.*

light infantry cap much like that worn by the earlier Rhode Island Train of Artillery, except it bore a much simpler fouled anchor device on the front flap.

2ND MASSACHUSETTS REGIMENT. This regiment apparently wore regulation uniforms in all details.

4TH MASSACHUSETTS REGIMENT. The men wore regulation uniforms, but their gaiter trousers were brown instead of white.

► **FIFER, NEW JERSEY REGIMENTS, 1779** *Another regulation uniform for musicians, again in reversed colours. Fifers might be boys too young to carry a drum, and they might also be a relative, such as a son or a younger brother, of someone in the regiment. They took their chances in combat and were usually armed as shown. Their fifes were carried in a leather tubular-shaped case that hung on the hip by a shoulder belt.*

◄ **PRIVATE, 2ND PENNSYLVANIA REGIMENT, 1779** *This is the enlisted version of the regulation uniform after 1779. Neat, functional, and very military in concept, in reality the coat might be made shorter, the troops put into light infantry caps and hunting shirts, as well as either coveralls of striped bed ticking or gaiter trousers.*

Mid-Atlantic

The regulations provided for dark blue coats faced and lined with buff (a bright light tan colour) for New York and New Jersey. Pennsylvania, Maryland and Delaware were authorized to wear dark blue coats with red facings and a white lining. Musicians would be in reversed colours (buff coats faced with dark blue and red faced with dark blue, respectively) and they would wear a light infantry style cap. Privates as well as the company grade officers would wear gaiter trousers in white, of different material for winter and summer. Belts would be of white or light buff leather, and the headgear would be the tricorne with the black and white alliance cockade. Privates would have their hats bound in white tape (except Delaware which had yellow tape), the officers in black.

The regulation light infantry companies would wear the same uniform but with light infantry distinctions such as the ubiquitous cap and wings on their shoulders.

Delaware Regiment. This unit had usually been dressed in regulation dark blue and red. Needless to say, the exigencies of serving in the South for extended periods tended to erode dress regulations. They did, however, maintain tricornes with yellow tape.

Marylanders had usually been uniformed in either blue faced red or brown faced red from the beginning of their service. They did not have to change very much to conform to new regulations, but the Maryland line had the same clothing problems in the South as the Delawares. Hunting shirts of various colours were probably worn, but some, especially the officers, undoubtedly maintained the regulation dark blue and red or scarlet.

The New Jersey troops, when inspected, had no hunting shirts, and they may or may not have been clothed in the new regulation uniform. They were apparently well clothed, but there is no way to know for certain what was worn between 1779 and 1781. Evidence is clearer for other units.

2nd New York Regiment. The men wore blue faced with white, instead of the regulation buff. The other regiments probably wore either what they could get or their older, now non-regulation uniforms, although some had both breeches and overalls on hand, which was fortunate.

1st Pennsylvania Regiment. This was apparently uniformed according to the new regulations by 1780.

2nd Pennsylvania Regiment. The regiment was also well uniformed according to regulation and had a combination of tricornes and light infantry caps in the correct

◄ **NCO, Virginia Regiments, 1779** *NCOs in the Continental Army were distinguished by small coloured epaulettes on their shoulders. They were armed and equipped in the same manner as the enlisted men and took their place in line of battle with them. They never carried a halberd as their European, particularly German, counterparts did, though in the pre-war provincial units that piece of equipment was common.*

► **Officer, Virginia Regiments, 1779** *At the beginning of the war, brown and dark blue were favoured for uniform coats. Facings would vary, but red was usually predominant. Virginia was unique in that its facing colour was also dark blue, which made for a rather sombre uniform but handsome nevertheless. In combat, officers probably would not wear the gorget as it made an excellent target.*

◄ **Drummer, Continental Artillery, 1779–83** *The reversed colours of this artillery drummer, specified in the 1779 uniform regulations, are an excellent example of the prevailing practice in uniforming musicians. The addition of a light infantry cap instead of the usual tricorne is another distinction that set the drummers apart from the rest of the unit for easy identification in combat, as well as for* esprit de corps *and pride.*

proportions for its companies. There is also a notation that the regiment had grenadier caps in mid-1779, but there is no record of what they looked like, or even that the regiment officially had a grenadier company.

The 5th Pennsylvania Regiment. The 5th had regulation coats, but had overalls of various colours, probably out of necessity as there was undoubtedly a cloth shortage in the correct colour. The 6th Regiment was in the same situation.

The South

The regulations provided for dark blue coats faced and lined with a dark medium blue, a shade lighter than the coats. The regiments from the Southern states were also to have white buttonhole lace, something that was not used for the Northern regiments. Musicians would be in reversed colours (medium blue coats faced with dark blue), and they would wear a light infantry-style cap. Privates and probably the company grade officers would wear gaiter trousers in white, of different material for winter and summer. Belts would be of white or light buff leather, and the headgear would be the tricorne with the black and white alliance cockade. Privates would have their hats bound in white tape, the officers in black.

The regulation light infantry companies would wear the same uniform but with light infantry distinctions such as the ubiquitous cap and wings on their shoulders. There is scant information available on the uniforms of the four Georgia regiments. Hunting shirts and gaiter trousers seem to have been the norm, but there is evidence that the 4th Georgia might have been in blue coats piped in white in 1779.

The North Carolina regiments were usually uniformed in hunting shirts and overalls, North Carolina being, as noted before, a poor state with little money to spare on uniforms. Like the Georgia units and those from the Carolinas, the Virginia Continental Line was captured at Charleston when that city was surrendered after a siege. They were probably not in the new regulation uniforms at that point, although there were plans to adopt them. Virginia initially issued the units with hunting shirts of various colours, those being uniform within the units. There is also contradictory evidence that blue coats faced red were worn.

► **NCO, Continental Artillery, 1779–83** *This was the uniform for the Continental artillery regiments according to the 1779 uniform regulations. It wasn't a drastic overall change from what had been worn before this date, but regularized the uniforms of the different Continental artillery regiments that had differed in some details and colours since the beginning of the war. The sergeant's rank is shown by his epaulettes. He was uniformed and equipped like the enlisted men.*

LEGIONS AND PARTISANS

Units that combined a number of branches of service, the most frequent combination being infantry plus cavalry, were popular. Some units also included artillery. Legions were the most common such units and were often raised by a wealthy volunteer – who became the unit's commander. Legions developed from Europe and were suited to warfare in North America. It was a fusion of practicality with necessity, and an admission that co-ordinating the operations of troops of more than one arm was a tactical development essential for success in combat operations, even at a basic level. It was also a practical method for the Continental Army, as the raising and maintaining of mounted units was expensive and difficult. This compromise held out the possibility that if enough horses were procured the unit could remount itself.

The Legions

Legions were often equipped and uniformed by their commander, and the unit's dress inevitably reflected the personal tastes of that individual.

The legion of 1781, organized from the four light dragoon regiments, consisted of a headquarters and staff and had four mounted and two dismounted troops (companies). The headquarters consisted of one colonel, one lieutenant colonel and one major supported by a staff of one surgeon, one surgeon's mate, one saddler, one trumpet major, one riding master, one paymaster, one adjutant and one quartermaster. The duties of adjutant, quartermaster, riding master, and paymaster were performed by officers. Mounted and foot troops were organized similarly, the only difference being that the mounted troops had a farrier (blacksmith). Each had four officers, eight NCOs, a trumpeter and 60 privates.

LEE'S LEGION. This was a combined infantry/cavalry force that worked well both as a regular unit and in combination

◀ **INFANTRYMAN, PULASKI'S LEGION, 1779**
Casimir Pulaski was the first commander of the American cavalry. A member of the Polish aristocracy, he was a skilled and experienced military leader who joined the American revolution in 1777. He took his legion south and was present at the Siege of Savannah in 1779. Courageous, loyal, and an excellent horseman and combat leader, he was killed in action leading his troops against the enemy; another gallant son of Poland who died far from his homeland.

▶ **OFFICER, ARMAND'S LEGION, 1780**
Armand was a French nobleman who formed a small legion for service with the Continental Army. The unit's reputation was not good, and they have been noted as an especially ill-disciplined lot, with a tendency to disappear when the going got a little too rough. Generally composed of foreigners and not native-born Americans, Armand commanded slackly when a firmer hand could have made his unit into a first-rate outfit.

with partisans; the legion's cavalry was very well mounted and the troopers described as young and eager. They fought alongside Francis Marion's partisan unit, and shared in several small successes in South Carolina. Lee's cavalry were uniformed in green round jackets with buckskin breeches. The leather equipment was black.

▼ OFFICER, LEE'S LEGION, 1780–1 *Lee's infantry initially wore purple coats and overalls, but were later uniformed in green coats and overalls, and wore the same headgear as the cavalry. They were otherwise equipped as regular infantry.*

PULASKI'S LEGION. This exotic unit was initially organized to contain not only cavalry, but also grenadiers and chasseurs in its infantry component. The cavalry was supposed to carry lances, and all of the infantry were finally organized as light infantry. Apparently the legion was uniformed in dark blue with red facings, white small clothes or overalls, and buckskin breeches for the cavalry. Both infantry and cavalry wore a type of light dragoon helmet in leather.

Pulaski was initially the commander of the cavalry component of the Continental Army. He wasn't suited for that command, and was given permission to form his legion, which was incorporated into Armand's Legion following Pulaski's death in action at Savannah in 1779.

ARMAND'S LEGION. This unit was not highly regarded; it was generally poorly disciplined, having an inclination not to stay on the battlefield when the situation became difficult. Officially, the unit was the Free and Independent Chasseurs, and they undoubtedly took this title just a little too literally. The unit was probably uniformed in blue and buff, with brass dragoon helmets for the cavalry and leather light infantry caps for the infantry. It was formed in 1778 and disbanded in late 1783.

Partisan Corps

The 1781 organization for the Partisan Corps was similar to that of the legions. The headquarters and staff were the same, and the only difference was in the number of troops, of which there were three mounted and three dismounted. They were organized similarly to the legionary troops of each type, except there were only 50 privates. The partisans' mission was twofold. First, it could act independently if necessary and engage in partisan warfare either on its own or with the independent partisan units that were active in the Carolinas. Second, it could take its place in the line of battle if necessary, as these units were Continental regulars.

▲ INFANTRYMAN, LEE'S LEGION, 1780–1 *Lee's Legion wore a dragoon helmet apparently patterned on the "Tarleton helmet". In fact, the whole uniform was very close to that of Tarleton's British Legion.*

There were two units re-designated as partisans while operating in the southern theatre. The first was Lee's and the second Armand's. Armand's, originally designated the Free and Independent Chasseurs, probably wore blue coats faced white, buff, or red.

CONTINENTAL CAVALRY

The American cavalry arm began by fits and starts, and was never large by European standards or particularly efficient as an organization. There were four light dragoon regiments, which were numbered consecutively from one to four and which were also known by the names of their respective commanding officers.

Light Dragoons

The Continental light dragoons had significant teething problems. Horses were always difficult to obtain and maintain, and saddles and harnesses, as well as suitable arms, were also difficult to come by. The light dragoons were raised for reconnaissance, escort duties and other such activities, and were seldom used for the typical knee-to-knee charges and aggressive action that European light cavalry were intended for. In the Southern army, however, under William Washington (the commander in chief's cousin and arguably the best cavalry commander of the war on either side), the 3rd Continental Light Dragoons were used on the battlefield, as cavalry should have been. Washington's appearance – that of a large and rather disgruntled cherub – belied his true character as an aggressive combat commander, and he led his light horsemen in hell-for-leather charges at Cowpens and Guilford Courthouse, which were devastating for the British infantry.

▶ **Trumpeter, 3rd Continental Light Dragoons, 1781** *American mounted units followed the European custom of uniforming their trumpeters in "reversed colours" and mounting them on white or grey horses. This was for easy identification in combat, especially when the unit was attempting to rally after a charge or being broken. Trumpeters also had the duty of watching their commander's back in a melée.*

Organization

The four Continental light dragoon regiments were authorized in 1777, and they were organized with a headquarters of one colonel (commander), one lieutenant colonel, one major and a staff of one chaplain, one quartermaster, one surgeon, one surgeon's mate, one paymaster, one riding master, one saddler, one trumpet major, one adjutant, and four supernumeraries. The latter were cadets who were being trained. There were six mounted troops in the regiments, each being authorized three officers, six NCOs, one trumpeter, one farrier, one armourer and 32 privates.

On 27 May 1778 the light dragoon regiments were reorganized with a headquarters of one colonel, one lieutenant colonel, and one major with a staff of one surgeon, one surgeon's mate, one adjutant, one quartermaster, one paymaster, one riding master, one saddler and one trumpet major. The roles of adjutant, paymaster and riding master would be performed by company officers "in addition to their other duties". There were still six mounted troops, each of four officers, eight NCOs, one trumpeter, one farrier and 54 privates. When the light dragoon regiments were converted into legions with some of the troops serving dismounted, those who were unhorsed were equipped as infantry, but retained most of their dragoon uniform and accoutrements. Their short coats, swords, and helmets were retained, but they were now issued overalls or gaiter trousers, supposedly in brown, but probably in any material that was at hand, including the utilitarian bed ticking. Infantry packs were issued, and the tin ammunition box was probably carried in addition to the belly box they used when mounted. Drums were substituted for trumpets in the troops, and undoubtedly there was much unhappiness among those troopers who now had to walk instead of ride.

▲ **Officer, 3rd Continental Light Dragoons, 1781** *This unit, along with the 2nd Continental Light Dragoons, developed into a crack outfit. Its performance in 1781 at Cowpens and Guilford Courthouse was exemplary and showed what well-led cavalry could do on the battlefield against infantry and cavalry. This uniform was prescribed in the regulations and used in practice.*

▶ **Private, 2nd Continental Light Dragoons, Dismounted Service, 1780** *Continental mounted units were plagued by a shortage of mounts and suitable saddles and harnesses during the war. One solution that was reached was to dismount some of the troops, converting the regiments into legions of horse and foot, which proved effective in the usual broken terrain of North America.*

Light Dragoons in Combat

The four light dragoon regiments were small and in themselves did not constitute an effective cavalry arm for the Continental Army. Cavalry acting in mass was a new concept for most American officers, as it had not been done before in America because of the heavily wooded terrain.

Initially, the four regiments were employed as couriers, escorts, and reconnaissance, but there were officers among them who knew how to use cavalry. William Washington, and Henry Lee, who acquired the nickname "Light Horse Harry", had definite ideas of how to use their horsemen, but initially they were junior officers in command of companies not regiments, and came off badly in nasty little fights with their more experienced opponents.

Lee was later allowed to build a legion around his mounted company, and when they were assigned to Greene's army in early 1781 they soon proved themselves an excellent unit. William Washington finally became the commander of the 3rd Continental Light Dragoons. Together with detachments from the 1st and 4th Continental Light Dragoons, he led the devastating charges they delivered so well at Cowpens and Eutaw Springs against British infantry, which often decided the issue.

Regulations and Uniforms

The cavalry was not affected by the uniform regulations as much as the infantry was and developed its own uniforms during the period.

1ST REGIMENT OF CONTINENTAL LIGHT DRAGOONS. The regiment was raised and commanded by Colonel Theodorick Bland and was the only one of the four light dragoon regiments with a comprehensive set of uniform regulations.

The regiment was to have worn a brown coat faced green, the trumpeters to be in reversed colours. Buff breeches were worn and, apparently, white waistcoats. Coloured hearts, brown for trumpeters and green for everyone else, were to be worn on the elbows. Trumpeters were supposed to have trumpet banners the colour of the regimental facings. Black leather light cavalry helmets were to be worn, but roundhats were apparently worn by some in the regiment.

Some of the cavalrymen probably wore a red coat faced blue, and it should be noted that all of the light dragoon regiments wore the hunting shirt, either as a primary garment or on top of the regimental coat from time to time. If at all possible riding boots were procured and worn, and typical horse equipment was issued for all four regiments.

2ND REGIMENT OF CONTINENTAL LIGHT DRAGOONS. This regiment was commanded by Colonel Elisha Sheldon and was probably originally

◄ **TRUMPETER, 4TH CONTINENTAL LIGHT DRAGOONS, 1780** *Once again this figure displays the practice of having cavalry trumpeters in reverse colours for quick identification in the smoke and noise of combat. The trumpet was able to pierce the ear-shattering din of battle, and the trumpeter, a trained soldier and not just a musician, was vital to keep the unit under control or to implement a rally.*

▲ **Trooper, 4th Continental Light Dragoons, 1780** *This regiment was initially uniformed with captured British infantry coats, but was finally given green coats faced red. It had the same teething problems as the other Continental cavalry regiments, though it served well. Like the 1st Regiment of this arm, a detachment served with Greene's army in the Southern campaign from 1780 onward.*

uniformed in short green coats faced white. Brass dragoon helmets with a light blue "turban" were ordered in 1778, and the usual uniform this unit is shown in is short blue coats faced in buff, buff small clothes and breeches.

3rd Regiment of Continental Light Dragoons. The 3rd, or Baylor's 3rd Regiment, might originally have been uniformed in a blue coat faced red, but the more common uniform described is of a short white cavalryman's coat faced light blue with a white lining. Leather belts were black for an interesting contrast, and the unit wore a black leather dragoon helmet. William Washington eventually became the unit's commander and it was he that led it to fame in the South.

4th Regiment of Continental Light Dragoons. Commanded by Stephen Moylan, the unit was dressed in scarlet coats with blue facings, a style that was undoubtedly confusing to both sides. Ordered to dye the coats to obtain a different colour, Moylan instead had hunting shirts of various shades issued to wear over the coats. New uniforms were eventually issued of green faced with red, in addition to a red waistcoat, buckskin riding breeches and a leather cap with a bearskin across the top.

The cavalryman's equipment included his sword or sabre, and two crossbelts of white, buff, or black leather. One belt held the sword, and the other held a carbine, which clipped on to the belt by a small swivel. His armament was completed by two pistols in holsters attached to the saddle. Trumpeters, in addition to wearing a uniform of reversed colours, were also supposed to ride white or grey mounts for easy identification.

▲ **Officer, 1st Continental Light Dragoons, 1780** *There are two uniforms that have been identified for this regiment. One was dark blue faced red, and the other was brown faced with green. The latter is pictured here. Hard service and the lack of horses reduced the already small regiments rather quickly, and few people in the Continental Army knew how to employ cavalry the way William Washington and Henry Lee did. A detachment of this regiment served under William Washington in the Southern theatre in 1780–1 and after.*

CONTINENTAL ARTILLERY

The United States had to build its artillery from scratch, and problems were inevitable. However, with impressive speed, by 1778 this branch of service was well regulated and effective. The Continental Army's artillery units were not affected by the uniform regulations as much as the infantry had been. The artillery would wear the same basic uniform throughout its service.

Types of Artillery

From the 14th century onward artillery development underwent repeated changes based on how generals intended to employ their guns. Three distinct types of artillery emerged for use in land operations: siege artillery, garrison artillery and field artillery.

Siege artillery generally consisted of large, heavy guns used to batter fortifications that were emplaced in fortified siege works to protect them from enemy counter-battery fire.

Garrison artillery was employed to protect fortresses and the guns were usually placed on specially designed carriages that were then mounted on the fortress wall. Neither of these types were suitable for use with field armies as they were too heavy and very difficult to move across country.

Field artillery was light and mobile and accompanied the armies in the field. The calibres employed were 3-, 4-, 6-, 8-, and 12-pounders, their designation being by the weight of the projectile they fired. These were long-barrelled cannon, and they were augmented by howitzers, which were short-barrelled weapons designed to fire at a higher angle than the flat trajectory fired by guns. The effective range for these direct fire weapons was about 1,000 yards. The ammunition used was roundshot, which was a solid cast-iron ball; canister, which was a tin can filled

◀ **Sergeant, 2nd Continental Artillery Regiment, 1781** *NCOs served either as gun captains or commanded gun sections in the gun companies. They, as the rest of the artillery, were uniformed and equipped as infantry and learned to fight for their guns to the last extremity, if need be. Losing a gun to the enemy was as large a disgrace to the artillery as it would be for an infantry regiment to lose its colours.*

▲ **Matross, 2nd Continental Artillery Regiment, 1781** *A matross was literally a gunner's assistant and was the neophyte in the artillery enlisted hierarchy. There was no American artillery school at this time, and artillerymen were trained by their officers and NCOs in the gun companies or "on the job" in combat. That the American artillery arm gained the high level of skill and reputation it did during the war is a testament to the dedication of the gunners that manned it.*

with small, cast-iron balls, which gave the effect of a giant shotgun when the piece was fired; and grapeshot, which was larger cast-iron balls that were arranged around a wooden "tree" and covered with some type of "bag". Roundshot had the same effect as canister. Both canister and grapeshot were anti-personnel rounds and were quite effective at 500 yards or less. Roundshot was used against earthworks, personnel and other artillery pieces.

Howitzers did not fire roundshot (although they did fire canister). Their round of choice was the exploding shell. A shell was a hollow cast-iron ball filled with gunpowder and set with a fuse that would explode either as the shell rolled along the ground at the end of its trajectory or in the air.

Continental Batteries

In 1781 the four artillery regiments were reorganized with a headquarters consisting of one colonel, one lieutenant colonel, one major, with a staff of one paymaster, one adjutant, one quartermaster, one surgeon, one surgeon's mate, one sergeant major, one quartermaster sergeant, one drum major and one fife major. The adjutant, quartermaster and paymaster were drawn from company officers already in the gun companies, as additional duties. There were ten gun companies consisting of six officers, 12 NCOs, a drummer and fifer, and 51 privates.

The basic artillery unit in the field was the company. It was usually issued between four and eight field pieces, and one company was assigned to each infantry brigade in the Continental Army. In most armies the artillery regiment was usually an administrative and not a tactical unit. In the Continental Army, however, General Knox used the regimental command and staff structure to control artillery employment on the battlefield. This gave the Continental Army an immense advantage in artillery employment over their opponents.

General Knox was an expert organizer and trainer. He also knew how to employ his artillery, a fact demonstrated by the American artillery employment at Monmouth in 1778 and Yorktown in 1781. In addition, Knox insisted that all of his artillerymen were trained properly in all of the different weapons in the inventory. Artillery companies were rotated among the different pieces used for different missions, making all of the gun companies able to handle field artillery, siege artillery, including mortars, and artillery in defensive works.

◀ **Colonel, 2nd Continental Artillery Regiment, 1781** *The Continental artillery units were considered elite from at least the Battle of Monmouth in June 1778. There, the American artillery outshot its British opponents and clearly demonstrated its skill. Field officers were usually mounted, and this being a regimental commander, the figure here is shown in regulation dress.*

America's Artillerymen

There were generally two types of enlisted artillerymen. Gunners were qualified men who were both well trained and experienced. Matrosses were a type of apprentice artilleryman still learning their trade while working at the job. Matrosses were used for the more manual type of labour associated with serving on a gun crew, such as moving the piece back into battery after firing, and emplacing and displacing the guns when they had to move. There were generally more matrosses on a gun crew than gunners. The gun captain and the pointer were always properly qualified gunners.

American artillery usually served well, especially after mid-1776. As the war progressed, and the amateur artillerymen learned their trade, they became a respected force on the battlefield. Their service contributed much to the Battle of Monmouth in June 1778, a fact remarked upon by the commander in chief.

Functional Uniforms

The change imposed on the artillery by the regulations was to make all four of the Continental regiments uniform in appearance as a branch of service and to do away with distinctions between the regiments. This happened in October 1779. The artillery adopted dark blue coats faced and lined with scarlet, with yellow (gold) buttons, yellow lace on the buttonholes and around the lapels, cuffs and turnbacks. The regulation tricorne was bound in yellow tape or lace. Small clothes were white, and when overalls were worn, they were also white. Prior to this, the artillery arm of the Continental Army had been

▼ Continental Artillery Kit, 1781–3

Artillery sidearms were the tools necessary to work a field piece. They were used to load and fire the piece, move the trail to aim, and to clean it after action. They were also very useful in close combat if the company was being overrun by the enemy. The rammers and handspikes made excellent "skull-crackers". 1 & 2 Two views of the fork lever. 3 The rammer and worm. 4 & 5 Two views of the straight handspike. 6 The rammer, staff and sponge. 7 & 8 Two views of the crooked handspike. 9 & 10 Two views of the ladle. 11 Tampion, or muzzle plug. 12 Portfire, a simple tool used to fire the piece. 13 Water bucket. 14 & 15 The bricole, a leather crossbelt, length of rope, metal ring and hook used to manoeuvre the piece by the gun crew without the horses from the limber.

▼ Gunner, Continental Artillery, 1781–3

A gunner, though the term can be used to denote all artillerymen regardless of rank or skill level, was a highly skilled artilleryman who "pointed" (aimed) the piece and was usually the second-ranking member of a gun crew. Pointing the gun was an acquired skill, and each gunner would come to know his particular piece, all of which had different characteristics when aimed and fired.

◀ **Officer, New York Continental Artillery Company, 1776** *This elite unit of 60 men was led by Alexander Hamilton, who started his military career as an artillery officer. He was an independently minded commander who fought with courage and skill, and served as one of Washington's aides-de-camp. At Yorktown he led the light infantry in their successful night assault against Redoubt Number 10, an action that is often given credit for bringing the war to a victorious close for the Americans.*

▶ **Sergeant in Winter Dress, New York Continental Artillery Company, 1776** *The ubiquitous blanket coat shown here was almost universal winter wear in both the Continental Army and the British forces in North America. Complete regimental uniforms would be worn underneath. The cap shown was also almost a uniform item in the winter on both sides.*

noted as always wearing dark blue coats, usually faced red. Some Continental units, such as Lamb's artillery company, wore blue and buff or other variations of the regulation uniform, but basically the Continental artillery wore something similar in colour and style to the regulation uniform throughout the war.

Mounted officers would wear the same uniform as prescribed and also wear riding boots with spurs. The horse equipment probably varied, and was most likely of the kind used by the cavalry, or whatever was available.

For winter either the service overcoats of various colours would be worn, or the typical blanket coat. The blanket coat was an excellent piece of winter clothing that was both utilitarian and warm, and was usually of the same pattern for all units.

Equipment

Artillerymen were issued with standard issue infantry equipment. They carried the regulation musket and bayonet, which after the French alliance became the excellent French Charleville musket. Shoulderbelts were white and were worn in the same manner as those worn by the men of the infantry. What were referred to as artillery "sidearms" were actually the specialist tools and equipment vital for working and manoeuvring the guns on the battlefield, rather than weapons.

The rammer staff was used to ram the round down the gun tube. The sponge was dipped in the water bucket, and the tube was rammed wet after firing to ensure there were no hot pieces of wadding or cartridge remaining in the piece that might cause a premature detonation of the new round when it was rammed. The worm was used to extract excess wadding that might build up after prolonged firing.

The pricker was a large metal needle that was inserted into the vent at the breech of the piece to pierce the powder bag before the primer or priming powder was put into the breech. The bricole was a leather crossbelt with a length of rope with a hook on the end that was used to manhandle the piece into position or to displace if the limber and horse team was not used. Handspikes were used to both move and "point" (aim) the piece and were also very handy, along with the rammer and sponge, as weapons if the company was overrun by the enemy.

SPECIALIST TROOPS

An 18th century army needed specialist troops trained for specific activities to function effectively in the field. More particularly, in a seige situation, when it served as either besieger or besieged, an army needed engineers, miners and sappers. Initially the United States suffered from a dearth of such army specialists but, with French assistance, they eventually created a corps of useful technical troops.

Engineers

When the war began, there were no native military engineers available in the fledgling United States. In this critical technical branch, foreign volunteers had to be completely relied on. The Continental Army was fortunate in that Louis Duportail, a highly skilled and dedicated officer, arrived from France and organized and led what became the engineering arm of the army.

The regulation engineer uniform was eventually to become a dark blue coat with buff facings, red turnbacks and buff small clothes.

Sappers and Miners

The three Continental companies of sappers and miners came into existence in May 1778 at the insistence of General Duportail. Each company was to consist of four officers, eight NCOs and 60 privates. These companies were to be known as a corps of engineers and when working on fortifications or in siege operations were to be augmented by drafts from the infantry regiments present. The corps of sappers and miners were uniformed in a style similar to the engineers and wore dark blue and buff. As they were combat troops, they were also armed, equipped and drilled like the infantry.

A sapper is a combat engineer employed in the construction of "saps", the French term for a

◄ **Officer, Engineers 1780–3** *The engineering arm of the Continental Army was established by European officers, as there was no comparable engineering education available in North America at the time. The Chevalier Duportail was the father of the American engineering arm, and this uniform was prescribed for engineer officers in the Continental Army.*

▲ **Officer, Artillery Artificers, 1780–3** *The artificers constructed and repaired the artillery equipment and vehicles. A specialist arm like the engineers, it was a small unit, though designated a regiment. This uniform is that of their commanding officer and is quite elaborate for the Continental Army. The formation of this unit indicated that the Continentals were becoming the army that Washington aspired to create.*

▲ **Private, Corps of Sappers and Miners, 1781** *This unit was the combat arm of the engineers. Miners and sappers were specially trained to serve in sieges as both the besieged and the besiegers, where they dug trenches, fortified posts, and fought as infantry when needed. They served well and ably in the Continental Army at the siege of Yorktown, and their contribution was a notable part of that victory.*

trench used in siege warfare. Sappers were used to build fortifications, were sent in the advance guard of armies on the move to clear obstacles in the path of the army and were also employed in the establishment of camps.

Miners were engaged in a particularly dangerous form of warfare: mining and counter-mining. A mine was a tunnel that was dug under the walls of an enemy's fortress, and then either set on fire or exploded, so that the wall would collapse and the fortress could be stormed. Counter-mining was to dig tunnels from the besieged fortress to try and intercept the enemy's mines. If found, they were to be destroyed. This underground warfare was extremely dangerous, and miners were considered elite troops.

The existence and performance of these engineer troops was vital to the Continental Army, and their formation, training and effective deployment, especially at Yorktown, was an indication that the Continental Army was a professional military force.

Artificers and Invalids

The Regiment of Artillery Artificers was formed and commanded by Colonel Benjamin Flower and was employed in constructing and repairing artillery gun carriages, limbers and other ancillary vehicles used by the artillery.

Artificers and invalids were uniformed and equipped as the artillery and wore dark blue coats, with red facings, waistcoats and breeches. For the type of construction and repair work they did, they were issued hunting shirts of various colours and types. The tricornes were bound in yellow tape, and their leather crossbelts were probably black. They may or may not have been issued half gaiters or overalls.

The Invalid Regiment was made up of men too badly injured to serve with the Continental Army, but who could still perform good and valuable service. They were employed to guard posts and prisoners, and the unit was also designated to act as a military school. They probably wore the uniforms of their old regiments, but there is evidence that they were issued and wore a green coat, white waistcoat and breeches and a red overcoat. There is also evidence that they might have worn captured British uniform coats that had been dyed brown.

▶ **Private, Corps of Invalids, 1780–3** *This unit was formed of men who had been too badly wounded to return to their regular units but were fit for light duties. There is a first-hand account of them wearing watch coats on duty, as shown here. They were armed as regular infantry and performed sterling service as garrison troops.*

SOLDIERS OF THE KING

With the defeat of France in North America, Europe, India in 1763, and wherever the writ of the British Empire ran, the prestige of the Royal Navy and the British Army reigned supreme. Their reputation was even greater, at least among their kinsmen in the North American colonies, than that of Frederick the Great's legendary Prussians. Twelve years later, however, those same colonists opened fire on the King's regiments, the now hated "lobster backs", who represented oppression not liberation. The British soldiers fought a gallant war in North America, and although they were defeated, they gave courageous and selfless service to their king and country.

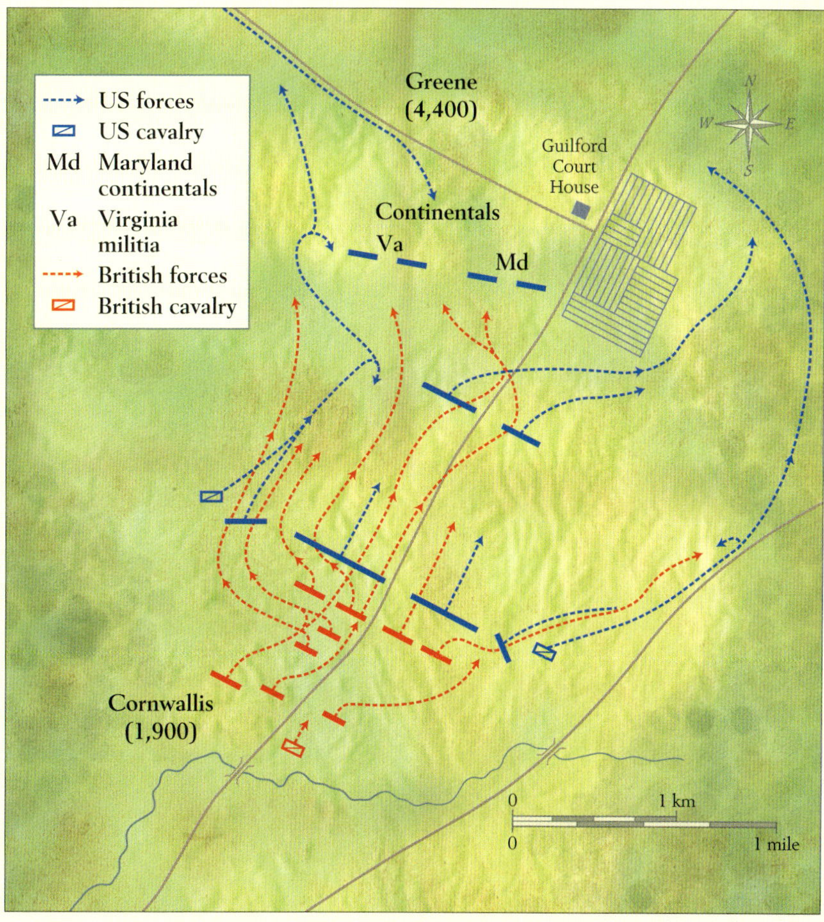

▲ *The battle of Guilford Courthouse was one of the hardest fights of the entire war; the British held the field, but some of their best units were severely mauled by the Continentals.*

◀ *This version of the third and final British assault on Breed's Hill shows the death of Joseph Warren. In reality Warren was shot in the final melée inside the redoubt.*

THE ARMY OF THE BRITISH EMPIRE

British soldiers had learned much during the bitter fighting of the French and Indian War but, inevitably, much of this wealth of experience had been forgotten by 1775. Even so, some important reforms had taken place, and this meant, for example, that each regiment was given a permanent light infantry company in the early 1770s.

In terms of acting as a cohesive body, armies in the field were a collection of regiments with no permanent higher units such as the brigade or division. The higher tactical units were formed on an ad hoc basis and commanded either by a brigadier general or the senior regimental commander. Still, as the French had discovered to their chagrin, it was a formidable force on the battlefield: well trained, generally competently led, and inured to hardship and campaigning. It was also to be supported by a large number of American Loyalists who, for one reason or another, remained loyal to the British Crown and hostile to those they termed rebels. The Loyalists formed a number of units, and some of these were extremely valuable to the British for their local knowledge and military competence. Other units were less capable, and their performance was, in contrast, lacklustre.

Organization

With the exception of the three regiments of Foot Guards, which were large regiments, a British regiment was organized with 10 companies (there were actually 12 companies in each regiment, but two of them were depot companies used for recruiting, one in England and one in Ireland). There were eight battalion companies and two elite companies (the grenadiers and light infantry). Grenadiers were picked for height, bravery and experience. Light infantrymen were picked for the ability to think independently and fight in open order. They were used for advance guard, flank guard and rearguard duties. The light infantry companies, which were found to be so useful in the French and Indian War, were abolished after the conflict, but were reinstated in 1771. It is for this reason that they are not mentioned in the 1768 Warrant.

The regiment had a staff of one colonel, one lieutenant colonel and one major as well as a chaplain, a surgeon, a surgeon's mate, an adjutant and a quartermaster. The last two functions were performed by junior

▼ *General James Wolfe dies on the Heights of Abraham, Quebec, 13 September 1759. His victory resulted in British control of Canada.*

British Regiments in America

Infantry:

1st Foot Guards
2nd Foot Guards (Coldstream)
3rd Foot Guards
3rd Foot (Buffs)
4th Foot (King's Own)
5th Foot
6th Foot
7th Foot (Royal Fusiliers)
8th Foot (King's)
9th Foot
10th Foot
14th Foot
15th Foot
16th Foot
17th Foot
18th Foot (Royal Irish)
19th Foot
20th Foot
21st Foot (Royal North British Fusiliers)
22nd Foot
23rd Foot (Royal Welch Fusiliers)
24th Foot
26th Foot
27th Foot (Enniskillen)
28th Foot
29th Foot
30th Foot
31st Foot
33rd Foot
34th Foot
35th Foot
37th Foot
38th Foot
40th Foot
42nd Foot (Royal Highland /Black Watch)
43rd Foot
44th Foot
45th Foot
46th Foot
47th Foot
49th Foot
52nd Foot
53rd Foot
54th Foot
55th Foot
57th Foot
59th Foot
60th Foot (Royal Americans)
62nd Foot
63rd Foot
64th Foot
65th Foot
69th Foot
70th Foot
71st Foot (Fraser's Highlanders)
74th Foot (Argyll Highlanders)
76th Foot
80th Foot
82nd Foot
84th Foot (Royal Highland Emigrants)
105th Foot (Volunteers of Ireland)

Cavalry:

16th Light Dragoons (Queen's)
17th Light Dragoons
Royal Artillery
Royal Irish Artillery
Royal Engineers

▲ *General Sir Thomas Gage, governor of Massachusetts and commander in chief of British forces in America at the outbreak of the war. His determined actions to stamp out patriotic American protests led to the clash at Concord on 19 April 1775 and the shot that was heard around the world.*

officers from the companies as an additional duty. The companies were more or less of the same authorized strength: three officers, six NCOs, two drummers and 56 privates. Three of the companies were Field Officer's Companies and only had a lieutenant and an ensign each. The two elite companies had two lieutenants rather than a lieutenant and an ensign. The grenadier company had two fifers.

Three of the authorized privates were known as "contingent men", who were fictitious but carried on the rolls anyway. Their pay was used as a regimental reserve fund to take care of widows and orphans.

The colonels commanding British regiments seldom took to the field as their post was largely ceremonial, somewhat like the Inhaber of a regiment in the German kingdoms and principalities. The lieutenant colonel was the de facto commander in the field, and it should also be noted that most British regiments consisted of a single battalion, and that the terms 'regiment' and 'battalion' in the British service were interchangeable. Few cavalry served in North America, as the cost of shipping horses was prohibitive and the war was such that mounted troops played a less significant role than they would have done in Europe.

British soldiers served honourably and effectively in North America during the Revolution, but were not recognized by their king and country during the period or after. High deeds were performed, and the efficiency, discipline, and effectiveness of the British soldier was proven time and again on the battlefield. Lessons learned in North America would be put to use in a later, larger conflict.

COMMANDERS AND STAFF

At the time of its entry into the war in North America, the upper hierarchy of the British Army was in a formative stage. Generals selected their staff from amongst relatives, friends or those they were keen to promote. Uniforms, too, could be influenced by personal taste.

Generals

British generals wore the ubiquitous red coat, although in their case it would be more bright scarlet than red. The facings would be dark blue, and there would be abundant gold lace on the lapels, buttonholes, pockets and cuffs. For wear in the field on campaign, a much simpler coat was worn, without most, if not all, of the gold lace. The general's rank would be indicated by the number of buttons, and by accompanying lace worn above the cuff. Gold epaulettes were worn on the shoulders.

White waistcoats and cravats were worn, as well as white breeches, stockings and buckled shoes. In the field, riding boots were worn, as the general officers were most often mounted. The cocked hat was bound with gold lace and had the British black cockade. A red sash completed the uniform, with the addition of an ornate officer's sword as a sidearm.

Some generals went into combat well dressed and in their best uniform. General William Howe was noted as wearing satin breeches at the Battle of Bunker Hill, which were splashed with the blood of his staff after the conclusion of the action. Indeed, all of his staff had become casualties by the time the battle ended. The general, who had been with them the entire time, was untouched.

A general officer's horse furniture would be the typical bridle of the period, along with the regulation British officer's saddle which would have two pistol holsters, probably fur covered, a popular affectation for most mounted troops and one that meant the holsters were also waterproof. The general officer's shabraque and saddle cloth were dark or royal blue, and trimmed in gold lace.

Staff Officers

Even though the British Army had campaigned in Europe and North America in the previous conflict, its staff organization at the time was still in the rudimentary stages of development. Generally speaking, a commanding general would be able to organize his staff to suit himself. His inner circle was not a planning staff in the modern sense, but a small organization dedicated to keeping the army supplied in the field and to carrying and supervising the general's orders in combat.

◄ **British General, 1772** *The lapels of the coat could be worn either turned back (as shown here) or buttoned closed in bad weather. The complicated rank system of chevrons and buttons on the forearms might confuse many; some troopers in certain cavalry regiments wore the same decorations. Note the crowned royal cipher GR (George Rex) in the rear corner of the shabraque.*

▲ **AIDE-DE-CAMP TO A GENERAL OFFICER, 1780** *Aides-de-camps (ADCs) were very often younger family members of the generals that they served; social status counted for more than skill in this position. Many regiments and corps of the British Army wore dark blue facings and golden buttons; this officer could easily have been mistaken as belonging to any number of them.*

Aides-de-camp were junior staff officers who took their commander's orders to the units concerned. They were usually detailed from regiments under the general's command and therefore wore their regimental uniforms. In 1767, regulations of a sort were issued for the uniforms of aides-de-camp. These officers were to wear red coats with blue facings and silver lace. By 1782, ADCs were to wear two gold epaulettes and gold lace.

Brigade majors, principal staff officers in the British Army at the time, were to wear the same red coat with blue facings, but with silver lace and epaulettes. All staff officers wore white small clothes and usually wore riding boots and spurs as they were frequently, if not exclusively, mounted when on duty in the field.

British Leadership

The English generalship during the war was adequate, many times competent, but seldom brilliant. The first commander in North America, Sir Thomas Gage, was relieved after Bunker Hill. His successor, Sir William Howe, had a string of battlefield successes to his credit, was respected by his men, but did not have the killer instinct of the true independent commander. Neither did his successor, Sir Henry Clinton, who commanded from 1778 to almost the end of the war, when he was replaced by Sir Guy Carleton, who had commanded in Canada since the beginning of the conflict.

Other senior British commanders were more effective. Artilleryman Sir William Phillips was an aggressive and imaginative officer. Sir Charles Cornwallis was probably the best of the lot: hard, unflappable, and a driving, aggressive commander who could have made the difference if he had been promoted to theatre command early in the war. Left with too few resources in the southern theatre, facing an equally talented commander in General Nathaniel Greene, he was fought to a strategic standstill and his army mauled at Guilford Courthouse. From there he withdrew to Yorktown in Virginia and final defeat and surrender.

The senior British commanders were not a band of brothers and sometimes failed to support each other when necessary. Howe failed Burgoyne in 1777, leading to Burgoyne's defeat and surrender at Saratoga. British armies in Virginia and the Carolinas did not co-operate after great initial successes that were later wasted when they could not be sustained. The British could have won early on, but after the French intervention they were on the strategic defensive.

▲ **STAFF OFFICER, ADJUTANT GENERAL, 1775** *Both the adjutant general and the quartermaster general wore silver lace and buttons on their tunics. If attached to cavalry formations, the single epaulette was worn on the left; if attached to infantry formations, it was worn on the right. This officer carries a cane and wears stockings and shoes, as if at a social occasion.*

INFANTRY

The Royal Clothing Warrant of 1768 formed the uniform regulations for the regular army of Great Britain. It governed all the uniforms and equipment issued to British soldiers in the field. In fact, the warrant went further as it covered what the soldiers were to wear and how they should wear their uniforms, and, in some aspects, how they were to be armed. As is true with all regulations, the warrant was to be more or less followed, but implementation suffered on active service. Regimental commanders still had a lot to say about what their regiment looked like, and on distant foreign service, especially, the uniform regulations could be ignored.

Officers' Uniforms

According to regulations, officers' uniforms were to be scarlet and faced in the regimental colour. Coats were to have round cuffs. Buttons were to have the regiment's number stamped on them. Embroidery or lace was not required. Waistcoats were to be plain. Grenadier officers wore an epaulette on each shoulder. Officers of battalion companies were to wear one epaulette on the right shoulder. The swords of each regiment were to be of the same pattern, and the hilts had to match the regiment's buttons, in gold or silver.

The tricorne hats were all to be of the same pattern and could be laced or bound in either gold or silver. Each officer was authorized a crimson silk sash, which was to be worn around the waist and knotted on the left hip. Gorgets matched the metal colour of the regiment (either silver or gold, sometimes referred to as "white metal" and "yellow metal", respectively). Gorgets were engraved with the king's arms and regiment number. Grenadier officers bore a fusil, a short musket, in addition to their swords. Battalion company officers bore spontoons.

NCOs and Privates

Sergeants were to have coats of the same design as the officers, although of a lesser material and probably more a shade of madder red than scarlet. Their sashes were to be of worsted cloth instead of silk, but of the same crimson colour. They also had a centre

◄ **NCO 29TH FOOT, 1770** *This figure wears typical garrison dress; at this date the hair was still powdered, curled and queued. The rectangular silver belt plate bore the lion within the crowned Garter and the motto:* Honi soit qui mal y pense *(Shamed be he who thinks evil of it).*

► **OFFICER, 29TH FOOT, 1770** *The old halberd was still carried as a badge of status by infantry NCOs. The 29th was involved in the so-called "Boston Massacre" of 5 March 1770, in which five patriots were killed. Henceforth, the regiment was known as the "Vein Openers".*

▲ PRIVATE, 29TH FOOT, 1770 *At the rear of his bearskin cap, this man wears a grenade with the number 29 on it. The star badge on the cartridge pouch represents the Order of the Garter. The buttons bore 29 within a ring.*

stripe of the regimental colour. Red-faced regiments had a white stripe on the sergeants' sashes. Grenadier sergeants were armed in the same manner as the officers. Sergeants of the battalion companies were issued with halberds and swords. Corporals had a silk epaulette on the right shoulder.

The grenadiers were to have coats with wings of red cloth on the shoulders and extra lace to denote their status. The men of the battalion companies had white lace on their buttonholes (the buttons were of white metal), and the regiments were distinguished by different coloured lines (straight or wavy, known as worms) and their arrangement on the white lace. Buttonhole lace was to be about half an inch wide.

All coats had round cuffs and lapels 3in (7.5cm) wide that were to reach the waist. Shoulderbelts were 2¾in (7cm) wide. Waistbelts were 2in (5cm) wide. The belt colour was usually determined by the waistcoat colour. Lace was white. Coloured stripes on the lace distinguished each regiment's buttonhole lace. Gaiters were of black linen with stiff tops, black buttons, black garters and black uniform buckles.

Musicians

The uniforms of the drummers and fifers of "royal" regiments, who all had blue facings as an indication of their royal titles, were to be red with blue facings and have royal lace. Musicians' small clothes and the lining of their coats were to be the same as for musicians in other ranks.

The drummers' and fifers' coats of regiments with red facings were to be white with red facings and lining. All of the other infantry regiments' drummers were to wear reversed colours, their coats being their facing colours and their facings being red. Small clothes of the regiments who had either white or buff coats were to have red waistcoats and breeches. All other regiments were to have them in the regiment's facing colour.

Distinctive Dress

Grenadiers, drummers and fifers wore black bearskin caps. There was a silver cap plate on the front of the bearskin with the king's crest. The bearskin cap was 12in (30cm) high and the regimental number, distinctions and badges were on the cap. Fusiliers also wore a bearskin, lower than that of the grenadiers. Battalion companies wore the tricorne. Sergeants' hats had silver lace. Corporals and other ranks had their hats bound in white tape. The lace was to be 2¼inches (6cm) wide, and all ranks had black cockades.

Sergeants and grenadier companies wore the sword. All ranks in the Royal Highlanders used a claymore, the traditional weapon of their clans. Drummers and fifers had short swords.

Pioneers carried an axe and a saw and wore a large leather apron, and a distinctive leather cap with a bearskin front carrying the king's crest.

▼ DRUMMER, 29TH FOOT, 1770 *The 29th regiment was one of the first to deploy African bandsmen, some ten slaves having been bought by the brother of the colonel in Guadaloupe and presented to him. Records indicate that in 1775 there were still four or five of these men serving. This tradition continued until Queen Victoria banned it in 1844.*

FOOT GUARDS

Britain's Guard units consisted of infantry and cavalry, and developed from units responsible for the personal safety of the monarch and protection of the royal residences.

Organization

The three Foot Guard regiments totalled seven battalions: the 1st Regiment having three, the 2nd and 3rd Foot Guards having two each. The 1st Foot Guards had four grenadier companies in its battalions, the 1st Battalion having two, and the other two battalions having one each. The rest of the regiment consisted of battalion companies, for a total of 28 infantry companies in the regiment.

The 2nd Foot Guards had a total of two grenadier companies and 16 battalion companies, which were sometimes referred to as "hat" companies, as all ranks wore the cocked hat and not the bearskin of the grenadier companies, for a total of 18 companies in the regiment.

The 3rd Foot Guards was organized like the 2nd Foot Guards: two grenadier companies, one per battalion, and 16 battalion companies. Officially, there were no light infantry companies in any of the Foot Guards.

The Household Troops in 1775*

Infantry
1st Foot Guards
2nd (Coldstream) Foot Guards
3rd Foot Guards

Cavalry
Horse Guards
Horse Grenadier Guards
Royal Regiment Horse Guards

*All of the Household regiments were stationed in England and were on the English Establishment.

▲ NCO, 2nd Foot Guards, Dress Uniform, 1775 *The seniority of this regiment was expressed by its members wearing their buttons in pairs. There are many depictions of officers and men of many armies of this period, which show the waistline "dropped" by about 4in (10cm); the resultant distortion places waistbelts in such pictures at hip level.*

◄ Officer, 1st Foot Guards, Dress Uniform, 1772 *The gold lace decoration on these uniforms was rapidly abandoned in field service, and the hats were cut down in size. As the 1st Foot Guards Regiment, they wore their buttons evenly spaced.*

Service in America

The Guards expertly prepared for field service in North America by adopting comfortable and practical dress before deployment, and by organizing light infantry for use in the North American terrain. Considered an elite unit and among the best in the army, their active service was honourable and the units did well. One of the battalions was mauled by Continentals at Guilford Courthouse in March 1781 and had to be extricated to avoid annihilation. However, they were tough, well-trained troops under competent commanders and did more than their assigned duty.

The Foot Guards' regimental full dress for the period is well known and detailed in contemporary records. This uniform was not, however, worn on active service in North America during the period; indeed, considerable thought and effort went into both organizing and modifying the Guards' uniforms resulting in an interesting and unusual uniform.

▼ **Officer, 3rd Foot Guards, field uniform, 1776** *The Scots Guards wore their buttons in threes. Officers' oval gilt belt plates bore the silver cross of the Order of the Thistle, with the golden motto* Nemo me impune lacessit *(No one attacks me with impunity) on a green collar. Their buttons bore "Gds" over "3".*

The Guards Detachment that was formed for American service was composed of 33 officers, 87 NCOs, 15 drummers, six fifers and 960 privates. The personnel were selected by a draft from the three Foot Guards regiments. The detachment's commander was to be Lieutenant Colonel Edward Mathew from the 2nd Foot Guards. Some 15 men were drafted from each of the 64 companies that made up the brigade. These troops were formed into a regiment of ten companies: one grenadier and, surprisingly, one light infantry company in addition to eight battalion companies. The grenadier company had a strength of 120 privates, the light infantry company had a strength of 96 privates and the battalion companies had 93 each.

The uniform selected for the detachment consisted of cut-down regimental coats with the lace removed from the lapels, making the red coats quite plain. Long trousers of drill or duck material with half gaiters over shoes were also provided. The grenadier and light infantry companies were issued "hat caps", which were essentially light infantry caps with a peak and plate in the front, a turban around the base of the cap and a feather on the left-hand side of the cap. The turban was tied into a bow in the rear. The battalion companies were issued with a type of roundhat with a feather on the left-hand side.

Arms and Special Equipment

The light infantry were also assigned special equipment such as ball bags, powder horns and "light infantry accoutrements". They also received a pair of bugle horns. Their musket was to be the Short Land Pattern Firelock (the "Brown Bess"), while the rest of the detachment carried the Long Land Pattern. Hatchets and bill hooks were also issued and were worn alongside the bayonets on a combination frog. The one crossbelt and waistbelt combination soon turned into two crossbelts to carry the cartridge box and bayonet for all of the companies. Finally, each man was issued a haversack as well as a pack, and it was ordered that 60 rounds of ammunition be issued to each man before landing in North America.

▼ **Private, 1st Foot Guards, Field Uniform, 1776** *The brass oval belt plate bore the crowned Garter badge. All white tape was removed from the facings, and the coat tails were shortened. The white edging was cut from around the hat, making it smaller.*

ROYAL REGIMENTS

The designation "Royal" on its own did not attach any elite status to the regiments concerned, but Royal regiments in the British service may have had more prestige than other line regiments. The designation was usually awarded as a battle honour or for long and distinguished service, but line regiments who were not faced in the "Royal blue" were just as proud of the facing colour that had become part of their particular regiment's service, traditions, and history.

As in other armies at other times, regimental commanders took liberties with the uniform regulations, especially as they applied (or not) to the flank companies (grenadiers and light infantry) and to the "heads of column" (drum major, drummers and fifers, pioneers, and the band if the regiment had one). Regimental commanders could spend lavishly to spruce up their regiments in order either to look more impressive on parade or to outdo a rival or neighbouring regiment. The exigencies of active service, especially in North America, took a toll on uniforms, and they seldom would last one campaigning season; a handsome regiment, for example, in March or April might be in rags by September/October. If the regimental staff did their job competently and efficiently, the unit might always be suitably clothed and uniformed. If not, then the troops might be at the mercy of the elements.

◀ **Grenadier Sergeant, 18th Foot, Royal Irish Regiment, 1776** *This figure is in full parade dress, complete with bearskin cap. His rank is shown by his crimson waist sash, which had a central stripe in the facing colour. The obsolete brass match case on his bandolier was a reminder of the days when grenadiers used to actually throw hand grenades in battle.*

▶ **Officer, 4th Foot, 1779** *The ancient regimental badge was the lion of England. As with many of the older regiments in the army, their facings were dark blue. Officers' oval belt plates bore a crown over a lion with "King's" above them and "own" below. Buttons bore "4" within a raised rim. The 4th Foot's nickname was "Barrell's Blues", taken from the name of their commander from 1734 to 1749.*

Royal Facings

There was no functional difference between such units and the rest of the British infantry, but there were some differences in costume.

The main Royal regimental distinctions were dark blue facings and a dark blue regimental colour. Not all the Royal regiments that served in America are listed here, as some of them come under different distinctions such as either fusiliers or Highlanders.

▲ PIONEER CORPORAL, 60TH FOOT, 1776 *The Royal American Regiment was raised in December 1755 as the 62nd and renumbered in 1757. The silver oval belt plate of the centre companies bore "60" within the crowned Garter. The buttons bore "60" within a rope rim. Facings were dark blue and the officers wore silver lace. The white shoulder knot was the corporal's badge of rank. Pioneers wore the special red cap plates.*

Royal Regiments

Reg't	Facings	Officers' Hat Lace	Lapel Lace*	Small Clothes
4	blue	silver	1 blue	white
8	blue	gold	1 blue, 1 yellow	white
60	blue	silver	2 blue	white

*All lace was white. What is listed in this column is coloured stripes on the lace which made each regiment's buttonhole lace distinctive.

All of the British infantry regiments serving in North America, with the exception of the Guards Detachment, were generally uniformed in the same manner. The differences between regiments were shown by facing colours and by different distinctions in the caps for the regimental light infantry companies.

Musicians

All musicians were combat soldiers and went into battle with their regiments. They were uniformed differently in order to stand out. Generally speaking, they wore uniforms with "reversed colours", the coat of the regimental facing colour and their facings red.

The uniforms of the drummers and fifers of "Royal" regiments, who all had blue facings as an indication of their royal titles, were to be red with blue facings and with royal lace. Small clothes and coat linings were the same as for other ranks. They wore the bearskin as did the grenadier companies and the fusilier regiments.

Campaign Variations

The 4th, 8th and 60th Royal Foot were all uniformed according to the 1768 clothing warrant when the war in North America began. Only later, when campaigning became long and a lot rougher in the varied and wild terrain, did uniform dress become much less formal, and regiments began to introduce variations and adaptations not only from the pertinent regulations, but from other similar units as well. For example, British infantry would adopt locally made cloth as trousers and coats wore out. In the south brown trousers often replaced regulation white. Sometimes with more subtle differences in tones and colours, these clothes rapidly departed from the uniform appearance that the authors of the 1768 warrant had envisaged.

▼ DRUMMER, 4TH FOOT, 1777 *The 4th was raised in 1680 and became The King's Own Regiment of Foot in 1715. In 1774 the men's oval brass belt plates bore the same badge as the officers, but their buttons bore the numeral IV within a ring of leaves around the edge. The regimental lace was white, with a black stripe on the inside. Drummers were often the sons of soldiers of the regiment.*

FUSILIERS

Fusiliers were originally raised to escort and guard the artillery train, and from there they developed into yet another form of infantry, though they were organized and trained in the same manner as other line units. They were armed with a shorter pattern musket, the fusil, from which their title was derived. To enhance their status, there were few fusilier regiments in the British Army, and they developed their own traditions, badges, and distinctions.

Fusilier Regiments Serving in North America

Reg't	Facings	Reg't Distinctions	Officers' Hat Lace	Lapel Lace*	Small Clothes
5th	green	Goslin green	silver	2 red	white
7th	blue		gold	1 blue	white
21st	blue		gold	1 blue	white
23rd	blue		gold	1 each blue, red, yellow	white

*All lace was white. What is listed in this column is coloured stripes on the lace which made each regiment's buttonhole lace distinctive.

Fusiliers were considered to be elite troops and were all issued bearskins, except for the light companies. They were also considered light troops, and their loss in combat or on campaign could be a body blow to the army. Cornwallis suffered the loss of the greater portion of his light troops at two battles in the Carolinas before Guilford was fought. His Loyalist troops were killed or taken at the Battle of King's Mountain, and most of the remainder were lost at the Cowpens debacle. One fusilier regiment was lost, as was the light infantry of the British Legion.

◀ **Officer, 23rd Foot, 1774** *The Royal Welch Fusiliers was raised in 1689 and converted to "Fuzileers" in 1702. Their badge was the Prince of Wales' crest of the three feathers within a coronet, with the motto ICH DIEN (I serve). Officers' oval gilt belt plates bore the three plumes, coronet and scroll with ICH DIEN over 23 in silver. Their buttons bore the same device within a peripheral ring of leaves. Their nickname is "The Royal Goats", due to their mascot, which comes from a royal herd. The 23rd advanced against French cavalry at the battle of Minden in 1759, for which they wear a red rose in their caps on 1 August.*

▶ **Drummer, 7th Foot, 1774** *We do not see here the usual reversed colours on the tunic, but, as a Royal regiment, those of the 7th wore red coats faced dark blue. Grenadier drummers wore a small brass drum on the back of their bearskin bonnets. They also had special black and silver plates to the fronts of these bonnets. The drums bore GR, the rose within the crowned Garter and the regimental number, which was also embroidered on the red backing of the fur cap.*

These losses were keenly felt during Cornwallis' pursuit of Greene in the Race to the Dan and are considered one of the reasons that Cornwallis failed to catch Greene and his army.

The term 'fusilier' (originally fuzilier) came from the long arm they carried, which was not as long or heavy as the normal musket issued to regular infantry regiments. When that role was no longer required, the term stuck and began to be considered an elite designation, hence the wearing of the bearskin, which was only slightly shorter than that of the grenadiers.

▼ **Sergeant, 7th Foot, 1772** *The 7th was raised in 1685 as the Ordnance Regiment to escort the artillery train. Officers' gilt belt plates were rectangular, with bevelled corners, bearing an eight-pointed star, having a rose within the crowned Garter. The buttons bore "7" within a double ring, enclosing tiny leaves. Black gaiters were often worn during the winter.*

Uniform Distinctions

The fusilier's hair was worn in a braided queue which was kept off the back of the jacket by black ribbons attached to the collar. The queue was later abolished – in 1808 – although the 23rd kept the black ribbons as a traditional distinction.

Fusilier regiments also contained light infantry and grenadiers. Light infantry wore a helmet, bearing the regimental badge, and this had a black "roach". On campaign this was frequently replaced by black felt round- or slouch hats. These were sometimes turned up at one side, in imitation of many German light infantrymen.

As with other regiments fighting in North America, when uniform clothes wore out they were replaced with local items. Brown trousers seem to have been worn by members of the 23rd Foot operating in the South.

Both the 7th and 23rd regiments were also Royal regiments, and were both highly regarded as infantry units, having a rich history to their credit. Their uniforms were generally identical. The 23rd Regiment was called Welch (sometimes spelled "Welsh"), and was referred to as the Royal Welch Fusiliers.

Both of these excellent regiments served in the South during the most crucial and decisive campaigns of the war, and both met defeat at the hands of the Continental Army. The 7th Regiment was caught up in the defeat at the Battle of Cowpens in January 1781, and their attack was broken up and the unit routed by a combined Continental regiment composed of veterans of the Maryland Line and the Delaware Regiment, who wanted revenge for being decimated at the Battle of Camden the previous August. Gallantly led into the attack by Lieutenant Colonel John Eager Howard of Maryland, the Continentals not only routed the 7th Foot, but also captured their colours. The Welch fought through the Southern campaigns only to be caught with Cornwallis at Yorktown in October 1781.

▼ **Private, 23nd Foot, 1777** *A light company figure, wearing the generally prescribed leather cap; there were several unofficial designs worn as well. The buttons bore "23" under the Prince of Wales' plumes. Grenadiers and the Light Company wings at the shoulder were edged and trimmed with the regimental lace; white with red, dark blue and yellow stripes. It is likely that the flank companies wore grenades or bugle horns on their belt plates.*

HIGHLAND REGIMENTS

Highland regiments contained tough fighting men, and their uniforms added colour and dash to any British army to which the Scots were attached.

Highland Regiment Distinctions

Reg't No.	Facings	Officers' Lace	Hat Lace*	Lapel	Small Clothes
42nd	blue	gold	1 red		white (kilt)
71st	white		1 red		white (kilt)
74th	yellow		1 red		white (kilt)
84th	blue		2 red, 1 blue		white (kilt)

*All lace was white. What is listed in this column is coloured stripes on the lace, which made each regiment's buttonhole lace distinctive.

Highlanders in America

England's rocky relationship with Scotland was finally brought under control after the Jacobite Rebellion of 1745, when the young Stuart Pretender, Bonny Prince Charlie, was defeated and went into permanent exile. The first Highland regiment in the British Army, the 42nd Foot (initially the 43rd Foot, but their number was later changed), was raised to police the highlands of Scotland and grew from an original four companies to a full regiment. Noted for exceptional service in North America during the French and Indian War and Pontiac's Rebellion, it had become a Royal regiment by the time of the Revolution.

Highland Dress

The regiment was initially uniformed in full Highland dress at the beginning of hostilities. Officers wore a kilt of belted plaid together with a sporran, and a Scottish bonnet. As the war went on, however, the dress became much simpler, and kilts were discarded. It is not certain exactly why the kilt was not worn later in the war, but it was for one of two reasons: either it was too

◀ PRIVATE, 42ND FOOT, FIELD UNIFORM, 1774 *Full Highland dress, complete with the claymore, a heavy, straight-bladed weapon. The bastion-ended white regimental lace had a red stripe near the outer edge; the pewter buttons bore "42" under a crown and within two sprigs each of a rose and a thistle.*

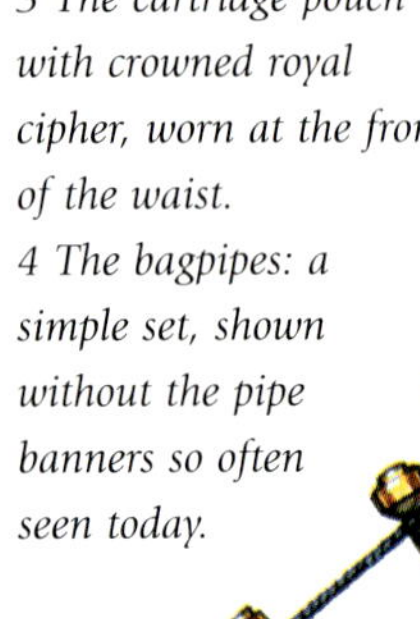

1

2

3

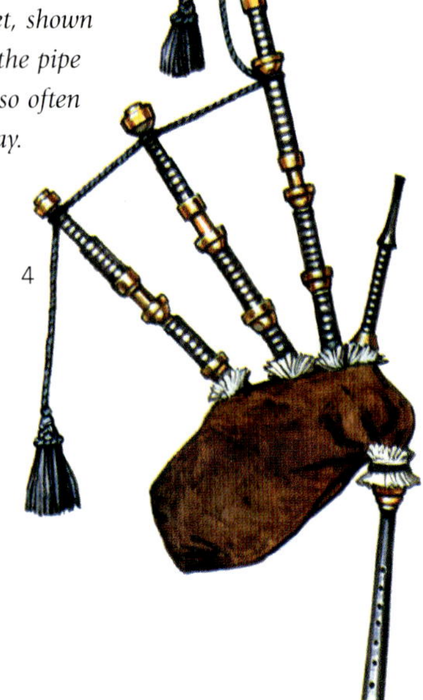

4

▼ 42ND FOOT, KIT, 1774 *1 The claymore, with steel basket hilt, lined in red. 2 The bastion-ended regimental lace and the button. 3 The cartridge pouch with crowned royal cipher, worn at the front of the waist. 4 The bagpipes: a simple set, shown without the pipe banners so often seen today.*

coats were retained, as was the custom of officers wearing a sash across the body instead of around the waist. The cartridge box remained the belly box until almost the end of the war, when it was replaced by a crossbelt.

There is no evidence that pipers were on the regimental lists. However, they were definitely present, undoubtedly at the express desire of the regimental commander and probably at his own expense.

The 71st Foot also dressed for active service in the full-belted plaid, and then in field dress of trousers and half gaiters. This was the case when they served in the Southern campaigns. These campaigns were unfortunate. One battalion was captured at Cowpens, the other at Yorktown.

▼ **Officer, 71st Foot, Field Uniform, 1775** *This regiment (Fraser's Highlanders) was raised in Scotland in October 1775 for service in America; it was disbanded there in 1786. Officers' oblong silver belt plates bore the crowned "71"; their buttons – and those of the men – bore "71", within a wavy ring. It seems likely that they wore the same tartan as the 42nd Highlanders.*

▼ **Officer, 42nd Foot, 1780** *The Government set tartan was prescribed for the regiment, when it was raised in 1725 at four companies to police the Highlands. The kilt and plaid were soon withdrawn from use in North America, and breeches were worn instead. Each Highland regiment had its own distinctive sporran, with varying numbers and tassels. Officers wore a sash over the left shoulder.*

▲ **42nd Foot, Piper, Field Uniform, 1782** *The bags of pipes were often covered in the regimental tartan, or the Royal or Stuart tartan, and it became customary for the drones to be decorated with pipe banners, usually in the facing colour and bearing the regimental badge. Descriptions of pipers from this period are rare and open to conjecture.*

difficult to resupply kilts for the regiment, or the rigours of campaigning demanded a more practical uniform of white trousers and half gaiters. The only reminder of traditional Highland dress was now the ubiquitous Scottish bonnet. Regulation

IRISH REGIMENTS

The war in North America was not popular back in England, either with Parliament or with the general public, and there was no patriotic zeal to join up and fight for king and country. Without the Irish, and not just specifically in the Irish regiments, the British Army would have run out of both recruits and replacements. In ethnic makeup, many of the "English" regiments were Irish in character if not in name, just as in the French and Indian War the British regiments in North America recruited heavily among the population of the colonies, and many regiments of British regulars were almost half filled with Americans.

The British Army was also made up of "Establishments". Some regiments were assigned to the Irish Establishment and stationed in Ireland. Others were on the English Establishment and stationed "at home". These rotated on foreign service, and undoubtedly, those regiments stationed in Ireland would have recruited heavily among the native population.

A number of British units recruited heavily in Ireland before and during

Regiments stationed in Ireland on the Irish Establishment at the Beginning of the War

1st Foot**	40th Foot*
2nd Foot	42nd Foot*
6th Foot*	44th Foot*
15th Foot*	45th Foot*
17th Foot*	46th Foot*
20th Foot*	49th Foot*
22nd Foot*	53rd Foot*
24th Foot*	54th Foot*
27th Foot*	55th Foot*
28th Foot*	57th Foot*
33rd Foot*	61st Foot
34th Foot*	62nd Foot*
35th Foot*	63rd Foot*
37th Foot*	68th Foot

*Served in North America 1775–1783

**This regiment had two battalions, one stationed in each "establishment". The 1st Battalion was on the Irish Establishment, and the 2nd Battalion was on the English Establishment.

◄ Sergeant, 27th Foot, 1777 *Raised in Ireland in 1689, this regiment was placed on the English military establishment within months and in 1751 became the 27th (Inniskilling) Regiment of Foot. Officers' oval gilt belt plates bore "27" over a scroll with "Inniskilling" under the castle of Enniskillen. The buttons bore the badge and regimental number.*

► Officer, 18th Foot, The Royal Irish Regiment, 1775 *This is an officer of the centre companies in parade dress, with a spontoon. This regiment was raised in 1684 in Ireland and received Royal designation in 1695. The matt oval gilt belt plate had a beaded edge and bore the gilt harp on a blue ground, within a crowned belt inscribed* Virtutis namurcensis praemium *(A reward for valour at Namur). Soldiers' buttons bore "RI" over "18", within a rope ring.*

the war in North America. Although such units took on something of an Irish character, their dress and equipment followed the pattern of the other British infantry regiments.

Regulation Dress

Although the 18th Foot was a Royal regiment, it has been listed here under the Irish regiments as there were technically only two Irish units serving in North America during the period. The uniforms of both the 18th and 27th Foot conformed to the 1768 Clothing Warrant. The 27th Foot was also known as the Inniskilling Regiment (or just as commonly the "Enniskillen"), and the service of only two Irish regiments is interesting in illustrating the recruitment for the British Army of the period.

Recruitment

Recruiting for the army was exceptionally difficult for the British during this unpopular war. There was much support for the Americans before and during the war, not only in Parliament, but among the British as a whole, for Americans, at least before 1776, and in many cases thereafter, thought themselves to be Englishmen. The British Army was forced to recruit among the lowest classes in Britain and among convicts in prison, who could have their sentences shortened or commuted if they volunteered to serve in the army.

The saviour for the British Army of the period was the large recruitment of Irishmen. So not only were the designated Irish regiments, such as the 18th and 27th Foot, Irish in fact and character, but many "English" regiments were also largely made up of Irish privates. There was a steady flow of Irish recruits into the Army during the period, and the same can be said for recruiting from Scotland, the second greatest source of recruits for the war in America.

▲ **Grenadier Private, 18th Foot, 1776** *This was a Royal regiment, therefore the facings were dark blue. As with most other infantry regiments, the 18th abandoned the long gaiters for the short spatterdashes, often black. This figure is in marching order and has an animal skin pack instead of the canvas item painted in the facing colour. The coat-tails have been shortened into a jacket.*

▼ **Drummer, 27th Foot, 1775** *Drummers were often the sons of soldiers of the regiment, serving from as young as 14 if strong enough. They shared all the perils of their fellows and often continued to serve as adults. Drummers' bearskin cap plates had a special design including two drums. Note the harp and crown as well as the cipher "GR" and the regimental number "XVIII" on the drum. The regimental nickname is "The Lumps".*

Irish Regiments Serving in North America

Reg't	Facings	Officers' Hat Lace	Lapel Lace*	Small Clothes
18th	blue	gold	1 blue	white
27th	buff	gold	1 blue 1 red	buff

*All lace was white. What is listed in this column is coloured stripes on the lace, which made each regiment's buttonhole lace distinctive.

ENGLISH REGIMENTS

The units serving in North America tended to comply with the 1768 uniform regulations, subject to local campaign variations. The selection of light infantry caps is an interesting feature in itself. Many regiments had a different style of cap, although there are many features in common. Three of the caps have turbans (5th, 36th, and 71st Foot), and most of the caps were modelled on light cavalry helmets with a peak, brim, or turned up front plate with a regimental badge, crest, or number (5th, 6th, 7th, 11th, 23rd, 62nd, 68th, 69th, and 71st). Two had "combs" with a horsehair falling plume (62nd and 71st), and one even had a rear flap (69th). There were still further variations. That of the 7th looked rather like the headgear of the Queen's Rangers. The 36th Foot has a cap very much like the light cavalry Tarleton helmet. The 13th Foot had the most unique headgear of all, looking quite unlike any of the others.

▼ **Officer, 3rd Foot, 1775** *The title of "The Buffs" was awarded in 1747 and reflects their facing colour. The green dragon was the ancient badge of the regiment, and is possibly of Saxon origin. The regiment's buttons bore a "3", within a series of three concentric rings.*

▲ **Private, 64th Foot, 1776** *The 64th regiment, later known as the 2nd Staffordshire Regiment, had black facings; their lace had a black line to the outside and a red central line. The pewter buttons bore "64" in a wreath. The same design, under a crown, was worn on the belt plates.*

▲ **Drummer, 25th Foot, 1775** *This regiment, raised in Scotland in 1689, was known as the Edinburgh Regiment in 1777; this later became The King's Own Scottish Borderers. It seems that officers' oval gilt belt plates bore the number under a crown; the same device was borne by the men.*

One of the first items of kit to wear out, then as now, was an infantryman's footwear. Regulations stipulated that infantrymen were to have gaiters made of black linen with stiff tops, black buttons, black garters and their uniform buckles in black. Gaiters were designed to prevent gravel and stones getting into the shoe, and kept mud and dust off the bottom of the white small clothes. The gaiter's stiff tops were obtained from cowhide or from painting the cloth black, the latter giving an element of waterproofing.

▼ PRIVATE, 28TH FOOT, 1777 *Raised in 1702, the regiment received the number 28 in 1751. Officers' buttons bore "28" under a crown and lion, within a ring of laurel leaves. The men's buttons just bore "28". The regiment earned the nickname "The Slashers" for their battlefield conduct.*

English Regiments Serving in North America

Reg't	Facings	Reg't Distinctions	Officers' Hat Lace	Lapel Lace*	SmallClothes
3rd	buff		silver	1 each black, yellow & red	buff
6th	yellow	deep yellow	silver	yellow, red	white
9th	yellow		silver	2 black	white
10th	yellow	bright yellow	silver	1 blue	white
14th	buff		silver		buff
15th	yellow		silver	1 red, yellow & black worm	white
16th	yellow		silver	1 crimson	white
17th	white	greyish white	silver	2 blue, 1 yellow	light grey
19th	green	deep green	gold	1 red, 1 green	white
20th	yellow	pale yellow	silver	1 red, 1 black	white
22nd	buff	pale buff	gold	1 blue, 1 red	buff
24th	green	willow green	silver	1 red, 1 green	white
26th	yellow	pale yellow	silver	1 blue, 2 yellow	white
28th	yellow	bright yellow	silver	1 yellow, 2 black	white
29th	yellow		silver	2 blue, 1 yellow	white
30th	yellow	pale yellow	silver	1 sky blue	white
31st	buff		silver	1 red, blue & yellow worm	buff
33rd	red		silver	1 red	white
34th	yellow	bright yellow	silver	1 red, blue and yellow worm	white
35th	orange		silver	1 yellow	white
36th	green		gold	1 red, 1 green	white
37th	yellow		silver	1 red, 1 yellow	white
38th	yellow		silver	2 red, 1 yellow	white
40th	buff		gold	1 red, 1 black	buff
43rd	white		gold	1 red, 1 black	white
44th	yellow		silver	1 each blue, yellow & black	white
45th	green	deep green	silver	red, purple worm	white
46th	yellow		silver	red & purple worm	white
47th	white		silver	1 red, 2 black	white
49th	green	full green	gold	2 red, 1 green	white
50th	black		silver	1 red	white
52nd	buff		gold	1 orange, red worm	buff
53rd	red		gold	1 red	white
54th	green	popinjay green	silver	1 green	white
55th	green	dark green	gold	2 green	white
57th	yellow		gold	1 black	white
59th	red	purple	silver	1 red, 1 yellow	white
60th	blue		silver	2 blue	white
62nd	buff	yellowish buff	silver	1 blue	buff
63rd	green	very deep green	silver	1 green	white
64th	black		gold	1 red, 1 black	white
65th	white		silver	1 black, red & black worm	white
70th	black		gold	black worm	white
76th	green			1 black	white
80th	yellow			1 red, 2 black	white
82nd	black			1 black	white

*Lace was white; listed in this column are coloured stripes on the lace.

COLOURS AND STANDARDS

Every British regiment had two colours. The 1768 Clothing Warrant specified colours of the Royal regiments and the senior infantry regiments, which were known as the "Six Old Corps". For each colour, the regimental crest was to be in the centre of the flag. Each regiment's drums would also carry the regiment's crest ("device" or "cipher") on the front of the drums, along with the regiment's number positioned underneath the crest. The Royal regiments were all to have the king's cipher on their colours, the other regiments having their own regimental badges, which were of ancient lineage.

The first colour of a regiment, the king's colour, is the Union flag. This had the regiment's badge in the centre. The second colour is the regimental colour, which was of a set design according to the facing colour of the regiment.

For Royal regiments this colour was dark blue. The Union was in the upper left hand corner, or canton, of the flag except for regiments whose facings were red or white. In that case, the flag had a white field with a red cross of St George with the Union as before. Those regiments with black facings were as for the red- and white-faced regiments, except that the upper left-hand canton had the Union, and the other three cantons formed by the cross were black.

Each colour had the regiment's number, badge or royal emblem. Those regiments that had only numbers (which were to be in Roman characters) had these surrounded by a wreath of thistles and roses. These emblems and devices could be either embroidered or painted on the flags. Finally, there were cords and tassels of mixed gold and crimson.

Each infantry regiment had to ensure its two colours were 6ft (1.8m) on the pike (wide) and 6ft 6in (2m) on the fly (long). The pike itself was 9ft 10in (3m), which included both the spear and spearhead (called a ferril or finial). Some key regimental distinctions were as follows:

1ST REGIMENT OF FOOT. The king's cipher inside the circle of St Andrew and a crown above it. In the three corners of the regimental colour, the thistle and crown. The distinction of the colours of the second battalion was a flaming ray of gold descending from the upper corner of each colour towards the centre.

2ND REGIMENT OF FOOT. The queen's

▶ **ENSIGN, 27TH FOOT, HOLDING THE REGIMENTAL COLOUR, 1774** *The regimental colour of the 27th bore the castle of Enniskillen in the centre, but no corner badges. The scroll bore the motto* Nec aspera terrent *(Nor hardships deter us). The honour of carrying the colours went to the two most junior officers in the regiment, a common practice in European armies.*

▼ *Regimental colour, 23rd Foot.*

▼ *King's colour, 1st Foot Guards.*

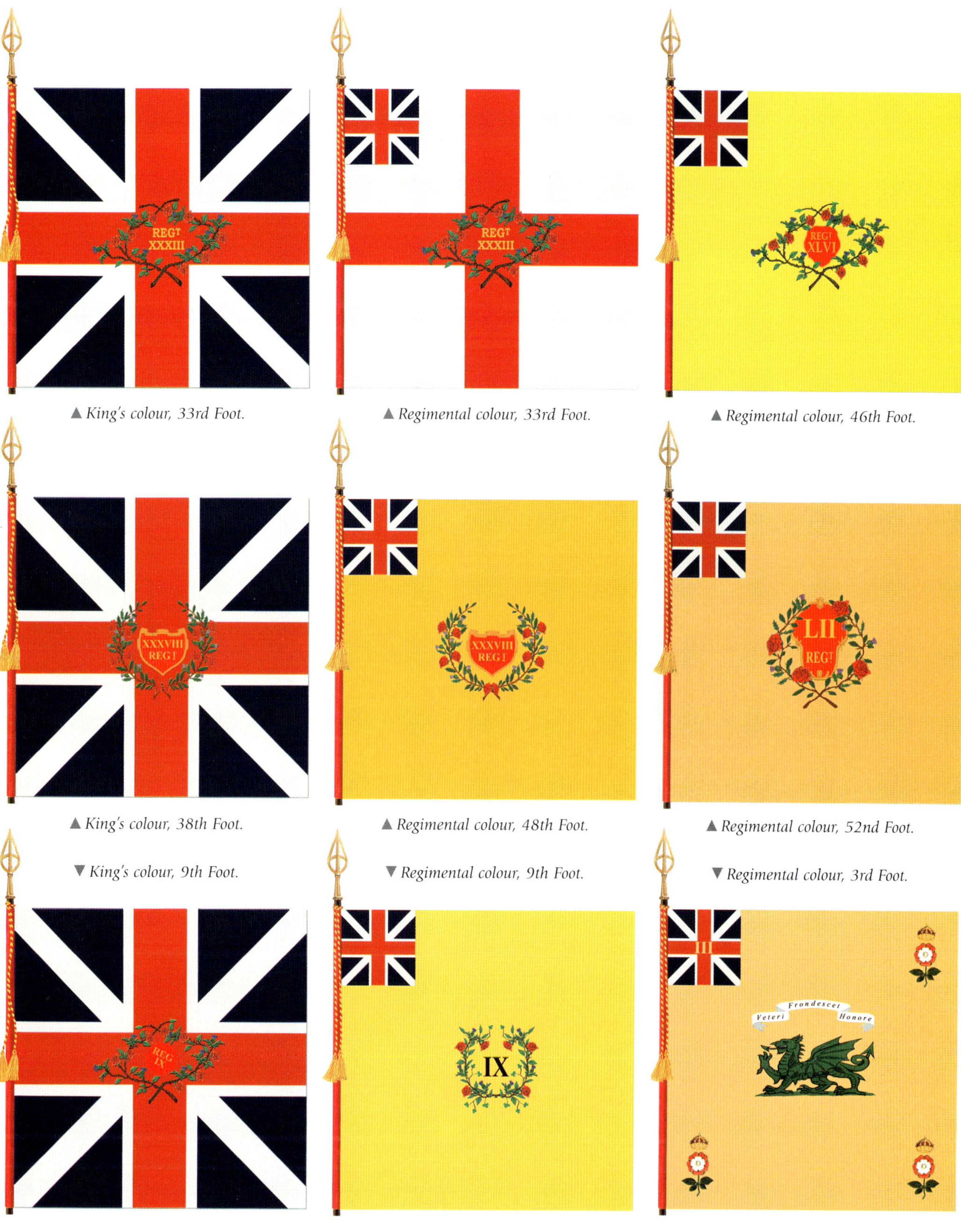

▲ *King's colour, 33rd Foot.*

▲ *Regimental colour, 33rd Foot.*

▲ *Regimental colour, 46th Foot.*

▲ *King's colour, 38th Foot.*

▲ *Regimental colour, 48th Foot.*

▲ *Regimental colour, 52nd Foot.*

▼ *King's colour, 9th Foot.*

▼ *Regimental colour, 9th Foot.*

▼ *Regimental colour, 3rd Foot.*

cipher on a red ground with garter and crown. The regimental colour has the lamb and badge in the three corners.
3RD REGIMENT OF FOOT. The dragon is the regimental badge with the rose and crown in the three corners of the regimental colour.
4TH REGIMENT OF FOOT. The king's cipher on a red ground with the garter and crown. The regimental colour has the English lion in the three corners.
5TH REGIMENT OF FOOT. St George (the patron saint of England) killing the dragon with the rose and crown in the three corners of the regimental colour.
6TH REGIMENT OF FOOT. An antelope is on the king's colour, and the regimental colour has the rose and

▲ *King's colour, 64th Foot*

▲ *Regimental colour, 64th Foot.*

▲ *King's colour, 55th Foot.*

▲ *Regimental colour, 55th Foot.*

▼ *King's colour, 4th Foot.*

▼ *Regimental colour, 4th Foot.*

crown in the three corners.

7TH REGIMENT OF FOOT. The regimental device was a rose, garter and crown. The white horse of Hanover is in the three corners of the regimental colour.

8TH REGIMENT OF FOOT. A white horse on a red ground within the garter, with a crown above it. The king's cipher and crown would be in the three corners of the regimental colour.

18TH REGIMENT OF FOOT. A harp in a blue field, with a crown above it. The regimental colours had William III's lion of Nassau in the three corners.

21ST REGIMENT OF FOOT. The colour bears a thistle within the circle of St Andrew with a crown above it. In the three corners of the regimental colours would be the king's cipher and crown. St Andrew is the patron saint of Scotland and the 21st was a Scottish lowland regiment.

23RD REGIMENT OF FOOT. This colour bears the Prince of Wales' crest of three feathers above the prince's coronet, with the badges of Edward the Black Prince in the three corners of the regimental colour. The three badges consist of a rising sun, a red dragon and the three feathers above a coronet. The regimental motto also appeared on the colour, *Ich dien* (German for "I serve").

27TH REGIMENT OF FOOT. The regimental device was a castle with three turrets. In addition it had St George's colour flying in a blue field with the title "Inniskillin" above it.

42ND REGIMENT OF FOOT. The king's cipher within the garter with a crown over it. St Andrew also appeared on the colour with the regimental device along with the motto, *Nemo me impune lacessit* (Nobody provokes me with impunity). The king's cipher and crown was in the three corners of the regimental colour.

51ST REGIMENT OF FOOT. This colour had a red background, with the rose and thistle device along with the garter and crown. The king's cipher and crown were in the three corners of the regimental colour.

60TH REGIMENT OF FOOT. This colour consisted of the king's cipher with garter and crown. The regimental colour had the king's cipher in three corners topped by a crown. The Second Battalion's colours were distinguished by a flaming golden ray descending from the upper corner towards the centre of the colour.

There were also small regimental flags, called camp colours, in the regiment's facing colour. These marked the area when in camp. They were 18in (45cm) square, with poles either 7ft (2.1m) or 9ft (2.7m) high.

GRENADIERS

The grenadier evolved from the men who were armed with a rudimentary form of hand grenade. They were adapted into a company of hand-picked experienced veterans for every battalion in an army. These elite troops were given the honour of forming for battle on the right of the line. Grenadiers were chosen from the largest and strongest men in a regiment, and their uniform was based on the original necessity of having to wear a hat that would not impede the arm when throwing a hand grenade.

The first cap that is recorded in use by the grenadiers of the British Army was the cloth mitre cap, embroidered with regimental badges. All British regiments had grenadier companies, as did the British marines, and all of the men wore the bearskin.

▼ GRENADIER PRIVATE, 42ND FOOT, 1782 *The officers' oval belt plate bore "42" within a ring, surmounted by St Andrew and his cross; above the saint the motto:* Nemo me impune lacessit *(Nobody provokes me with impunity); below the regimental number was a spray of roses and thistles.*

▼ GRENADIER OFFICER, 38TH FOOT, 1779 *The yellow facings and silver lace marked out this regiment. The officers' silver, oblong belt plate bore the crowned royal cipher between "XXXVIII" and the regiment number. Buttons bore either "38", or a crowned "38", within a wreath of peripheral laurel leaves.*

▼ GRENADIER PRIVATE, 3RD FOOT, 1774 *The men's brass belt plates of this regiment seem to have been oblong, with rounded corners, bearing a winged dragon. Those of the officers were silver, with a similar design.*

LIGHT INFANTRY

British light troops proved themselves essential in the fighting in America. They were elite troops, and their uniforms were adapted from regulation dress to meet local conditions.

Along with the grenadiers, the light infantry might be massed from the available regiments and formed into "Sunday punch" battalions either for specific missions that required a high degree of experience and skill or for an entire campaign. Sir William Howe, who was a light infantry officer in the French and Indian War, did exactly this for the Bunker Hill mission in June 1775. The light infantry regiments of Howe's force were formed into a special striking force that was ordered to flank the American position on Breed's Hill and get into their rear. They assaulted an American position astride the Mystic River beach, and were slaughtered by John Stark's thoroughly prepared men, who hammered out three volleys on to the assaulting British companies. Howe's light infantry was decimated, and the grenadiers lost heavily in the frontal attack against the main American position. This tactic was nearly universal, and its advantages were also a liability in that it took away from the commanders their most experienced, and often their toughest troops.

◀ **Private, Light Company, 16th Foot, 1777** *The unusual yellow facings mark out this regiment. Amazingly enough, most regiments retained the antiquated, unhygienic powdered hairstyle throughout the war. The oval belt plates seem to have borne "16"; the grenadiers' were surmounted with a grenade, while those of the light company had a stringed bugle. Buttons bore the regimental number within a rope rim. The regimental lace was white with a red stripe near the outer edge. The regimental nickname was "The Old Bucks".*

▶ **Officer, Light Infantry at Germantown, 1777** *This figure is based on contemporary paintings and the uniform reflects the simplified "battledress" that was adopted by many officers for their daily patrols, involving scrambling through woods and thickets. The coat has been cut down, the lace has been removed and it is now single-breasted. Pointed cuffs were popular, although completely against regulations. The rakish hat and feather added further panache to the character. The regiment is not specifically identified, but the green facings narrow the possibilities.*

Light Infantry Companies

After the war, the British light infantry were abolished. In 1771 the light infantry arm was resurrected, and each infantry regiment was authorized a light infantry company. Again, all British infantry regiments, this time with the exception of the three Foot Guards regiments, were entitled to a light infantry company. British light infantry

▲ **Cavalry and Light Infantry Caps**
In 1768 the light dragoon regiments of the British Army adopted the dashing, crested helmet shown in figures 1 and 4. The skirmishing in rough woodland that formed a major part of the warfare in America gave the light infantry companies the perfect excuse to plead that their tricornes were too bulky for field service and they were allowed to leap on to the bandwagon of fashion. All regiments were keen to have their identities clearly shown, and figures 2 and 3 show the cap style originally approved, with three rings of white metal chain around the crown and a metal tip. Variations then appeared, some of which are shown here. 1 17th Light Dragoons. 2 6th Foot. 3 10th Foot. 4 16th Light Dragoons. 5 71st Foot. 6 11th Foot. 7 23rd Foot. 8 5th Foot. 9 69th Foot. 10 62nd Foot.

distinguished itself for dash and gallantry on every field of the war. It was British light infantry that made the deadly assault on General Anthony Wayne's encampment at Paoli outside Philadelphia, during the 1777 campaign. Hitting Wayne's camp at night, with only the bayonet and unloaded muskets, the British silenced the American sentries and overran the camp, catching the Americans asleep and inflicting heavy losses.

Uniform Conformity

As with other regiments, uniforms were changed or modified to fit the North American theatre of war, and many articles of Indian clothing, such as Indian leggings, were used by British light troops. These innovations meant they did not always appear as regular troops, and they were certainly not the best at conforming to regulation uniform. The different types of light infantry caps have already been detailed, and it should also be noted that the 4th Foot's light infantry company retained the cocked hat.

Practical Uniforms

The light infantry companies started the war in regulation dress. By 1777 light infantry dress had evolved into a uniform that was both practical and elegant. White overalls were worn with a red short coat or sleeved waistcoat, and the leather equipment was blackened. Instead of drummers, the light infantry used cornets for signalling, and the instrument was usually in the shape of a large hunting horn. This became the light infantryman's symbol, as the grenade was for the grenadier.

The officers and men alike carried long arms, and the headgear worn was a roundhat with a feather on the right or left side, depending on personal taste. This uniform was also adopted by the battalion companies of many regiments, the difference being that the "hat men" kept the white leather equipment along with white breeches, stockings and half gaiters in place of the overalls.

CAVALRY

Cavalry was expensive to raise, maintain, and train. Deployment and tactics had to be practised continuously, and the horses had to be scrupulously cared for or they would be unfit for service. The British had poor to average reputations as horse masters, and – especially in the Southern theatre – were mounted on inferior animals to the Continental cavalry units under Henry Lee and William Washington. This showed up clearly on campaign, especially on the Race to the Dan in early 1781. The American cavalry were always one jump ahead of Tarleton's troopers, and they continuously kept them away, not only from the infantry of Otho Williams' light corps, but also from Greene's main body. Tarleton was unable to break through to give Cornwallis definite information on where Greene's main body was located.

The commander of the 16th Light Dragoons, William Harcourt, formed a dismounted detachment of his regiment, which operated as light infantry. It gave the regiment the form and substance of a legion, a combination of horse and foot, and made it a more flexible organization suited for campaigning in North

Cavalry of the English Establishment

1st Dragoon Guards	3rd Dragoons
2nd Dragoon Guards	4th Dragoons
3rd Dragoon Guards	6th Dragoons
1st Dragoons	7th Dragoons
2nd Dragoons	10th Dragoons
	11th Dragoons
	15th Dragoons
	16th Dragoons*

*Served in North America during the period 1775–83.

◀ **Officer, 16th Light Dragoons, 1776**
The horse was not native to America, and only two regiments of British Light Dragoons took part in the war; this was definitely an infantryman's struggle. The queen's cipher (C) was worn within the crowned garter and the motto: Aut cursu aut cominus armis *(Either in the charge, or hand to hand). The buttons bore "Q" over "LD" all over "16", within a ring of leaves.*

▶ **Trooper, 17th Light Dragoons, Attached to the British Legion, 1776**
Together, these two units made up an effective force in the guerrilla war of the vast American forests. Instead of the regimental red turbans, these detached men wore white sheepskin around their helmets. Being dragoons, they carried the straight-bladed sword instead of the lighter hussar sabres that were soon to become so popular. The badge on the holsters was "XVII" over "LD". Members of the regiment seem to have adopted Indian leather buckskin trousers and hunting shirts for the field.

Cavalry of the Irish Establishment

1st Horse	9th Dragoons
2nd Horse	12th Dragoons
3rd Horse	13th Dragoons
4th Horse	14th Dragoons
5th Dragoons	17th Dragoons*
8th Dragoons	18th Dragoons

*Served in North America from 1775 to 1783

America. When the regiment was sent home after the Battle of Monmouth, only the officers and NCOs left, the remaining enlisted men and horses were given to the 17th Light Dragoons.

By all accounts, the 17th was an outstanding unit. A detachment was sent to serve with and alongside Tarleton's British Legion in the South, but bluntly refused to give up their regimental dress in exchange for the green uniforms of the Legion. They retained their own uniforms, undoubtedly patched and repatched when necessary.

Uniform Distinctions

Both the 16th and 17th Light Dragoons were dressed in red with light cavalry helmets. Privates wore cloth epaulettes in the regimental colour. Buttons for both units were of white metal, and the small clothes were white.

16TH LIGHT DRAGOONS. The 16th had dark blue facings. The 16th had a small dismounted troop which wore the regimental coat, overalls, and a Tarleton-style helmet, and was equipped and trained as light infantry. The regimental trumpeters were uniformed in red faced dark blue with yellow lace.

17TH LIGHT DRAGOONS. Men of the 17th wore white facings. The regiment was known as the "Death or Glory Boys" and bore this motto beneath a white skull and crossbones on their helmet and shabraque. The 17th's trumpeters were stunningly uniformed in white with cocked hats instead of helmets.

When part of the 17th Light Dragoons was detached to serve with Tarleton's British Legion in the Southern theatre, they retained their own uniform. They would also wear a light, white "overcoat", which helped with the Southern heat and humidity. Their turbans were replaced with sheepskin, as they were away from any regimental resupply.

Horse furniture was standard issue, and each regiment had the regimental badge on the shabraque (the queen's cipher: a "C" for Queen Charlotte for the 16th and the skull and crossbones for the 17th). Dark horses were preferred while trumpeters were supposed to ride greys.

▶ **TRUMPETER, 17TH LIGHT DRAGOONS, 1778** *In later years this regiment was amalgamated with the 21st Lancers in 1922, to become the famous "Death or Glory Boys". The hogged manes and the docked tails were characteristic of British cavalry. The death's head badge is reputed to have been adopted at the death of General Wolfe at Quebec; originally it seems that the crossed bones were above the skull. The buttons bore "17" over "LD" in a ring in an eight-pointed star.*

ARTILLERY

The Royal Artillery was not part of the administration of the British Army during this period. It belonged to the Master General of the Ordnance, which gave it the advantage that promotions were within the artillery and were based on experience and merit, not on the ubiquitous purchase system that the Army employed.

Service in America

The Royal Artillery has always had a reputation for skill and competence, and its service during this war was exemplary. One of the best general officers in the service, William Phillips, was an artilleryman and is famous for his artillery successes on the European continent during the Seven Years' War, especially at the Battle of Minden in 1759, at which point Phillips was only a captain. He is famous for a comment to John Burgoyne during the investment of Fort Ticonderoga on Lake Champlain in 1777. Phillips wanted to emplace a battery of artillery on Mount Defiance, which overlooked Ticonderoga, in order to fire into the fort without receiving counter-battery fire from the American garrison. Burgoyne told Phillips that it was impossible as the mountain was too steep. Phillips replied, "Where a goat can go a man can go; where a man can go he can drag a gun." Needless to say, a battery was emplaced, and the Americans hastily abandoned the fortress.

The standard field piece of the period was the British light 6-pounder, used by both sides. It was an excellent weapon with a sturdy and effective carriage. It was pulled by horses in tandem harnessed to a limber that moved the gun effectively. The horses and drivers were hired civilians, which could pose a problem, as they usually didn't like getting shot at and might take "French leave" and abandon the gun and its crew when they were needed most. This unsatisfactory situation was not remedied until 1794, when the artillery train was militarized. Crew drill was performed like a military ballet. A well-drilled crew

► **Officer, Royal Artillery, 1774** *The dark blue uniform, red facings and yellow buttons emphasized the fact that the artillery was governed by the Board of Ordnance and not by the Horse Guards, who controlled the line infantry and cavalry. The household troops were managed by the sovereign himself. The saddlery used was of the heavy cavalry style.*

could deliver two aimed rounds a minute, and more per minute for short periods of time, such as in an emergency. Artillerymen were usually big men picked for intelligence as well as strength, and they were considered elite troops.

British Artillery Companies Serving in North America

	1775	1776	1777	1778	1779	1780	1781	1782	1783
Canada	1	4	2	1	3	3	3	4	8
Boston	5	7							
Florida	1	1	1	1	1	1	1		
Caribbean				3	2	2	2	2	12
Elsewhere			10		10	12	12	12	9

Personnel

The Royal Artillery was organized into four battalions of ten companies each until mid-1779, when an invalid regiment of ten companies was formed. Two of its companies came from the numbered battalions, and two were newly formed. Companies from the 3rd and 4th battalions were deployed to America, while the companies stationed on Gibraltar came from the 2nd Battalion. In 1783 these were replaced with companies from the 1st Battalion and rotated home. Most of the 1st Battalion companies and half of the 2nd were stationed in Great Britain, mostly at Woolwich, the artillery's home, although some of the 1st Battalion's companies did go to the West Indies.

Practical Uniforms

The Royal Artillery and its sister arm, the Royal Irish Artillery, were uniformed identically in dark blue faced red. The Royal Artillery wore the cocked hat, and the Royal Irish artillery, when in the field with Burgoyne's expedition in 1777, wore a light infantry-style cap. The Royal Irish Artillery was formed in 1755 and disbanded in 1801.

► **Gunner, Royal Irish Artillery, 1772** *Although a separate military establishment from the Royal Artillery, there were few visible differences in dress between these two corps. The Irish corps was founded in Dublin in 1755 and absorbed into the Royal Artillery in 1801. The uniform differences from the Royal Artillery were that the Irish wore their brass buttons in pairs and had four buttons on each sleeve, with the red cuffs cut out in a slight "V" at the top. The gunner holds a ramrod, used for ramming home charges and ball with the solid end and for mopping out any burning residue with the wet mop after every firing.*

◄ **Gunner, Royal Artillery, 1772** *The artillery could be recognized by their powder horns or flasks, long picker needles (for clearing the touch holes of debris and piercing the cases of gunpowder charges) and the smouldering matchstick, or portfire, which would be planted in the ground beside the gun when in action. This figure is in normal drill order.*

SPECIALIST TROOPS

An 18th-century army relied on a number of specialists to enable it to undertake operations in the field and, more particularly, any kind of attack on or defence of a fortified position. British engineer officers served capably and well during the war, and conducted sieges and the defence of fortified places throughout North America. The lines of defence at Yorktown were expertly laid out and constructed (and can still be seen today, as they are largely preserved), and the defence of Savannah in 1779 was accomplished with energy and skill, holding the city against all the odds.

Royal Engineers

The Royal Engineers were like the Royal Artillery, a specialist formation that did not come under the cognizance of the army, but under the Board of Ordnance. It was an organization made up completely of officers, and these men were educated, well trained and efficient. Promotion was by seniority and merit, and there was no purchase system for either commissions or promotion as there was in the infantry and cavalry.

▶ **Officer, Royal Engineers, 1782** *This mounted officer of the Royal Engineers wears the new, dark blue coat with black facings, which replaced the red coat faced black (some sources say dark blue) that was previously worn. The facings were of velvet, possibly a reference to the Hanoverian and Prussian engineers, who also wore black velvet facings. The royal engineer's waistcoat and breeches were originally buff, later becoming white. Riding boots and the tricorne were worn.*

The engineer uniform was of red faced black, and the buttons were silver. Small clothes were buff originally but were white during this period. Mounted officers always wore riding boots and spurs, and the cocked hat was bound in gold lace.

As the British engineer arm had no privates, drafts from the local infantry units were used when siege or fortification work was needed. When erecting the defensive works at Yorktown, the British employed black slaves from the area, who were promised their freedom if they worked for the British. That promise, and the hopes of those who worked for their freedom, came to nothing when the British surrendered.

Regimental Pioneers

The regimental pioneers were another type of elite soldier in the regiment. The nearest equivalent to them today would be a combat engineer. The pioneer was usually a picked NCO who carried out minor engineering duties such as clearing roadways and obstacles, and they were employed in attacks on fortifications to clear the way through any obstacles. Many pioneers wore a small version of the grenadier bearskin cap. The badges of their office and rank were the pioneer's apron and the axe. Other items might be carried, such as saws, bills and other handy tools. While the number of pioneers was not usually fixed by battalion, five to eight per unit would not be unrealistic. High gaiters with stiff tops for the protection of knees were usually worn.

Seconded Officers

The British are never given enough credit for the work and excellent relations they maintained with the Iroquois during the period. British officers lived and worked with the tribes; some men such as Lieutenant John Caldwell of the 8th Foot, stationed in Quebec, were assigned as liaison officers with Indian warriors. Many wore full Indian regalia.

▼ **Regimental Pioneer, 59th Foot, 1775** *Pioneers sported a full set of whiskers, which arose from the fact that they were often way ahead of their battalion, in the rough of the forests, unable to spend much time shaving and cleaning kit. It is still the custom in the British Army today that the sergeant of pioneers wears a beard and moustache.*

▼ **Regimental Pioneer Kit** *1 Picker and chain. 2 Artilleryman's pouch. 3 The wooden interior of the infantryman's cartridge box, with the holes drilled to hold the cartridges. 4 Bottom tray of the pouch with clearing tool, flints, muzzle plug. 5 Axe. 6 & 7 Saw and its case.*

▼ **Officer, 8th Foot, in Indian dress, 1780** *This is based on a portrait of Lieutenant John Caldwell, of the 8th Foot. In the last year of this war, he was mainly employed in treating with the Indians to gain their support for the British against "the rebels".*

AMERICAN LOYALIST INFANTRY

Loyalists, or Tories as they were also called, formed a considerable proportion of the American population, and it was inevitable that a number of Loyalist units were raised for service alongside the British. These varied in quality and commitment.

Authorized Units

There were approximately 100 Loyalist units listed as being authorized or raised during the war. Most of these never reached active service and were only paper units. However, two of the infantry regiments, the Volunteers of Ireland and the Royal Highland Emigrants, became regular British Regiments during the conflict, the former winning a distinguished reputation. Others, such as the Queen's Rangers, Butler's Rangers and Tarleton's British Legion also became famous for their exploits in the field of battle.

Loyalist units initially wore green with varied coloured facings, but later in the war they changed to red. Exceptions to that rule were Tarleton's British Legion and the Queen's Rangers who retained their green uniforms.

Recruitment Problems

Loyalist units had one major recruiting problem throughout the war. While it was relatively easy to procure officers for the numerous Loyalist units, the recruiting of privates to fill the ranks was more difficult. Consequently, many of the Loyalist units in existence were not at full, or authorized, strength, and if they suffered losses on campaign or in combat, they often found it difficult to replace them.

KING'S AMERICAN REGIMENT. This regiment was raised and initially commanded by Edward Fanning. Fanning was a lawyer, practising in North Carolina, and was a considerable adventurer who offered his services to the British. Fanning was granted

◄ **DRUMMER, KING'S AMERICAN REGIMENT, 1776** *Like their British brothers-in-arms, Loyalist drummers wore reversed colours, the coat the colour of the regiment's facings and facings in red or scarlet. This drummer wears the traditional bearskin cap. Drummers were considered to be combat soldiers, and while some were young, they took their chances on the battlefield with their armed comrades.*

▲ **OFFICER, KING'S AMERICAN REGIMENT, 1776** *This unit's full title was the King's Regiment of Foot (4th American Regiment). The men were initially probably clothed in whatever could be procured locally and at short notice. Eventually they wore a simple green uniform with crossbelts that were probably in black leather. The officer pictured here is dressed in what became the final evolution of the regiment's uniform.*

Effective Loyalist Units and Dates of Service

Infantry

The King's American Regiment (4th American Regiment) 1776–82
The Newfoundland Regiment 1776–82
Royal Highland Emigrants 1775–84
Volunteers of Ireland (2nd American Regiment) 1776–87
Delancey's Brigade 1776–83
King's Royal Regiment of New York
Loyal American Regiment 1776–81

Cavalry

Queen's Rangers (1st American Regiment) 1776–83
The British Legion (5th American Regiment) 1778–82
Tarleton's Dragoons 1776–83
King's American Dragoons 1780–3

Rangers

Butler's Rangers 1777–84
Queen's Rangers 1777–84

authorization to raise this two-battalion regiment in December 1776. The regiment was stationed in New York and Rhode Island until 1780, when it was sent to Virginia with the British expedition that was raiding that state. The regiment remained in the south of America, and attrition reduced the unit to 271 in all ranks. Throughout all this campaigning, Fanning remained in New York, the regiment being commanded in the field by Lieutenant Colonel George Campbell. In 1783 the unit became the 4th American Regiment, and was disbanded the next year. The uniform worn in the South was red faced green with white small clothes or gaiter trousers. Coats were lined in white, and the cocked hat was worn, bound in white lace for the privates and in gold for the officers.

NEWFOUNDLAND REGIMENT. This unit was raised for service in Canada, but throughout the war it saw no action. Its uniform was dark blue faced red and lined with white. Arms and equipment were like those of a regular British unit.

◀ **PRIVATE, THE NEWFOUNDLAND REGIMENT, 1780–3** *This uniform is a "possible", there is no complete description of the Legion's infantry uniform, one of the reasons being that they were either killed or taken at the Battle of Cowpens. The only description found is of a dark green coat with a black collar and cuffs. This figure has been depicted to comply with the Legions' overall uniform and shows how the Legion was sometimes mistaken for Lee's Legion in the Continental Army.*

▶ **INFANTRYMAN, THE BRITISH LEGION, 1780–1** *The full title of this regiment was His Majesty's Newfoundland Regiment of Foot (Pringle's). It was organized in late 1780 to garrison Newfoundland in Canada against any attack from the French, but was never in combat. Instead of the usual red, it wore dark blue with the traditional bearskins.*

▲ **Officer, Royal Highland Emigrants, 1775** *This regiment's official name was the 84th (Royal Highland Emigrants) Regiment of Foot. They were formed in 1775 and were uniformed in complete Highland dress. The pattern of tartan used for the kilt was the Government Tartan, which was also worn by the 42nd Foot, the famous Black Watch. Officers carried the Highland broadsword, the claymore, as well as the ubiquitous Scottish dirk. The full, belted plaid, a traditional cloak that doubled as bedding for the Highland warriors for many years, was worn.*

Drummers wore reversed colours and the cocked hats of the privates were bound in white tape, those of the officers in silver lace. Buttons were of white metal.

Royal Highland Emigrants. This regiment was later entered into the British line as the 84th Foot for good and faithful service. It wore full Highland dress on active service, and with minor changes in uniform items it appeared in a uniform almost identical to that worn by the Black Watch when they had come to North America and before changing to campaign dress. The full belted plaid and Highland bonnets were worn, as were sporrans, the dirk and claymore. As a Royal regiment, the unit had dark blue facings.

Volunteers of Ireland. The Volunteers of Ireland was formed as a Loyalist unit in Philadelphia, Pennsylvania, in 1777. Most of its active service was spent in the Southern theatre, where it gained a reputation as a tough, hard-fighting unit. It was granted regular status as the 105th Regiment of Foot in the British line. Its members distinguished themselves at the Battle of Camden in August 1780 and at Hobkirk's Hill in April the same year, remaining in the Carolinas for the remainder of the war, thereby missing the debacle at Yorktown in October 1781. They embarked for England at the end of hostilities in 1783 and were disbanded the next year. The regiment was uniformed in a red coat and white lace in place of lapels. Small clothes were white, and brown long gaiters were worn over shoes. Standard infantry equipment was used, and the regiment probably wore a light infantry cap with the regimental badge of the Irish harp on the front, with a short red plume on the left side. Cuffs were green.

Delancey's Brigade. This unit was a three-battalion regiment, hence the term "brigade" in its title. It was uniformed as a Royal regiment in red faced blue, with coats lined in white. They were equipped as regular infantry and wore white small clothes with half gaiters. For foreign service in hot and humid climates they might wear a white roundhat with a feather on the left side.

► **Private, Volunteers of Ireland, 1780** *This volunteer unit served with great distinction throughout the Southern campaigns of the war, and was a regular regiment. Their full title was the Volunteers of Ireland (2nd American Regiment), and they were later honoured with the number "105" in the British Army list. They were disbanded in early 1784.*

▲ **PRIVATE, DELANCEY'S BRIGADE, 1778** *While termed a brigade, this unit was actually a three-battalion regiment. The men received their red uniforms around 1778, along with most of the rest of the Loyalist line, and were also awarded the dark blue facings of a Royal regiment. The unit wore coveralls of red, blue, or brown wool in the winter, along with woollen caps. The white roundhat shown here was worn during the summer months and was quite distinctive.*

▲ **OFFICER, REGIMENT OF PENNSYLVANIA LOYALISTS, 1779–81** *This regiment, along with the Regiment of Maryland Loyalists, was part of the British garrison of Pensacola from 1779 to 81 and took part in the defence of Pensacola against the Spanish. By this time in the war, Loyalist units served with their British counterparts in different theatres of war and served well and capably. Some of the best British units, such as the Queen's Rangers, were Loyalist units.*

▲ **PRIVATE, KING'S ROYAL REGIMENT OF NEW YORK, 1776** *This was one of the best and most effective of the Loyalist units fighting for the British, and they served at times with Butler's Rangers on the northern frontier. They were originally uniformed in green with facings of various available colours, but were re-uniformed in red coats with dark blue facings, as they designated a Royal regiment, after 1778. The regiment was disbanded in 1784 after the war.*

KING'S ROYAL REGIMENT OF NEW YORK. This unit frequently operated with Butler's Rangers in upper New York state. Initially uniformed in green with white facings and small clothes, the unit was re-uniformed in red in 1778. The gaiters shown with the green uniform came to the knee, and the headgear was a roundhat bound in white tape, which was similar to the original uniform of the King's American Regiment.

LOYALIST CAVALRY

In addition to the Loyalist infantry units, a small number of local Loyalist mounted units were raised to support the British effort in North America. The cost, in effort and money, of raising and maintaining the horses for these and other mounted troops was high, but they were assisted by the issue of distinctive British uniforms and special equipment.

Mounted Rangers

The rangers were first organized by Robert Rogers of French and Indian War fame. For many reasons he proved unsuitable in this capacity and was replaced by Major Christopher French after the rangers were surprised by the Americans in October 1776 at Mamaroneck and lost heavily. French reorganized the unit, replacing many unsuitable personnel, and was followed in May 1777 by Major James Wemyss. He was efficient, and the rangers were enlarged and under Wemyss' command became an excellent unit. Wounded at the Battle of Germantown, Wemyss was replaced by Major John Graves Simcoe in October 1777, the unit's last and best commander. It was Simcoe who organized the cavalry arm of the rangers, and under his command it became a crack unit that served throughout the war until it surrendered at Yorktown in October 1781. At the peak of its efficiency as a combat unit, the rangers was

◀ **Dragoon, Queen's Rangers, 1778** *The other cavalry component of the rangers was a unit of dragoons. Originally made up of mounted infantrymen who fought on foot, and rode inferior horses, the regular dragoons that served in North America were actually light cavalry and were usually termed light dragoons in both the British and American armies.*

▼ **Hussar Officer, Queen's Rangers (1st American Regiment), 1778** *The all-green uniform was retained after most of the Loyalist units converted to the more traditional scarlet or red. The hussars wore this very simple uniform topped off by an impressive busby that marked them as hussars – descended from the Hungarian light horsemen, who inspired most if not all European armies in the 18th century.*

a vest-pocket task force that included infantry, cavalry, and artillery. It retained its original green uniforms when most Loyalist units were re-uniformed in red/scarlet.

British Legion

This was another green-uniformed Loyalist unit that spurned changing to red/scarlet and they were at their best when operating in the South, usually in an anti-partisan role. Skilled in raiding and ambushes, the legion was responsible for annihilating Abraham Buford's command at the Waxhaws, reputedly refusing them quarter.

Tarleton and his legion had a very bad day at Cowpens in January 1781 when they were destroyed by Daniel Morgan and his picked force. The legion infantry ceased to exist after that action, and the legion cavalry fled the field, with Tarleton just missing getting killed or captured by William Washington.

Mounted Tories

QUEEN'S RANGERS. The Queen's Rangers included both hussars and dragoons. All were uniformed in green, the hussars wearing a tall black busby with a green bag on the left side and a crescent crest on the front. The light dragoons wore the Tarleton helmet. Officers and men generally wore the same uniform. The round coatee was green, with a green collar, facings, lining and green breeches. The coatee was double-breasted. Equipment was of black or brown leather, and black leather boots were worn. The saddle and accoutrements were of the usual British issue, and the pistol holsters were covered in black bearskin.

BRITISH LEGION. Banastre Tarleton, the commander of the feared British Legion in the Southern theatre, developed, wore, and equipped his troopers with a cavalry helmet with a comb or crest along its centre line which retains his name to this day. The Tarleton helmet continued to be worn by British light dragoons until 1810 and by the British horse artillery until after the Napoleonic Wars.

KING'S AMERICAN DRAGOONS. These troops wore a uniform which was a little more official in character. They had red coats with blue facings, yellow lace and yellow buttons, and wore light dragoon caps. The unit was commanded by Benjamin Thompson and was disbanded in Canada in 1783. Trumpeters in this unit were black.

◀ **OFFICER, BRITISH LEGION, 1780** *This elegantly uniformed officer is taken from a portrait of the commander of the legion, Banastre Tarleton. The distinctive cap was allegedly designed by Tarleton and was widely copied during the period and after.*

▶ **TROOPER, 17TH LIGHT DRAGOONS, 1780–1** *A 50-man detachment of this regiment served in the south with Banastre Tarleton's British Legion. The weather in the South being unbearably humid, the troopers donned a white smock either in lieu of their regulation tunic or over it. They adamantly refused to wear the legion's green uniform and preferred to keep their own unit identity. This was a crack unit with a proud history, and after service in the Napoleonic Wars it was converted to a lancer regiment. In the Crimea in 1854, they were part of the Light Brigade, who charged at Balaclava.*

RANGERS

The Loyalist rangers fighting in North America had a well-deserved reputation as highly effective light infantrymen, who became adept at raids and skirmishing.

The infantry of the Queen's Rangers consisted of eleven companies made up of light infantry, riflemen and grenadiers. They were uniformed in green, and they had a small detachment of light artillery attached to the rangers. There was also a Highland company, which also wore green uniform coats, with a blue Highland bonnet with a black plume. The kilt was the McNab tartan.

Stealth and Camouflage

The unit was capable of fighting in line of battle or in partisan or irregular warfare. Their last commander, John Graves Simcoe, who had already seen service in North America in New York, Brandywine and Philadelphia with the 40th Foot Regiment, insisted on realistic training based on experience of fighting in North American terrain. The unit was expert in raids, ambushes, and the use of the bayonet, and individual marksmanship was stressed. Simcoe also insisted upon physical endurance, constant activity, and handpicked officers, together with a healthy diet and personal cleanliness.

Butler's Rangers were originally a ranger company of General Sir John Johnson's King's Royal Regiment of New York under the command of Major John Butler. They were later reorganized and expanded to regimental size on the orders of Sir Guy Carleton to serve with and lead the Iroquois forces of Joseph Brant against the Patriots, and they served on the northern frontier. Buter's Rangers were expert in irregular warfare and took part in

◀ **Rifleman, Queen's Rangers, 1778** *The rifleman shown here undoubtedly used the short German Jäger rifle instead of the American long rifle, and he is wearing a light and short-sleeved waistcoat instead of a regulation coat. Long coveralls were probably worn by many in the rangers, and it appears they were "regulation" for the riflemen. His tall hat was the same as was worn by the light infantry arm of the rangers.*

▶ **Officer, Light Infantry, The Queen's Rangers, 1778** *This light infantryman wears a regulation coat in green and is equipped as a British light infantry officer would be. Noteworthy are the black leather equipment that was common among light troops, and the stockings and half gaiters he wears instead of breeches. He could also have been equipped with gaiter trousers, as the rifleman.*

several "massacres" supporting the Indian contingents. They ranged as far as Detroit and Kentucky in the west. In their operations, they were not above settling old scores with former neighbours and were reluctant to grant quarter in combat. They expected none in return.

Uniform Distinctions

BUTLER'S RANGERS. Primarily raised for employment in raids and for working with the Indians, the unit's experience in the war meant that they quickly became an efficient and well-commanded and disciplined force, feared by its opponents and respected for its combat power and efficiency. The unit was in battalion strength and had six companies in 1778.

The uniform was green, either with a coat of regulation cut, in which case it was faced and lined with red, or a hunting shirt. The men wore a simple light infantry cap with a brass badge on the front flap. Leather equipment was buff, brown or black, and the men were equipped with muskets and bayonets, as were the officers. Scalping knives and hatchets were common equipment in the battalion. The battalion was raised to eight companies in 1781 and was disbanded in June 1784.

QUEEN'S RANGERS. The Queen's Rangers saw extensive action during the Philadelphia campaign, including a successful surprise attack (planned and executed by Simcoe) at the Battle of Crooked Billet. In 1779, Simcoe was captured by the Americans, but was released in 1781, just in time to see action at the Siege of Yorktown. The unit was uniformed in green throughout its service life, the usual type of dress being a green round coat with green facings. White overalls were generally worn by all ranks, although officers might have had a regulation cut coat, faced and lined in white, and with white lapels. White small clothes would be worn with shoes and half gaiters, along with the usual officers' crimson sash.

▲ **OFFICER, BUTLER'S RANGERS, REGIMENTAL DRESS, 1778** *Ranger officers could have been dressed like their men, especially in the field, or they may have been dressed in the regulation uniform coat that is pictured here. Officers carried long arms as the men did; these should have been rifles, but that was not universal throughout the unit, as muskets were also carried. Various additional pieces of American Indian equipment, weapons or dress, such as the beaded shoulder sash worn by the officer pictured here, were often adopted by the rangers.*

◄ **PRIVATE, BUTLER'S RANGERS, IN HUNTING SHIRT, 1778** *Most, if not all, of the ranger enlisted men were dressed like this figure from Butler's Rangers. They were required to clothe, arm, and equip themselves, so the dress and equipment could be different from company to company, and quite possibly from man to man. The distinctive light infantry-type cap seems to have been universal throughout the unit, but that probably also varied according to what was actually available.*

LOYALIST MILITIA

The British had a number of Canadian militias to hand. The Quebec militia had fought hard against the American invaders under Montgomery and Arnold in 1775–6 and were instrumental in their defeat. In addition, in the early years of the war, a small number of American units remained loyal, mostly at the instigation of commanding officers.

Loyalist militia units were formed for such duties as coast-watching and coastal defence, as well as defending their home villages and towns. They also performed garrison duty in outlying towns and districts, freeing regular troops to be assigned to the army on campaign. Some units, such as the Quebecois, were uniformed very well, and some were not, with only the officers and NCOs having anything approaching a uniform, and the enlisted men resembling their rebel cousins in their civilian dress and armed as circumstances allowed.

Southern Loyalist militia units had a much harder time. The South was more sparsely populated than the North, and except in the cities, units were spread out over the countryside. A first attempt at supporting the British in the Carolinas was defeated at Moore's Creek in 1776. When the British returned and took both Savannah and Charleston in 1779 and 1780 respectively, Loyalists turned out to support the British, but this was largely discouraged by Loyalist units being defeated, and sometimes savagely annihilated, at such places as King's Mountain, when Ferguson's command was not only defeated, but the prisoners taken were hanged out of hand afterwards by the victors for unknown reasons.

Henry Lee and his legion stumbled upon a Loyalist unit that mistook the Americans for the British Legion, as both units were similarly uniformed. The Loyalists actually thought that Lee was Tarleton until the point at which the Continentals turned on them and massacred them. Such was the nature

◀ **Private, Quebec Militia, Winter Dress, 1775** *This was common winter dress in the Northern colonies and Canada. The private wears a blanket coat, which was warm, comfortable, and practical for field service. He wears a worsted sash and a cap, or "tuque", made out of wool. His sash is typical of militia units raised in Canada. He wears Indian-style leggings and moccasins.*

▲ **Sergeant, 11th New Hampshire Provincial Regiment, 1774** *This pre-war militia unit had somewhat outdated uniforms, more akin to those of the French and Indian War period than to the British 1768 Clothing Warrant for the infantry. NCOs were properly uniformed, down to the regulation sash and halberd, both signs of rank. There is no record of an enlisted man's uniform.*

of the war in the South, pitching American against American.

As with the American militia, there was a great deal of variety in terms of dress and behaviour in the ranks of the Loyalist militia.

QUEBEC MILITIA. The Quebec militia was inherited from the French when Canada was conquered by the British in 1759–60. The uniform was dark green with the same colour facings for both officers and men. Coats were lined in white and small clothes were buff. Officers wore the crimson sash, and their cocked hats were bound in silver lace, while the privates' were bound in white tape. Privates wore the usual white leather equipment. Officers wore riding boots, while the men wore half gaiters over shoes. For winter a white blanket coat was worn, with a broad sky-blue stripe around the lower quarter of the blanket. Various kinds of winter headgear were worn, either fur caps or red stocking caps. The leather equipment would be worn around the outside of the coat. A red and white sash might also be worn with Indian leggings and moccasins.

11TH NEW HAMPSHIRE PROVINCIAL REGIMENT. The 11th New Hampshire was formed in 1774, and although initially loyal to the Royal Governor, and hence the Crown, it inadvertently gave rudimentary military training to men who would eventually end up at Bunker Hill facing the British regulars.

Only the officers of this regiment were properly uniformed. Coats were red, lined, faced and cuffed in sky blue. Gorgets were silver, and a small aiguillette was worn on the right shoulder. The cocked hats were bound in black lace. Sergeants usually had a similar uniform, probably also wearing white long gaiters that came above the knee and that were fastened below the knee with a black strap. They carried swords on a buff shoulderbelt that went over the right shoulder, as well as the old-fashioned halberd. No uniform was provided if privates came to duty in anything suitable from home.

LOYAL QUEEN'S COUNTY MILITIA. This home guard unit was formed in December 1776 for duty on Long Island, New York. Only the officers were uniformed, with red coats lined white and faced with sky blue. Small clothes were white, as was the lace binding the officers' tricornes. The red sash was worn at the waist.

◄ **OFFICER, QUEBEC MILITIA, 1774** *This militia officer's brown uniform was prescribed in a general order of 7 February 1780. Each officer was to provide his own uniform at his own expense and undoubtedly was also expected to arm himself. There is no record of an enlisted man's uniform for this unit, and it is highly probable they turned out in civilian dress. NCOs at least tried to look the part, but they probably were not as elegant as the officers.*

► **OFFICER, QUEBEC MILITIA 1774–5** *This dapper officer was a member of the Canadian militia drawn from the city of Quebec. English-speaking members of the unit were organized in "British companies", and the French-speakers were in the "Canadian Militia". The elegant uniform has both British and French features, and was common to both officers and enlisted men.*

AMERICAN INDIANS

Britain had loyal allies among the American Indian population and was able to draw upon a number of warriors to serve as auxiliaries, scouts and guides.

The Iroquois

Though the Iroquois were not the only Indian nation to be allied to the British forces during the war, they proved to be the most steadfast and loyal, thanks to the efforts of the Mohawk leader, Joseph Brant. Indians were active with British regular forces and Loyalist units such as Butler's Rangers. They fought primarily along the frontier in New York state and in the South. The Iroquois themselves lived around New York and were a prosperous and well-governed people. Iroquois was not the name of a single tribe, but that of a confederation of six tribes.

Joseph Brant and the Iroquois served the British loyally, raising a united force of around 300 Indians and 100 white Loyalists to fight when summoned. In the 1777 campaign, Brant led his men in support of Barry St Leger's expedition against Fort Stanwyx, and they engaged in the savage and bloody Battle of Oriskany, where they ambushed a relief column of well-armed and led militia, stopping them from reaching the fort. However, Indian losses were heavy as well, and when it was rumoured that a large force of Continentals was on the way to relieve Stanwyx, Indian resolve melted away and many left the field. Not even a leader of Brant's calibre could hold them in place. Because of this exodus, St Leger had to abandon his siege and retire back into Canada.

◀ **Iroquois Warrior, 1775–83** *The Iroquois fighters usually could be found dressed in red and blue "traders cloth", which they then decorated with beads and quills, which could be quite elaborate. The Iroquois, like other Indians, painted their faces and bodies for combat and were armed with a combination of Indian and European weapons. The headdress is noteworthy in that it is not only striking but would have been easily identifiable from a distance; it also gives the wearer the appearance of additional height that might throw an opponent's shot off the mark.*

▲ **Iroquois Warrior, 1775–83** *This is a more traditionally dressed warrior. Leggings and moccasins were worn, as were breechclouts and sometimes a type of kilt. The club shown was sometimes carved from the root of a tree and was quite effective in close combat. Steel knives and muskets were much prized and were either traded or taken from the Americans and British. Trade with the Indians was sometimes unfair and often illegal, as the weapons gained by the Indians could be used against the colonial entrepreneurs. Hatchets were also carried.*

Sullivan's Expedition

The Iroquois' worst days were probably the result of General Sullivan's expedition into their territory with a force of 4,000 men, mostly well-trained and disciplined Continentals.

▼ JOSEPH BRANT, 1780 *One of the most noted Indian leaders was Joseph Brant. Brant's Mohawk name was Thyandanega, and he was a protégé of Sir William Johnson, the British director of Indian Affairs. Brant's sister, Molly, married Sir William, and Brant was employed by Johnson before the war. He served in the field with Butler's Rangers.*

The Iroquois were excellent scouts, knew how to live, navigate and fight in the rough North American terrain, but they had neither the strength nor the ability to take on the large enemy force that was sent to destroy them. They tried to ambush the Americans once, but were outmanoeuvred and outfought, and from then on they merely hung on the flanks and rear of the column as it moved through their territory. They could do nothing as their well-kept towns and land were methodically destroyed by the American troops. Iroquois lands were so completely devastated by this punitive expedition that they retired into Canada, fed and supplied by the British, and they remained there after the war, as did many Loyalist allies, never returning to their ancestral lands.

Tribes of the Iroquois Confederation

Tribe	Possible Warrior Strength
Mohawk	100
Oneidas	200
Tuscarora	200
Onondonga	230
Cayuga	220
Seneca	650
Total	1,600

Traditional Dress

Indian warriors wore a combination of native clothing and European items. They generally looked formidable. Largely dependent on the British for arms and accoutrements, they prized steel knives and hatchets highly. Indian warriors were completely familiar with the musket and other firearms, and generally were considered good shots. Individually they were tough fighters, but the warfare they engaged in was not a fight by European standards. They fought expertly in the woods of their native land, and would manage to subsist where an inexperienced European would starve to death. However, they were easily discouraged, and if they could see no point to a campaign or they incurred heavy losses with nothing to show for it, they would pack up their kit and leave for home.

◀ RED JACKET, 1780 *Red Jacket was a Seneca, one of the tribes of the Iroquois Confederacy, and served the British loyally throughout the war. Indian dress of this period was a combination of Indian and European/American elements, and picturing Red Jacket in the ubiquitous hunting shirt is undoubtedly correct.*

THE FRENCH, GERMANS AND SPANISH

The French Alliance, negotiated by Benjamin Franklin in Paris in late 1777, was the decisive event of the war. The French had already been supporting the Americans clandestinely with money and munitions, and now they placed their reborn fleet and army in the war against the British. The Spanish later joined in with the Americans and French, and the only allies the British had were the faithful Germans they had hired as auxiliaries in 1776.

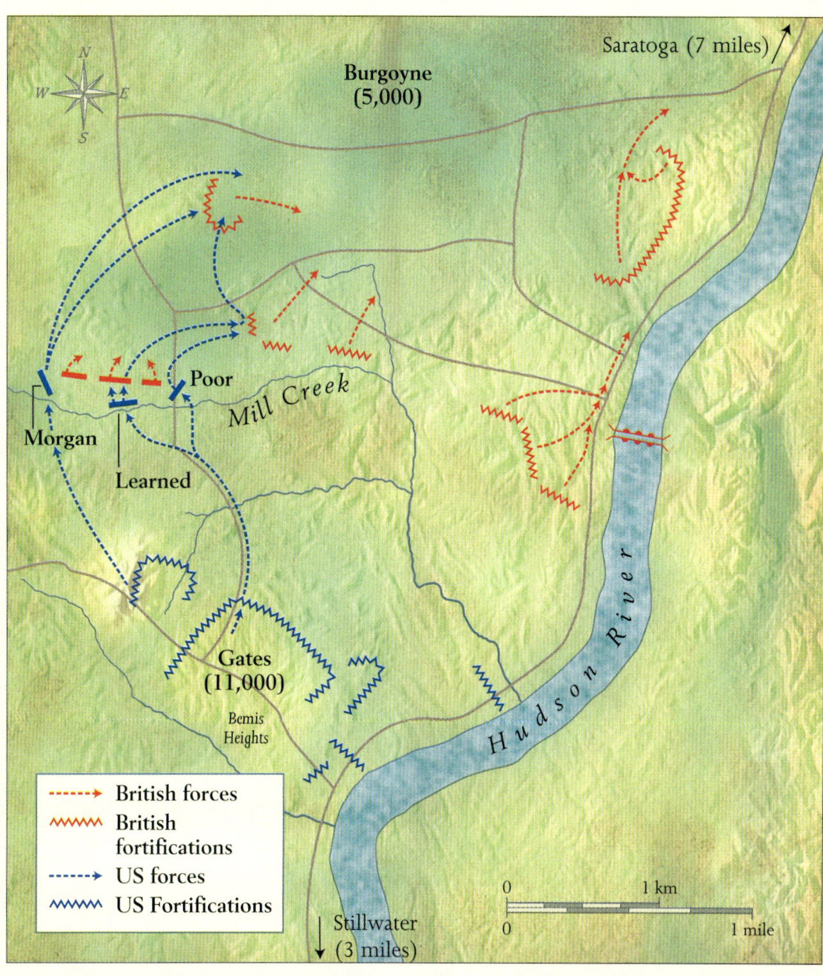

▲ *The action at Bemis Heights saw the last hope of the Anglo-German force of General Burgoyne dashed, as they failed to break through the American lines.*

◀ *General Burgoyne surrenders his sword to General Horatio Gates, whose terms of capitulation were honourable and generous, after the battle of Saratoga. His outnumbered, starving, surrounded command, low on ammunition, was in a hopeless position.*

ALLIES AND MERCENARIES

The American alliance with France was to prove a decisive factor in the war. The French Army had had experience fighting in North America and used the sharp lessons inflicted on it during the Seven Years' War to effect. Other nationalities involved in the conflict were the Germans and Spanish; the German contingents fighting for Britain, and a small number of Spanish troops defending their country's interests in the Southern theatre of war.

France

The performance of the French Army during the Seven Years' War, with a few notable exceptions, had been dismal. The development of French tactical doctrine was an evolutionary process that emerged from the ashes of that disaster. Theorists and those with practical experience had their input; thoughtful officers were clever enough to realize that something had to be done to correct the inherent weaknesses in the French Army, which had proved fatal. The French infantry regulations went through several modifications, practical experiments and manoeuvres were conducted, the artillery arm was completely revamped, a staff corps and college were organized and combined infantry–artillery co-operation was taught in the excellent French artillery schools. By the time of France's entry into the conflict against Britain, fighting alongside the young United States, its army was prepared to take the field and was the best army that France had produced since the days of Louis XIV and of Turenne's famous white coats.

The 1776 regulation (the *règlement*) was a step in the right direction, and the Americans were to gain more from it in the short term, and from the training camp of Vaisseaux, than the French themselves. The French expeditionary force which set out in 1780, and which ultimately made the victory of Yorktown possible in 1781, was well trained and disciplined, well led and well organized. Its commander, Jean-Baptiste Donatien de Vimeur, comte de Rochambeau, who had been involved at Vaisseaux, was undoubtedly the right choice to lead it. He was an officer of character, determination, courage and experience.

▲ *Rochambeau was an ardent supporter of the reforms undertaken in the French Army following the Seven Years' War.*

His spirit of co-operation with his American ally, and his willingness to work towards an allied victory, not only made the victory at Yorktown possible but ensured the independence of the United States of America.

▼ *Fatally wounded Hessian Colonel von Rall surrenders Trenton garrison to Washington.*

German Troops

In the mid-18th century, Germany was not a single nation or political unit. It was made up of a vast number of independent kingdoms, principalities, electorates, bishoprics and other territories that were attempting to retain their independence from Prussia, on the one hand, and a grasping Austria, on the other. Both Prussia and Austria were expanding empires. To the west was an aggressive, and equally expansionist, France, which continually engaged in a series of wars from the late 17th to the early 19th century and was slowly extending its eastern borders to its "natural frontier", the River Rhine. These smaller states all had armies of various sizes. Most of these were modelled on Prussia as an example of a successful

▲ *This picture of the Spanish fleet at Naples in October 1759 shows how Spain was still an impressive sea power at the time.*

▼ *Portrait, c.1761, of King Charles III of Spain during the time of the war in America.*

German kingdom and the Prussian model, especially after Prussia's impressive victory over all comers in the Seven Years' War, served as the best example of military organization. A few states modelled their armies on Prussia's enemy Austria, but by far the greater influence in central and western Germany was Prussia.

Most of these minor states were loosely grouped into the German Reich, collectively known as the Holy Roman Empire. The titular emperor of this entity was the Austrian emperor, and obedience to this ruler varied from state to state and from occasion to occasion. A number of smaller states were in the habit of supplying contingents of their troops for monetary gain, and the British had considerable experience of hiring such mercenaries to bolster manpower in their wars in Europe. By the early stages of the war in North America, they took the step of enlisting the support of a number of units of German mercenaries. These would fight throughout the war.

Spanish Soldiers

Spain was well past its heyday of empire by the middle of the 18th century. Its influence in Europe had waned substantially, and since the War of the Spanish Succession, at the beginning of the 18th century, its ruling house had been the House of Bourbon, related to the kings of France. Spain still had an extensive overseas empire in Central and South America, with a substantial fleet to protect that empire, and its army was still capable of effective action, but its interests in European affairs were limited to its own survival. By the time it entered the war on the side of France and the United States it was a secondary power.

FRENCH COMMANDERS AND STAFF

The French Army was a leader in the development of a modern staff system, and French staff officers were skilled professionals who were highly qualified in the duties of running an army in the field. The general staff of the army were, in essence, the commander's management team – a reflection of the administrative and planning functions to be found, then as now, in all hierarchical social, commercial, religious and military organizations.

Generals

The uniform that was worn by General Rochambeau was typical of those used for all French general officers. He wore a dark blue coat, lined and cuffed in dark blue, and outlined in gold braid, with two rows of gold braid at the cuffs and one at the collar. His waistcoat and breeches were white, and generally he wore black riding boots that came to the knee, with gilt spurs. The coat buttons were also of yellow metal, and his cocked hat was bound with one row of gold braid. French generals had field dress and also full dress, which was similar to the field dress, but more ornate, with the amount of gold braid more pronounced.

Army Staff

Staff development and practices matured through the myriad wars of the 17th and 18th centuries in Europe, the main object being to allow the commander to concentrate on the larger issues of managing an army on campaign and in combat. The chief of staff of an army ran the staff and was responsible to the commander for its functioning and organization.

The outstanding French staff officer of his day was General Pierre Joseph Bourcet, who not only developed modern staff practices, but

◄ **Officer, Staff Corps, 1780**
This figure is based on Louis-Alexandre Berthier, later to become famous as Napoleon's chief of staff, who acted as aide-de-camp to Rochambeau in the Staff Corps, with the rank of colonel. His official title was 'Sous-Aide Maréchal des logis', which, roughly translated, means an assistant to Rochambeau's chief of staff. The royal blue coat, with a small, standing collar, bears the two gold bullion fringed epaulettes of his rank. This uniform, with its red waistcoat and breeches, was rather similar to that of French naval officers. Note the black and white alliance cockade.

▲ **Rochambeau as General-in-Chief of the French Expeditionary Force, 1780**
This figure is wearing the handsome undress uniform of Jean-Baptiste Donatien de Vimeur, Comte de Rochambeau, in his rank of lieutenant general, with the red ribbon and star of the Grand Cross of the Order of Saint Louis, which Rochambeau received in 1771. The coat is edged with a spiral ribbon pattern of gold lace.

opened the French staff college for the training of staff officers at Grenoble in 1764. Bourcet's influence in staff operations and planning are still felt to this day and his procedures were further developed during the wars of the French Revolution. Louis-Alexandre Berthier, who was Napoleon's chief of staff from 1796 to 1814, was an officer on Rochambeau's staff in North America from 1780 to 1782, distinguishing himself in that role and in combat, and he left a valuable journal of his experiences.

Topographical Engineers

French topographical engineers were cartographers, responsible for making and maintaining maps. Examples of their excellent work in North America are preserved, and the quality is outstanding for the period. They were among the best map-makers in Europe, and their work was invaluable. They were uniformed in a dark blue coat, lined white, with aurora (a yellowish orange) facings, collar and cuffs.

The French had a fondness for interesting facing colours, and some of them, such as aurora (*aurore* in French) were mixed by a combination of dyes. The waistcoat and breeches were white, as were the epaulettes. Tall riding boots would be worn due to their usually being mounted in the field. The cocked hat was bound in white lace. The French cockade was normally white, but in America they wore the alliance cockade, white with a black centre (the opposite of the American cockade).

Staff Officers

The staff officers' uniform was dark blue, with a dark blue collar and cuffs, and with gold lace on the pockets. The eight buttonholes on the front of the coat were embroidered with gold lace that extended in rows across the front of the coat. The cuff buttons were embroidered in the same pattern. The breeches and waistcoat were both scarlet, the cocked hat was bound in thin gold lace, and riding boots were worn. This was the uniform the young Colonel Berthier would have worn, pictured left. His title as a staff officer was *Sous-Aide Maréchal des Logis*, a French military term that can be translated as a staff assistant to the chief of staff.

◀ **Officer, Topographical Engineers (Ingenieurs-Geographes), 1780**
The orange facings, silver buttons, epaulettes and lace embroidery distinguished this branch of the general staff. He wears riding boots as his job of surveying uncharted territory meant that he was often in the saddle for days at a time. These officers were specially trained to record the terrain and their maps were closely guarded secrets, available to only a few officers.

▶ **Commissaire des Guerres, 1780**
The iron-grey coat and red small clothes mark this officer out as being a non-combatant. The gold embroidery on the coat was in the form of stylized acanthus leaves. As commissaire des guerres *(military commissary general), his duties were the organization of logistical supplies for the army, such as fodder, accommodation and food. The uniform may have lacked panache, but this official's task was vitally important for the maintenance of any army.*

FRENCH INFANTRY

The French infantry sent to North America during the war were dressed in a transitional uniform, as they were caught between the 1776 and 1779 regulations.

The New and the Old

Uniforms and equipment were given a period of grace in which they were worn until they were worn out, and French commanding officers were not inclined to discard any item of clothing or equipment that was still serviceable.

French Infantry Uniforms in 1776

Regiment	No.	Facings	Lapels	Collar	Cuffs	Buttons
Champagne	3	silver grey	silver grey	silver grey	silver grey	yellow
Austrasie	4	silver grey	silver grey	red	silver grey	white
Armagnac	6	sky blue	sky blue	aurora	sky blue	white
Auxerrois	12	black	black	crimson	black	yellow
Agenois	14	pink	pink	green	pink	white
Bourbonnois	15	crimson	crimson	crimson	crimson	yellow
Auvergne	17	violet	violet	violet	violet	yellow
Gatinois	18	violet	violet	yellow	violet	yellow
Cambresis	20	violet	violet	pink	violet	white
Viennois	22	red	red	green	red	yellow
Touraine	34	steel grey	steel grey	yellow	steel grey	white
Soissonais	41	red	red	sky blue	red	yellow
Hainault	51	crimson	crimson	yellow	crimson	yellow
Royal-Comtois	76	sky blue	sky blue	crimson	sky blue	yellow
Saintonge	85	aurora	aurora	sky blue	aurora	white
Foix	86	dark green	dark green	yellow	dark green	white
Dillon*	90	yellow	yellow	white	yellow	yellow
Walsh*	95	blue	blue	yellow	blue	yellow
Enghien	96	aurora	aurora	red	aurora	white
Royal Deux-Ponts**	104	crimson	crimson	crimson	crimson	white

*These regiments wore red coats **This regiment wore light blue coats

Therefore some units sent to America were probably dressed in uniforms from the 1776 regulations while others wore the new 1779 dress. Others probably wore a combination of the two. It is quite probable that Rochambeau's expeditionary force was uniformed according to the 1779 regulations, but perhaps not exclusively.

The "metropolitan" French units, those from mainland France, wore white uniforms with coloured facings and piping. Any German, Swiss and Irish regiments in French service wore sky blue and red respectively. The colonial regiments were not subject to the same uniform regulations and were usually uniformed in dark blue.

◀ ARMAGNAC REGIMENT, CHASSEUR, 1779
Prior to the uniform regulations of this year, the cuffs of this uniform had been sky blue, as were the lapels, and an orange collar had been worn. Some French regiments in America presented a mixed appearance, with both old and new uniforms worn together.

GUADELOUPE REGIMENT. This unit was one of the colonial regiments that served in North America, and was present at the failed Siege of Savannah in 1779. They were uniformed in a dark blue coat without lapels and with red cuffs, collar and epaulette straps. The coat was lined with white, so the turnbacks would be white. Waistcoat and breeches were white, as were the grand gaiters, and the cocked hat was bound in white lace.

ARMAGNAC REGIMENT. A standard line regiment, this unit was typically uniformed in white with sky blue lapels and cuffs, with a yellow collar. The coat was lined with white, and the waistcoat and breeches were white. The grand gaiters were black and the cocked hat bound in white lace. Epaulette straps were white.

HAINAULT REGIMENT. This line regiment was uniformed in white lapelled in red with red cuffs and a yellow collar. White epaulette straps ended in red tufts for the grenadiers. Waistcoats and breeches were white, the grand gaiters black. According to the 1779 regulations bearskin caps for grenadiers were abolished. As they were authorized by the 1776 regulations, the "wear out" period had probably only just begun. French commanders had their own opinions of how their troops should be uniformed, and undoubtedly the bearskin continued to be worn after the new regulations went into effect. The plume on the cap was white with a red tip, and the cap cords were also white.

DILLON REGIMENT. Men and officers were uniformed in the traditional red of the Irish regiments in French service. The Irish Brigade was part of the "Wild Geese", who left their homeland to fight against the English in support of the Stuart cause. Lapels and cuffs were yellow, the collar white. The cocked hat was bound in black lace. The waistcoat, breeches, and grand gaiters were white. Buttons were white metal. The four cuff buttons, outlined in white lace, were set in a herringbone pattern that went up the sleeve.

▲ **OFFICER, DILLON REGIMENT, 1778**
As one of the Irish regiments of the French army, Dillon wore red coats. The golden epaulettes mark this figure out as a lieutenant. While on duty, he wears the gold gorget with the royal lilies of France.

◄ **SERGEANT, GUADELOUPE REGIMENT, 1780**
The silver braid at the top of the cuff was the sergeant's badge of rank. The anchor badges on his coat turnbacks indicate that this colonial regiment was administered by the Admiralty. The silver buttons bore the regimental title.

► **GRENADIER, HAINAULT REGIMENT, 1779**
Prior to the new uniform regulations of this year, Hainault wore crimson lapels, and this man would have worn grenades on his turnbacks. There were two or three different patterns of grenadier cap plate.

COLOURS AND STANDARDS

Regiments from all nationalities carried some form of colour or standard, and these varied according to regulation, the taste of a commanding officer or even the availability of cloth.

◀ *Regimental colour for the Santo Domingo Volunteer Infantry, Cuban Militia, Louisiana Regiment. The crest is Spain's, complete with the collar of the Order of the Golden Fleece.*

French Colours

The French had no national colour during the period. The Bourbon colour was white, and eventually a white flag with gold fleur-de-lis would be adopted as a national colour. French regiments had a colonel's colour of a white flag with a spear point finial and a white cravat hanging from the staff directly under the finial. This cravat had been a French symbol and rallying point since Henry IV fought to gain the throne in the 16th century.

The other colours for the infantry regiments were ordnance flags for each company. The designs for all of these flags were based on a large white cross centred on the colour, dividing the flag into four quarters, these then bearing a particular design for each regiment. The colours of the foreign regiments in French service could be of very different design as was the case for the colours of the Regiment Deux-Ponts, which distinguished itself at the Siege of Yorktown.

The Irish regiments in French service had ordnance colours in the same design as the native French infantry regiments. The main difference in these colours was the motto *In hoc signo vinces* (In this sign conquer).

German Colours

Most infantry regiments of the petty German principalities, kingdoms and electorates had two colours per regiment. One was the sovereign's colour and the other the regimental colour. The flags of Brunswick and Hesse-Cassel were similar to those of Prussia and can be distinguished by the device in the centre of the colours:

▼ *The regimental colour of the Hesse-Cassel line infantry. The motto* Nescit pericula *means "Regardless of dangers".*

▼ *The colour of Regiment Royal Deux-Ponts, a design in stark contrast to the geometric patterns of other French regiments.*

a white galloping horse facing to the left and on a red circle surrounded by a laurel wreath for Brunswick, and a rampant lion on a blue circle brandishing a sword and with the ubiquitous laurel wreath for the Hessians. Both regimental flags had the same design but were coloured differently. The central design on both was topped by a crown; crowned ciphers were in each corner.

Hesse-Hanau had a pink colour with the crowned arms in the centre. Crowned ciphers were again in the

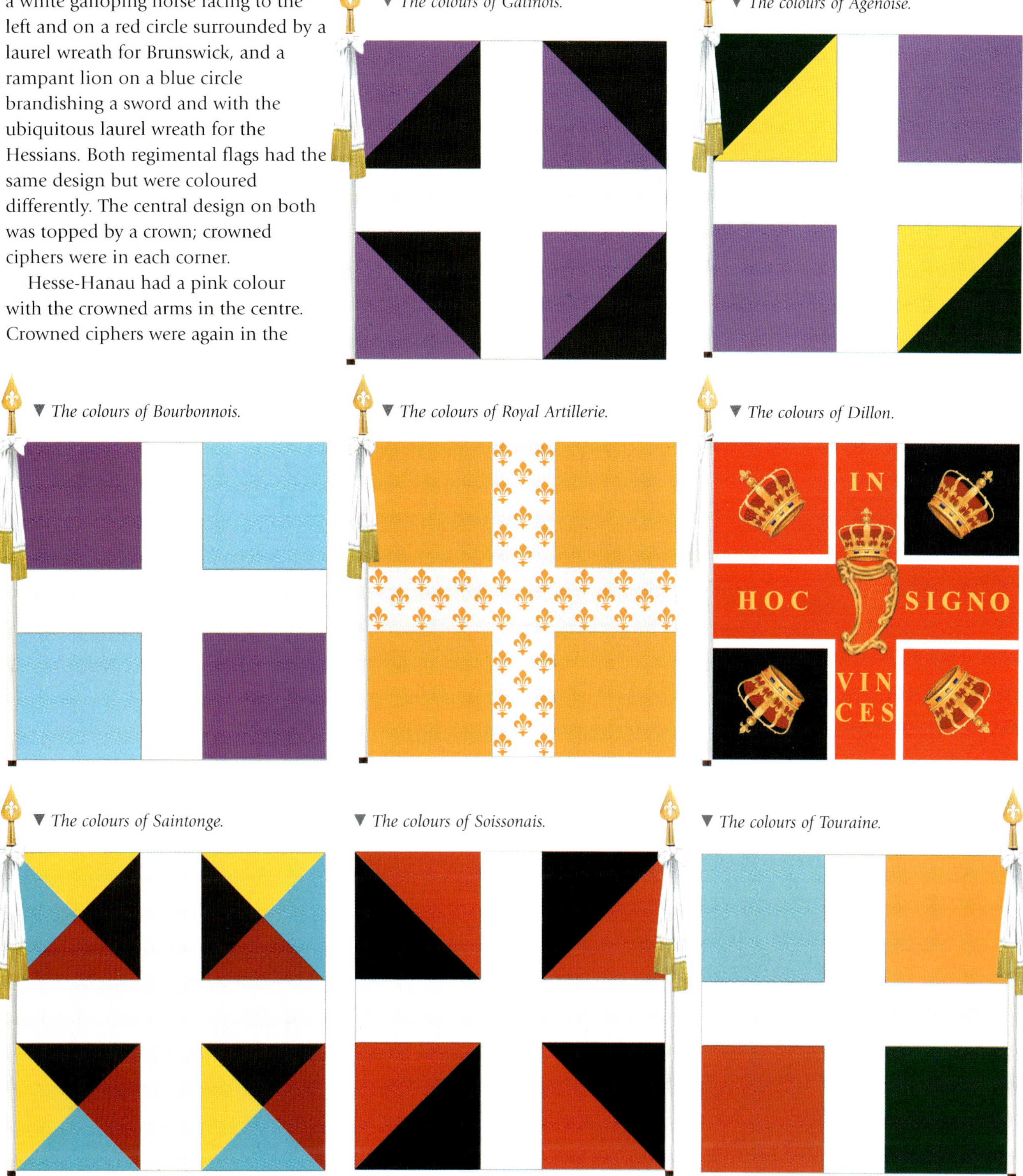

▼ *The colours of Gatinois.*

▼ *The colours of Agenoise.*

▼ *The colours of Bourbonnois.*

▼ *The colours of Royal Artillerie.*

▼ *The colours of Dillon.*

▼ *The colours of Saintonge.*

▼ *The colours of Soissonais.*

▼ *The colours of Touraine.*

centre of the colours. Unlike the colours of Brunswick and Hesse-Cassel, there was no overall cross design on the colours.

The colours of Ansbach-Bayreuth were of white damask with a crowned cipher in the centre, surrounded by a laurel wreath.

Spanish Colours

Each Spanish infantry battalion carried two colours: the king's colour and the regimental colour. Spanish colours generally followed a simple design of a white field upon which was a red Burgundian cross. The king's colour carried the royal arms of Spain surmounted by a crown. In the corners was a crowned crest of the province city from which the regiment had been recruited. The crowns could be pointing inward, outward, or be vertical. The regimental colour had the regimental crests, as on the king's colour, but did not carry the royal arms of Spain.

ROCHAMBEAU'S EXPEDITIONARY FORCE AND COLONIAL TROOPS

The deployment of the French expeditionary force to the United States in 1780 was competently led by Jean-Baptiste Donatien de Vimeur, comte de Rochambeau. The expedition was a well-disciplined and planned venture that was handled with professionalism and excellent organization, even down to rosters for the units and the ships to which the troops would be embarked. Over 5,000 French troops were embarked, and they landed in Rhode Island on 11 July 1780.

French Infantry Uniforms in 1779

Regiment	Number	Facings	Lapels	Cuffs	Buttons
Armagnac	6	sky blue	sky blue	white	
Champagne	3	sky blue	white	sky blue	
Austrasie	4	black		black	black
Auxerrois	12	black	black	white	white
Bourbonnais	13	black	white	black	white
Agenois	16	violet	white	violet	yellow
Auvergne	17	violet	violet	violet	
Gatenois	18	violet	violet	white	white
Cambresis	20	steel grey	steel grey	steel grey	
Viennois	22	steel grey	white		steel grey
Touraine	34	rose	white	rose	white
Soissonnais	41	crimson	crimson	crimson	yellow
Hainault	51	crimson	white	crimson	white
Rouergue	59	silver grey	silver grey	silver grey	
Royal-Comtois	76	royal blue	white		royal blue
Saintonge	85	dark green	white	dark green	yellow
Foix	86	dark green	dark green	dark green	white
Dillon*	90	yellow	yellow		yellow
Berwick*	91	black		black	black
Walsh*	95	blue		blue	blue
Enghien	96	white		white	white
Royal Hesse-Darmstadt **	97	capucine	capucine	capucine	
Royal Deux-Ponts**	104	yellow		yellow	yellow

Note: Regiments that had white coats and had either lapels, cuffs or collars in white had them piped in the facing colour.

* These regiments wore red coats. ** These regiments had light blue coats.

◀ **Officer, Saintonge Infantry Regiment, 1779** *Under the 1776 uniform regulations, this regiment had orange lapels and cuffs and a sky blue collar. This figure is shown in the later uniform, off duty, carrying the cane or walking stick, which was also a badge of officer rank.*

The 1779 French uniform regulations grouped most of the line regiments into ten "classes" of six regiments each. The exceptions were the Royal regiments, the Regiment of the Princes and the Picardie Regiment. Each class was divided further into two "divisions", each of three regiments. The first division of each class had yellow metal buttons, and the second division had white metal buttons.

The first regiment of each division had their lapels and cuffs in the regimental colour. The second regiment also had lapels in the regimental colour, but cuffs were white and trimmed in regimental braid. The third regiment had cuffs in the regimental colour with the lapels in white, which were also outlined in braid (piping) of the regimental colour.

Coat pockets in the first division would be horizontal with three buttons and outlined in regimental piping. The second division regiments would have vertical pockets, with three buttons each, and piped in the regimental colour. Royal regiments all had dark (or royal) blue as the facing colour. The Regiment of the Princes

had red as a distinguishing colour. Bearskin caps for the grenadier companies were banned by the 1779 regulations, but this was largely ignored. Grenadiers were supposed to wear a red pompom on the cocked hat. Chasseurs, who were the light infantry companies in the regiments, were to have a green pompom in the hat. The battalion companies' pompom colours were dark blue for the 1st Company, aurora for the 2nd, violet for the 3rd and crimson for the 4th Company. Buttons were stamped with the regimental number, and epaulettes for the battalion companies were white piped in the regimental colour. Grenadiers had red epaulettes piped red, and chasseurs green epaulettes piped white. The turnback ornament for the coats consisted of a flaming grenade for the grenadiers, a hunting horn for the chasseurs and a fleur-de-lis for the battalion companies. Regimental drummers wore the king's livery.

▼ **Drummer, Soissonais Infantry Regiment, 1778** *This uniform was worn by most French infantry drummers. Interestingly, the chain-pattern red and white lace was also worn by Spanish drummers. Lapels were in the regimental facing colour.*

▲ **Fourrier, Saintonge Infantry Regiment, 1779** *A fourrier in the French Army was responsible for some of the logistical duties in his company. The grade was between corporal and sergeant and not in the direct line of promotion to those grades. The billet was a combination of company clerk and supply sergeant. As well as the red stripes over the cuff, he wore a red diagonal bar on the upper sleeve. Note that he wears only the white, French cockade, not the black-within-white alliance pattern.*

► **Chasseur, Soissonais Infantry Regiment, 1780–3** *This man wears the costume worn for drill and fatigue duties (without the musket, bayonet and pouches). The chevron on the upper sleeve denotes five years of service. Black gaiters were usually worn in winter.*

Rochambeau's Men

The force included the infantry regiments Bourbonnois, Saintonge, Soissonais and Royal Deux-Ponts, as well as Lauzun's Legion of infantry and light cavalry, which included the equivalent of an artillery battalion and attached engineers.

When the force deployed to Virginia in the autumn of 1781, on the way to Yorktown with Washington and the Continental Army, Rochambeau was met by the Marquis de Saint-Simon with a further 3,000 French troops brought from the West Indies by the comte de Grasse's French fleet. This force included the infantry regiments Touraine, Agenois and Gatenois, and they set sail with 3,000 men from Saint-Dominique. De Grasse landed his reinforcements in Virginia, and immediately afterwards decisively defeated the British fleet in the Battle of the Chesapeake in September 1781. This decisive victory over the Royal Navy by the French fleet prevented the British from resupplying the forces of General Lord Cornwallis at Yorktown, Virginia. It also prevented interference with the supply of troops and provisions from New York to the armies of George Washington through Chesapeake Bay, as De Grasse blockaded the coast until Lord Cornwallis surrendered.

Service of Colonial Regiments

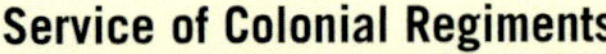

Unit	Location
Regiment du Cap	St Domingue (Haiti)
Regiment Port-au-Prince	St Domingue (Haiti)
Regiment Martinique	Martinique
Regiment Guadeloupe	United States and Guadeloupe
Volontaires de Bouille	Martinique
Cadets de St-Pierre	Martinique
Cadets du Gros-Morne	Martinique
Volontaires étrangers de la Marine	United States and West Indies
Chasseurs Volontaires	St Domingue (Haiti)
Grenadiers Volontaires	St Domingue (Haiti)
Corps de Travailleurs	Guadeloupe
Chasseurs Royaux	St Domingue (Haiti)
Volontaires Libres	Guadeloupe and Martinique
Cannoniers Bombardiers	St Domingue (Haiti), Martinique, and Guadeloupe

◀ **Grenadier private, Royal Deux-Ponts Infantry Regiment, 1779** *Under the old regulations, this regiment wore crimson collar, lapels and cuffs to the sky blue coat. This figure wears the old-fashioned bearskin cap with the distinctive brass plate of a grenadier company, bearing the flaming grenade, which was the symbol of those elite troops.*

▶ **Drummer, Royal Deux-Ponts Infantry Regiment, 1779** *This is the usual French line infantry drummer's uniform, with the lapels in the regimental facing colour, and the distinctive, chain patterned, red and white coloured lace.*

French Infantry in the Caribbean

Year	Location	Units Involved
1778	Dominica	Auxerrois, Viennois, Martinique
	St Lucia	Martinique, Royal Artillerie, Armagnac
1779	St Vincent	Champagne, Viennois, Martinique
	Grenada	Dillon, Auxerrois, Martinique, Foix, Cambresis, Hainault, Champagne, Royal Artillerie, 1st Legion Volontaires étrangers de la Marine
1780	St Vincent	Auxerrois, Viennois
1781	St Lucia, Tobago	Viennois, Brie, Dillon, Armagnac, Auxerrois, Walsh, Royal-Comtois
	St Eustatius	Auxerrois, Royal-Comtois, Dillon, Walsh
1782	St Kitts	Armagnac, Agenois, Auxerrois, Touraine, Viennois, Brie, Royal-Comtois, Dillon, Royal Artillerie, 1st Legion Volontaires étrangers de la Marine
	Demerara	Armagnac, 1st Legion Volontaires étrangers de la Marine
	Montserrat	Auxerrois

Facing Colours for each Class

Class	Colour	Class	Colour
1	sky blue	6	yellow
2	black	7	crimson
3	violet	8	silver grey
4	iron grey	9	aurora
5	rose	10	dark green

Colonial Regiments

France's colonial regiments were recruited for service abroad, often in the terribly unhealthy climates of West Africa or the Caribbean. Consequently, they did not always attract the best men. The regiments fought, for the most part, in the Caribbean. They were often accompanied by detachments from regular line regiments.

The men of the colonial regiments were uniformed in dark blue coats without lapels but with red cuffs, collars and epaulette straps. The coat was lined with white and the turnbacks were therefore white. Waistcoats and breeches were also white, as were the grand gaiters. The inevitable cocked hat was bound in white lace.

◀ **Officer, Bourbonnois Infantry Regiment, 1779** *The uniform regulations of 1776 gave this regiment crimson collar, cuffs and lapels and yellow buttons. This officer is a lieutenant on duty, so he wears the gorget. At the time, the French Army was so large that groups of regiments shared the same facing colour, being differentiated by button colours, horizontal and vertical pocket flaps and lapels in the coat colour for some of them.*

▶ **Chasseur, Lauzun's Legion, 1778** *As with all legions in the French Army at this time, it included an infantry component. The anchors on the coat turnbacks denote that this unit belonged to the Admiralty. The equipment was standard line infantry issue. There were three legions raised from foreign volunteers; all wore light blue coats, the 1st had lemon yellow collars and epaulettes, the 2nd had white and the 3rd had red.*

FRENCH CAVALRY AND LEGIONS

The war in North America involved comparatively few mounted troops. France did not send large numbers of cavalry to the Americas, dispatching only a few selected light troops.

Dragoons and Legions

In addition to one company each of the dragoon regiments Belsunce and Condé, deployed to Santo Domingo in October 1777, France also sent the 1st and 2nd Légions Volontaires étrangers de la Marine to America.

These two units were mixed cavalry and infantry, and belonged to the French Navy because the Ministry of the Navy had responsibility for the French colonies. Eight of these legions of foreign volunteers were planned, but only three came into existence. The 1st Legion served in the West Indies from 1779 to 1782, when it was disbanded. The 2nd Legion became the famous Lauzun's Legion, deployed to the United States with Rochambeau, and the cavalry of the legion eventually became the 5th Hussar Regiment. The 3rd Legion served in India until 1783. Some of the cavalry of the 1st Legion came north with Saint-Simon and served attached to the 2nd Legion at the Siege of Yorktown. It undoubtedly appreciated campaigning in Virginia more than it did in the West Indies, where disease was rife, and units could be destroyed by disease in a single campaign. The 2nd Legion was a compact force of infantry and cavalry that could be employed in a variety of missions. On campaign, the infantry was sometimes mounted with the cavalrymen, two men to a horse, for speed of movement of the entire unit. It was ideally suited for war in the American South, and all three armies – British, French, and American – employed the legion organization during the war. The legion in American service would later be modified and expanded into a division-size unit of all arms that

◄ **Hussar Officer, Lauzun's Legion, 1778** *This entire uniform reflects the Hungarian origin of the hussars, complete with light, curved sabre, complex braid decoration, dangling sabretache and short light cavalry boots. Instead of the fur cap (colpack), a coloured felt Mirliton, or winged cap, was often worn by French hussar regiments. The sabretache was decorated with the crowned, reversed, entwined royal cipher "L". The traditional, ornamental white pelisse was seldom worn in America.*

▲ **Grenadier Private, 1st Volontaires Etrangers de la Marine, 1778** *Together with the light blue coat, with naval anchor decorations on the turnbacks of the coat, this figure wears the trappings of the grenadier, including the bearskin and the red sabre strap. Grenadiers usually also wore red epaulettes. The French termed the grenadier companies "elite companies", and they were excused from fatigue details and received extra pay.*

would be renamed the Legion of the United States and employed successfully in combat against the Indians of the Old Northwest.

Hussars

The cavalry of all three legions were uniformed as hussars and were classed as light cavalry. Hussars originated in Hungary and were irregulars who engaged in small-scale operations such as raids, ambushes and fighting behind enemy lines. The traditional Hungarian garb these irregulars wore eventually evolved into a colourful and striking uniform; different regiments were assigned different colours (for the dolman, pelisse, collar, cuffs, etc.) for identification.

The hussars of the 1st Legion wore a dolman of sky blue, with a light blue collar and yellow cuffs. The elaborate hussar lace was white. The tight Hungarian breeches were yellow with white lace. Boots were black, as was the winged cap (the *mirliton*), the distinctive hussar headgear of the period. The troopers were armed with light cavalry sabres, two pistols and a carbine. The horse furniture (saddle cloth or shabraque) was sky blue.

The hussars of Lauzun's Legion, the former 2nd Legion, were similarly uniformed, except braid and lace was yellow and the breeches were red. Unusually, half of the cavalrymen were armed with lances.

The first French hussar units were organized and employed as irregulars for the "petite guerre", the war of ambush and raid. They proved successful eventually, though they had a hard time matching the superb irregular units in the Austrian Army. Hussar regiments were later authorized as regular light cavalry, and their duties included reconnaissance, screening, and intelligence-gathering. They were the ideal light cavalry to send to North America during the war. Campaigning there was impractical for large bodies of cavalry; however, smaller cavalry operations were feasible, from traditional light cavalry roles to charges on the battlefield.

Legion Infantry

Half of the legions were composed of infantry. These troops were also uniformed in sky blue faced yellow. The 1st Legion had yellow collars as well, and Lauzun's infantrymen had white. Waistcoats and breeches were white, as were the grand gaiters. Cocked hats were bound in white tape, and they wore the alliance cockade of white and black.

The infantry was armed and equipped as regular infantrymen.

▶ **Hussar, Lauzun's 2nd Legion Volontaires Etrangers de la Marine, 1780** *The hussars of the 1st Legion wore yellow breeches, Lauzun's wore red. This figure wears the* mirliton, *popular in many hussar regiments at this time. The costume, weapons, equipment, saddlery and harness were all copied from Hungarian originals. Equipping half the hussars with lances led to the unit becoming known as Lauzun's Lancers. Only the first rank of Polish lancer regiments carried lances.*

FRENCH ARTILLERY

Companies from these two artillery regiments (there were seven in the French Army at this time) served with some distinction in North America. French artillery had always enjoyed a reputation for skill and discipline and had usually been the leader in European artillery development. This pre-eminence had been lost, however, in the 1740s and 1750s because of new artillery developments in Prussia and Austria. This problem was addressed at the conclusion of the Seven Years' War in 1763, and by the mid-1770s a new artillery system, now the best in Europe, had been officially adopted by the French Army. The new system had been designed by noted French artilleryman Jean-Baptiste Vaquette de Gribeauval.

Artillery Uniforms

All wore the same uniform of a dark blue coat and breeches, blue collar and lapels piped red and red cuffs. The coat was lined with red. Black grand gaiters were worn in winter, and white in summer, and white waistcoats were worn as well as dark blue. The cocked hat was bound in black tape. The artillerymen were equipped and armed as infantry but, in addition, as they were classed as elite troops, they carried the short artillery sword in a frog with their bayonet, with the belt worn over the right shoulder.

◀ **Gunner, Metz Artillery Regiment, 1780** *All regiments of the French artillery wore the same uniform. In 1779 their distinctive red waistcoats were changed to dark blue. The dark uniform colours did not show the discoloration caused by the black powder as much as the white of the infantry. As a side arm this figure carries a short, straight-bladed sword with a brass hilt in the form of an eagle's head. Gunners were also usually armed with shorter muskets than those issued to the infantry.*

▶ **Officer, Auxonne Regiment of Artillery, 1780** *The artillery lost their red waistcoats in the 1779 regulations, when they were replaced with blue; undoubtedly, however, many could be seen for years after this official change. The two fringed epaulettes denote a field officer, the artillery using the same rank badge system as the line infantry.*

Artillery Systems

The French artillery in the Seven Years' War used the Vallière System of 1732. Although the calibres of the pieces were standardized, there was no distinction between field and siege artillery. Further, there was no standardization for the artillery vehicles required to move and supply the gun companies (limbers, caissons, ammunition wagons and so on). This

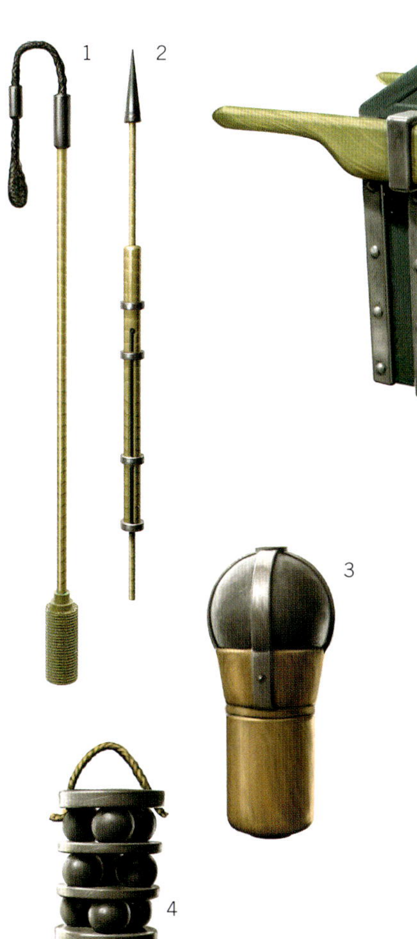

▲ **Artillery Ammunition and Sidearms, 1779** *1 Rammer with rope loop to aid extraction. 2 Linstock. In the field the pointed end would be stuck into the ground, and a length of slow match, with one end lit, would be wound around it. Fire was thus always available to ignite the powder charge and fire the piece. 3 A ball cartridge strapped to its charge. This technique simplified and speeded up the loading of the gun in action. 4 A form of canister shot. Firing these projectiles into dense infantry or cavalry formations at close range could cause terrible havoc. The effects dropped off rapidly as the range increased.*

▲ **Ready Ammunition Box, 1779** *The "coffret", or ready ammunition box, held various types of ammunition, depending on the calibre of the gun. It was carried on the trails of the gun when the piece was limbered up for movement and could be carried by two men. In action it was placed on the limber.*

put the French artillery, once Europe's finest, at a great disadvantage when compared to Austria and Prussia, which had more modern artillery arms, as well as to Britain.

Jean-Baptiste de Gribeauval, a skilled French artilleryman, had made a study of the Prussian artillery before the Seven Years' War, and was seconded to the excellent Austrian artillery during that conflict. After this experience, when he came home after the war, Gribeauval was determined that France would develop a modern artillery system that would be superior to anything they would face in combat. This brought him into direct conflict with Vallière junior, who was determined that his father's artillery system would remain the standard in the French Army.

So began a series of tests, arguments and court squabbles between *les rouges*, the artillerymen who supported Vallière (and the retention of the old artillery uniform, which included red breeches), and those more reform-minded gunners who supported Gribeauval's intention to modify the French artillery, including giving the gunners blue breeches (hence their nickname, *les bleus*).

Eventually Gribeauval and his supporters won the debate, and the new artillery system was eventually fully adopted, and was implemented by the mid-1770s.

▲ **Water Bucket, 1779** *The gunners' water bucket was designed as a truncated cone to make it difficult to tip over. The lid helped limit water loss when attached under the gun carriage during movement.*

▶ **Gunner, Metz Artillery Regiment, 1781** *This figure wears the alliance cockade in black and white, and white summer gaiters. The gunner's coat was of line infantry cut; weapons and equipment were the same as those issued to infantry regiments.*

THE GRIBEAUVAL ARTILLERY SYSTEM

Artillery was a key supporting arm in 18th-century wars, a time of great technical and organizational advances in artillery. Wars in the second half of the 17th century revolved around the siege, and French artillery development reflected that emphasis. However, warfare was changing in the first half of the 18th century, and the French were slow to adapt their artillery arm to reflect this. As already noted, they were bypassed by other, more innovative artillery systems, and by 1760 were outclassed. The French defeat in the Seven Years' War was devastating. Reform was needed, and thoughtful, reform-minded officers were determined to completely overhaul the artillery from top to bottom. Everything was addressed by the new system, from uniforms to organization, as well as formal education for both officers and non-commissioned officers. By the time Rochambeau's expeditionary force embarked for America in 1780, the French artillery arm was probably the best in Europe.

The Gribeauval System

Artillery units had been organized into batteries or companies by the great Swedish king and soldier Gustavus Adolphus in the first half of the 16th century. The first artillery systems, as such, did not come into existence for another century.

▶ **Gunner, 1780** *This French gunner, at ease, holds his rammer and water bucket. Apart from his musket, sword, rammer and bucket, this busy gunner also wears the bricole over his right shoulder. A gun crew equipped with bricoles could move the piece about the battlefield (within reason) without the need for horses. Note the alliance cockade and the white, summer gaiters.*

The French, Prussians and Austrians all contributed greatly to the development of artillery as an arm, but the greatest advance in artillery in the 18th century, and the system of the most subsequent influence, was the Gribeauval System, introduced in 1764.

Jean Baptiste Vaquette de Gribeauval had entered the French artillery in 1732, underwent training at the artillery school at La Fère and was commissioned in 1735. Gribeauval's skill as an artilleryman and his expertise gained him a reputation for the design and construction of ordnance. During the War of the Austrian Succession (1740–8) he fought in Germany and Flanders.

The French, having recognized the advances in field artillery being made in Prussia, and that the Prussian artillery now completely outclassed the Austrian artillery, despatched Gribeauval to Prussia to study and observe their light artillery. He brought back plans of the Prussian pieces, and constructed one for testing. When the Seven Years' War broke out, France answered an Austrian request to send competent artillery officers. In 1757 Gribeauval was seconded to the Austrian artillery for service against the Prussians. The Austrians had responded to the Prussian field artillery reforms and, under the direction of Prince Wenzel Lichtenstein, developed a new, simple artillery system that was the first complete artillery system in Europe.

Lighter Guns

Gribeauval, having served during the Seven Years' War, was determined to give France a newer, better system that would incorporate the best of the Prussian and Austrian systems he had seen, while keeping the best of the older Vallière system of France.

Gribeauval designed his field pieces to be light and manoeuvrable while at the same time retaining the hitting power of the older, heavier Vallière pieces of the same calibre. He tested his new guns at Strasbourg in 1765. The guns proved to be accurate and robust and were easy to manoeuvre by either horse team or the gun crew.

Gribeauval also introduced a number of new innovations that were standard on his field pieces, including stronger, improved gun tubes for field artillery; the prolonge, which allowed the piece to be transported over rough ground, loaded and readied to fire, without having to limber up to displace; the iron axle for field artillery vehicles and gun carriages; the bricole, a leather strap, with a rope and hook at the end of the rope that allowed the gun crew to move the gun manually; a new moveable rear gun sight that did not have to be detached from the gun tube when firing; the standard elevating screw; a technologically advanced searcher to ensure gun tubes did not have internal defects after being cast or after prolonged firing; and new, improved gun carriages for field artillery. Gribeauval ensured that all of the new gun tubes were cast solid and then bored out with the new boring machine that had been developed by the Swiss Jean Maritz. This ensured that the line of the bore was in the centre of the gun tube.

▼ **THE GRIBEAUVAL ARTILLERY SYSTEM**
1 An early form of grapeshot for close-range use against infantry or cavalry. The balls were held in bags of sacking. 2 Canister shot, using small iron balls packed with sawdust in a tin can. 3 Tiered grapeshot; a more modern form of the round than that pictured in (1). 4 One of the wooden discs that held the grapeshot in place.

▼ *5 Sponge for a 4-pounder, with attached handle and rope to assist rapid extraction from the gun barrel after having washed it out. 6 Combined sponge/rammer for the 8- and 12-pounder field pieces. 7 Ladle for inserting black powder into gun tube. This was an older, less safe method that was rendered obsolete by the invention of the powder cartridge in the 1740s by French General Brocard. 8 Searcher, used for checking for defects inside the gun tube.*

▼ *9 The barrel of the 18-calibre Gribeauval field piece. The handles on the top of the barrel were termed "dolphins", as they were originally cast in that form. They were used to hoist the gun tube off the carriage with the use of a gyn. 10 The limber for an 8-pounder field gun had no ammunition box or seats incorporated into it and was a light, simple piece of equipment. 11 8-pounder Gribeauval field gun, with coffret on the trails.*

HESSE-CASSEL INFANTRY

The German principality of Hesse-Cassel sent the best-disciplined and uniformed German contingent to North America to fight on the side of the British. The Hessians had a tradition of military service and were frequently sent as mercenaries away from their homeland. They had been

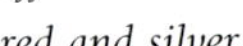

▼ **Officer, Musketier Regiment von Knyphausen, 1777** *The centre companies in musketeer regiments wore the tricorne, edged in lace in the regimental button colour. The gorget bore the red-and-white-striped Hessian lion on a royal blue ground and the officer's sash and sword strap were in red and silver.*

Hesse-Cassel Infantry Regiments

Regiment	Coat	Facings	Small Clothes	Buttons	Button Lace	Hat
Du Corps	blue	yellow	yellow	white	white	F-silver
Erbprinz	blue	crimson	white	white	none	F-silver
Prinz Carl	blue	red	white	yellow	yellow	H-white
Ditfurth	blue	yellow	white	white	white	H-white
Donop	blue	straw	straw	yellow	none	H-white
Lossberg	blue	orange	white	yellow	none	F-brass
Knyphausen	blue	black	straw	yellow	none	F-brass
Trumbach	blue	white	white	yellow	none	H-white
Mirbach	blue	red	white	white	white	H-white
Rall	blue	red	straw	yellow	none	F-brass
Wutginau	blue	red	straw	yellow	none	H-white
Wissenbach	blue	white	blue	white	none	H-white
Huyne	blue	yellow	blue	white	none	H-white
Bunau	blue	crimson	blue	white	none	H-white
Stein	blue	orange	blue	white	none	H-white

Classification of Hessian Infantry Regiments

Type	Name
Musketeer	Leib (Life)
Musketeer	Erbprinz (Crown Prince)
Musketeer	Prinz Carl
Musketeer	Donop
Musketeer	Trumbach (von Bose 1778)
Musketeer	Mirbach (von Jung-Lossberg 1780)
Musketeer	Wutginau (Landgraf)
Grenadier	Rall (von Wollwarth 1777, von Trumbach 1778, von Angelelli 1779)
Grenadier	von Linsingen (made up of companies from the 2nd and 3rd battalions of the Guard Regiment as well as the grenadier companies of the Leib Regiment and the Regiment von Mirbach; this unit was a battalion in strength)
Grenadier	von Block (von Lengerke 1777, made up of grenadier companies of the regiments Wutginau, von Donop, von Trumbach and Prinz Carl, this unit was a battalion in strength)
Grenadier	von Minnegerode (von Lowenstein 1780, made up of grenadier companies from the regiments Erbprinz, von Ditfurth, von Lossberg and von Knyphausen, this unit was of battalion strength)
Grenadier	von Kohler (von Graff 1778, von Platte 1782, made up of the grenadier companies of the Regiment von Rall and the garrison regiments von Kloblauch, von Seitz and von Bunau, this unit was a battalion in strength)
Fusilier	von Ditfurth
Fusilier	von Lossberg
Fusilier	von Knyphausen
Garrison	von Bunau
Garrison	Huyne
Garrison	von Stein (von Seitz in 1778)
Garrison	Wissenbach (von Kloblauch in 1780)

hired by Great Britain before, for example during the Jacobite Rebellion in 1745, and were, by all accounts, excellent troops when competently led.

A Hesse-Cassel infantry regiment in 1776 was organized with a regimental staff and five companies. The headquarters consisted of a colonel, a lieutenant colonel and a major, and the staff consisted of an adjutant, a quartermaster, a judge advocate, a chaplain, a surgeon, a wagonmaster, a drum major, six musicians, an armourer, a provost, an assistant provost and two drivers.

Each company had four officers, 12 NCOs, a junior surgeon, three drummers, a clerk, four servants for the officers and 105 privates. Two of the five companies would only have three officers, as their commanders were field-grade officers. Upon arrival in America, the officers and NCOs carried spontoons and pikes that were rapidly discarded in favour of short muskets, the bandolier and cartridge pouch.

▼ **Private, Fusilier Regiment von Ditfurth, 1776** *The brass or tin plates worn by the Hessian grenadier and fusilier regiments were of different patterns for each regiment, just as in the Prussian army. They all bore the rampant Hessian lion as part of the design. The fusilier cap plate was shorter than that of the grenadier and was in the regimental button colour. The top of the headpiece formed the top half of a flaming grenade.*

▼ **Pioneer, Garrison Regiment von Stein, 1777** *Hessian garrison regiments wore no lapels and, apart from the pioneers, wore tricornes. The regimental facings of this regiment were orange. This figure, armed with a short musket, wears a leather apron and carries a hatchet, axe and saw. The initials "FL" on his pouch stand for Friedrich Landgraf, ruler of Hesse-Cassel until 1783.*

▼ **Private, Grenadier Regiment von Rall, 1776** *The Prussian character of this uniform is obvious. The brass cap plate bears the Hessian lion over a cartouche enclosing the cipher "FL". As before, the breeches are made out of mattress ticking. Note the match case on his bandolier.*

HESSE-CASSEL ARTILLERY

The Principality of Hesse-Cassel also deployed a significant artillery contingent of three artillery companies to North America, almost 600 of all ranks, sent at the behest of their British paymasters. This was the entire artillery contingent of the state, and two of the companies had to be recruited and trained to fulfil the treaty obligations with Great Britain. The Hessian artillery arm was a skilled, well-trained unit, which served well alongside their British comrades.

◀ **Hessian Artillery NCO in Charge of a Gun Section, 1776** *A* Feuerwerker, *or Bombardier, would be in charge of a pair of guns. The gold braid around the hat and at the top of the cuffs, his sabre strap and the stick he carries were all the marks of a skilled professional.*

Artillery Companies

The gun companies were probably equipped with 4-pounder guns, which were painted medium blue with black ironwork. Each company was made up of five officers, 14 NCOs, three drummers and 129 privates. They served faithfully and competently in all the major campaigns. The artillery commander was Lieutenant Colonel von Heitel, with Major Pauli as his second in command. The artillery companies were probably assigned to the infantry regiments on campaign. They could be assigned by company or in smaller detachments. Artillery was seldom massed in large numbers in battles on the North American continent. In the late 18th century, North America was not considered to be artillery country. The pieces themselves were moved on the battlefield by hired civilian drivers and horse teams. The gun-shy civilians would and did leave the gunners on their own to survive and operate as best they could.

There were two ways to move a field piece on the battlefield without the use of horses. The first was by the use of drag ropes. These were long ropes attached to the guns and pulled by three men each. The British used this method which was, by the time of the War of Independence, becoming obsolete. The other method was by the use of the French-developed bricole. This piece of equipment consisted of a leather shoulder belt to which an iron ring had been attached. To that ring was attached a rope with an iron hook on the other end. The shoulder belt was worn by the gunners as a crossbelt and the hook would be attached to hooks or rings on the gun carriage, and the gun crew would then operate as a "man-team" and manoeuvre the field

▲ **Hessian Gunner with Powder Flask, 1777** *This man wears the Hessian artillery's canvas version of the leather shoulder harness, used to move the gun for limited distances on the battlefield without the need for horses to be brought forward. The flask in his hand allowed him to place measured amounts of powder in the vent near the breech.*

piece on the battlefield. The German gun companies were equipped with this simple but effective piece of equipment, as were the French when they deployed to North America.

Artillery Uniforms

The uniform for the artillery was a basic dark blue with red facings. The coat was lined red, so the turnbacks would be red. Artillerymen of most armies of the period did wear dark blue. The German gun companies, along with the British and Americans all did, and it would take a keen-eyed observer to tell the difference on a smoke-shrouded battlefield. Buff breeches and waistcoat were worn along with black grand gaiters. An artilleryman's sword was worn on a waistbelt, together with a cartridge box for his musket, on a white broad buff leather shoulderbelt. The German version of the bricole was made of canvas, and was usually white in colour instead of plain leather as in the French Army. Its use and purpose were the same. A cocked hat bound in white lace was worn with a red pompom. Many German units wore striped overalls, as did the Americans, instead of breeches and gaiters as the war continued and initial stocks of clothing wore out. Buttons were yellow metal. The German NCOs carried canes both as a symbol of rank and as the means to inflict on-the-spot nonjudicial punishment, not unusual in the German armies of the period.

Officers wore gold instead of yellow metal, and their hats were bound in scalloped gold lace. Sashes were silver and red, as were their sword knots.

All ranks carried metal canteens, and if the officers were mounted, for example the field officers and the company commanders, they would wear high riding boots, similar to those worn by the cavalry, and spurs. Officers' spurs would be gilded.

Gunners' Kit

The gunners all carried extra equipment, which included several interesting items besides the bricole. The gunner who used the pricker to puncture the powder bag from the vent at the breech of the piece wore a special belly box that carried primers to ignite the powder bag after it was pricked. The pricker would be carried on the outside of the belly box.

◀ **Gunner Carrying Side Arms, 1777** *This plate shows an artilleryman, who might have come from almost any army of the day, with the equipment he wears dictated by the universal job on the battlefield. The long, brass pickers on the shoulder strap were held by chains to prevent their loss in the heat of the action.*

Although different nations had different styles of artillery sidearms, the rammers and sponges all performed the same function, and a worm, which was a corkscrew fixed on a long staff, was used to extract excess pieces of the charge and wadding after the round was fired.

Artillery cartridges were now the norm in loading the piece, and ladles, which were used to put loose powder down the tube when loading, were still carried. This was an inherently dangerous job as the gun tube was usually warm and there were often hot or burning remnants of powder in the piece even after firing. Premature detonations were not unknown, which could cause terrible wounds for the members of the gun crew.

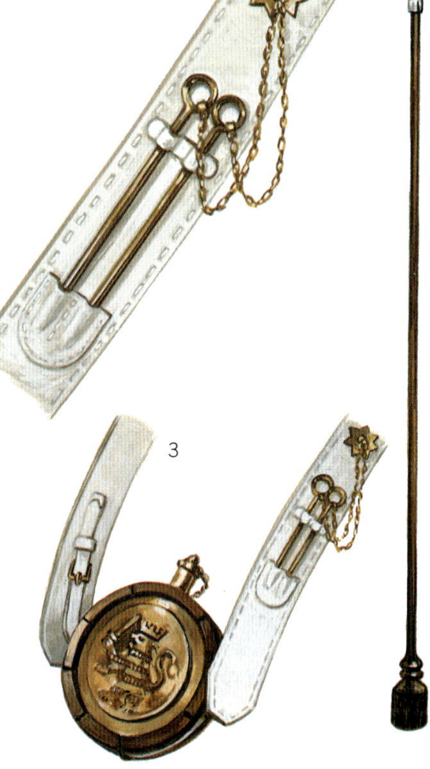

▲ **Gunner Kit** *1 Detail of gunner's picker, for clearing the touch-hole and piercing the bagged charge or the cartridges.*
2 The combined rammer/extraction tool. This could be used to load the gun and to extract any ball or cartridge if it was decided not to fire the piece after it had been loaded.
3 Detail of a Hessian gunner's powder flask, embossed with the rampant Hessian lion.

BRUNSWICK INFANTRY

The Duke of Brunswick, Charles I, was a relative by marriage to George III. The Duke's son had married a sister of the king. The duchy was in financial trouble, and the British proposition for troops was a windfall for the duke. This was the first treaty that the British entered into for troops to fight in the American war. The treaty was more than favourable to the duke, and the Brunswick contingent was the first to march for various ports of embarkation.

They marched in two contingents through Hanover, crossing that state without difficulty as it was in the possession of George III, and arrived in America in excellent shape with the infantry dressed in their splendid uniforms. Their smart, regulation appearance, however, was soon showing signs of wear as the rough fighting conditions and distance from home took their toll.

The Brunswickers spent the winter of 1776–7 in Canada, where their commander, General Baron von Riedesel, kept them occupied with drills whenever possible in the harsh winter conditions. He was especially concerned with their marksmanship, having made a trip to New York and witnessed first-hand the expert shots in the American troops, who patently outclassed his own.

This conscientious insistence on proper training would bear fruit in the coming campaign. Riedesel took 3,958 Brunswickers south from Canada alongside Burgoyne's invasion army, and he and his men performed well during the campaign. The disaster at Bennington was not of his making; his contingent was a well-trained, well-led force, and it deserved far better than being led to such disaster by Burgoyne.

The Brunswickers were uniformed on the Prussian model, as were all of the German contingents except for that of Anhalt-Zerbst.

Regiment von Rhetz. This regiment was elegantly uniformed in dark blue with white facings, waistcoat and breeches. The lapels had no lace. Either white gaiter trousers or grey grand gaiters were worn.

◄ **Field Officer, Infantry Regiment von Rhetz, 1777** *The scalloped gold hat lace, silver and yellow sword strap and waist sash, the gorget with a springing white horse on a red ground and the cane with silver and yellow cords all mark this man out as a field officer. He wears the gorget as he is on duty. The Brunswick contingent was the only one to have just four buttons on their lapels.*

► **Private, Infantry Regiment von Rhetz, 1777** *This musketeer is in field service order, with his calfskin pack on his left hip, together with his white canvas haversack. His sabre knot was in the company colour. The combination trouser-gaiters were popular with many armies of this period.*

The coats were lined red for both privates and junior officers, while field officers wore blue breeches and high riding boots with manchettes.

The officers' sashes were silver and yellow. Cocked hats were bound in white lace for the other ranks and in gold for officers; the field officers had scalloped lace.

REGIMENT VON SPECHT. This regiment, again in dark blue, was faced in red. The details are as for the Regiment von Rhetz from which this unit originally formed the 2nd Battalion.

◀ SERGEANT, LIGHT INFANTRY REGIMENT VON BARNER, 1776 *The four companies of this regiment were armed with rifles and sometimes operated as skirmishers, in open order. Their black facings reflect their light infantry role, but little else of this costume does. The hat pompom is in the colours of the Duchy of Brunswick.*

▶ OFFICER, INFANTRY REGIMENT VON SPECHT, 1777 *The gorget shows that this officer is on duty, and the simple gold edging to the hat marks him out as a junior officer, although he is dressed for mounted duty. The Brunswick colours of silver and yellow are borne in his sash, sword strap and cane cord.*

Brunswick Headgear

Some of the Brunswick units had unique accoutrements. Regiment von Riedesel's light company had special helmets with a prominent red and white plume.

The musketeers wore the tricorne. Grenadiers wore a metal mitre cap, and the fusiliers wore a smaller, more round type of mitre cap, as did the troops from Hesse-Cassel. As has already been stated, many of the Brunswick troops favoured striped overalls, which after a few months into the fighting were probably made locally out of bed ticking, as would Continental troops in the Southern campaigns when their supply situation became critical. The Brunswick contingent used their ingenuity to overcome the disadvantage of being the worst supplied and uniformed of the German troops from their home duchy.

The von Rhetz and von Sprecht regiments fought gallantly and well with Burgoyne in the 1777 campaign and were finally taken at the surrender at Saratoga. It appears that Burgoyne foolishly treated the German troops that were assigned to him as inferiors, not even taking von Riedesel into his confidence.

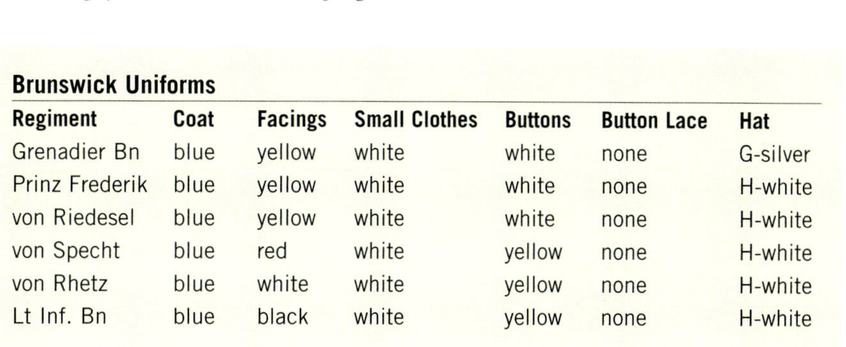

Brunswick Uniforms

Regiment	Coat	Facings	Small Clothes	Buttons	Button Lace	Hat
Grenadier Bn	blue	yellow	white	white	none	G-silver
Prinz Frederik	blue	yellow	white	white	none	H-white
von Riedesel	blue	yellow	white	white	none	H-white
von Specht	blue	red	white	yellow	none	H-white
von Rhetz	blue	white	white	yellow	none	H-white
Lt Inf. Bn	blue	black	white	yellow	none	H-white

BRUNSWICK CAVALRY

Only one cavalry regiment was supplied by the German princes to fight under British command. This should not come as a surprise as cavalry was expensive and difficult to export for many of the land-locked minor states. It is interesting that the British either wanted or accepted a German cavalry regiment, as there were enough light cavalry or dragoon regiments on the British Establishment to offer support to the war effort in North America.

The Brunswick Regiment of Dragoons was, therefore, in that sense unique. It can be found listed as the Brunswick Regiment of Dragoons, the Brunswick Dragoon Regiment, or the Dragoon Regiment Prince Friedrich. While this was a cavalry regiment, it was sent to North America without mounts and served dismounted on active service. With the rest of the Brunswick contingent, along with that of Hesse-Hanau, it was sent to Quebec and was part of Burgoyne's ill-fated expedition in 1777.

Brunswick Dragoons

The Dragoon Regiment Prinz Friedrich, to give the unit its correct title, was a four-squadron regiment commanded by Lieutenant Colonel Friedrich Baum, who was mortally wounded at the Battle of Bennington in August 1777. The regiment was part of a foraging and horse-hunting expedition, and many reliable sources have reported that the dragoons wore their cavalry accoutrements, including heavy boots, on this expedition. As they were serving dismounted on this campaign it is doubtful that they would don boots and spurs, and were undoubtedly wearing coveralls and shoes. Spurs could fit quite well over this type of footwear, so it is highly probable that they were not wearing cavalry boots at Bennington. It was at Bennington that they were surprised and defeated by John

◀ **Officer, Brunswick Dragoons, 1776** *The white and yellow plume is in the Brunswick colours as are the figure's sash and sword strap. The aiguillette on the right shoulder is in the button colour – silver. The silver gorget that he wears bears the white springing horse on a red ground.*

▶ **NCO, Brunswick Dragoons, holding a Regimental Guidon, 1776** *As a dragoon regiment, this unit was authorized to carry a swallow-tailed guidon on a lance-style staff. The bandolier reflects the Brunswick colours of silver and yellow. This figure's NCO status is shown by the silver cuff edging and his sword knot.*

▲ **Drummer, Brunswick Dragoons, 1777** *It was the original rule that dragoon regiments had drummers instead of trumpeters, due to their role as mounted infantry. Quite a few regiments that fought in America acquired black musicians, and some accounts state that the Brunswickers kitted theirs out with white turbans. Marching any distance in heavy, jacked boots and a turban and carrying a very heavy drum must have been very tiring and uncomfortable.*

Stark and his militiamen, the expedition failing in its objective and most of the personnel killed or captured. The regiment's usual field and fatigue wear was the same as the infantry. The regiment was uniformed in sky blue coats faced and lined in yellow. Breeches were buff leather, and high-topped cavalry boots were worn for mounted service with manchettes. The cocked hat was worn by all ranks and was bound in black lace. White over yellow, and/or yellow over white cut feather plumes were worn over the black cockade.

All ranks wore a white aiguillette on the right shoulder. Although cavalry officers did not usually wear a gorget, the officers of this regiment did, undoubtedly because they were serving as infantry. There is evidence that some of the drummers may have been black and, although they wore the regimental uniform, they may have worn a type of white turban with a yellow over white plume.

Field Service

For field service the breeches and boots were left behind, and the dragoons wore white and blue striped overalls, which were quite elegant and made out of the ubiquitous bed ticking. The cloth may very well have matched the coat colour. The troops were armed and equipped as infantrymen, although they retained their long cavalry broadswords.

Some of the troopers acquired mounts during Burgoyne's campaign and were put to good use for outposting and patrolling the rear of the army. The regiment was severely tested in the Saratoga campaign and finally surrendered with Burgoyne's army. Even so there were almost 300 present for duty in Canada in 1779. The Americans recruited among the German contingents' prisoners after Saratoga, and although some of the Brunswickers did join the Americans, particularly Armand's Legion, many of them deserted as soon as possible.

The regiment did not bring its colours to North America. Four guidons in sky blue bearing the usual Brunswick arms were brought and were saved from the Saratoga surrender. The Brunswick contingent commander, General Baron von Riedesel, had the guidon staffs burned, but had the guidons themselves hidden. He then reported to General Gates, the American commander, that he had burned the guidons as well. They were later smuggled back to the British lines in New York.

▶ **Dragoon in Field Service Dress, Brunswick Dragoons, 1777** *This unit never went into action as a mounted unit in a cavalry role, but it seems to have insisted on keeping its traditional heavy, dragoon-pattern* Pallasch, *or long, straight-bladed sword, which must have been roundly cursed as they marched. The figure wears the striped trouser-gaiters so popular with the German auxiliaries in America.*

ANSPACH-BAYREUTH, ANHALT-ZERBST AND WALDECK

These small German territories formed effective, disciplined contingents for the British. Generally they began the war dressed in Prussian-style uniform or, in the case of Anhalt-Zerbst, in Austrian-influenced attire.

Anspach-Bayreuth

Anspach-Bayreuth provided two infantry regiments to the British for service in North America. They may well have replaced their own uniform items with British stock as the conflict progressed and supplies dwindled.

1st (Anspach) Regiment. This was uniformed in Prussian-style dress of dark blue coats faced with red. Officers and privates had white waistcoats and breeches, NCOs had straw-yellow small clothes. Gaiters, which reached above the knee, were either white or black. Grenadiers wore the mitre cap, musketeers the cocked hat bound in white lace. Buttons were of white metal. A field uniform for later in the war consisted of striped trousers over half gaiters and shoes, the rest of the

◄ **NCO, 1st Anspach-Bayreuth Infantry Regiment, 1776** *This man, with his spontoon, is a senior NCO in parade dress, complete with a Malacca cane, suspended from a tunic button. His rank is shown by the silver hat edging, the silver edging to the collar and cuffs, the cane, and the sabre strap. After a few weeks fighting in America it was decided that the spontoons and pikes of the officers and NCOs should be consigned to the quartermaster's stores. This regiment was recruited largely within Anspach.*

► **Musketeer Private, 2nd Anspach-Bayreuth Infantry Regiment, 1777** *The 2nd Regiment wore black facings and was recruited within Bayreuth. This figure wears his calfskin pack on his left hip, in Prussian style. Beneath it is his grey canvas haversack. It is likely that both regiments used Prussian muskets and sabres.*

Uniforms of the Smaller Contingents

Regiment	Coat	Facings	Small Clothes	Buttons	Button Lace	Hat
Anspach-Bayreuth						
1st Regiment	blue	red	white	white	none	H-white
2nd Regiment	blue	black	white	white	none	H-white
Light Inf. Co.	green	red	white	yellow	none	H-black
Anhalt-Zerbst						
Infantry Rgt	white	red	white	yellow	none	H-white
Waldeck						
3rd Regiment	blue	yellow	white	yellow	none	H-yellow

uniform remaining the same. Officers had silver lace, and their cocked hats were bound in silver. NCOs wore the belly box for ammunition.

2ND (BAYREUTH) REGIMENT. This unit wore dark blue faced black. The general appearance is very similar to the 1st Regiment except for the facings. Striped gaiter trousers were worn in the field, and the belly box was probably used by officers and NCOs. Small clothes for all ranks were white.

Anhalt-Zerbst

The German principality of Anhalt-Zerbst sent one infantry regiment to North America. Contrary to the Prussian influence of the other five contracted states, Anhalt-Zerbst's troops were uniformed in Austrian-style uniforms and colours. Most of the officers and men recruited by the ruler of this principality were mercenaries, as the required contingent could not be filled with natives.

The uniform was a white coat lined and faced with red. Buttons were of yellow metal, and the grenadier caps were very much like the Austrian equivalent and were of bearskin. Black grand gaiters were worn, as were white waistcoats and breeches. A field uniform of 1778 was described as having a mostly red waistcoat, buff trousers, white half gaiters over shoes, a black cocked hat with a white plume and the regulation coat. The bayonet with a short sword was worn on a waist belt, and a broad white shoulderbelt over the left shoulder bore the cartridge box.

The uniform of a contingent that arrived in 1781 in New York looked like a cavalry unit, although they were infantry. The regimental coat was the same, although cavalry-style boots coming to the knee were worn with white breeches, along with a waistcoat and a red and yellow sash. They wore a cylindrical high felt cap akin to that worn by the Queen's Rangers, together with the white plume worn on the left side of the hat.

Waldeck

The Waldeck 3rd Infantry Regiment was uniformed in a very Prussian style. The coat was dark blue, lined red. Facings were yellow, and the waistcoat and breeches were white. Black grand gaiters were worn. The short sword and bayonet were worn on a waistbelt and the cartridge pouch was worn on a broad white belt over the left shoulder.

▲ GRENADIER PRIVATE, ANHALT-ZERBST INFANTRY REGIMENT, 1775 *The Austrian influence in this uniform is plain to see, with the bearskin grenadier bonnet and the typical white tunic and breeches. The grenade on the cap plate bears the cipher "FA" for Friedrich August, the ruler of the principality. The back of the grenadier's bearskin was in red, piped in yellow.*

► MUSKETEER PRIVATE, 3RD WALDECK INFANTRY REGIMENT, 1775 *This man is in full service marching order and the popular ticking trouser-gaiters are worn. As with the armies of many of the minor German states of this period, Prussian influence is clear in the uniform and equipment used. Waldeck also provided troops for Dutch service.*

Anspach-Bayreuth Artillery

The German state of Anspach-Bayreuth sent one company of artillery to North America, where it always served with the two Anspach-Bayreuth infantry regiments that formed the rest of the state's contingent.

The contingent was uniformed in Prussian-style attire. The artillery was dressed in the usual dark blue coats, and looked very similar to the Hesse-Cassel artillery companies. The coat was lined in red, and the waistcoat was white. Striped gaiter trousers made out of bed ticking were undoubtedly worn on campaign, and the artillerymen carried the normal artillery equipment and sidearms as described for Hesse-Cassel. All ranks would wear black grand gaiters in the field.

The canteen was of the round wooden type, and the cocked hat was bound in white lace and had a white pompom above the black cockade. The guns the company served may have been from Anspach-Bayreuth, or they may have been issued British pieces, such as the excellent light 6-pounder.

Artillery Drivers

It should be noted that during this period in military history the drivers for the artillery were not soldiers, but hired civilians. This was a major handicap for any artillery arm in the field. When civilians were contracted for this duty they usually brought along their own horses and harness, which they had a vested interest to preserve. If the situation became desperate, or rounds flew too close to the hired civilians, they would depart at the crucial moment, leaving the artillerymen to do as best they could with no horse teams to manoeuvre, advance or withdraw their pieces.

Crew Drill

Artillerymen were usually picked for size and intelligence, as the artillery was a technical arm. Not only did they have to manhandle and serve the field piece in action on a day of battle, but they had to practise their crew drill to become proficient. Survival on the battlefield could rest on their technical expertise as well as how swiftly they served the piece. Lastly, after the action was over, the piece had to be cleaned and maintained and any damage repaired. The gun tube would be fouled with powder and cartridge residue, which had to be scrubbed out, and brass field pieces had to be carefully maintained on the outside of the gun tube, as the metal oxidizes over time. Lastly, the bore had to be checked for wear and flaws to ensure the piece was serviceable.

Crew drill itself took long hours of practice. It has been described as a type of military ballet. Muzzle loading artillery had to be relaid after each shot, as there were no recoil mechanisms yet developed that would maintain the piece in the same position after firing. The entire piece recoiled when fired. After firing the gun crew had to manhandle the piece back into position, re-lay the gun, and the gunner would "point" (the period

1

2

3

◀ **Ansbach-Bayreuth Gunnder, 1776** *This gunner wears the shoulder strap used by the crew to move the piece on the battlefield.*

◀ **Ansbach-Bayreuth Artillery Kit, 1776** *1 Combined sponge/rammer for cleaning out the barrel after each discharge and ramming home the next charge. 2 Shoulder belt with powder flask. The roundel bears the eagle, and the initials of* Markgraf *Christian Friedrich Carl Alexander. 3 The leather strap used to pull the gun carriage.*

artillery term for aiming) the piece at its target. First, the command to load would be given, and one of the cannoneers would step up to the muzzle of the piece and hand a round to another gunner, who would place the round in the bore. Between the gunners would be a wooden sabot (shoe) that fitted the roundshot and would help seat the round in the bore after being rammed. The rounds were usually carried one at a time in a leather pouch carried on a shoulder strap. After delivering the round, the cannoneer would return to fetch another round. The gunner with the sponge/rammer would place the rammer into the bore and ram the round down the gun tube. It would be "seated" in the bore, usually with a very satisfying "thunk", which let the gunners know the round had reached the end of the bore.

Next, at the breech of the piece, another cannoneer would insert the pricker into the vent, which was a hole at the top of the gun tube that went all the way through to the bore of the piece and pierced the powder bag. Then, either very fine powder, or most probably a fuse, would be inserted into the vent. The gunner pointer would then step behind the breech and aim the piece by turning the elevating screw to adjust the height and signalling to the one or two cannoneers at the trail of the piece, manning handspikes in the trail, to move the piece laterally (called deflection in artillery parlance). The gun was now ready for firing.

The crew would step clear, and the gunner holding the portfire would approach the breech, ensuring that he was not in the way of the wheels of the piece so he would not be run over when the piece recoiled. At the command "Fire" he would touch the portfire to the vent, and the gun would go off. Then the process would be repeated until the command "Cease Fire" was given. A well-trained gun crew could do this without missing a beat, in combat and while incurring losses. The only command that would be heard after the initial command to load would be the command to fire. Crew fatigue would slow things down, and this type of firing could not be kept up for long.

◄ **Officer, Anspach-Bayreuth Artillery, 1776** *Because this was a foot artillery company, the officer wears gaiters, just like the men. His officer status is indicated by his sash, sword and sword strap, the edging to his hat and the long skirts to his coat. The whole outfit would have been of much finer cloth and workmanship than those of the enlisted men.*

► **Senior NCO, Anspach-Bayreuth Artillery, 1776** *This figure holds the spontoon, carried in the early stages of the war by senior NCOs. The braid edging of the collar and cuffs is in the button colour, the gauntlets, sword strap, hat edging and cane are all indications of his rank. The position of the cane on the left-hand side of the coat is unusual; they were normally hung from a button on the right-hand lapel.*

HESSE-HANAU

A small territory in south-western Germany, Hesse-Hanau sent a small contingent of infantry and artillery to fight in North America. The contingent was made up of the infantry Regiment Erbprinz (Crown Prince), a battalion of *Jägers* and a company of artillery. As with other German contingents, the Hesse-Hanau troops were of a high quality.

Infantry

The Erbprinz regiment was uniformed in dark blue faced red with white lace on the lapels. The coat was lined in red. Buff waistcoats were worn as were white breeches with black grand gaiters. Gaiter trousers of white or striped material were generally worn in the field. NCOs wore a belly box, and the sword was usually worn on a waistbelt, but this was sometimes slung as a shoulderbelt. Gauntlets of white were worn by both officers and NCOs. Grenadiers wore a silver metal mitre cap, musketeers the cocked hat laced white. Officers' lace was silver, and their waist sash was silver and crimson. NCOs carried halberds and canes as signs of rank; the canes were also a sign of their duty to administer corporal punishment to anyone deemed to need it.

The Artillery Company

At a distance it would have been difficult to tell the difference between the German artillery companies. The Hesse-Hanau gunners wore a dark blue coat faced and lined with red, yellow metal buttons and a cocked hat bound in white lace. They wore artillery short swords on a white waistbelt, and their cartridge pouches on a buff leather belt slung over on the left shoulder. They had round wooden canteens and might wear their muskets slung crossways on their backs in the field. They wore the German-style bricole of canvas. Striped gaiter trousers or breeches with grand gaiters were worn.

The Hesse-Hanau troops, even though the rulers of Hesse-Cassel and

▶ **Musketeer, Regiment Erbprinz, 1776**
This regiment is noted in old documents as having worn both red and pink facings in America. This, together with the bewildering changes of titles during the period, makes research difficult. The uniform is standard for musketeers.

◀ **Grenadier, Regiment Erbprinz, 1784**
This man wears the cipher "WL" (Wilhelm Landgraf) on his pouch; Wilhelm IX succeeded Friedrich II to the throne of Hesse-Cassel in 1783, but this regiment wore "WL" as opposed to the "FL" worn by the Hesse-Cassel regiments. There were confusing similarities between this regiment and the Fusilier Regiment Erbprinz. His cap plate bore the Hessian lion and the cipher "WL".

Hesse-Hanau were related, were not part of the same army and did not travel or embark together. In fact, they didn't serve together in North America. The Hesse-Cassel contingent disembarked in New York in the summer of 1776 with General Sir William Howe's army and served with it for the remainder of the war, though some units, such as the Regiment von Bose, served in the South.

The Hesse-Hanau troops, as previously mentioned, were sent to Quebec and were lost at Saratoga in October 1777.

Frederick II, the Landgrave of Hesse-Cassel, was Wilhelm, Count of Hesse-Hanau's father. The two men did not get along, and the two courts were not on good terms with each other. Both men were alike, and Wilhelm was still Frederick's heir apparent. This has led to some confusion about two of the regiments that were sent to North America. The Hesse-Cassel Regiment Erbprinz "belonged" to the hereditary prince of Hesse-Cassel, who was Wilhelm. The Hesse-Hanau infantry regiment that was furnished by Wilhelm was also named Erbprinz.

The Hesse-Hanau Regiment Erbprinz was a musketeer regiment, and there is primary source material available for its uniform during the Saratoga campaign. The Hesse-Cassel Regiment Erbprinz was initially a fusilier regiment, but was later renamed a musketeer regiment. To add to the confusion in identifying and naming the German regiments, many were known by the name of their commander, and these could change frequently, especially in combat. Some German regiments had as many as three commanders during the war, to the confusion of researchers. The Hesse-Hanau contingent served well and ably in the north. Von Riedesel's lively wife, the Baroness von Riedesel, accompanied her husband on the Saratoga campaign, and she left an excellent diary of her experiences. She had the reputation of a good and virtuous lady, and an ideal soldier's wife, and her observations and opinions make interesting reading.

One other German state supplied troops to Great Britain during the war. They were not, however, mercenaries. King George III was also head of state of Hanover, and seven Hanoverian infantry regiments saw service with the British during the war. Two regiments served in India, three in the Gibraltar garrison and two were lost on the island of Minorca.

◀ **Officer, Regiment Erbprinz, 1775** *The full, Prussian style of Hessian uniforms is plainly evident here. The coloured enamel centre of the gorget shows the rampant, red and white striped Hessian lion, with a sword, on a royal blue ground. The cipher "WL" can be seen on the blade of his spontoon.*

▶ **Gunner, Artillery company, Regiment Erbprinz, 1777** *This figure is dressed for gun drill, complete with pickers, powder flask and the combination mop/rammer. His musket is slung over the shoulder so that his hands are free to work the gun but he is still able to defend himself quickly if necessary.*

GERMAN *JÄGERS*

German *Jägers* were recruited from experienced hunters and foresters, and were armed with the famous short German hunting rifle. They were the best of the German troops, and were excellent light infantrymen, outstanding shots, and also excelled at skirmishing, scouting and ambushes. The *Jägers* were greatly feared by the Americans. They did not have bayonets for their rifles, so they were issued short swords and were also supported by musket and bayonet-armed light infantry in the field. This was to make up for the shortcoming of using the slow-loading rifle, a lesson the Americans had to learn the hard way.

Their most famous officer, who might have been the best light infantry officer in the British Army, was Captain Johann Ewald, who commanded the 2nd *Jäger* Company of the Hesse-Cassel contingent. He left valuable memoirs and a useful treatise on light infantry organization and tactics. Ewald admired his American adversaries and noted that the American officers actually studied the theories of their profession, whereas his British colleagues were generally not disposed to consulting books. He greatly admired General Cornwallis, and eventually became a general officer himself in the Danish Army during the Napoleonic Wars.

Hesse-Cassel *Feldjäger* Corps

The *Jägers* were uniformed in green, faced crimson, and their buttons were yellow metal. As with all the *Jäger* contingents, they wore the cocked hat, usually with a green cut-feather plume on the left side over the cockade. They did not wear lace. Some Hessian *Jägers* were mounted and wore buff leather breeches and knee boots.

Once in America, those *Jägers* serving on foot replaced their issue knee boots with long brown leather gaiters. Belts were brown or buff. Detachments of this corps were present

◄ **Jäger, Anspach-Bayreuth, 1777**
The similarity in costume among all Jäger *units in America extended to such units in the service of almost all German states. There are differences in the hilt of the* Hirschfänger, *but its function as a sword-bayonet was the same as for the companies from Hesse-Cassel. In later years, the 5th Battalion of the 60th Foot of the British Army was recruited from among German* Jägers *to a great extent.*

► **Jäger, Hesse-Cassel, 1777** *These heavy, jacked boots would have been far too cumbersome for dismounted duties; black cloth gaiters and shoes would have been worn in practice. The sword-bayonet that this figure carries is called a* Hirschfänger; *attached to the scabbard of the main blade is a smaller knife, used for skinning game when out hunting. This must have been one unit which never went hungry.*

in every theatre and every action of the war. It was difficult, if not impossible, to distinguish the different *Jäger* contingents as their uniforms were almost identical. At their greatest strength, the Hessian *Jägers* had five foot companies and one mounted company. Their first commander was the very competent Colonel Carl von Donop. After he was fatally wounded in October 1777, he was replaced by Colonel Adolphus von Wurm.

Anspach-Bayreuth *Jägers*

The *Jäger* contingent from Anspach-Bayreuth was uniformed like the Hesse-Cassel *Jägers*, wearing dark green and crimson. Their buttons were of yellow metal. They served with St Leger's expedition against Fort Stanwyx in 1777 and subsequently were returned to Canada.

Brunswick *Jägers*

The battalion of Brunswick *Jägers*, sometimes referred to as a light infantry battalion, was efficiently commanded by Lieutenant Colonel von Barner. They fought with Burgoyne in 1777 and distinguished themselves in the tough fighting in difficult terrain.

The battalion consisted of five companies and they were uniformed in the usual dark green with crimson facings with yellow metal buttons. They had buff waistcoats and breeches, and wore long gaiters that were usually of brown cloth. They wore cocked hats in the usual manner. The battalion carried no colours and usually operated by company.

Hesse-Hanau *Jägers*

The company of Hesse-Hanau *Jägers* wore dark green coats, faced red, with yellow buttons. They had green cockades on their cocked hats. Waistcoats were white, belts and breeches were buff.

▶ **MOUNTED *JÄGER*, HESSE-CASSEL, 1776** *All the* Jäger *companies that served in America in this war wore the same uniforms, except for differing legwear for mounted and dismounted duties. In time of peace, it was their working dress, as they were gamekeepers for the ruling houses. Some few were mounted and used as scouts and couriers. This man carries a curved, light cavalry-style sabre. The saddle furniture closely reflects the rider's uniform colours. The mounted* Jägers *were not cavalry, and were not counted as such. The horse was used for mobility and the men usually fought on foot, even though they were armed with two pistols and a light cavalry sabre. The high cavalry boots could have been a hindrance when dismounted, and it is possible they swapped them for gaiters when fighting.*

SPAIN

The Spanish Army traditionally wore white coats, and various adjustments were made for those units serving in the North American or Caribbean theatre. Regimental distinctions were well established in the Spanish Army of the period. In the tropics an all-white uniform, including white lining for the coats, would be worn. It was cut in the same pattern as the regulation uniforms listed. Small clothes would also be white, but the regimental facings would be in the colours listed in the table.

Spanish Infantry

Spanish regiments had two battalions of nine companies each. There were no light infantry companies, but one grenadier and eight battalion or fusilier companies. The regulation uniform was a white coat, single-breasted, with a white waistcoat and breeches. Equipment was of white buff leather, and grand gaiters could be white or black. Cartridge pouches were black without any device on the outside for identification purposes.

Grenadiers wore a black bearskin without a front plate, but with a "bag" hanging down the back on to the soldier's shoulders, in the regimental facing colour. Centre companies wore cocked hats with the Spanish red cockade. This was often worn with the French white cockade to create a version of the alliance cockade. NCOs and grenadiers carried a short sword and the grenadiers wore a brass "match case" mounted on a shoulderbelt.

◀ **Private, Santo Domingo Volunteer Infantry, White Companies, 1778** *Due to the tropical climate of the West Indies, tunics were usually made of white linen, and the coloured cuffs and collars were buttoned or hooked on, so that the garment might be washed without the dye running or fading too quickly. The Spaniards had a well-developed system of raising local militia for the defence of their colonies.*

▶ **Officer of Cuban Militia, Battalion of Havana, 1779** *The Spanish gentry living in the colonies would provide the officer corps of the locally raised defence forces. This officer of the Cuban militia's colourful costume shows a very unusual style of collar and lace ornamentation.*

NCOs carried canes just as their German counterparts did and the rank insignia of the NCOs was worn on the cuff edging in the unit's button colour. Sergeants and sergeant majors wore epaulettes, sergeants wearing one on the right shoulder in the unit's facing colour and sergeant majors wearing them on both shoulders. Sergeants usually carried spontoons. Regimental sappers wore grenadier uniforms

Spanish Regimental Facing Colours and Distinctions

Unit	Coat	Cuffs	Collar	Lining	Waistcoat	Breeches	Buttons
Rey	blue	red	red	red	red	blue	yellow
Soria	white	red	red	white	red	red	white
Navarre	white	red	red	white	red	red	yellow
Hibernia	red	green	none	red	red	red	yellow
Aragon	white	red	white	white	red	red	yellow
España	white	green	green	white	white	white	yellow
Flanders	white	blue	blue	white	blue	blue	yellow
Principe	white	red	red	white	white	white	yellow
Guadalajara	white	red	none	white	red	white	white

and buff leather aprons along with the usual axes, saws and hatchets. Junior officers' rank insignia was either cuff lace or epaulettes. Cocked hats were bound in either gold or silver lace. Epaulettes were either gold or silver, depending on the button metal colour of the regiment. Golden gorgets were worn on duty and had the royal crest topped by a crown. Off-duty officers carried canes to show rank.

Infantry Musicians

Musicians (drummers and fifers) had dark blue coats with scarlet facings and turnbacks. Facings were edged in red and white lace. The regiments of the queen, however, wore reversed colours (red faced blue) with blue and white lace. Swiss regiments in Spanish service wore the colonel's livery. A unit's drums were either painted blue or in the regiment's facing colour. The regimental crest was on the front of the drum. The Spanish Louisiana Regiment was an exception to this practice. The drummers of the regiment wore the same uniform as the rest of the unit with the addition of red and white lace around the cuffs, turnbacks, collar, and the pockets on the coat tails. The drum was the same blue as the regiment's facings, with red trim along the top and bottom. The Spanish coat of arms was on the front of the drum.

◀ **Private, Santo Domingo Volunteer Infantry, Black Companies, 1777** *It seems from the unit titles that both newly freed and able-bodied slaves were called upon to serve in the militia. The authorities must have been very confident of the loyalty of the slaves before equipping them with muskets. The darker colour of the coat is unusual for the climatic conditions.*

▶ **Private, Cuban Militia, Free Negroes of Havana, 1778** *This man wears the red-within-white alliance cockade, which declares his co-operation and affiliation with the French. Again, the coat was made from linen, to allow for climatic conditions. Weapons and equipment were basic and of practical design.*

Spanish Cavalry

The Spanish cavalry in the Americas consisted of three units. Firstly, a squadron of carabiniers (*Carabineros*) that was organized in New Orleans in 1779 by Bernardo de Gálvez, the successful Spanish commander in North America and the man who besieged and took Pensacola from the British garrison of British, German and Loyalist troops in 1781. Their coats were crimson, lined and faced white, with white breeches and waistcoats. They wore white or buff leather equipment, high cavalry boots, and their cocked hats were bound in yellow lace.

Two other Spanish mounted units also served in North America: the Regiment of Dragoons of America and the Regiment of Dragoons of Mexico. The first was uniformed in yellow coats with a dark blue waistcoat and breeches. The coat had no lapels. The second unit was in dark blue coats faced red and lined with white, with blue breeches and red waistcoats.

Spanish Artillery

The men of the Spanish artillery wore the usual dark blue coats and breeches with red facings and turnbacks. The coats were lined in red. Their cocked hats were bound in yellow lace. Their waistcoats were red, and their coats had yellow metal buttons. The men were armed and equipped as infantry, and they eventually adopted the French Gribeauval artillery system.

Spanish Engineers

Spanish engineers were an all-officer branch during this period. Their uniform was very similar to that of the artillery except that the lace was silver and the buttons were of white metal.

▶ **Colonel, Louisiana Regiment, Full Dress, 1779** *A rather splendid figure, whose uniform shows much more colour than normally seen on Spanish colonial uniforms. He wears a gilt gorget and is on duty; the absence of a gold sword strap and tassel or a gold cord to the cane are unexplained. Note the rank stripes on the cuff.*

◀ **Drummer, Louisiana Regiment, 1778** *This figure's tunic is decorated with the same distinctive red and white chain-link pattern that was worn on the clothing of drummers in the French Army of this period. On the drum is the regimental crest set between Spanish flags.*

Spanish Staff Officers

The various senior officer ranks in the Spanish Army had been indicated by gold lace on the cuffs since 1768. General officers had additional gold lace on the collar, the front edges of the uniform coat and also on the red waistcoat. The only Spanish officers who wore waist sashes during this period were the generals.

General officers wore red breeches, but if they were to be mounted they exchanged these for buff leather riding

Uniforms of Spanish Colonial Regiments

Unit	Coat	Cuffs	Collar	Lining	Waistcoat	Breeches	Buttons
Habana	blue	yellow	yellow	blue	yellow	blue	yellow
Louisiana	white	blue	blue	blue	blue	blue	white
Voluntarios de Cataluña	blue	yellow	yellow	blue	yellow	blue	white

breeches worn with riding boots with spurs attached. Staff officers wore a dark blue coat and breeches, coats were lined in red, and had red facings and red waistcoats. Buttons were gold, as was the lace depending on rank.

Spanish Colonial Units

All of the European colonial powers raised and maintained units that were not on the official army establishment for service in their colonies. The Spanish were no exception. Units of varying quality were formed in all of the Spanish colonies in the Americas, and many of them saw active service. Their primary function was to serve as reliable garrisons, usually in the major ports and facilities, and undoubtedly the quality of the units varied from place to place. On campaign, colonial units served alongside Spanish regulars. One advantage they had was that they were accustomed to serving in the tropics and were less vulnerable to the diseases that decimated Europeans. Cuban militia consisted of both white and black units, and the uniforms were meant to conform to the June 1764 regulations.

◀ FUSILIER PRIVATE, LOUISIANA REGIMENT, 1778 *This was the normal duty dress of the Louisiana Regiment. According to the regulations, small clothes were to have been blue, but that colour cloth was often in short supply, so many men wore white. It was calculated by the government that the battalions of troops sent out to serve in the West Indies would all have died of yellow fever and other diseases after two years. Thus fresh units were sent out on this regular basis. The same, chilling, calculations were carried out in the French and British War Offices, with the same, detached attitude.*

▶ FUSILIER PRIVATE, WHITE BATTALION OF CUBA AND BAYAMO, 1778 *The unusual coloured braid across the chest of this figure's tunic seems to have been confined to units that had been raised in Cuba. The equipment issued was simple, the total ammunition supply being limited to the small pouch on the front of his waistbelt.*

Jackets were usually single-breasted and white, with dark blue collars and with cuffs trimmed in white. Belts were buff leather, and they wore a belly box. The men wore black felt caps with the front flap turned up. Knee breeches were worn with white stockings and half gaiters. Blue overcoats were carried slung in a blanket roll over the shoulder. Arms were regulation musket and machete.

THE NAVAL FORCES OF THE WAR

Naval power has decided the fate of nations and empires since ancient times, and its use in the American War of Independence was crucial. The French Navy went down to defeat and destruction during the Seven Years' War but rose again, phoenix-like, to announce a treaty of alliance with the new United States in 1778. The Continental Navy was founded on 13 October 1775, followed by the Continental Marines on 10 November of that year. Victories were won against the Royal Navy, but the British were more experienced and had a much larger force, and consequently had either sunk or captured most of the Continental ships by 1781. Still, a new tradition and naval power had been born. The United States Navy was established in the 1790s, along with a new Marine Corps, and that navy would be small but of excellent quality.

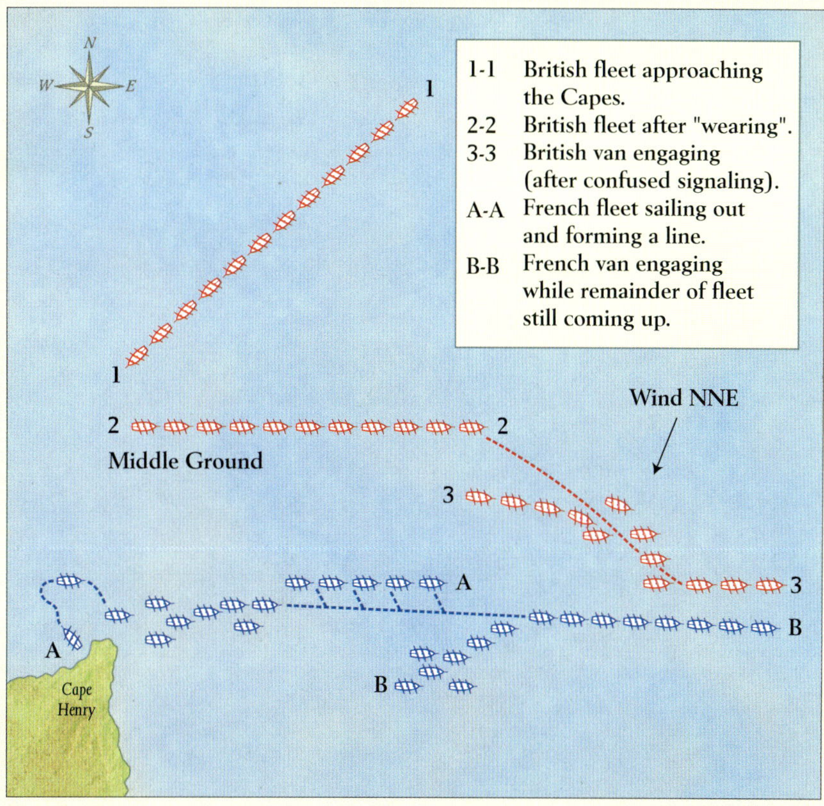

▲ *The Battle of the Virginia Capes, 5 September 1781, the action that sealed Cornwallis' fate at Yorktown, and for all intents and purposes ended the war in favour of the Americans.*

◀ *The desperate fight between John Paul Jones'* Bon Homme Richard *and HMS* Serapis *off Flamborough Head was won by Jones in spite of being outgunned by the British.*

THE WAR AT SEA

America's bid for independence was largely decided by who could control the oceans. Britain's powerful Royal Navy was initially challenged only by a nascent American Navy and then, with France's entry into the war, by a far more formidable foe.

Just as the French campaigns on land had ended in complete defeat and disgrace at the end of the Seven Years' War, so did it end in the same way at sea. The French Navy, so painstakingly built up during the reign of Louis XIV, had been disastrously defeated and all but destroyed at the Battle of Quiberon Bay in November 1759. Reforms, however, were begun and new ships were designed and built.

The Treaty of Paris of 1763, which ended the Seven Years' War, ensured that Great Britain was the greatest colonial power in the world and also confirmed its status as ruler of the waves. Great Britain's navy unwisely rested on its victorious laurels.

Warship Development 1690–1783

The warships that made up the navies of the European colonial powers were standardized into categories by the time of the war in North America.

The basic types were the ship of the line, a vessel designed to take its place in the line of battle and participate in fleet actions. These were subdivided into three basic types, or rates.

Frigates were the cruisers of their day, designed to be fast and well armed, and were used as the "eyes of the fleet" and for escort duty. Their armament was increasing, but they generally fought similar ships or smaller vessels. They seldom engaged a ship of the line, and, even then, rarely from choice.

Sloops, sometimes called ship sloops, formed, along with brigs, the next class of warship. They were smaller than frigates, although similarly constructed. While the sloop might have looked like a miniature frigate, actually the brig only had two masts instead of three. Sloops were escorts and raiders, and were perfect warships for the type of naval warfare that would initially take place in North American waters.

▼ *The Battle of Cape St Vincent took place on 16 January 1780. This action, begun late in the day and fought into the night, is also known as the Moonlight Battle and it was won by the British.*

Warships were first given "ratings" by Jean-Baptiste Colbert (1619–83), who was one of the most capable ministers of Louis XIV of France. Colbert is usually considered to be the father of the French Navy. The fleet he built was the one that was destroyed in 1759 at Quiberon Bay. What followed was an entirely new fleet that would pose a serious challenge to the Royal Navy, and would actually emerge victorious after the war.

The Rating System

There were actually four ratings for ships of the line when the war began. However, only the first three ratings were considered strong enough to be employed in the line of battle. Fourth rates, which were usually "two-deckers" (they had two gun decks and looked like small ships of the line), were now used as flagships on colonial stations and as convoy escorts. When war erupted in 1775, ships of this class were the most numerous of the Royal Navy ships assigned to America.

Warship Construction

Wooden warship design and construction was an art. It was also an industry. The Royal Navy, for example, had six great dockyards (Portsmouth, Plymouth, Sheerness, Chatham, Deptford and Woolwich) for building ships and where ships were maintained, repaired and constructed. France had a similar system of "military ports", such as Toulon and Brest, which were the main dockyards for the Mediterranean and Atlantic respectively. The royal dockyards employed over 10,000 people and would maintain the entire Royal Navy for the war, no matter where the ships were employed. It was an immense effort and was largely successful, although the long 3,000-mile (5,000km) voyage to a dockyard from the North American station was demanding.

Naval dockyards were a maze of different shops with different responsibilities: dry docks, magazines for ordnance and ammunition, the shipyards themselves, ropewalks, sail lofts, lumber yards and storehouses. The dockyard workers were men of different skills and specialities: various types of carpenter, naval architects, construction crews, sail-makers, riggers, woodcarvers and caulkers. All of these worked under the theoretical supervision of the dockyard director, but the captain of a ship would have his own ideas on how to fit or rig the vessel under his command. Further, he might also arm the ship to his own satisfaction and not to how the warship was rated. This could make the ship top-heavy and liable to roll in anything but a perfectly calm sea.

▲ *Naval shipyards had to be well organized and efficiently run. No navy could exist without a well-thought-out system of naval dockyards where ships were built, fitted out for active service, repaired and overhauled.*

Royal Navy Ships' Rating in 1700

Rate	Guns	Designation
1st	100	ship of the line
2nd	90	ship of the line
3rd	70	ship of the line
4th	54–60	ship of the line
5th	30–40	frigate
6th	18–24	frigate

Royal Navy Ships' Rating in 1775

Rate	Guns	Designation
1st	100+	ship of the line
2nd	90–98	ship of the line
3rd	64–80	ship of the line
4th	50–60	command ship/convoy escort
5th	30–44	frigate
6th	20–28	frigate

▼ *John Paul Jones raising the first US flag to be flown from a Continental Navy warship. Jones later made a name for himself as a daring sea captain and raider.*

SHIPS OF THE LINE AND FRIGATES

Powerful navies were built around large numbers of ships of the line supported by frigates. Ships of the line were most effective in fleet actions, when combinations of heavily armed battleships could, literally, tear their opponents apart. Frigates were more versatile and, by the time of the war in North America, essential for the effective operation of any fleet.

Ships of the Line

Not merely the battleship of her day, a ship of the line was also the most technologically advanced weapons system of the period. This warship evolved in less than a century from a high-sided, and somewhat top-heavy, ship with a large number of guns into a lethal weapon with effective armament. It was truly terrifying to face such a ship at any time, but they really excelled in a fleet action.

The most common types of ships of the line to be constructed were the 74-gun ship of the line and the 80-gun ship of the line. Eventually the "74" triumphed over its rival and became the most popular. The 74-gun ship of the line became the workhorse of the battle fleets of both Great Britain and France. It was a powerful fighting machine, and generally had excellent sailing characteristics. French ships tended to be better sailers than their British counterparts, but this was partly offset by the British adoption of copper plates that were attached to the underwater hull of the warship. This slowed the growth of marine life on the hull as well as protecting and preserving the wooden hull. Wooden hulls in seawater tended to rot, sometimes with catastrophic effects. At least one British warship had her keel fall out, the ship sinking rapidly while at anchor. The strength of a navy was judged by the number of ships of the line in service, and no other single nation in the period had the same line of battle strength held by the Royal Navy.

▲ *Naval actions were usually a combination of gun actions and close actions where the fighting was fierce, grim, and bloody.*

▼ **Continental Navy 32-gun Frigate, the *Raleigh*** *The Continental Navy's newly built frigates were of three main designs. This is the spar and sail plan of the frigate* Raleigh. *Although she looks like one of the Royal Navy's frigates, she was not a copy but an original American design; her hull was designed for speed and she was specifically laid down and completed as a frigate.*

The Frigate

Frigates developed out of the need to have well-armed cruisers that were fast enough for scouting and screening missions and strong enough to take care of themselves when alone. In addition, they had to be able to outrun anything bigger that they could not fight. By the mid-17th century, the frigate had not only evolved, but had become a new class of warship.

Fleet Actions

There were two major fleet actions in the war that might be considered to be decisive: the Battle of the Virginia Capes and the Battle of the Saintes. The former was fought between a French fleet under the Comte de Grasse and a British fleet under Admiral Graves. It took place during the allied investment of General Cornwallis' British Army at Yorktown.

The French mission was to close Chesapeake Bay to prevent any attempt by the British to relieve Cornwallis. The British fleet arrived, the French came out to fight, and an indecisive tactical engagement followed, where ships on both sides were damaged, but none were sunk.

Ship of the Line Classes 1740–83

Class	Rate	Country	Guns	Gun Decks
Northumberland	3rd	Great Britain	64	2
Invincible	3rd	France	74	2
Sandwich	2nd	Great Britain	90	3
Bellona	3rd	Great Britain	74	2
Ville de Paris	1st	France	90+	3
Victory	1st	Great Britain	100	3
Santissima Trinidad	1st	Spain	120	3
America	3rd	United States	74	2

Frigate Classes 1740–83

Class	Country	Guns	Type	Gun Decks
Medée	France	26	8-pounders	1
Unicorn	Great Britain	28	9-pounders	1
Hermione	France	26	12-pounders	1
Southampton	Great Britain	32	12-pounders	1
Belle Poule	France	32	12-pounders	1
Santa Margarita	Spain	40	8-pounders	1
Hancock	United States	32	12-pounders	1
Randolph	United States	32	12-pounders	1
Flora	Great Britain	36	18-pounders	1
Alliance	United States	36	18-pounders	1
Hebe	France	40	18-pounders	1

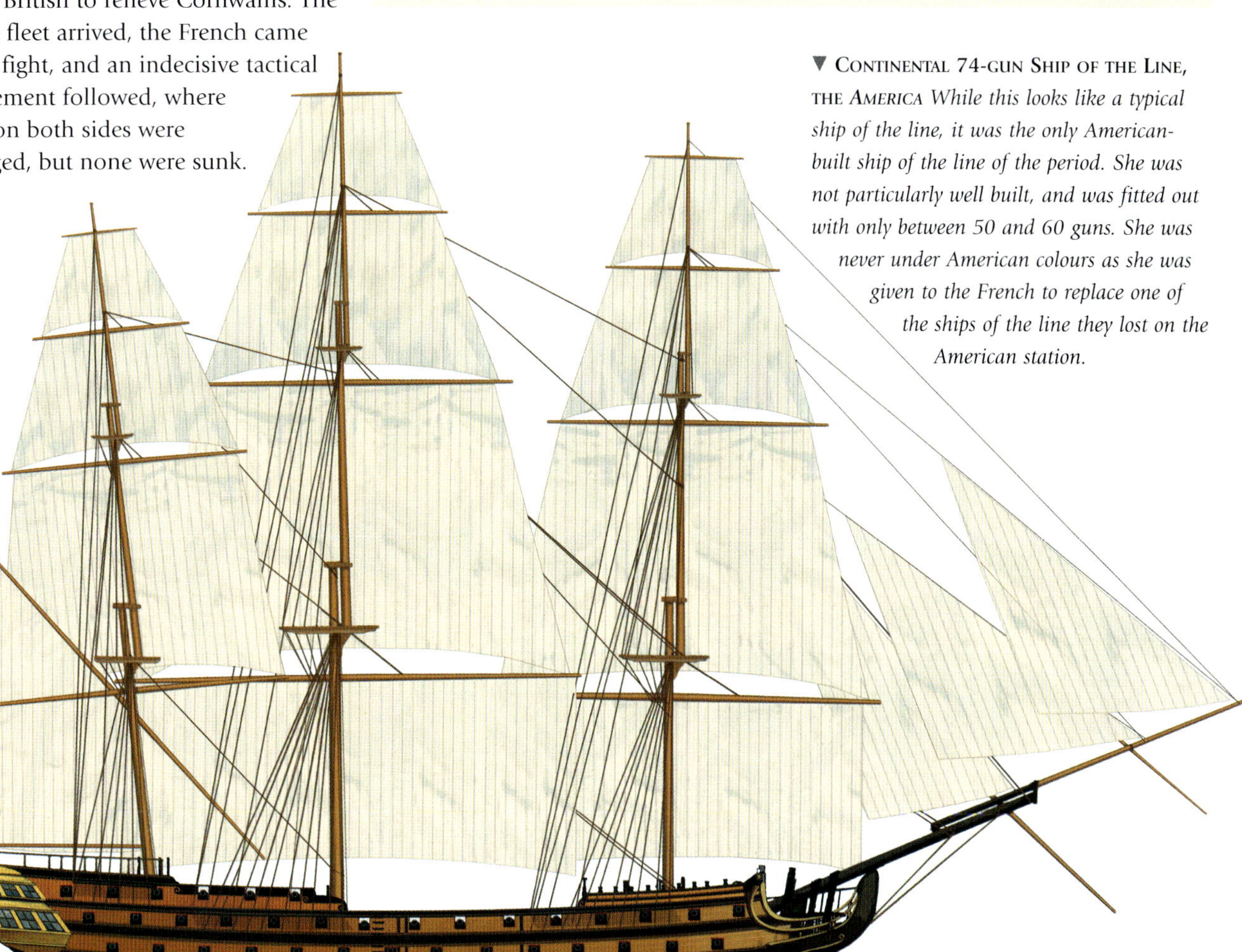

▼ CONTINENTAL 74-GUN SHIP OF THE LINE, THE AMERICA *While this looks like a typical ship of the line, it was the only American-built ship of the line of the period. She was not particularly well built, and was fitted out with only between 50 and 60 guns. She was never under American colours as she was given to the French to replace one of the ships of the line they lost on the American station.*

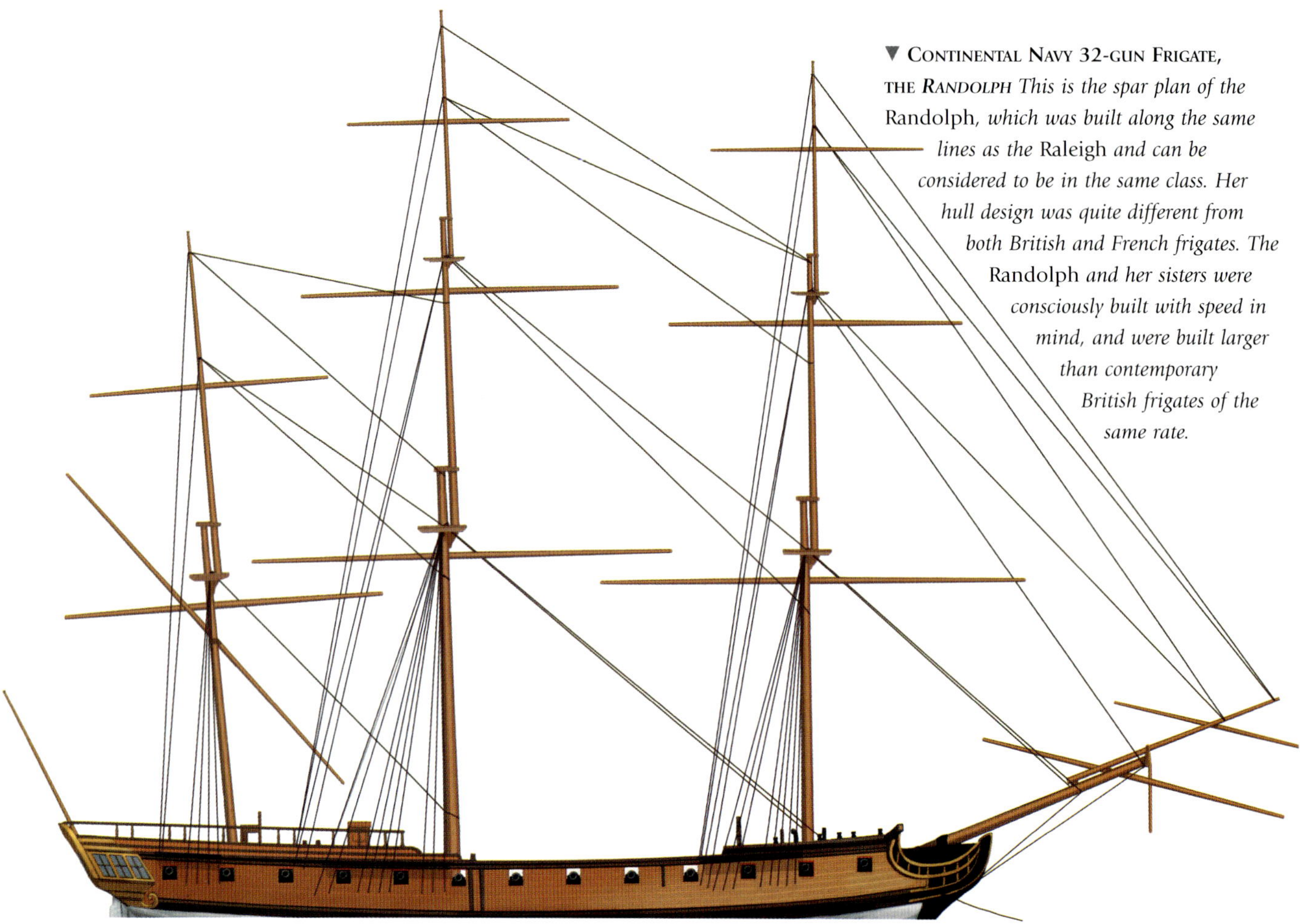

▼ CONTINENTAL NAVY 32-GUN FRIGATE, THE *RANDOLPH* *This is the spar plan of the* Randolph, *which was built along the same lines as the* Raleigh *and can be considered to be in the same class. Her hull design was quite different from both British and French frigates. The* Randolph *and her sisters were consciously built with speed in mind, and were built larger than contemporary British frigates of the same rate.*

Battle of the Virginia Capes

British Order of Battle

Ship	Type	Guns
Alfred	sol*	74
Barfleur	sol	90
Monarch	sol	74
Centaur	sol	74
America	sol	64
Resolution	sol	74
Bedford	sol	74
London	sol	98
Royal Oak	sol	74
Montague	sol	74
Europe	sol	64
Terrible	sol	74
Ajax	sol	74
Princessa	sol	70
Alcide	sol	74
Intrepid	sol	64
Shrewsbury	sol	74

French Order of Battle

Name	Type	Guns
Pluton	sol	74
Bourogne	sol	74
Marseille	sol	74
Diadème	sol	74
Reflechi	sol	64
Auguste	sol	80
St Esprit	sol	80
Caton	sol	64
César	sol	74
Destin	sol	74
Ville de Paris	sol	98
Victoire	sol	74
Sceptre	sol	74
Northumberland	sol	74
Palmier	sol	74
Solitaire	sol	64
Citoyen	sol	74
Scipion	sol	74
Magnanime	sol	74
Hercule	sol	74
Languedoc	sol	80
Zélée	sol	74
L'Hector	sol	74
Souverain	sol	74

*sol: ship of the line

The British did have to destroy one ship of the line after the action, because she had been badly beaten up by French gunfire.

This was, however, the decisive naval action of the war as the British fleet now returned to New York for repairs and Cornwallis, without hope of relief and with the allied siege lines getting closer to Yorktown, surrendered to the allies on 19 October 1781, virtually guaranteeing American independence.

The Battle of the Saintes took place in the Caribbean in April 1782 between the French fleet of the Comte de Grasse and the British fleet of Admiral George Rodney. Both admirals were competent, aggressive commanders, but de Grasse was failed by some of his captains who refused to close with the British.

The capable Rodney went in after the French ships, breaking their line and forcing five French ships of the line to strike their colours, including de Grasse's flagship, the *Ville de Paris*. De Grasse was captured and became a

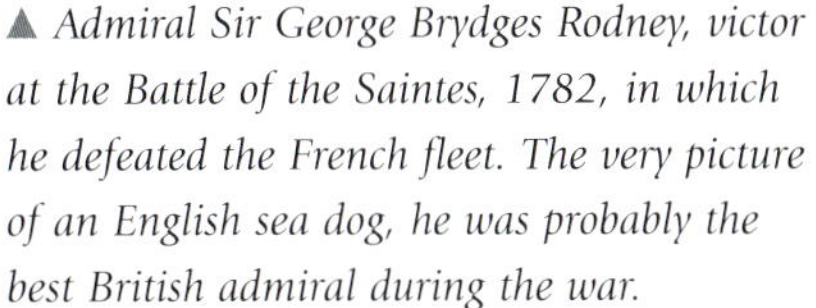

▲ *Admiral Sir George Brydges Rodney, victor at the Battle of the Saintes, 1782, in which he defeated the French fleet. The very picture of an English sea dog, he was probably the best British admiral during the war.*

▲ *John Paul Jones' ship* Bon Homme Richard *engaging the British* Serapis. *One of Jones' ships, the* Alliance, *commanded by the French Captain Landis, fired on the* Richard *during the action instead of assisting her.*

prisoner of war. This action was a decisive one in that it gave the British a much-needed victory in a failing war and thus more influence at the peace negotiations.

The Royal Navy's assets were stretched to the limits protecting the Empire and supporting land operations on the North American continent. It was challenged by the newly reborn French Navy, whose efforts during the war surpassed its performance in previous wars. Thanks to admirals such as Rodney and Hood, the Royal Navy survived, but it didn't win in the final tally, and the question of who controlled the sea lanes would be left to a much longer and much more bitter conflict in the years to come.

The war gave birth to a new naval service, and though the Continental Navy would be disbanded after the war, it would later be reborn as the genesis of the greatest naval force in military history, which would guard the sea lanes and man ships that could not even be imagined in the 1780s.

▼ Continental Navy Frigate, the Confederacy *This is the spar and sail plan of the* Confederacy, *which was built for speed and was larger than many contemporary frigates. She was also very ornate and was noted as being a "handsome" warship. However, she was not a lucky ship, and was finally captured by the British in 1781.*

SLOOPS, CORVETTES, BRIGS, SCHOONERS AND PRIVATEERS

Most of the naval war in American waters was on a much smaller scale. Individual ships, or modest combinations of vessels, fought and battered their way through the conflict.

Raiders

The British supply line to its army and fleet in North America was over 3,000 miles (5,000km) long. Re-supply vessels, the overwhelming majority carrying merchantmen, were usually grouped in convoys for protection, with escorts provided by the Royal Navy. Before the French entry into the war in early 1778, frigates or small

Sloop/Brig/Corvette Classes 1728–83

Class	Rate	Country	Guns	Type	Gun Decks
Nymphe	corvette	France	14	4-pounders	1
Wolf	sloop	Great Britain	14	4-pounders	1
Favourite	sloop	Great Britain	16	6-pounders	1
Calypso	corvette	France	16	4-pounders	1
Swan	sloop	Great Britain	14	6-pounders	1
Childers	brig	Great Britain	10	4-pounders	1
Naiade	corvette	France	20	8-pounders	1
Ranger	sloop	United States	18	6-pounders	1

▲ SCHOONER, THE *MARBLEHEAD*, 1768 *This is the plan of an excellent vessel, designed for speed and probably with a design based on the Bermuda sloop. Vessels of this type were used by both sides during the war and were excellent as revenue cutters, sloops used for scouting, and for privateers. It was a popular design and was continually improved upon through the War of 1812.*

▼ CONTINENTAL NAVY PRIVATEER, THE *RATTLESNAKE*, 1781 *This ship was an outstanding example of an American privateer designed with "extreme" lines because she was built for speed and not as a warship that would be able to slug it out in a ship-to-ship engagement. The* Rattlesnake *was captured by the Royal Navy in 1781 and was renamed by them as HMS* Cormorant.

Estimated Losses of Ships

Year	British		Allies	
	*M'men	P'teers	M'men	P'teers
1775	0	0	0	0
1776	229	5	19	6
1777	331	0	51	18
1778	359	5	232	16
1779	487	29	238	31
1780	581	15	203	34
1781	587	38	277	40
1782	415	1	104	68
1783	98	1	11	3
Total	3,087	89	1,135	216

* Merchantmen and Privateers

two-deckers of 44–50 guns were an adequate defence against the frigates of the Continental Navy and the privateers that sailed from American ports to prey on the British merchant fleet. Captain John Paul Jones, one of the best of the American captains, was a Scotsman, and a former slaver, who was successful at raiding close to the British Isles. His famous fight with HMS *Serapis*, a small two-decker, was the result of his attack on a British merchant convoy.

The entry of France into the war saw the first appearance of the newly rebuilt French fleet on the high seas, and this much more serious naval threat, along with the Spanish fleet, made the Royal Navy's mission much more difficult. The Royal Navy now faced a definite naval threat, and French warships were better designed and usually better sailers than their British counterparts.

Privateers from both sides of the Atlantic raided British commerce unmercifully, and the losses inflicted on the British merchant fleet were heavy, if not crippling.

▼ **Cutter, the *Lee*, 1776** *Originally American, but captured and put into service by the British, the* Lee *had one mast, was square rigged with a large spanker, and was not as good a sailer or fighting ship as the* Loyal Convert. *She was about the same size as a gundalow, but was fitted out as a larger vessel, which compromised her sailing abilities. She had both a raised quarterdeck and gunports.*

▲ **British Navy Brig, HMS *Carleton*, 1776** *This is one of the larger warships that was employed by the British on Lake Champlain. Brigs were two-masted vessels that worked very well on the large American lakes. Lake naval warfare was interesting in that the ships could be built with a shallower draft than seagoing vessels, although with the same features for types of ships, such as brigs and sloops. They also didn't need to carry as much on board, such as provisions for the crew, as they didn't stay away from port for such long periods of time. Control of the lakes was vital in North American warfare, a fact that became painfully evident to the British in the War of 1812.*

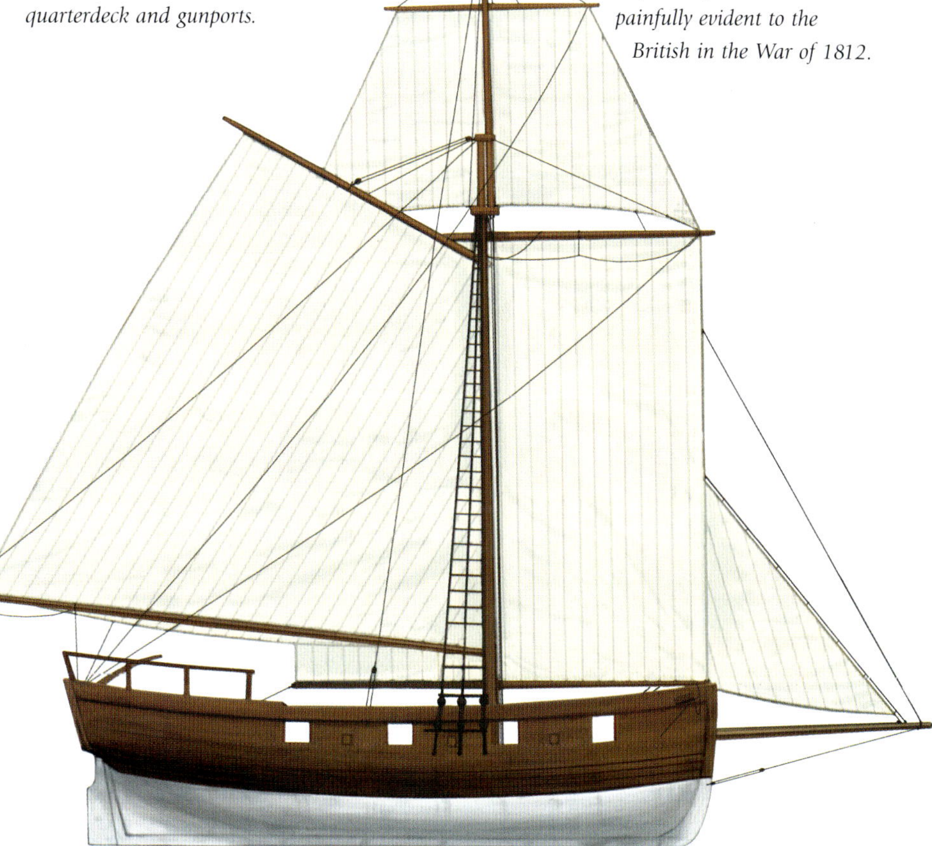

GUNBOATS, GUNDALOWS AND GALLEYS

Naval warfare was not confined to the high seas. The Great Lakes also saw action throughout the conflict, and fleets were built and destroyed on these expanses of freshwater.

Lake Champlain

Naval hostilities on Lake Champlain began on 11 October 1776, with the action at Valcour Island. The Americans, under Benedict Arnold, had a captured schooner, the *Royal Savage* (8 guns), his own schooner, a sloop, four galleys and eight gondolas or flat-bottomed boats.

The British had the schooner *Inflexible* (with 18 x 12-pounder guns it was the most powerful ship on the lake, and was dismantled and brought overland from St Lawrence), the *Carleton* (12 x 6-pounders), *Maria* (14 x 6-pounders), *Thunderer* (a *radeau*, or raft, with six 24-pounders, six 12-pounders and two howitzers), the *Loyal Convert* (seven 9-pounders) and 20 gunboats, each with a 24-pounder.

Schooner-rigged Vessels 1740–83

Class	Nomenclature	Country	Guns	Type
Mediator	sloop	Great Britain	10*	unknown
Mystique	xebec	France	18	unknown
Barbados	schooner	Great Britain	14	3-pounders
Fly	cutter	Great Britain	12	unknown
Chaleur	schooner	Great Britain	6**	3-pounders
Éclair	bark	France	18	6-pounders
Puce	cutter	France	6***	3-pounders
Espiegle	lugger	France	8	4-pounders
Lee	cutter	United States	6	mixed****
Levrette	cutter	France	18	6-pounders
Pigmy	cutter	Great Britain	10	4-pounders
Providence	schooner	United States	12	unknown
Fly	schooner	United States	6	9-pounders

* plus 18 swivel guns ** plus 7 swivel guns *** plus 10 swivel guns
**** probably carried a mixture of 4-, 9-, and 12-pounders

▼ **British Gunboat on Lake Champlain, 1776** *Control of the lakes, especially Lake Champlain, was vital to any army campaigning in the Northern states, as it was far easier to transport supplies by water than overland, where the few roads were no better than dirt tracks at the best of times. Gunboats were used by both sides for control of the lakes, and usually carried only one gun as shown.*

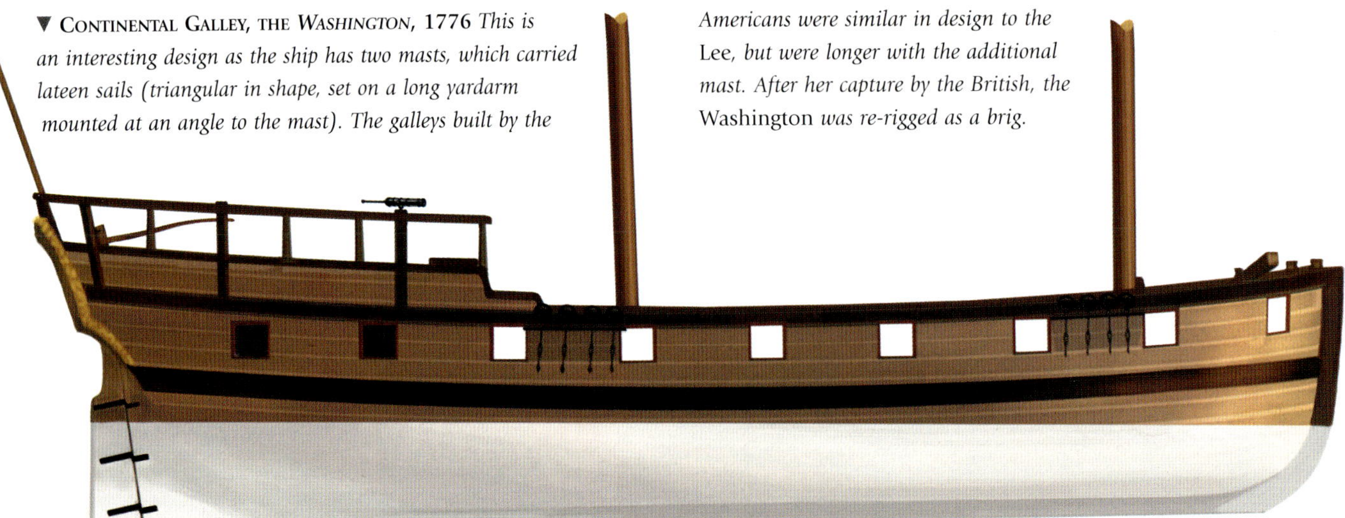

▼ **Continental Galley, the Washington, 1776** *This is an interesting design as the ship has two masts, which carried lateen sails (triangular in shape, set on a long yardarm mounted at an angle to the mast). The galleys built by the Americans were similar in design to the* Lee, *but were longer with the additional mast. After her capture by the British, the* Washington *was re-rigged as a brig.*

Lake Champlain was back under British control, but the year was now too far advanced for an effective invasion of the rebellious colonies to be mounted. The British withdrew north to St Johns on the River Richelieu and went into winter quarters. This was the end of the war on Lake Champlain. By enterprise and daring from a handful of colonists, the invasion of America from Canada had been thwarted. From a minor tactical defeat sprang a great strategic victory.

Both sides proved innovative on the lakes regarding the different types of warships used, getting the crews to man them, and building the different types of vessels far from shipyards, supplies, and shipwrights. The only plentiful supplies were trees. The operations required leadership of a high order as well as the ability to innovate, train landsmen to be sailors, and fight against hopeless odds. These skills were displayed by both sides.

▲ **HULL AND SAIL PLAN OF THE *LOYAL CONVERT*, LAKE CHAMPLAIN, 1776** *The* Loyal Convert *was a captured American gundalow for use on the lakes, and this is the hull and sail plan of that vessel. Gundalows were popular with the Americans, and captured vessels were also put to good use by the British. When the British captured an enemy vessel, they made detailed plans of her for the Admiralty. These plans are still in existence and give a highly accurate log of the ships involved in the war.*

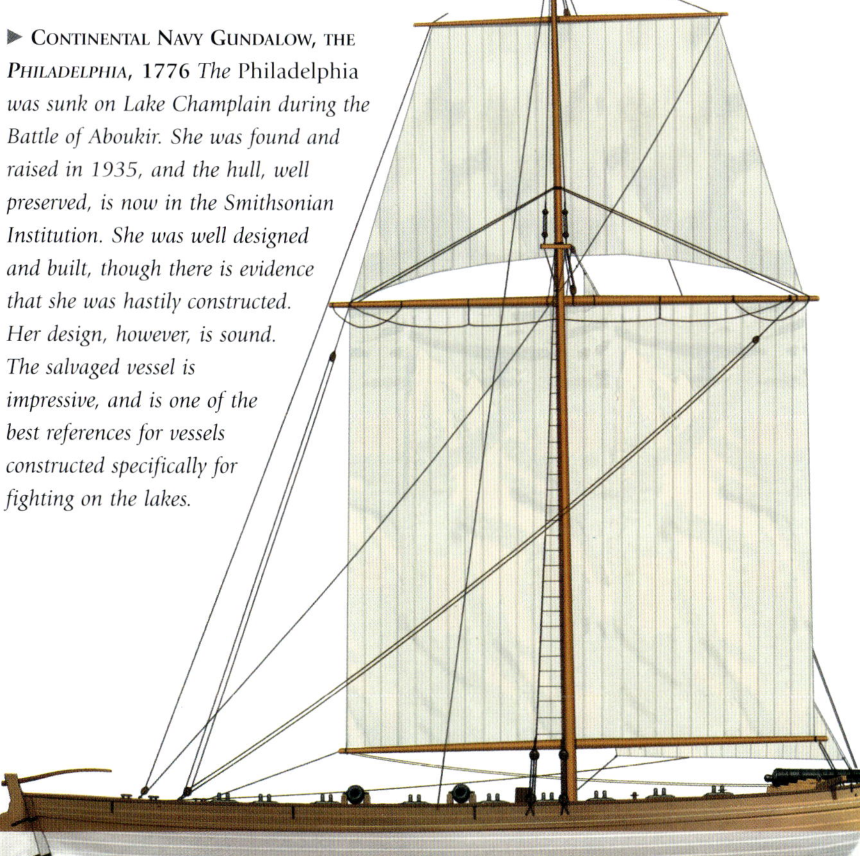

► **CONTINENTAL NAVY GUNDALOW, THE *PHILADELPHIA*, 1776** *The* Philadelphia *was sunk on Lake Champlain during the Battle of Aboukir. She was found and raised in 1935, and the hull, well preserved, is now in the Smithsonian Institution. She was well designed and built, though there is evidence that she was hastily constructed. Her design, however, is sound. The salvaged vessel is impressive, and is one of the best references for vessels constructed specifically for fighting on the lakes.*

During the action, the *Royal Savage* was taken by the British, but then burned and sunk; a gondola was also sunk. The Americans escaped south to Schuylers Island that night, but two more gondolas were so badly damaged that they had to be scuttled.

Captain Pringle then gave chase and forced Benedict Arnold to beach and set fire to two galleys and four gondolas. The Americans also lost over 80 killed and wounded; the British lost less than 40 men.

ROYAL NAVY OFFICERS

Unlike the American Navy, Britain's naval personnel benefited from a long-standing organization of distinguished lineage and established traditions.

Military Dress

In general, during this period, the officers of the Royal Navy were uniformed in blue and white. Uniforms were finally being standardized, and officers were to appear on deck in uniform at all times. Until recently, it had been quite normal for Royal Navy officers to sometimes wear civilian dress when at sea, but this practice was officially abolished in the mid-18th century.

Senior Officers

Admirals were authorized a dark blue coat, cut somewhat wide and meant to be comfortable to wear. There was no collar as such, but the top of the coat around the neck was edged with two bands of gold lace. The lapels and cuffs, both much wider than their army counterparts, were white. The coat was worn full – that is, there were no turnbacks. The waistcoat was long and generously laced with gold. The buttons of the coat were gold, marked out by gold lace, and the lapels were edged with gold lace. The pockets of the coat were also "picked out" in gold lace. The cuffs matched the lapels in that the buttons were gold, with gold buttonhole lace and edged with even more gold lace. The entire ensemble of coat and waistcoat therefore presented an impressive appearance, as it was undoubtedly intended to do.

The breeches and stockings were white, of very fine cloth, and the footwear consisted of the normal buckled shoe. Boots were not worn onboard ship. The cocked hat was the normal tricorne of the period and was bound with a broad band of gold lace. The national cockade,

◀ **Admiral, Undress, 1775–83** *The uniforms for officers of all ranks of the Royal Navy at the time of the American war were relatively simple, quite elegant and eye-catching, and had gone through a simplification process since the Seven Years' War. Orders dated 13 July 1767 and 23 January 1768 go into considerable detail on uniform requirements, stating how much lace would be worn by what grade. The admiral's dress was an all-purpose uniform, worn for almost every occasion. Lapels and cuffs were reduced in size, as was the gold lace.*

▶ **Captain, Full Dress, 1775–83** *This handsome and functional uniform was also prescribed by the 1767 regulations. Waistcoats and breeches were to be white and the buckled shoes were the same as those worn in civilian life. There were three items that were still up to the wearer to choose and were not laid out in the regulations. Stocks and cravats were numerous and varied, and it was up to the officer to choose the sword that he wore. Many officers probably had a dress sword, and they undoubtedly had a more sturdy one, along the lines of a cutlass, for combat.*

▲ LIEUTENANT, 1775–83 *Junior uniforms were of the same general design and pattern as those of their senior officers, but were much simpler, with less gold lace, narrower lapels, and cuffs of a different design, known as slashed cuffs. They may or may not have had cuff flaps as are shown here. Both captains and lieutenants would have undress frock coats, which were worn aboard ship and in combat. Hats were bound in black lace, unlike those of captains and flag officers, which were bound in gold lace. The cockade was the typical black British cockade, worn by the Royal Navy, the Marines and the Army. As in the case of his senior officers, a lieutenant's small clothes and stockings were white.*

black, was worn. Two items were left up to the individual: his sword and his cravat. Undoubtedly, the admirals of this period used a traditional and old-fashioned style of cravat. Swords could come in various forms: the hunting sword, rapier, or the military hanger would all have been in use.

Captains had a simpler uniform with the same general cut as the admirals', but the lace on the cuffs, lapels and collar would be thinner. The waistcoat would not, in all likelihood, have been laced in gold but would have been plain white and probably shorter. The hat lace would have been thinner, and the breeches, stockings and shoes would have been the same as the flag officers'. Hair styles for both were supposed to be powdered and clubbed, but at sea that practice was undoubtedly abandoned by the practical officers.

Junior Officers

Commanders and lieutenants would have worn a uniform of the same style as that of their captains, although the gold lace would again have been thinner on all parts of the uniform for the commander. Lieutenants would not have worn lace on their white lapels and cuffs. The tricornes of commanders would have had a thin band of gold lace; the lieutenants had no gold lace on their tricornes. They would arm themselves as they saw fit with respect to sidearms, unless their captain had a definite idea as to what sword they should wear. Most officers probably had at least two swords, one for full-dress occasions and one for sea duty and combat.

Midshipmen, many of whom were mere boys sent to sea to earn their way in the navy, were uniformed simply in blue and white with no gold lace. Buttons were gold, and the coats had no lapels but had white cuffs. The cocked hat had the usual cockade but no gold lace. They would only be awarded their gold lace after promotion to lieutenant.

▶ MIDSHIPMAN, 1775–83 *Midshipmen, most of whom started as boys as young as 12 years old, were first issued a uniform as early as 1748. However, nothing "official" is actually mentioned about their dress until 1787. Their small clothes were the same as the regular officers', and their coats were dark blue and unlaced. They had slashed cuffs and gold buttons (as all the officer ranks did). They wore a midshipman's dirk, which was a glorified knife, but in combat undoubtedly armed themselves with cutlasses if they were big enough to wield them effectively. They could have worn the hat as shown or an unlaced tricorne with a cockade. The instrument shown is a speaking trumpet which was used to magnify the voice for commands during combat or to hail other ships at sea.*

ROYAL NAVY SEAMEN

Working a sailing vessel became much more difficult as ships became larger. It was also dangerous, and death and injury were familiar hazards for all crews in all seasons.

Personnel

During this period the seamen of any one nation might very well be a polyglot force from some or all nations. Seamen drifted from one ship to another, and from one navy or merchant marine to another. It was also a very dangerous profession, whether or not there was a war going on, and there was inevitably pressure to fill the ranks and keep the crews up to strength. Captains could not always be too fussy about where their crew came from.

Petty Officers

The petty officer was the NCO of the naval services, and if the captain of the ship was considered supreme in power and authority, the petty officers were certainly as important for the enlisted sailors themselves. It was the petty officer who dealt with the men on a daily basis, and his authority was absolute. They were trusted, veteran seamen who taught the new sailors in a very hard school but drilled into them how to work the ship. If they were just, they took as good care of the ordinary seamen as they could. It was a hard life at sea, and it took proven professionals to do it.

Royal Navy petty officers were well-trained, experienced, professional seamen who were the effective backbone of the

◀ **Seaman, 1775–83** *There was no prescribed uniform for British seamen in the Royal Navy. Some crews merely wore their civilian clothes at sea. Others, who weren't cared for by their captain, merely wore rags. Treatment of this type is what led to the famous mutinies at Spithead and the Nore in the 1790s. This "jolly Jack" is dressed in clothing from the "slops", or the slop chest, which was "issue" clothing carried aboard ship. It is typical seagoing dress of the time, with the addition of a striped vest worn over a shirt. The ubiquitous clay pipe was undoubtedly a universal piece of equipment aboard ship, though fire was feared on a wooden warship more than anything else. The dried wood, tarred rigging, and ammunition magazine were all subject to the lethal spark that could destroy an entire ship.*

▶ **Seaman, 1775–83** *This is the popular view of the British sailor of the period. He is without a jacket here to show the typical checked shirt that would have been worn by a well-dressed crew. The captain of a ship was the closest thing to an absolute monarch who was not a crowned head. He had the power of life and death over his crew and ship and his skill as a combat leader and seaman, as well as how he treated the men in his charge, could determine if anyone came home in one piece or came home at all after a voyage.*

service. They undoubtedly adopted a type of uniform for themselves in an era when none was defined by regulations. A coat was worn, probably dark blue to match that of the officers. Waistcoats were also common, possibly red or brown in colour, and wide-cut trousers, which were very baggy, would extend to just below the knee. Stockings and the typical buckled shoes would also be worn. Neckerchiefs were traditional in the navy, and these would in all probability be black, although chequered patterns might also be worn. Petty officers would not usually be armed, unless the ship was going into combat. Headgear of some type would also be worn, either a tricorne or some type of locally manufactured boarding helmet made of leather, without a brim or peak. Petty officers usually carried a cane or a rope end to deal with any unenthusiastic sailors or the stubborn individual who needed some kind of "encouragement".

Seamen

What seamen wore was entirely up to the captain of the ship. There was no monarch in Europe who had the absolute and total authority that was enjoyed by the captain of a ship at sea. On some ships the seamen might be dressed in nothing but the remains of the civilian clothing with which they came on board. On others they might be issued with whatever was in the ship's "slop chest". Either way, they often presented a motley appearance.

Typical issued wear for the Royal Navy from ships' stores could be very similar to what the petty officers were wearing: wide trousers, stockings and buckled shoes, a waistcoat of red, brown, or even striped material, and a blue or brown coat of some type without lapels or cuffs. Buttons would be of yellow metal.

Another option might be a short blue coat, again with no lapels or cuffs, with yellow metal buttons, along with white or striped trousers extending to the ankle. The enlisted seaman, like the petty officer, would also wear some type of neckerchief, probably black, in order to hide the tar stains that came with working onboard ship. Ship wear, or "seagoing", was cut wide to be comfortable and to allow unimpeded movement, enabling the sailors to work the ship without being constrained by their clothing.

◄ **Seaman, 1775–83** *This is another type of universal seaman's dress in the Royal Navy. Aboard ship the sailors would seldom be armed unless they were going into combat. Arms were kept under lock and key for fear of mischief by the crew, which was one of the reasons marines were stationed on board warships. Royal Navy seamen had worn brown jackets for years, but blue was becoming popular during this period. There were no regulations governing the dress of seamen during this period and would not be for some time to come.*

► **Ship's Cook, 1775–83** *Life at sea was a dangerous occupation. Ships could be gone from the home ports for years at a time and men were killed or hurt both in peacetime and during war. This veteran, in the typical wide trousers and blue coat of a well-commanded ship, has had his share of hardship and undoubtedly combat. Veterans might be kept on by a loyal captain to serve as a cook or other supporting role.*

BRITISH MARINES

A ship's crew was composed not only of sailors but also some kind of naval infantry. The latter were to protect the ship's crew, board enemy ships and form landing parties. The Royal Navy had, since the 17th century, used marines for this purpose.

Marines in America

The British marines dated from 1664. They were not designated a Royal regiment until the early 19th century, when they were awarded this honour for their steadfast loyalty and performance during the great fleet mutinies at Spithead and the Nore during the French Revolutionary wars of the 1790s.

▲ **Naval Colour** *These are the colours flown by the triumphant John Paul Jones on the captured HMS* Serapis *as she was taken from the British as a prize into Texel, Holland, after the Battle of Flamborough Head on 23 September 1779.*

▼ **Naval Colour** *This is the so-called Gadsden Flag which was the colour of the commander in chief, Continental Navy. The rattlesnake had been a popular American emblem since Benjamin Franklin had done his "Join or Die" engraving urging the colonies to unite to fight against Britain.*

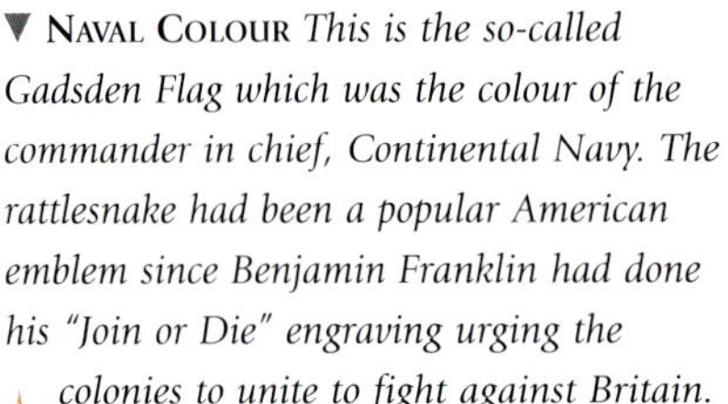

◀ **Private, British Marines, 1775–83** *Unless it is pointed out, it is nearly impossible to tell the difference between troops of an army regiment and those of the British marines. The uniform and equipment was the same, but the military function was not. Marines not only fought in land and sea battles, but also kept order aboard ship, always providing the captain with a group of highly disciplined, loyal men who would die to the last man rather than give up the ship they sailed on to any enemy, foreign or domestic.*

▲ **Naval Colour** *These two colours are British naval ensigns during the period. There was a third ensign flown, which consisted of a plain blue field, with the Union Jack in the upper left canton as the other two.*

The marines were a reliable, well-trained and disciplined force employed for maintaining discipline on board ship and for employment ashore as needed. Detachments on board ship were usually commanded by captains or senior lieutenants, and there were two battalions of marines stationed in Boston at the beginning of hostilities in 1775. They took part in the abortive mission to Lexington and Concord in April of that year, and in the bloody assaults on the American fortification on Breed's Hill in June.

The marines' respected and beloved commander, Major Pitcairn, was mortally wounded in the third and last assault on the Breed's Hill redoubt. Major Pitcairn had also been the senior

After the evacuation of Boston in early 1776, marines no longer served with the army ashore and resumed their normal duties as detachments onboard ship and were constantly employed as landing parties throughout the war.

Infantry-style Uniforms

The marines were armed and uniformed as infantry, and appeared, at first glance, to be very similar, if not identical, to regular British infantrymen. Marines, however, were different and separate from the army with separate regulations, traditions and functions. They were organized into companies and battalions, and they were assigned in detachments to the six rates of ships of the fleet. The smaller ships, such as sloops, brigs, bomb ketches, etc., did not carry marine detachments.

The marines' uniform during this period was cut in the same style as the army, was red or scarlet in colour, and was faced and lined in white. Collar, cuffs, lapels and turnbacks were all white, as were the waistcoat, breeches and stockings. Buttons were of white metal, and officers' lace was silver, as were their gorgets if worn. For duty ashore the privates, and probably the junior officers, wore black half gaiters. Field officers might wear boots, with spurs if mounted, as Major Pitcairn had at Lexington. Onboard ship all ranks would probably wear stockings and buckled shoes.

Equipment was the same as that for the regular army: two crossbelts, one for the cartridge box, the other for the bayonet. The grenadier companies might also carry a short sword, although this was undoubtedly not worn onboard ship. Grenadier companies would wear the bearskin cap, the cap plate bearing the motto *Nec aspera terrant* (Difficulties do not daunt), along with a fouled anchor device (an anchor with a length of rope wrapped around it). The light infantry companies had a kind of light infantry cap which was unique to them. It was in the shape of a pill box with a flat top and a flap that turned up in the front. Both grenadier and light infantry companies had "wings" on their shoulders to denote their elite status. The officers wore cocked hats with the usual British black cockade and the hats were bound in black lace. Privates of the battalion companies also wore cocked hats like those of the officers.

▲ **British Marine, 1775–83** *The marines also had flank companies as the army regiments of foot had. This is a marine grenadier and he would be uniformed in this manner for service ashore. Aboard ship the bearskin might be awkward to wear, especially if the grenadiers were in the fighting tops, but it would be worn as a mark of pride and of being in an elite company.*

officer on Lexington Green in April and the one who had ordered the rebels to disperse. This precipitated the "shot heard around the world" that started the war.

► **Officer, British Marines, 1775–83** *At this time, the British Marines were not yet a "Royal" formation, so their facing colours were not dark blue but white. They wore a simple, handsome uniform similar to their army contemporaries', with only specifics, such as buttons, denoting the differences.*

FRENCH ROYAL NAVY

France's Royal Navy was formed from an experienced body of men and equipped with excellent fighting vessels. It would prove a formidable opponent for the British.

Senior Officers

The French corps of naval officers, termed the *Grand Corps de la Marine* (and referred to as *officiers rouges*), were mostly, if not exclusively, drawn from the nobility. They believed firmly that their ships had to be preserved at any cost, regardless of the outcome of a sea action. Only a few of the senior commanders, such as de Grasse, Latouche-Treville and Suffren, believed in going in and finishing a fight gun-to-gun and ship-to-ship.

The basic French naval officer uniform was a dark blue coat with no lapels or collar, cuffed and lined with red. In full dress, admirals were authorized a dark blue coat with generous amounts of gold lace in a leaf pattern design. Three gold bands or rows in this pattern were around the cuffs, two rows along the coat edge, and one row along the seams of the sleeves. Gold epaulettes were on the shoulders to denote rank.

The gold trim extended around the colour from along the front of the coat, and there was also gold trim of the same pattern on the waistcoat. The pockets of the waistcoat and blue coat were also outlined in the patterned lace. The cocked hat was bound in gold tape, but solid, not in the pattern on the coat and waistcoat. The French cockade was white, the Bourbon colour. The Bourbons were the ruling house of France until 1792. The

◄ **Captain, Full Dress, 1778–83**
Besides the expensive full dress uniform authorized in 1756 French naval officers also had a less elaborate, cheaper undress uniform that was worn at sea and "on duty". It was the same basic cut, but was simpler in design and was definitely not as expensive. However, on a day of battle, if the captain actually owned full dress, he might well wear it and if he fell, would make a handsome corpse. French naval captains, while having the same life-and-death authority over their crews, were an independent lot and might or might not obey the orders of their admiral. They could very well be of a higher "nobility" rank than their admirals, which could make for a difficult command relationship.

▲ **Admiral, Full Dress, 1778–83**
The uniform for French flag officers was handsome and literally dripped with gold lace. It was also expensive and could very well set back their owners who, even though they were of the nobility, might not have the finances to back up the new purchase. The new uniforms were authorized in 1756 at the beginning of the Seven Years' War. The embroidery which marked the rank of French naval officers was very similar to that of their peers in the army.

waistcoat and breeches were red, and riding boots were worn, along with a white manchette at the top to protect the breeches. Hair was worn powdered and clubbed, as was the fashion, especially among nobles. If stockings and buckled shoes were worn, the stockings would be of white silk.

French captains wore two gold epaulettes on their shoulders and had only two rings of gold lace around their cuffs. One row of lace outlined their dark blue coats, and their pockets were outlined in patterned gold lace, in the same manner as the admirals. Red waistcoats were outlined in patterned lace along the outside and the pockets, following the admirals' style. Silk stockings and buckled shoes were worn, and the captains' cocked hats were the same as the admirals'. A white swordbelt was worn over the right shoulder, and swords were formal.

Junior Officers

French junior officers wore a single epaulette on one shoulder and had a single row of patterned lace along their coats and collars. They had a single band of gold lace at the cuff, and, like the captains, had no lace along the seams of their coat sleeves. Waistcoats were again red but laced in a much more simple and elegant manner, denoting their status as commissioned officers. Their breeches were blue, with white silk stockings and buckled shoes. Their cocked hats had no gold lace, but, like all officers, they wore the white cockade. They, and the captains, wore their hair powdered and clubbed, but on foreign service, certainly in the Indian Ocean with Suffren, they probably kept it their natural colour. Their swords were of the usual officer pattern, but on active service and in combat a more versatile weapon, such as a hanger or cutlass, or perhaps even a light cavalry sabre, was employed.

French midshipmen, known as officer candidates (*élèves de la marine*), were uniformed along the lines of a commissioned officer, but without the gold lace. Their uniform, like those of the British and Americans, was most likely blue apart from white stockings and buckled shoes. The navy functioned as an academy and the *élèves* learned their profession at sea, enduring the same hardships as the lowliest seaman. If they were competent enough, they could expect to be commissioned as a lieutenant.

◀ **Lieutenant, Full Dress, 1778–83** *Junior French naval officers had the same cut of uniform as their nominal superiors, with less corresponding lace to denote their naval rank. Again, they might be of a "higher" nobility than their senior officers, which could lead to discord aboard ship unless the captain was a tough, no-nonsense seaman who could discipline the crew and officers.*

▶ **Lieutenant, Naval Infantry, Full Dress at Sea, 1778–83** *While this officer is in naval dress, he is actually an officer of the naval infantry, another arm of the French navy. This naval officer would usually only wear his infantry uniform when leading troops ashore. When at sea he would dress like his companions who had regular officer billets aboard ship.*

FRENCH SEAMEN

The seamen who served in the French Navy were drawn from all over the maritime world, and the French Navy actively recruited men from among their allied nations and even among captured crews. France's own maritime traditions had ancient roots, strongest around Bordeaux (Gascony) and Brittany. It was these areas, together with Normandy, that provided a solid stream of enthusiastic recruits.

Petty Officers

The veteran petty officer was the equivalent of the sergeant in the land forces. Like their British counterparts, the French petty officers undoubtedly adopted a type of uniform that would set them apart from the privates for reasons of *esprit de corps* and to make themselves recognized both to the quarterdeck and to the privates. The petty officer was an authority to be obeyed at all times. Disobedience or showing disrespect to a petty officer were serious offences. The crime of striking one could result in the sentence of death. Their power over the crew was absolute.

French petty officers of the period had their work cut out for them. They not only had to train new crews, but had to endure the manner of the officers, most of whom were nobles, *petit* or otherwise, who made up the French naval officer corps. Commanders such as de Grasse and Suffren were few and far between, and the French captains maintained a great gulf between themselves and the lower deck, including the petty officers. In many ways the French petty officer found himself between the world of the privates and that of the officers, and he was not generally liked or trusted by either group.

As with their Royal Navy counterparts, they had no uniform regulations to go by. They wore much the same as a well-turned out enlisted sailor might wear, and probably carried a cane or rope end to persuade reluctant individuals from the lower deck to do their bidding. A coat of dark blue was undoubtedly worn, of better quality than an enlisted sailor might wear.

◀ **Petty Officer, 1778–83** *This is a typical French enlisted sailor of the period. Blue is probably the universal naval uniform colour. The tricorne for enlisted men is somewhat unusual, except for the French, and the sash is a typical piece of "equipment" for French sailors. French seamen usually enlisted by each cruise the particular ship would make, and French crews would not be either permanent or "militarized" until Napoleon became French head of state in 1799 and launched significant naval reforms.*

▶ **Ship's Boy, 1778–83** *Ship's boys were common aboard vessels of all navies. They were used as "powder monkeys" bringing ammunition to the gun decks from the magazine deep in the ship. Bare feet were also common aboard ship, and before going into action, decks might be sanded so that the sailors would not slip in the blood and mess that accompanied actions at sea.*

▲ **SEAMAN, 1778–83** *Another typical French seaman, although this figure is wearing sabots, the wooden shoes, or clogs, which were commonly worn by the working class of France. Sabots were quite practical, more comfortable than they looked, easy to take care of, and long-lasting. French soldiers would also wear them on campaign once the Revolution got well underway in the 1790s.*

Trousers, stockings, buckled shoes and a hat would also be worn. Neckerchiefs, again, would be worn by both the sailors and petty officers, and any petty officer worth his salt would endeavour to stand out in the crew to denote his rank and status.

Seamen

How seamen were clothed was entirely up to the captain of the ship. The captain's authority being absolute, having the power of life and death over his crew, the seamen were generally at his mercy in all matters. If seamen of the period from the navies of Great Britain, the United States and France were seen together, there would be no outstanding difference in their dress by which to tell them apart. They might be in a combination of civilian and naval attire. Sometimes, however, because of the care the captain might take on his ship to have everything in a neat and naval appearance, the enlisted sailors might all be wearing similar clothing and actually have a uniform.

The best French seamen came from Normandy and Brittany. Apparently, the best bosuns (boatswains) came from Gascony. They were reputed to be always full of brag and talk, but tough and enduring.

Common items that were worn included some type of headgear, either of tarred or boiled leather for protection on board ship and in combat. The hat could have some kind of ship's device on it, such as the ship's name. A coat of some type, usually blue with either yellow or white metal buttons, buckled shoes (stockings optional), and some variety of trousers completed the costume. The popular types of trouser were those that came to the knee or just below the knee, cut very wide for comfort and ease of movement, or longer trousers to the ankle that could be white, white with red or blue stripes, or any colour that was available. Waistcoats were usually worn for warmth and protection and could be red, white, brown, or blue. Chequered or striped waistcoats were also worn. Shirts could be plain, chequered or striped. Leather belts were worn around the waist to keep the trousers up and to hold tools or weapons when in combat. Weapons were only issued to the privates when combat was imminent, as mutinies could be a convenient way of ridding a ship of an unpopular captain or to relieve boredom.

▲ **SEAMAN, 1778–83** *Seamen would only be this well armed if they were called on for a close action at sea, or to join a cutting-out party, or become part of a landing party. For the rest of the time arms would be kept locked away. Sailors as well as the naval infantry or army "garrisons" of warships were used aboard ship as marines to fire from the fighting tops or to lead boarding parties against a still hostile enemy. The blue and white checked shirt was commonly worn by seamen of many nationalities at this time, as were the striped trousers, made from strong, hardwearing cotton. Black neckerchiefs were also a universal naval item, as black material hid tar stains.*

FRENCH NAVAL ARTILLERY AND NAVAL INFANTRY

French seamen were, for the most part, a very unmilitary group of men, possessing a well-developed sense of individuality, which could make them a challenging group to command and lead. To make things more complicated, two very different organizations made up the Royal Navy of Louis XVI: the Corps Royal de l'Infanterie de la Marine and the Bombardiers de la Marine. The first organization was naval infantry (and it was not a marine corps in the sense that the British and Americans had marines) and the second was the naval artillery arm.

Besides having an odd organization, the French navy had a very odd philosophy of combat. French officers were taught to save their ships at all costs, even if it meant losing a battle. This was completely foreign to the traditions of the Royal Navy, whose captains were expected to win at any cost and could very well face a court martial if they lost, no matter what the circumstances were.

There were aggressive French commanders: de Grasse in the West Indies and Suffren in the Indian Ocean are fine examples of admirals who did more than their assigned duty, but many times they were failed by the captains under them, and robbed of decisive victories over their British opponents.

Corps Royal de l'Infanterie de la Marine

In 1772 there were eight regiments of naval infantry raised to serve as ship's detachments of infantry. This structure proved somewhat unwieldy, and in December 1774 they were reorganized as 100 companies of naval infantry to serve as ship's garrisons (*garnisons*). These companies were stationed at the

◄ **Officer, French Navy (Corps Royal de l'Infanterie de la Marine), 1775–83** *The French were unusual among the great naval powers in that they did not have marines or a marine corps during this period. This officer belongs to the naval infantry who were actually sailors, not marines. The difference may be subtle, but is important. Officers of the naval infantry possessed both naval and infantry uniforms. Their naval uniforms were worn when they were embarked and/or afloat, while for service ashore they wore their infantry uniform.*

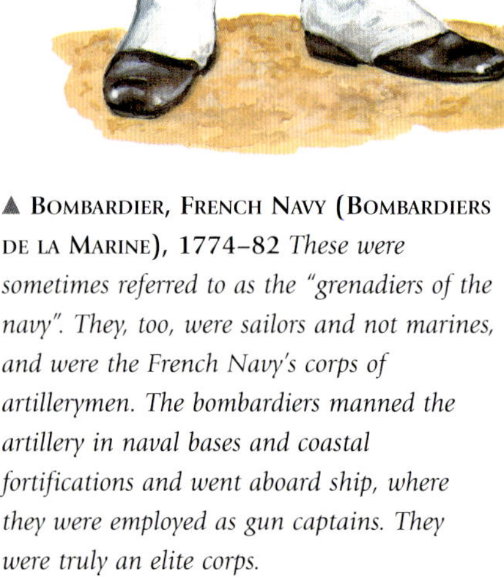

▲ **Bombardier, French Navy (Bombardiers de la Marine), 1774–82** *These were sometimes referred to as the "grenadiers of the navy". They, too, were sailors and not marines, and were the French Navy's corps of artillerymen. The bombardiers manned the artillery in naval bases and coastal fortifications and went aboard ship, where they were employed as gun captains. They were truly an elite corps.*

three great French naval ports of Brest, Toulon and Rochefort. Fifty companies were sent to Brest, and 30 to Toulon. Rochefort got the remaining 20. Company strength was three officers and 118 other ranks. All of the companies were sent to sea during the war, and some served ashore during the Siege of Yorktown.

The uniform of the Corps Royal de l'Infanterie de la Marine consisted of dark blue coats and breeches, the coats being lined blue. Collars, cuffs, lapels and epaulette straps were red and buttons were of yellow metal. Long white grand gaiters were worn that reached above the knee. One shoulderbelt was worn and this carried the cartridge box and bayonet scabbard, and a waistbelt that carried an infantry short sword (*briquet*) was worn. Cocked hats bound with yellow tape were worn with the French white national cockade; officers' hats were trimmed in gold lace. Officers' buttons were gold. Waistcoats could be either blue or red.

Officers wore the same uniform as the men did when they were ashore and would wear navy uniform onboard ship. Officers wore a sword on a white waistbelt, and had a pair of gold epaulettes and a gold gorget with a silver device embossed in the centre.

Drummers wore the king's livery of dark blue coats with Bourbon lace, along with a red waistcoat.

Artillerymen and Gunners

The Bombardiers de la Marine were artillerymen and were considered elite troops and wore the grenadiers' bearskin because of it. All ranks wore the bearskin. The uniform was similar to that of the naval infantry with the following differences: all ranks wore red waistcoats, and the dark blue uniform coats were lined red, so the coat turnbacks were red. The bearskin cap had a brass plate on the front with an embossed flaming grenade, the symbol of elite troops, in the centre of the plate. There were only three companies of these artillerymen, and they were either employed as artillerymen or grenadiers when in the infantry role. Both the artillery and naval infantry were armed with the Charleville musket.

◄ **DRUMMER, FRENCH NAVAL INFANTRY, 1775–83** *This musician is in royal livery, as the naval infantry were designated a royal regiment. The emblem on the front of the drum would be the arms of France. Note the method for carrying the drum on the march or for coming aboard ship, which was typical of any infantry unit. The rope, or leather straps, that hung from the bottom of the drum were made to order for this function.*

► **FUSILIER, FRENCH NAVY (CORPS ROYAL DE LA MARINE), 1775–83** *This is an enlisted naval infantryman. In French, the term "marine" means "of the navy", and not marine as it does in English. They served aboard ship and were employed ashore. During the Yorktown campaign the French fleet landed 800 naval infantrymen to support the operations ashore. While the uniform is similar, except in colour, to infantry uniforms of the regular army, the buttons and turnback ornaments, if any, would be naval in character.*

NAVAL GARRISONS

The French Navy of the period had no marines on the model of either the British Marines or the Continental Marines. They did have naval infantry (*l'infanterie de la Marine*), and the naval artillery arm was an elite branch of the service that either went to sea on French warships or manned artillery ashore. However, the shortage of suitable troops to serve as marines was taken up by *garnisons* of detachments from infantry regiments of the army.

When the *Bon Homme Richard*, named after Benjamin Franklin's *Poor Richard's Almanac*, was commissioned by John Paul Jones, his detachment of marines was formed by 140 officers and men from France's Walsh Regiment. These were Irishmen in French service. They were uniformed in the usual red uniforms of Irish regiments and formed a reliable core for Jones' crew in their epic fight with HMS *Serapis*. The Dillon Regiment also served on board ships.

WALSH REGIMENT. This was numbered 95 in the French line, was uniformed in red (or scarlet) with blue lapels and cuffs, yellow collar and yellow metal buttons. The Irish regiments in the French service had an excellent reputation, especially distinguishing themselves at the Battle of Fontenoy in 1745 under Maurice de Saxe. These were the famous Wild Geese, who had fled their native Ireland rather than fight for the English. At this point in their history, they were not purely an Irish regiment any longer, and privates of other nationalities were enlisted to keep their strength up. However, the cadre was undoubtedly solidly Irish, which kept the character of the regiment intact.

◄ COMPANY GRADE OFFICER, FRENCH INFANTRY REGIMENT WALSH, 1775–81 *Many times regular French infantry regiments provided naval "garrisons" aboard ship, for service as marines. A detachment from the Irish Regiment Walsh, one of the original Wild Geese émigré regiments from Ireland, who refused to serve the British in the late 17th century, was assigned to Captain John Paul Jones for his flagship. They served gallantly in the deadly fight with HMS* Serapis *and suffered heavy losses. Petty officers were usually seamen who had risen from the ranks. Many carried rope ends to "encourage" recalcitrant crew members in their duties.*

French Regiments with Detachments at Sea

Regiment	Regimental Number
Champagne	3
Austrasie	4
Armagnac	6
Normandie	9
Auxerrois	12
Agenois	14
Fores	16
Auvergne	17
Gatinois	18
Viennois	22
Brie	25
Poitou	26
Dauphin	30
Touraine	34
La Sarre	52
Condé	56
Royal Artillerie	64
Beauce	71
Monsieur	78
Foix	86
Dillon	90
Walsh	95
Enghien	96

DILLON REGIMENT. This was numbered 90 in the French line and they also wore the traditional red coats, had yellow lapels and cuffs, a red collar and white metal buttons. This regiment also served at the failed Siege of Savannah in 1779, where it again distinguished itself.

Uniforms On Board Ships

Aboard ship, troops of the *garnison* would usually wear a seagoing uniform when off-duty or on fatigue duty (from which grenadiers were exempt). It usually consisted of a light overcoat (*capote* or *redingote*), white in colour with collar and cuffs in the regimental facing colours, the pokalem fatigue cap, a pair of trousers, usually undyed (so they would look buff in colour, as the wool was left in its natural appearance), socks and buckled shoes, usually an older pair. The *capote* would have epaulette straps the colour of the coat, and the men would probably be wearing their crossbelt as if for drill.

▼ **Private, French Infantry Regiment Walsh, *Bon Homme Richard*, 1775–81** *The Irish regiments that formed the famous Irish Brigade in the service of France stayed in French service until the Revolution. By this time it is doubtful that the Irish regiments, were still made up of native Irish, but they still wore the same distinctive uniforms.*

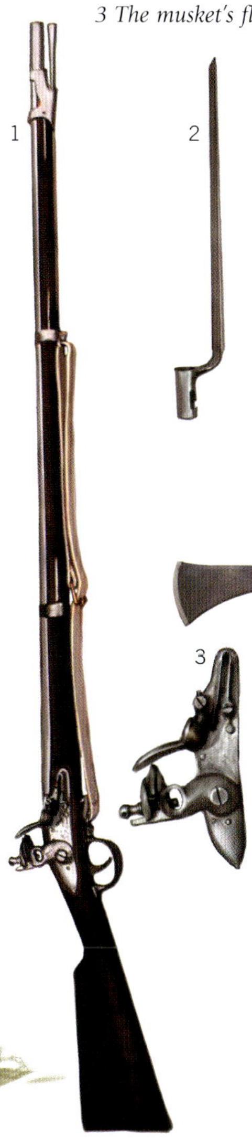

The regular French regiments that had detachments serving at sea as *garnisons* on warships is shown in the table, left. Additionally, detachments from Bombardiers de la Marine, Corps Royal de l'Infanterie de la Marine, 1st Légion Volontaires étrangers de la Marine, Volontaires de Bouille, Canoniers-bombardiers des Iles-du-Vent, 3rd Légion Volontaires étrangers de la Marine, Volontaires de Bourbon, and the Regiment Ile-de-France, as well as sepoys from India served as ship *garnisons* during the war in different theatres.

▼ **Private, French Infantry Regiment Walsh, Kit** *1 The French-issue musket, commonly called the Charleville from one of the factories in which it was manufactured. Many sources consider it superior to the British Brown Bess. 2 The issue bayonet. 3 The musket's flintlock mechanism.*

1

2

3

4

5

▲ **Fusilier, French Navy, Barrois Regiment, Shipboard dress, 1775–81** *This is a typical working uniform for soldiers assigned as garrisons aboard French warships. It is practical and comfortable and saves wear and tear on regimental dress.*

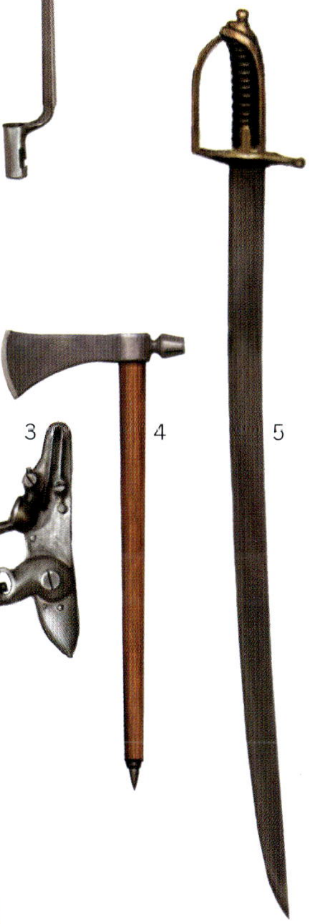

◀ **French Infantry Weapons used on Board Ship, 1775–81** *4 A tomahawk or hatchet. The naval term was "boarding axe" and this weapon could be useful in the rough fighting when boarding an enemy vessel. It could also be used to cut away damaged rigging during and after a sea fight. 5 Naval cutlass, a preferred weapon for officers and enlisted men alike.*

CONTINENTAL NAVY OFFICERS

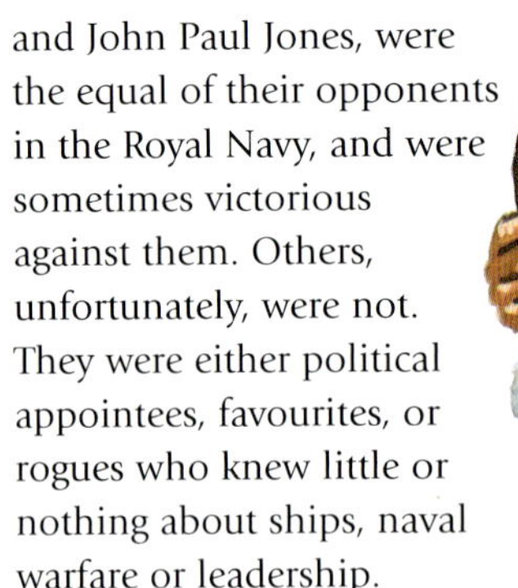

America's navy was born and raised in the war and went from nothing to an experienced and relatively capable force in a matter of years. Everything, from uniforms to rank designations, was started from scratch.

Officers of the New Navy

American naval officers were selected by Congress and should have been either experienced merchant captains or officers with combat experience, of which there were undoubtedly few. The better American officers, such as John Barry, Joshua Barney and John Paul Jones, were the equal of their opponents in the Royal Navy, and were sometimes victorious against them. Others, unfortunately, were not. They were either political appointees, favourites, or rogues who knew little or nothing about ships, naval warfare or leadership.

The Continental Navy was not initially a war-winning force, but there were victories and successes from time to time that allowed the Americans to build a tradition of excellence that would reap rewards in later conflicts.

Senior Officers

There were no admirals in the Continental Navy, the highest rank being commodore, which was an appointment for a senior captain in command of more than one vessel at sea (a flotilla or squadron), rather than an actual rank. In such a case, the designated officer would wear his captain's uniform. While there were uniform regulations for American naval officers, they were certainly not followed in all cases. John Paul Jones was an outstanding example of individualism, wearing a uniform of his own choice. The regulation captain's uniform consisted of a dark blue coat lined red, with red collar, cuffs and lapels. A red waistcoat with gold braid along the outline of the garment and the pockets, much like that of a French captain, was accompanied by dark blue breeches, white silk stockings and buckled shoes and a cocked hat with a black cockade

▶ **Captain in Regulation Dress, 1775–81** *This is an example of the regulation uniform of a Continental Navy captain. It is handsome and lavishly decorated with gold buttons and braid. It is basically modelled on the captains' uniforms of the Royal Navy, with the exception that the facing colour is red or scarlet instead of white. American Continental Navy captains, however, were allowed to design or adapt their own uniforms, as John Paul Jones did.*

◀ **Midshipman, 1775–81** *Midshipmen's uniforms were simple, and American midshipmen had the same purpose as those in the Royal Navy. They were apprentice officers and were there to learn their trade before sitting for their commissions. At sea and in combat, these boys endured the same dangers and hardships as the rest of the crew.*

bound in black lace. Buttons were of yellow metal.

John Paul Jones was uniformed in a striking outfit comprising a dark blue coat faced and lined with white, much on the pattern of a British captain. That choice on his part might have been influenced by his operations around the British coast. He also uniformed his marine detachment in red and white. His vessels could quite easily pose as a British warship in those waters.

Jones' uniform coat was unique, and he outdid his British counterparts in elegance and flamboyance. The dark blue coat had no collar, but had two gold epaulettes and also had gold buttonhole lace. The buttons were of yellow metal. The breeches and stockings were white, and he wore the usual buckled shoes. He carried the usual officers' sword. The white waistcoat was trimmed in gold lace, including the pockets, and the white cuffs were treated the same as the lapels, with gold buttonhole lace, and trimmed in gold. His cravat was white. His black tricorne was the only regulation part of his uniform, bound in black lace and with a black cockade.

A hard, driving commander, and a relentless fighter, Jones overcame great odds in his old *East Indiaman* fighting the newer, faster HMS *Serapis* off Flamborough Head in a desperate attempt to capture the Baltic convoy. His guns included some the French had condemned, and some in his main battery exploded at the beginning of the fight, killing their crews. He refused to surrender when summoned by his British counterpart, and fought on with the smaller quarterdeck guns until he toppled the *Serapis*' main mast. The British captain, his deck swept by American fire and many of his crew dead or wounded, asked for quarter. After abandoning the sinking *Bon Homme Richard*, Jones and his surviving crew watched her slide beneath the sea, old and worn out, yet gallant in victory.

◀ **Junior Officer, 1775–81** *Junior naval officers had a less ornate version of the captain's uniform, and it was quite handsome in appearance, again modelled on that of the Royal Navy. At sea, hair would not be powdered, but left its natural colour. At this time, though, the fashion of powdering hair was starting to disappear.*

▶ **Captain John Paul Jones, Continental Navy, 1779** *John Paul Jones was born in Scotland. Before the war, he had been a merchant seamen and a slaver, and knew his profession thoroughly. He was intelligent, combative, insubordinate, tough, maintained strict discipline, loved to fight, and never lost an engagement at sea. Unfortunately, the Continental Navy had too few captains of Jones' calibre. This blatantly non-regulation uniform was typical of Jones.*

Junior Officers

The authorized uniform for junior American naval officers was much the same as for captains. They wore a dark blue coat lined and lapelled in red with yellow buttons. A red waistcoat and dark blue breeches completed the outfit, which had no gold lace or epaulettes. Cocked hats were the same for all officer grades.

Midshipmen wore a dark blue coat cuffed blue and lapelled in sky blue. They had a red waistcoat and on board ship wore white trousers like the enlisted seamen. Their hat was a black roundhat without lace or cockade; they wore buckled shoes and were armed with a midshipman's dirk or a cutlass.

PETTY OFFICERS AND SEAMEN

Fortunately, the American colonies could draw on experienced seamen and a maritime tradition as they sought to organize a united navy. However, it would take time, and bitter experience, before a capable, centralized force emerged.

Birth Pangs

The Continental Navy was born on 13 October 1775. The new United States was a seagoing nation, accustomed to the maritime arts and with thriving seaports at Boston, New York, Charleston, Savannah, Wilmington and Philadelphia. In addition, there was no lack of qualified seamen for the new Continental Navy.

The Americans were also no strangers to shipbuilding, either merchant vessels or warships. The first warship built for the Royal Navy in the colonies was in 1690 when HMS *Falkland* was built in Portsmouth, New Hampshire. Colonial shipwrights and designers were fully capable of building warships, and the sturdy frigates that they would turn out for the Continental Navy were an outstanding class of ships. It is a pity that most of the officers that commanded these vessels were not up to the challenge. But with these hard beginnings would come experience that would bear fruit later.

Petty Officers

The most telling lack in both the Continental Army and Navy was a solid NCO corps. If there was one great weakness in the Continental Navy, it was the lack of experienced petty officers to assist in running the ship and training the crews. As the war went on, good petty officers came to the fore, and good captains, such as Jones and Barney, would not have achieved anything without petty officers who knew their business. They had to be tougher than the seamen they were in charge of.

American petty officers were probably uniformed in a double-breasted dark blue coat of "naval" cut with a white or chequered shirt underneath. The typical sailor's black neckerchief was also worn and the

◄ PETTY OFFICER, 1775–81 *Petty officers ran the ships for the officers and had to be efficient, tough men. They were usually professional seamen who had risen from the ranks. Many carried rope ends to "encourage" the recalcitrants in the crews to demonstrate more zeal in the performance of their duties.*

► SEAMAN, 1775–83 *Seamen were multi-national and American crews also had black freedmen as part of their crews. This became a tradition, and after the war, merchant ships sailed from US ports, especially in New England, with freed slaves being a significant part of the crews. The US Navy never had problems enlisting black sailors and during the Civil War 30,000 of them served in the United States Navy.*

buttons were of yellow metal. Long, loose trousers of white or buff colour were worn with stockings and buckled shoes, along with a hat of leather or perhaps straw. Again, the cane and rope end were not only badges of rank, but symbols of company punishment.

Seamen

Again, what seamen wore was entirely down to the whim of the captain of the ship. Good captains would ensure that there was a supply of serviceable clothing on board ship to issue to new crewmen. Dark blue or brown coats were usual, and a shirt and waistcoat combination was usually worn underneath the coat. Shoes were usually of the buckled type, although laced shoes could also have been worn.

Trousers were loose, of white, red or blue striped white, or light brown material, and were comfortable to wear. Well-dressed and uniformed seamen could be seen on some Continental Navy vessels, dressed like the petty officers described above.

Some captains would neglect their sailors, and did not care about their dress or appearance, and the seamen would end up dressed in rags. This could lead to trouble, indiscipline or worse, and the intelligent officer would ensure his crew was well taken care of and looked after, as the terms of the day went.

▲ **Seaman, 1775–81** *This well-outfitted seaman would be considered lucky to be dressed this well at sea. The dark blue jacket is typical naval wear, as are the warm woollen socks and the wide cotton duck trousers.*

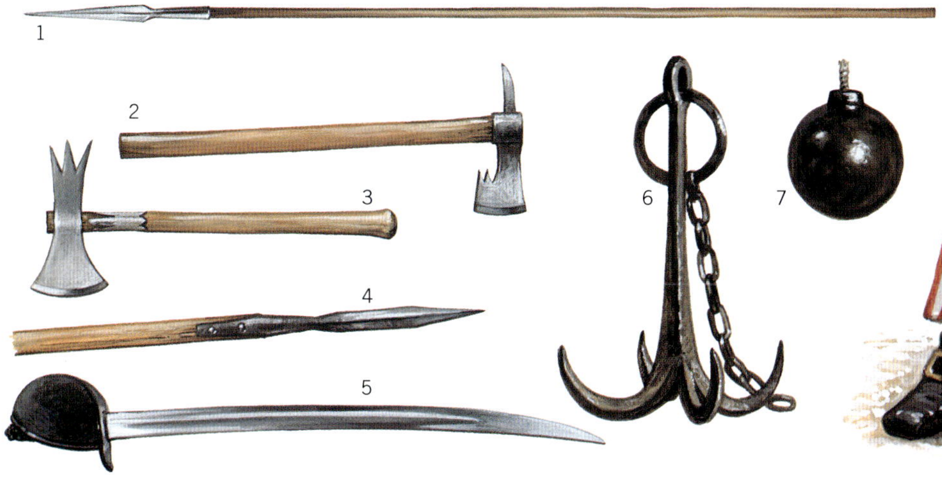

► **Seaman, 1775–81** *Another example of a well-dressed seaman, this time in a green jacket and striped trousers that could have been made out of bed ticking, which was popular in the army as well. It was tough material that could be expected to last throughout the rough work in which sailors engaged at sea, in storms, and in combat.*

▼ **Boarding Party Weapons** *1 A boarding pike – very useful when defending a ship against the enemy's boarders. 2 & 3 Two more examples of boarding axes. These are double-bladed, so either end can be used. 4 Detail of the tip of the boarding pike. 5 Another type of naval cutlass. 6 Grappling hook, used when boarding another ship. It was attached to a rope and was thrown across to the other ship, holding the ships together. 7 Hand grenade. The fuse was lit, and the bomb thrown at the opponent's ship.*

1 2 3 4 5 6 7

CONTINENTAL MARINES

America's marines were raised just a month after the Continental Navy had been established. They were to provide the sailors with armed support, defending the ships or going onshore as landing parties.

The Continental Marines were formed on 10 November 1775 in Tun's Tavern in Philadelphia, and were the only armed service of the United States to be founded in a bar. As Marine Corps tradition would have it, the men were recruited in the traditional British manner, by way of the recruiting party, with a fifer and drummer, literally "drumming up" recruits in the streets of Philadelphia and leading them to the tavern where they were plied with drink by the recruiting officer or sergeant. They were then "primed", given a shilling (in this case not a king's shilling but undoubtedly one issued by Congress), signifying their voluntary enlistment. Whether or not any of them were allowed second thoughts or to express reluctance when they sobered up the next day is not recorded.

Organization

The marines were initially authorized as a battalion in strength, and generally kept at that level throughout the war. They were modelled on the British marines and their initial traditions, kept until the present time, were also modelled on their British forebears. They were a well-disciplined and trained arm of the service and served at sea as ships' detachments, and were also engaged at times on land with the Continental Army. They served ashore in the Trenton/Princeton campaign and were noted for their useful service by Washington.

Service Afloat

The Continental Marines performed the same function as that of the British marines. They served as detachments onboard warships that manned the

◄ **Officer, Continental Marines, 1775**
The Continental Marines were raised on 10 November 1775 at Tun's Tavern in Philadelphia. They were always a small organization, and were known for the smartness of their uniforms, their discipline, and their fighting ability. They served both at sea and ashore, and fulfilled the same duties as their British forebears. The officer's uniform was the same as that of the enlisted men, except for the headgear.

▲ **Private, Continental Marines, 1775**
Dark green was chosen as the marines' uniform colour, faced and lined with white. It was simple, elegant, and completely functional. The handsome roundhat, jauntily turned up on one side, was an excellent choice for service at sea. More utilitarian and comfortable than the usual tricorne, it was also very military in appearance.

"fighting tops" in the masts and rigging during combat and sometimes, if necessary, served as gun crews. They made up the bulk of the landing parties that went ashore either to raid or to take objectives. They formed the disciplined portion of the landing party, and also assisted the ship's officers in keeping the crew in good order when at sea.

Their uniforms were of the same cut as those designated for the Continental Army. They were green coats faced and lined initially in white, the facings later being changed to red in 1778 or 1779. Their equipment was the same as that used by the army, as were their arms and accoutrements. It was difficult at times to procure enough material for such items as the crossbelts for privates' equipment, so only one belt might be worn for the cartridge box, and the bayonet would then be carried on a waistbelt frog. Buttons were of white metal, and the officers' lace and distinctions were silver. Rank distinctions were the same as for the Continental Army.

The privates wore a roundhat, turned up on the left side, with the black cockade also on the left. The hat was bound in white tape. Officers wore the tricorne bound in black lace with the black cockade. All ranks wore white waistcoats, light buff breeches, and grey stockings (although these were white for officers), along with black buckled shoes.

Drummers did not wear reversed colours, but the same uniform coat as everyone else. The device displayed on the drum itself was a coiled rattlesnake, with the motto "Don't Tread on Me" on a white background.

Service Onshore

For service on dry land, marines would wear black half gaiters, but when on board ship stockings and shoes would be the normal wear. Interestingly, John Paul Jones' marine detachment on board the *Ranger* was probably uniformed in red and white for "tactical" purposes, although they have also been portrayed in the regulation uniform, in order to make them seem like British troops.

The Continental Marines were disbanded at the end of the war, in 1783, but came roaring back in 1798, renamed the United States Marine Corps, which is still in existence today. The American Navy undoubtedly needed a few good men to keep discipline on board ship once again.

◀ **Drummer, Continental Marines, 1775** *Curiously, Continental Marine musicians did not wear reversed colours as those in the army did, but wore the same uniform as officers and enlisted men. Playing the drum aboard ship to any kind of regular rhythm must have been an interesting exercise. Note the emblem on the drum, which is a Continental Navy crest also used on naval ensigns. The motto reads "Don't tread on me".*

▶ **Private, Continental Marines, 1779** *In 1779 the facing colour of the Continental Marines was changed to red and remained so for the rest of the war. The Marines were disbanded after the war along with the navy. They would be re-raised in 1798 as the United States Marines, and the uniform colour would be changed to dark blue, with a temporary return to dark green in the 1820s.*

GUN CREWS

Manning and firing an artillery piece on a moving platform requires technical training and repetitive drill to be effective. The first priority is to load and fire the piece safely without injuring any friendly crewmen or damaging your own ship. Speed in loading and firing comes with practice. In action, when it seemed as if all hell had broken loose, especially on gun decks inside the ship, the smoke and noise would be terrifying, and only well-trained and well-drilled gun crews would be effective.

Crew Drill

The guns would be attached to the side of the ship by a system of blocks, tackles and stout ropes. These would retard the recoil of the piece as there was no recoil system on period artillery. The entire piece recoiled, i.e. went to the rear violently, when the piece was fired. The blocks and ropes also enabled the crew to quickly get the piece back into battery – the position to load and fire again.

The normal gun crew onboard ship consisted of six men. The gun captain commanded and pointed (aimed) the piece, and ratings would be numbered in the crew to carry and load the round, ram the round, stop the vent, fire the piece and swab the gun tube after firing. The ammunition consisted of a powder charge and the round itself, which would go down range after firing, and hopefully hit the target. To load the piece the powder cartridge went in first, then a piece of wadding, the round and another piece of wadding (wadding was usually made from yokum and then tied up with twine). Then the powder bag was pierced with the vent pricker, so that the primer or priming powder, when lit, would ignite

▼ CANNON *This is a typical piece of naval ordnance aboard ship complete with its tackle. This clearly demonstrates how a gun carriage was attached to the side of the ship at the gunport. The ropes and tackles retarded the gun's recoil and by pulling on the ropes the gun could quickly be pulled back into battery for the next broadside, even in rough seas.*

► GUNNER *This is a naval gunner as he would appear at sea, possibly at night on watch or making his rounds on the gundeck. Fire was a constant fear at sea, and the ship itself was a fire hazard. Tarred rigging and the dried-out wood made people careful, and even the small flame from the candle in a lantern could cause problems. Working in and around the magazine required having nothing, including shoes, that might cause a spark, and special slippers were issued.*

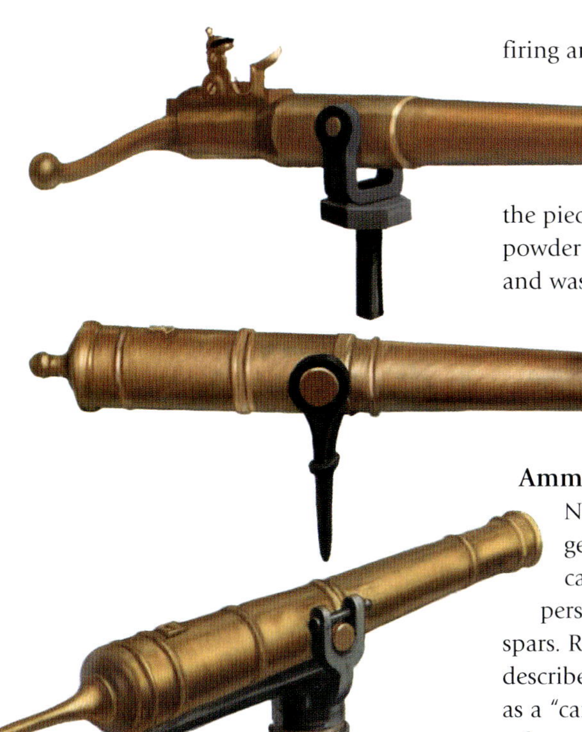

▲ SWIVEL GUNS *These swivel guns are a selection of those employed during the period. They could be of brass or iron and were anti-personnel weapons of small calibre. They were also used in a ship's fighting tops to fire down on the opponent's decks.*

the powder cartridge. The primer was inserted into the vent after the powder cartridge was "pricked" and the piece was then pointed by the gun captain.

At his command, the piece was fired by the application of a slow match to the vent, and the powder train would be ignited. The piece would fire and recoil. The gun tube was then swabbed out with the sponge, which had been dipped in the water bucket in order to ensure there were no hot or burning powder embers still in the bore, which could prematurely detonate the next round. As the next round was loaded, a designated crew member would "thumb" the vent. He would wear a leather thumbstall over his thumb (as the piece would get very hot during firing and could sear his thumb to the bone). This would preclude any air entering the piece's chamber where the powder charge would be rammed, and was an added precaution against premature detonation. Then the firing process would begin again.

Ammunition

Naval artillery ammunition was generally of three main categories: anti-ship, anti-personnel and anti-rigging and spars. Roundshot was exactly as described and is sometimes referred to as a "cannonball". This is a cast-iron sphere the weight of the rated gun that would fire it. It was designed to be fired at a ship's hull to cause enough damage for the ship either to surrender or to be so badly damaged she would sink. It was very effective, especially with the larger calibres of long guns. Anti-personnel ammunition was either grapeshot or canister. Grapeshot consisted of a number of cast-iron balls that were arranged around a wooden frame or "tree" and then had a bag of serge or other material that would cover it. When fired from a long gun or a carronade, it would act like the round from a giant shotgun and literally blow away anything in its path. Canister was a similar round, being cast-iron balls smaller than grapeshot that were placed in a tin can with an iron lid and base. It had the same effect, if not a more deadly one, than grapeshot as there were more balls to a canister round. Both of these types of ammunition were used at short range, probably less than 500 yards (460m). The bigger the piece, the more balls to each round. The grape and canister rounds for the carronade were large and very effective.

Anti-rigging rounds were many and varied, but all based on the same principle: to tear up an opponent's rigging so the supports for the masts would be gone, leaving the ship useless. The following types were employed: chain-shot, bar-shot, link-shot, expanding bar-shot, and knife-bladed shot. All were used, and all were very effective against both ships and personnel.

▼ CARRONADE *This was a short-ranged, large-calibre naval weapon that was developed by the British during the period. It was nicknamed "the Smasher" because of the damage it could inflict. It was designed as an anti-personnel weapon, but was equally deadly against the ship within its range.*

AMERICAN STATE NAVIES

Most of the states, just as they had state troops for home defence, also organized state navies for the same purpose. As with the state troops mentioned earlier, the state navies varied greatly in quality.

Navies and Marines

Some state navies were employed for offensive operations against the British, the disastrous Penobscot expedition being an excellent example. While the state navies performed useful service, overall they detracted from the effort of the Continental Navy and pulled off experienced seamen and officers that could have been better employed in the Continental service.

States that organized and employed their own navies usually either organized state marine units to go along with them or used state troops to serve as marines on board the vessels of the state navy. Again, while giving good and useful service, this drew valuable resources away from the national effort, and given that the inducements to join the state units were usually much higher than going into the Continental service, this caused problems. In addition, the Continental enlistments were for three years or the duration of the war, whereas state enlistments were shorter.

Officers

There are reliable records from at least two of the state navies, those of Virginia and South Carolina. Generally, the ships manned were sloops, brigs, brigantines and smaller vessels such as galleys. Virginia state officers wore a simple uniform of a dark blue coat without facings, blue cuffs and yellow metal buttons. Small clothes were white, and the typical buckled shoes were worn with white stockings. Hair may or may not have been powdered, according to personal choice. The cocked hat was bound in black lace with the usual cockade worn by the United States.

South Carolina officers wore a similar but generally more martial uniform consisting of a dark blue coat lined and faced red. The rest of the uniform was similar to that of the Virginia Navy.

◀ **Virginia State Navy, Ship's Carpenter, 1775–83** *Carpenters were essential specialists in any navy. They not only helped construct warships, but they and their mates maintained the ships at sea and repaired them after a battle of any and all damage. In their own way they were artists, and good ones were worth their weight in gold.*

▶ **Boatswain, South Carolina Navy, 1775–83** *A state navy's version of a petty officer, complete with rope end. The short wide trousers are almost skirt-like in appearance. Petty officers would always be comparatively well uniformed compared to the rest of the crew, to reinforce their status and authority.*

Crews

Virginia state sailors seemed to have favoured dark brown short coats worn with red waistcoats and chequered shirts, and appear to have been so similarly attired that their costume amounted almost to an official uniform. Long trousers were worn of a light buff colour, although breeches were also worn in various colours. Short blue naval jackets were also favoured. A variety of headgear was worn at sea, including roundhats, cloth hats, and even Scots bonnets, the Southern states having a significant Highland Scottish immigrant population.

▶ **Boatswain, Virginia State Navy, 1775–83** *This well-uniformed petty officer, with keys and armed with a cutlass, is uniformed simply in a coat, vest, and striped trousers. Apparently brown was a favourite colour among the seamen of the day and was seen almost as often as dark blue.*

Petty officers would be attired similarly to the seamen, and might favour striped trousers over plain ones. Cocked hats were usually worn and, as a badge of rank, and for practical use, they were usually armed with a cutlass on a black leather swordbelt worn over the right shoulder.

South Carolina seamen wore blue, brown or white jackets, with multi-coloured waistcoats of white and different shades of blue. Multi-coloured neckerchiefs were worn by both sailors and petty officers, and the trousers worn were the usual mixture of styles as in the Continental service. Boatswains and petty officers seem to have worn cocked hats and carried the ubiquitous rope ends for the procrastinators in the ranks.

South Carolina naval ensigns are interesting and were made up of at least three different varieties. One ensign featured the familiar red and blue striped "Don't Tread on Me" pattern, the stripes being horizontal on the fly and having the rattlesnake motif in the centre. Another ensign was modelled on the South Carolina state flag of a dark blue field with the state crescent in white in the upper left-hand corner. The third ensign was a medium blue-coloured field with the palmetto tree (the state tree) in the centre, surrounded by 13 stars (for the 13 rebellious states) arranged around the tree.

◀ **Seaman, Virginia State Navy, 1775–83** *Seaman with boarding pike. This gives a very good picture of the length of a boarding pike and clearly demonstrates the advantage defenders would have against boarders trying to take their ship. The hat illustrated here would be tarred to withstand the elements. The neckerchiefs and hats were usually black, as the sailors worked around tar on a daily basis.*

It is interesting to note that there were black sailors employed in both the Virginia and South Carolina state navies. This was one way for a slave to perhaps earn his freedom (although this was not always honoured after the shooting stopped) and sometimes a slave was sent to serve in his owner's place. Black sailors have a long and honourable history in the American naval service, both merchant marine and navy, and were accepted for service at sea from the start. This was not always the case on land.

▲ PRIVATE, MARYLAND STATE MARINES, 1775–83 *Maryland uniformed its state marines in the blue hunting shirts that were also worn by their infantry units. Maryland's marines were useful for defence of the coastline, which was extensive for a small state, and to embark aboard any state warships that might be employed for defence.*

▲ PRIVATE, PENNSYLVANIA STATE MARINES, 1775–83 *Pennsylvania mobilized troops for the defence of the state and marines were part of that mobilization. There was considerable fighting along the Delaware River in 1777, including defending the river forts against the Royal Navy. Brown for coats was popular among Pennsylvania troops.*

▲ PRIVATE, VIRGINIA STATE MARINES, CAPTAIN POLLARD'S COMPANY, 1775–83 *This simple uniform was both comfortable and practical. The Virginia state units were mobilized for state defence, although they sometimes served out of state with the militia or Continental troops. They could be considered to be state regulars.*

State Marines

There were at least three states with a marine corps: Pennsylvania, Maryland and Virginia. None were uniformed alike but all were equipped as infantrymen and were capable of service afloat and ashore. The Pennsylvania contingent was uniformed in brown coats faced red and lined white, much in the style of the Pennsylvania Line of the Continental Army. Collar, cuffs and lapels were red, and the coat turnbacks were white. The cocked hat was bound with white tape for privates and with black for officers, and the usual cockade was worn. Waistcoats were white, breeches were buff. Stockings were white, and half gaiters were meant to be worn. Equipment and weapons were the same as for the Continental infantry. Officers wore a red sash as a badge of rank and a white swordbelt over the right shoulder.

State Navies 1775–83

State	Ships	Sloops	Brigs*	Schooners	Gunboats**
Connecticut	1	2	2	2	3
Georgia					4
Maryland	1		11	2	8
Massachusetts	3	7	4	1	1
New Hampshire	1				
New York		2		1	
North Carolina			3		2
Pennsylvania	2	2	2	2	52
Rhode Island		4			3
South Carolina	4	4	4	14	8
Virginia	9	1	8	1	19

* This category includes brigantines.

** This includes galleys, gunboats, fire ships, store ships, armed boats, floating batteries, accommodation vessels, and guard boats.

The Maryland state marines had a smart appearance with a dark blue hunting shirt worn over buff breeches, white stockings and half gaiters. The privates would wear the usual equipment for infantrymen and be armed either with the British Brown Bess musket or the French Charleville. The cocked hats were bound in white tape for privates, and in black lace for officers, with the usual black cockade.

Virginia state marines wore a very simple uniform of a light tan shirt, perhaps a simplified hunting shirt design, that was worn over brown breeches, grey stockings and buckled shoes. The cocked hat was bound with black tape, with the black cockade, and there was probably only one crossbelt that carried the cartridge box. The bayonet and scabbard were worn suspended from a frog on a waistbelt.

Other states would embark detachments of regular regiments as marines, as the French did. South Carolina was one such case, the 5th South Carolina Regiment of the Continental Line being employed in this manner. They were uniformed in dark blue coats, faced and lined red, and they resembled the South Carolina naval officers except that they were equipped as infantry. Small clothes were white and black half gaiters were worn over buckled shoes. The cocked hats were bound in black tape.

State Navy Reputation

All of the states save two, Delaware and New Jersey, maintained state naval forces, and some of these included marines. Some did good service, as when the Pennsylvania ship *Hyder Ali*, under that daring swashbuckler Joshua Barney, captured HMS *General Monck* under the nose of a British frigate. Other state naval operations were less effective, such as the one in Penobscot Bay that was mounted by the state of Massachusetts against the British forces stationed in Maine, which was then part of Massachusetts. Some Continental naval forces were assigned to the expedition under the leadership of the largely incompetent Dudley Saltonstall, and the operation was a complete disaster, with most of the American ships being either burnt or captured by the British.

All told, the state navies were a drain on local assets, both material and personnel, which could have found better use spent on the Continental service. For all of its problems, the Continental Navy was more professional and better led than the state navies, whose quality in both ships and personnel varied greatly.

► **Boat's crew, South Carolina Navy, 1775–81** *This nattily dressed sailor is a member of a boat's crew, possibly for the captain of one of the larger vessels in the state fleet. He is outfitted in white, which was actually the easiest to keep clean as it was undyed and could be successfully washed. For permanent stains, pipeclay or chalk could be applied to the cloth to quite satisfactorily cover the stain. This method is still used today to cover small stains on white military uniforms.*

NAVAL ORDNANCE

Naval artillery equipment varied from ship to ship and from navy to navy. Different calibres and types of gun were employed for different purposes, and no one nation had any particular advantage in the manufacture or design of naval weaponry.

Carronade Calibres

Calibre	Length (feet)	Weight (pounds)	Calibre (inches)	Powder Charge (pounds)	Range at 5 degrees (yards)
68-pounder	4.1	3600	7.9	5.5	1,280
42-pounder	4.3	2220	6.7	3.5	1,170
32-pounder	4.0	1710	6.1	2.6	1,087
24-pounder	3.0	1150	5.6	2.0	1,050
18-pounder	2.3	850	5.1	1.5	1,000
12-pounder	2.2	590	4.4	1.0	870

Carronades

The carronade was a short-barrelled, large-calibre piece of ordnance that fired a very large ball, usually grape or canister. It was introduced in 1781, and its name was a development of the foundry in which it was developed, the Carron iron foundry at Falkirk in Scotland. The carronade was used at close range and was a devastating weapon that was nicknamed "the Smasher" for obvious reasons.

The carronade was much lighter than the long gun and was easy to operate and move if necessary. The weapon also required fewer sailors to man it. Its effectiveness and firepower were reduced at long range, and because of its design it was inaccurate at anything but short distances. A ship armed solely with carronades would be at a grave disadvantage in a fight with a ship equipped with long guns or a mixture of long guns and carronades.

The advantage of the carronade was that the powder charge was less than the long guns, the recoil was less, and at close range it could ruin a large boarding party and quite literally carry away large sections of an opposing ship. In short, at close range and well aimed, the carronade could be decisive in a ship-to-ship engagement.

Long Guns

The long gun was the standard naval weapon. Generally speaking, the higher the ship's rate and the larger the ship, the larger the calibre of long gun she would be armed with.

Naval guns were usually made of iron, rather than of the brass or bronze that army field guns were cast from. A gun's calibre was calculated from two things: the width of the bore (except for the French, who calculated it from the width of the shot), and the weight of shot. Long guns, or more commonly cannon, were called or named by the weight of the shot they "threw". Hence, a gun that fired a 12-pound roundshot would be a 12-pounder.

As ships developed, the different classes would tend to mount heavier guns, which would be more effective in a ship-to-ship engagement, and would cause more damage per round to the opposing ship. For example, frigates mounting 6- or 8-pounders in 1763, at the end of the Seven Years' War, would mount 12- or 18-pounders during the war in North America.

Warships, especially ships of the line, were mobile, floating gun platforms that were to be used to fight it out at relatively close range. The ship of the line was the height of military and naval technology of the period and its design and specification was still being improved upon as a type of fighting ship during the period of the American War.

Frigates were also being improved, and the tendency was to develop larger frigates with heavier guns, as well as a greater number. This class would eventually develop into the large

◄ 12-POUNDER LONG GUN, 1775–83 *This is a typical naval gun and gun carriage of the period, made from cast iron. The trucks, or wheels, of the carriage were constructed small in an attempt to reduce recoil aboard ship. The term "loose cannon" came from gun carriages that came loose from their moorings at sea and rolled around the deck, a very dangerous proposition for the crew, especially those who had to tie down the gun carriage before it caused too much damage.*

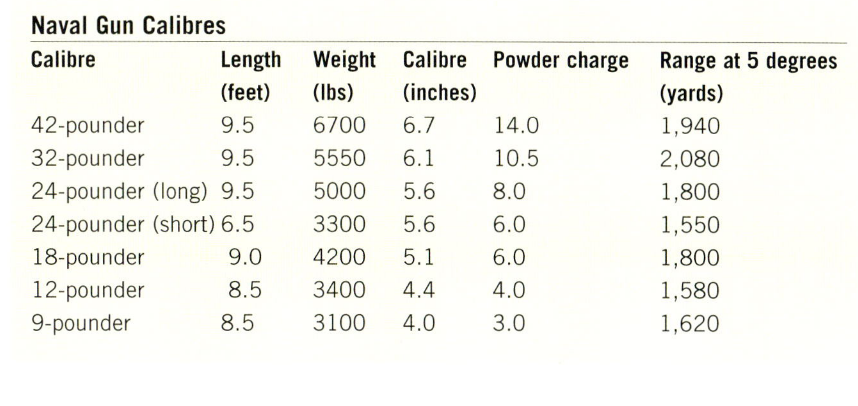

Naval Gun Calibres

Calibre	Length (feet)	Weight (lbs)	Calibre (inches)	Powder charge	Range at 5 degrees (yards)
42-pounder	9.5	6700	6.7	14.0	1,940
32-pounder	9.5	5550	6.1	10.5	2,080
24-pounder (long)	9.5	5000	5.6	8.0	1,800
24-pounder (short)	6.5	3300	5.6	6.0	1,550
18-pounder	9.0	4200	5.1	6.0	1,800
12-pounder	8.5	3400	4.4	4.0	1,580
9-pounder	8.5	3100	4.0	3.0	1,620

American frigates of the War of 1812 that did so well against the British Royal Navy. That tendency was already becoming obvious with the fine, bigger frigates that the Americans designed and launched during the War of Independence.

Several improvements in naval architecture came out of this war. Some of these included common sense innovations, such as putting copper bottoms on warships so they would be more hardy and last longer, and the invention of the short-range and deadly carronades. Both innovations that came from the Royal Navy, but were adopted universally. British naval supremacy, hard-won in 1759 at Quiberon Bay, was lost to the French in the American war, but was reasserted during the French Revolutionary Wars, and held until the Second World War.

▼ *Different pieces of iron British naval ordnance of the period. From top to bottom: ¾-pounder swivel gun, 4-pounder, 6-pounder, 9-pounder, 12-pounder, and 18-pounder. Note the size of each weapon and compare it to the size of the ball it fired. The projections about halfway down the gun tubes are the trunnions, by which the gun tubes were attached to the gun carriages.*

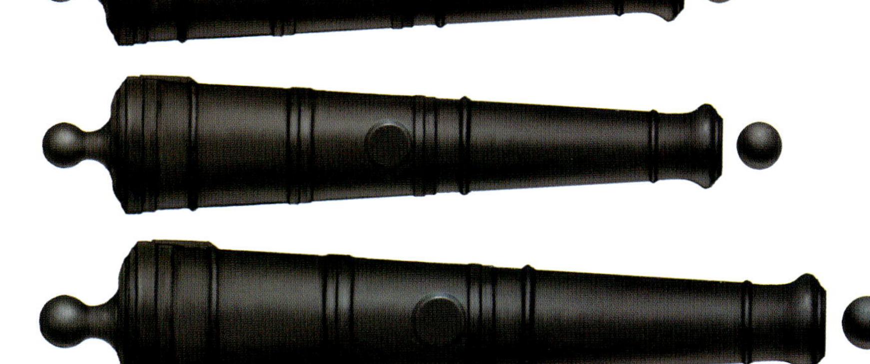

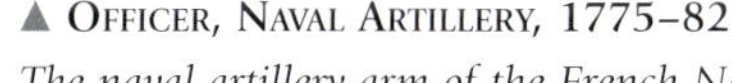

▲ Officer, Naval Artillery, 1775–82

The naval artillery arm of the French Navy was its most professional section. It was made up of professional artillerymen who could also be used as infantry if the need arose. The bearskin cap denotes the elite status of these gunners, who would be stationed on board ship – with at least one officer per gun crew acting as gun captain – and ashore, stationed in the fortresses that guarded the French naval bases.

LANDING PARTIES

Navies made large-scale or punitive raids possible, and the war in North America saw a number of such operations. Indeed, the movement of troops by sea proved vital to the success of many of the campaigns.

Amphibious Operations

Transporting and landing troops from the sea can give an enormous advantage in warfare. In North America in the late 18th century the most reliable method for transporting large cargoes and large bodies of personnel was by water, either by river or sea. A fleet of ships disappearing over the horizon posed enormous problems for an enemy commander with little idea as to where the troops were destined.

The size of an amphibious operation can range from a small raiding party sent from a single ship, as performed by Captain John Paul Jones in his famous Whitehaven raid on the coast of Great Britain, to moving an entire army across the Atlantic Ocean to land on a hostile shore, as the British did in the combined operation against New York City in 1776, dispatching the largest army they had ever deployed in combat.

The British were experts in conducting amphibious operations, and this was best exemplified in their amphibious assault against Newport, Rhode Island, in 1779. The landing force was quickly and efficiently loaded into the fleet's boats, and under the cover of a naval bombardment, swiftly made its way to shore and overwhelmed any opposition it met on the beach. The British also understood how to counter a naval and amphibious assault and displayed that expertise in their tenacious defence of their naval base of Gibraltar, which underwent three sieges by the Spanish (sometimes aided by their French allies). The base was held against all comers, and the allies were frustrated by the tough defenders and the expert British naval commanders, such as Admiral Richard Howe, who hammered into the fortress with a relief convoy in 1782.

The French also became proficient in amphibious operations during the war in the West Indies. They gallantly defended their possessions in the Sugar Islands, although not always with success, and skilfully attacked and seized islands held by the British. It is worth noting that these Caribbean islands were sources of great wealth for the colonial powers of the 18th century, although they subsequently lost that value and importance.

Landing Parties

Ships' landing parties, which were usually made up of both sailors and marines, were armed with a variety of

Amphibious Operations in the Caribbean 1778–83

Year	Location	Result
1778	Dominica	French capture island
	St Lucia	British capture island
	St Vincent	French capture island
	Grenada	French capture island
1780	St Vincent	French defend island against a British assault
1781	St Lucia	French feint to cover the attack on Tobago
	Tobago	French victory
	St Eustatius	French victory; Saba and St Martin also captured
1782	St Kitts	French capture
	Demerara	French capture
	Nevis	French capture
	Montserrat	French capture

▲ PRIVATE, BRITISH MARINES, LANDING PARTY, 1775 *This figure is from a battalion company of British Marines, equipped for a landing party. The arms and equipment he carries is the same as he would have for land operations, and the marines that served at Bunker Hill in 1775 would have looked like this, probably with the addition of a pack together with the haversack shown. American Continental Marines would have been kitted out in the same manner.*

▶ *Landing parties consisted of a mixture of sailors and soldiers, crammed into long boats that were carried by ships for this purpose. It was a dangerous operation, as the boats could be sitting targets. The British were particularly skilled at these amphibious assaults.*

▼ **Sailor, Landing Party, 1775** *This fully equipped and heavily armed sailor may or may not have taken the boarding pike ashore, but he surely would have taken the cutlass and boarding axe, along with a pistol and perhaps a musket. A naval landing party would generally present a mixed appearance. The marines would be uniformed alike, but not the sailors, who might well resemble pirates rather than naval personnel.*

small arms. The marines would be armed as infantrymen. The privates would have musket and bayonet, and the officers would be issued with sword and pistols. The sailors would be armed with a combination of cutlass, boarding pikes and axes, pistols and muskets, and some undoubtedly would take anything handy, such as belaying pins (stored along the sides of the ship or at the base of the masts and used to tie off the running rigging) for close combat. The marines would be armed uniformly, and the sailors in a much more haphazard fashion. The navy officers (both marines and officers were categorized as naval personnel) would be armed with an edged weapon, sword or cutlass, and probably pistols.

▶ **British Junior Officer, Boarding Party, 1775** *This officer is equipped to lead a landing party ashore for King and Country. He is armed with sword and pistol. Some officers would probably carry a sturdy cutlass like the sailors they were leading, in preference to the sword shown here.*

GLOSSARY

Adjutant: a staff officer usually found at the regiment or brigade.
Aide-de-camp: a junior officer on the personal staff of a general officer. Often used as messengers from one general to another.
Aiguillette: usually a gold or silver cord worn on the left or right shoulder, to denote special status.
Artificers: workmen tasked with small-scale engineering tasks, usually the repair of vehicles. During this period they were being militarized.
Artillery: heavy, towed weapons, firing heavy, often explosive projectiles.
Bateauxmen: men serving boats and barges, charged with transporting troops, equipment, or military supplies on the lakes or rivers.
Battalion: a unit of two or more companies, usually of about 600 men. In the British Army the term was used interchangeably with 'regiment.'
Battery: during this period this term designated an artillery emplacement of any number of guns. The basic artillery unit was termed a company at this time, the term battery replacing it in the first half of the 19th century.

▼ *The battle of Cowpens, 1781, showing one-to-one combat between Colonel Banastre Tarleton and Colonel William Washington.*

Bayonet: a spear-like attachment to a musket that was attached by a socket at the base of the weapon.
Bearskin: a tall fur cap.
Bicorne: a round, black felt hat with the wide brim folded up on two sides.
Braid: narrow, coloured cloth that might be used to outline facings on the uniform coat.
Breeches: close-fitting leg wear that came to just below the knee.
Bricole: a leather crossbelt with rope attached; used for manhandling artillery pieces.
Brigade: a unit of two or more regiments.
Briquet: a French short sword used by grenadiers as a sidearm.
Cape: another term for collar.
Carbine: a light firearm, shorter than a musket, carried by cavalrymen.
Cartouche: a small pouch for pistol cartridges, usually worn by officers.
Cartridge: for infantry, ball and powder wrapped in paper for small arms ammunition; for artillery, it could be the powder charge contained in a paper or cloth container alone, or as a complete round attached to the roundshot or canister.
Cazadores: Spanish light infantrymen.
Chasseur: French word for hunter, denoting light troops – i.e. troops dressed or armed for skirmishing; a French light infantryman.
Cockade: a bow or rosette worn on the hat, usually in the national colours.
Colonel: an officer of senior (field) rank, immediately below a general.
Colour: an infantry regimental flag, used as a reference and rallying point on the battlefield, highly prized as a trophy. British regiments carried two, as did French units.
Company: the basic unit in infantry, cavalry, and artillery. Two or more would constitute a battalion.
Comb: a vertical piece on top of a helmet, usually surmounted by a crest.
Crest: a badge or coat of arms; a piece of fur or horsehair, on top of a helmet.
Dolman: a waist-length jacket worn by hussars, heavily decorated.
Dragoon: originally an infantryman, mounted to improve mobility, and equipped to fight on foot.
Engineer: a specialist trained in the construction of defences, bridge building, and siege warfare.
Ensign: the most junior English commissioned officer in the infantry; also a term for a flag.
Epaulettes: shoulder straps with fringes to the outer ends.
Facings: the lapels, collar, and cuffs of a uniform coat, usually in a different colour to the coat itself.
Farrier: military name for blacksmith.
Free Corps: non-regular units raised as light troops during time of war, usually engaged in partisan operations.
Frog: an attachment to a waistbelt used to carry a sword, bayonet, or hatchet. Some were combinations that could carry more than one weapon.
Frogging: the lace across the chest of hussar dolmans and pelisses.
Fusil: a light musket.
Fusilier: French term for the troops of a non-elite company in a regiment.
Gaiters: cloth coverings of the lower legs, which kept the stockings clean. 'Grande' gaiters covered the knee; half gaiters came up to just above the ankle or just below the knee.
Gaiter trousers: a one-piece garment that combined trousers and gaiters, also known as overalls.
Gorget: a metal collar plate worn by officers on duty as a badge of office.
Grenadier: elite soldiers originally trained to carry and throw grenades.
Guidons: small flags used by companies or squadrons.
Halberd: an ancient weapon from the middle ages relegated to a badge of rank for European NCOs.
Hanger: a light combat sword.

▲ *A heroic image of Washington and his Continentals crossing the Delaware River.*

Haversack: a light pack worn on a crossbelt by the troops to carry food and personal items.
Horse furniture: saddle, portmanteau, shabraque, and saddle bags.
Howitzer: a short-barrelled artillery piece designed to fire projectiles in a high trajectory, to reach targets hidden from direct view.
Hunting shirts: Loose and baggy shirts with large collars, made from hard-wearing material.
Hussar: originally the Hungarian name for irregular light cavalrymen, meaning robber, or corsair. Subsequently a type of light cavalryman.
Jäger: originally the German word for hunter, usually trained for skirmishing duties and armed with rifles.
Limber: the vehicle to which a field gun trail was attached to enable the gun to be moved by a team of horses.
Light infantry: Elite infantrymen trained to fight both in line of battle and in open, or skirmish, order.
Line infantry: the bulk of a regiment that fought in line of battle.
Loyalists: Americans who stayed loyal to the British, also known as Tories.
Major: the lowest rank of field officers, usually commanding a battalion.
Manchettes: pieces of cloth worn by cavalrymen or mounted officers around the knee to protect it.
Marines: specially trained "soldiers of the sea", assigned to a naval ship.
Matross: an apprentice artilleryman.
Militia: American citizen or temporary soldiers who were mustered for service for the short term or emergencies.
Minutemen: American militia meant to be available at a minute's notice.
Mirliton: a peakless high-winged cap worn by hussars with a strip of cloth wound around it or floating freely.
Mitre cap: a peakless cap, often made of metal, and worn predominantly by German grenadiers and fusiliers.
Musket: the main long arm of the armies of the period, muzzle loading, could be fitted with a bayonet.
Overalls: *see* gaiter trousers.
Partisans: the period term for guerrillas. They were irregulars who seldom, if ever, fought in line of battle.
Pelisse: fur-lined and trimmed outer jacket of the hussar, usually worn over the left shoulder and seldom, if ever, worn in combat.
Piping: narrow cloth edging, usually in a contrasting colour.
Portmanteau: small saddle bag or valise, attached to the saddle.
Provost: an individual charged with maintaining discipline.
Regiment: a unit of two or more battalions or squadrons.
Rifle: a long arm that was slow-loading but very accurate. It could not be fitted with a bayonet.
Roundhat: a hat that was not turned up at all on the sides or had only one side turned up.
Sabretache: a highly decorated pouch, attached to a cavalryman's waistbelt.
Sapper: troops equipped and trained to dig field defences and siege works. In the French service, an elite soldier whose modern equivalent would be combat engineer.
Shabraque: a saddlecloth, derived from the Turkish word *tschprak*.
Sidearms: the tools used by artillerymen to work their field pieces.
Small clothes: vest, or waistcoat, breeches, and stockings.
Spontoon: a spear-like weapon used as both a badge of rank and a weapon.
Standard: small square regimental flag used by the cavalry.
Swallows' nests: *see* wings
Tarleton helmet: low-crowned helmet with a front peak and bearskin crest.
Tricorne: hat turned up on three sides.
Turnbacks: the skirts of a coat, turned back to show the lining.
Wings: decorated arcs of cloth on the shoulders. Termed 'swallows' nests' in German units.

INDEX

Page numbers in *italics* refer to captions.

A
Adams, John 21, 30
Adams, Sam 21, 30
America 6–7, 9
colonial rule 16–17, 20–1
colonization and emigration 12–13
founding 10–11
French and Indian War 14–15
American Army 22
1st Canadian regiment 62
1st Connecticut Regiment 97, *99*, 108
1st Continental Regiment 59
1st Continental Light Dragoons 116, *117*
1st Maryland Regiment *108*
1st New Hampshire Regiment *96*, 108
1st Pennsylvania Regiment 101, *101*, 110
2nd Battalion of New York Provincial Forces 50–1, *51*
2nd Canadian Regiment *62*, 62–3, *63*, 105, *105*
2nd Continental Artillery Regiment *118*, *119*
2nd Continental Light Dragoons *115*, 116–17
2nd Maryland Regiment 97, *97*
2nd Massachusetts Regiment 109
2nd New Hampshire Regiment 96, 108
2nd New York Regiment 110
2nd Pennsylvania Regiment *109*, 110–11
2nd Rhode Island Regiment 73, *73*, 108–9
2nd Virginia Regiment 97, *98*
3rd Continental Light Dragoons *114*, *115*, 117
3rd Massachusetts Regiment 97, *99*
3rd New Hampshire Regiment 108
3rd New Jersey Infantry Regiment 74, *75*
3rd New York Regiment 65, *65*, 96, *97*
4th Continental Light Dragoons *116*, 117, *117*
4th Maryland Independent Company *84*
4th Massachusetts Regiment 104, *104*, 109
4th New York Regiment 97, *98*
4th South Carolina Regiment (Artillery) *86*
5th Pennsylvania Regiment 101, *101*, 105, *105*, 111
6th Connecticut Regiment 108
6th Virginia Regiment *74*, 74–5
7th Connecticut Regiment 108
7th Pennsylvania Regiment 73, *73*
12th Continental Infantry Regiment *72*, 73
14th Continental (Glover's Marblehead) Regiment *64*, 64–5, *65*
18th Continental Infantry Regiment 73, *73*
Armand's Legion *112*, 113
artificers and invalids 123, *123*
Baltimore Independent Cadets *60*
Baltimore Light Dragoons *56*, *57*, 66
black soldiers *98*
Cantwell's Regiment 57, *67*
cavalry 114–17
Charleston Battalion of Artillery *87*
Charleston Regiment, South Carolina Militia *50*, 51
colours and standards *69*, *102*, 102–3, *103*
commanders and staff *92*, 92–3, *93*
Continental Army 22–3
Continental Army numbers 65, 72, 77, 79, 90, 91, 107
Continental regiments 1776 72–5

▼ *French artillery ready box, or "*coffret*".*

Continental Regiments in 1777 76–9
Continental Rifle Corps *58*, *59*
Dabney's Virginia State Legion *84*
De La Porte's French Company *71*
Delaware Militia 57
Delaware Regiment 61, 110
Dover Light Infantry Company 57, *66*
drill 90–1
engineers 122, *122*
Fairfax (Virginia) Independent Company of Volunteers *50*, 51
first Continentals 58–61
frontier regiments 70–1
Hall's Delaware Regiment 61, *100*, 101
Hartley's Regiment 77, *77*
Haslet's Delaware Regiment 61, *61*
headquarters troops 94–5
Henley's Regiment 79, *79*
infantry 96–101
Kirkwood's Delaware Battalion 104, *104*
kit *63*, *83*, *120*
Lee's Legion *113*, 112–13
Lee's Regiment 76–7, *77*
legions and partisans 112–13
light infantry 104–5
Maryland Regiments 61, *108*
Massachusetts and New York Continentals 64–6, *106*, *107*
militia 47, 48–9, 50–1
militia artillery 67, *67*
militia cavalry 66–7
militia infantry 54–7
minutemen 52, 52–3, *53*
Morgan's rifle corps 60–1
musicians 74, 75, 107, *107*, *108*, *109*, *111*, *239*
New Jersey Regiments *109*
New York City Independent Militia 51, *51*
New York Continental Artillery Company *121*
North Carolina Militia 56–7, *57*
over-the-mountain men 82–3
Philadelphia Associators *80*, 81, *81*
Philadelphia City Troop of Light Horse *68*, 68–9, *69*
Pulaski's Legion *112*, 113

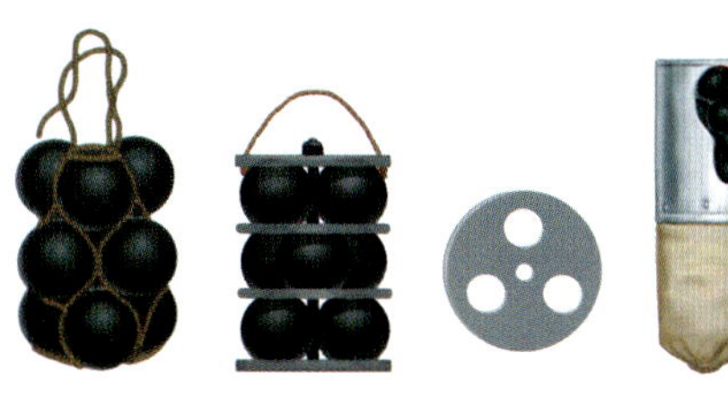

▲ *Artillery anti-personnel ammunition, grapeshot on the left, canister on the right.*

Rhode Island Regiment *98*
Rhode Island Train of Artillery *66, 67*
Richardson's Regiment *55*
riflemen *58, 59,* 82–3, *83*
sappers and miners 122–3, *123*
Sherburne's Regiment 76, *76*
Smallwood's Maryland Regiment *60,* 61
South Carolina Light Dragoons *85*
South Carolina Light Horse 66–7
specialist troops *122,* 122–3, *123*
Spencer's Regiment *78, 79*
state artillery units 86–7, *111,* 118–21, *120*
state troops 84–5
Stockbridge Indians 29, 82, 82
uniform regulations of 1779 106–11
Virginia Frontier Independent Company *71*
Virginia Light Dragoons *70*
Virginia Militia *54,* 54–5
Virginia Regiments *110*
Virginia State Artillery Regiment *87*
von Heer's Provost Company *94*
Warner's Green Mountain Boys *54*
Washington's Guard *94, 95*
Webb's Regiment 78, *78*
American Indians 6, 7, 9, 10, 11, 12, 29
French and Indian War 14–15
Indian Wars 13
Pontiac's uprising 16–17
American Navy 44, 210
black seamen *236,* 243
colours *224*
marines *238,* 238–9, *239*
Maryland state marines *244*
officers *234,* 234–5, *235*
Pennsylvania state marines *244*
petty officers and seamen *236,* 236–7, *237*
South Carolina navy *242, 245*
state marines 244–5
state navies 242–3
Virginia state marines *244*
Virginia state navy *242, 243*
American Revolution
Albany 1777 34–5
Battle of Camden 1780 39
Battle of Cowpens 1781 41
Battle of Guildford Courthouse 1781 42
Boston 1775 30
Brandywine 1777 32
Canada 1775 30–1, 62–3
Charleston 1776 32
Charleston 1780 38–9
Germantown 1777 33
Greene's Southern Campaign 1781 40–1, 99–101
Lexington and Concord 52–3
Loyalist and Rebel clashes 1780–1 38
Monmouth 1778 36
naval war 44–5, 213–15
New York and Princeton 1776 31
Newport, Rhode Island 1778 and Penobscot Bay 1779 37
Philadelphia 1777 32
Saratoga 1777 35
Siege of Yorktown 1771 43–2
Stony Point and Paulus Hook 1779 37
Valley Forge 1777–8 35
Amherst, Jeffrey 15
Anhalt-Zerbst 197
Infantry Regiment *197*
Anspach-Bayreuth
1st Infantry Regiment *196,* 196–7
2nd Infantry Regiment *196,* 197
artillery 198–9, *198, 199*
Jägers 202, 203
Arnold, Benedict 30–1, 35, 38, 164, 219
artillery (weaponry) 118–19, 121
naval *240,* 240–1, *241,* 246, *246–7*
American *120*
French 184–5, *185,* 186–7, *187*
German 190–1, *191, 198,* 198–9
Austria 18, 170, 171

B
Barney, Joshua 44, 234, 245
Barry, John 44, 234
Berthier, Louis-Alexandre *172,* 173
Bouquet, Henry 17
Bourcet, Pierre Joseph 172–3
Braddock, Edward 14
Brant, Joseph 29, 166, *167*
Broglie, Victor-François de 26
Brunswick
Brunswick Dragoons *194, 195*
cavalry 194–5
infantry 192–3
Infantry Regiment von Rhetz *192,* 192–3
Jägers 203
Light Infantry Regiment von Barner *193*
Regiment von Specht 193, *193*
Burgoyne, John 25, 29, 34–5, 129, 152, 153

C
Canada 9, 11, 28, 30–1, 34
Carleton, Sir Guy 31, 129, 162
Carrington, Edward 40, 100
Clark, George Rogers 70, 71
Clinton, Henry 24–5, 34, 35, 36, 129
Cornwallis, Charles 24–5, 31, 39, 41, *41,* 42–3, 45, 100, 101, 129, 136–7, 150, 180, 213

D
D'Estaing, Hector Charles 37
Declaration of Independence 6, *7,* 21, 51, 57
Duportail, Louis Lebèque 23, 90

E
Europe 7, 14, 18–19
Ewald, Johann *82,* 202

F
Ferguson, Patrick 41, 164
Forbes, John 15
France 6, 7, 9, 10–11, 18–19
American Revolution 30, 33, 35, 37, 43, 44–5, 169, 170
French and Indian War 14–15
Franklin, Benjamin 7, 23, 35, 81, 90, 91, 169, *224*
Fraser, Simon 35

▼ *French field piece, Gribeauval artillery system.*

▲ *German artillery acoutrements.*

Frederick the Great 18, 26, 35
French Army 26–7
 1st Volontaires Étrangers de la Marine *182*
 Armagnac Regiment 174, *174*
 artillery 184–5, 186–7
 Artillery Regiment Metz *184*, *185*
 Auxonne Regiment of Artillery *184*
 Bourbonnais Infantry Regiment *181*
 cavalry 182–3
 colours and standards *176*, 176–7, *177*
 generals and staff 172–3
 Guadaloupe Regiment *175*
 infantry 174–5
 kit *233*
 Lauzun's Legion *181*, *182*
 Lauzun's 2nd Legion *183*
 legions 182–3
 musicians *179*, *180*, *231*
 Regiment Dillon 175, *175*, 232
 Regiment Hainault 175, *175*
 Rochambeau's force 178–81
 Royal Deux-Ponts Infantry Regiment *180*
 Saintonge Infantry Regiment *178*, 179
 Soissonais Infantry Regiment *179*
 topographical engineers 173
French Navy 11, 19, 44
 Barrois Regiment *233*
 Bombardiers de la Marine *230*, 231, *247*
 Corps Royal de l'Infanterie de la Marine *230*, 230–1, *231*
 naval garnisons *232*, 232–3, *233*
 officers *226*, 226–7, *227*
 Regiment Walsh 232, *232*, *233*
 seamen and petty officers *228*, 228–9, *229*

G
Gage, Thomas 24, 30, *127*, 129
Gálvez, Bernado de 28, 206
Gates, Horatio 35, 39, 41, 55, 56, 85, 195
George III 16, 17, 21
Germany 7, 28, 49, 169, 170–1
 Anhalt-Zerbst 197
 Anspach-Bayreuth 196–7, 198–9, 203
 Brunswick 192–3, 194–5, 203
 colours *176*, 176–7
 Hesse-Cassel 188–9, 190–1, 202–3
 Hesse-Hanau 200–1, 203
 Jägers 202–3
 kit *191*
 Waldeck 197
Gist, Mordecai 39, 40
Grasse, François Joseph Paul de 37, 43, 180, 213, 214–15, 226, 230
Great Britain 6–7, 9, 10–11
 American Revolution 30–43, 49
 colonial rule in America 16–17
 French and Indian War 14–15
British Army 24–5, 125, 126–7
 1st Foot Guards *132*, *133*
 2nd Foot Guards *132*
 3rd Foot *142*, *147*
 3rd Foot Guards *133*
 4th Foot *134*, *135*
 7th Foot *136*, *137*
 8th Foot *155*
 11th New Hampshire Provincial Regiment *164*, 165
 16th Foot *148*
 16th Light Dragoons *150*
 17th Light Dragoons *150*, *151*, *161*
 18th Foot *134*, *140*, *141*
 23rd Foot *136*, *137*
 25th Foot *142*
 27th Foot *140*, *141*, *144*
 28th Foot *143*
 29th Foot *130*, *131*
 38th Foot *147*
 42nd Foot *138*, *139*, *147*
 59th Foot *155*
 60th Foot *135*
 64th Foot *142*
 71st Foot *139*
 American Indians 155, 166–7
 American loyalist cavalry 160–1
 American loyalist infantry 156–9
 American loyalist militia 164–5
 American loyalist rangers 162–3
 British Legion *157*, 161, *161*
 British regiments in America 127
 Butler's Rangers 163, *163*
 caps *149*
 cavalry 150–1
 colours and standards *144*, 144–6, *145*, *146*
 Delancey's Brigade 158, *159*
 English regiments 142–3
 Foot Guards 132–3
 fusiliers 136–7
 generals and staff *128*, 128–9, *129*
 grenadiers 147
 Highland regiments 138–9
 infantry 130–1
 Irish regiments 140–1
 King's American Dragoons 161
 King's American Regiment *156*, 156–7,
 King's Royal Regiment of New York 159, *159*
 kit 138, 155
 light infantry 148–9
 Loyal Queen's County Militia 165
 musicians 131, *131*, 135, *135*, *139*, *141*, *156*
 Newfoundland Regiment *157*, 157–8
 Quebec Militia *164*, 165, *165*
 Queen's Rangers *160*, 161, *162*, 163
 Regiment of Pennsylvania Loyalists *159*
 regimental pioneers 154–5, *155*
 Royal Artillery *152*, 152–3, *153*
 Royal Engineers 154, *154*
 Royal Highland Emigrants 158, *158*
 Royal regiments 134–5
 specialist troops 154–5
 Volunteers of Ireland 158, *158*
British Navy 44, 210
 British marines 224, 224–5, *225*, *248*
 colours *224*

▼ *Light infantry cap, pack and tin canteen.*

officers *220*, 220–1, *221*, *249*
seamen and petty officers *222*, *222–3*, *223*
Greene, Nathaniel 38, 39, 40–1, *41*, 42, 43, 55, 56, 71, 83, 85, 94, 99–101, 129, 137, 150
Gribeauval, Jean-Baptiste Vaquette de 19, 26, 43, 185, 186–7

H
Henry, Patrick 21, *53*
Hesse-Cassel
artillery 190–1, *190*, *191*
Feldjäger Corps 202, 202–3, *203*
infantry 188–9
Regiment von Ditfurth *189*
Regiment von Knyphausen *188*
Regiment von Rall *189*
Regiment von Stein *189*
Hesse-Hanau 200–1
Jägers 203
Regiment Erbprinz *200*, *201*
Holland 10, 11, 12, 19, 30, 44
Howard, John Eager 39, 40, 100, 137
Howe, William 24, 30, 31, 32, 34, 35, 36, 87, 128, 129, 148
hunting shirts 7, 49, 60

I
Iroquois 29, 155, 166–7, *166*, 167

J
Jefferson, Thomas *6*, 39, 84, 85
Jones, John Paul 44, *215*, 217, 232, 234, 235, 235, 239, 248

K
Kalb, Johann de 23, 39, 56, 90
Kirkwood, Robert 40, 61, 100
Knox, Henry 22, 30, 59, 87, 119
Kosciuzko, Tadeuz 23

L
Lafayette, Marie Joseph 32, 43
Lee, Charles 36
Lee, Henry 37, 37, 38, 40, 100, 116, 150, 164
Lincoln, Benjamin 39

M
Marion, Francis 38, 39, 41
Miro, Esteban 28
Montcalm-Grozon, Louis-Joseph 15
Montgomery, Richard 30–1, 164
Morgan, Daniel 35, *40*, 40–1, 49, 60

▲ *Military bass drum of the period.*

N
naval warfare 210–11
boarding party weapons *237*
carronades *241*, 246
fleet actions 213–15
gun crews *240*, 240–1
Lake Champlain 218–19
landing parties 248–9
ordnance 246–7
raiders 216–17
swivel guns *241*
warship development 210–11

O
Otis, John 30

P
Phillips, Sir William 34, 38, 129, 152
Pickens, Andrew 38, 41
Pigot, Robert 37
Pitt, William, the Elder 15
Portugal 10
Prussia 16, 18, 170–1
Putnam, Israel 22

R
Riedesel, Baron von 195, 201
rifles 59, 83
Rochambeau, Jean-Baptiste 26, 27, 37, 43, 101, 170, *170*, 182
Rodney, Sir George 45, 214–15, *215*
Rogers, Robert 15, 48, 160
Russia 18

S
Saltonstall, Dudley 37, 245
Sampson, Deborah 104, 108
Simcoe, John Graves 25, 162, 163
slavery 12–13, 16, 20
Spain 10–11, 19, 28
American Revolution 30, 44, 169
artillery 206
black companies *205*
cavalry 206
colonial units 207
colours *176*, 177
Cuban militia 204, *205*
engineers 206
infantry 204–5
Louisiana Regiment *206*, *207*
musicians 205, *206*
Santo Domingo Volunteer Infantry *204*, *205*
staff officers 206–7
White Battalion of Cuba and Bayamo *207*
St Leger, Barrimore 29, 35, 166, 203
Stark, John 22, 34–5, 148
Steuben, Friedrich Wilhelm von 23, 35, 59, 80, *90*, 90–1
Stevens, General 55, 56
Stockbridge Indians 29, 82, 82
Sullivan, John 29, *37*, 167
Sumter, Thomas 38, 41

T
Tarleton, Banastre 25, 38, 41, 150, 161, 164

W
Waldeck, 3rd Infantry Regiment *197*
Ward, Artemius 22
warships 210–11
brigs 210, *217*
construction 211
cutters *217*
frigates 210, *212*, 213, *214*, *215*, 216
galleys *218*, 219
gunboats 218
gundalows 219
privateers *216*, 217
rating system 211
schooners *216*, 218
ships of the line 212, 213, *213*
sloops 210
Washington, George 7, 7, 14, *92*
Continental Army 22–3, 58, 89, 90, 106–7
militia 47, 49
Washington, William 40, 41, 94, 99, 101, 114, 116, 150, 161
Wayne, Anthony, 32, *33*, 36–7, 101, 149
West Indies 7, 44–5
Williams, Otho Holland 39, 40, 100, 150
Wolfe, James 15

ACKNOWLEDGEMENTS

The study of military uniforms is an inexact science. What soldiers wore at any particular time in military history is a subject of constant debate and is subject to at least three influences: what the pertinent regulation stated that they were supposed to wear; what period eyewitnesses have told us that they wore; and what the soldiers actually wore on the parade ground and in the field. In compiling this volume, we have tried to depict both what the soldiers were supposed to wear and what they actually did wear. Both primary and reliable secondary source material has been used, and it is certain that variations within the units depicted also existed. Each uniform is a snapshot of a particular unit, and may or may not reflect what was worn for the period covered in this book.

This is the first time I have worked with a co-author, and none can be better than Digby Smith, an eminent scholar and historian. He has helped me immeasurably over the past eight years. A good project manager is essential to the success of any writing project, and Joanne Rippin is a Desk Editor of the first rank. Patient, enduring, witty and supportive, she has put up with my many failings and deftly guided this project, and my thoroughly cluttered mind, through the writing and picture process in a Herculean manner. Thanks too to Jonathan North, an outstanding author, historian, and publisher in his own right, a dear friend and colleague to whom I owe a debt that can never be repaid. The artists who have illustrated the book have come through the fire with flying colours, and the talents of Simon Smith, Nick Spender, Jim Mitchell, Rob McCaig, Carlo Molinari, and Giuseppe Rava are evident on these pages.

Thanks also to the late Colonel John Elting, authority on the Grande Armee and American military history, professional soldier and teacher, who was the source of my desire to become a military historian. He was my dear friend and mentor, and the nearest thing I had to a father for thirty years. Last, but definitely not least, this book is dedicated to my dear wife, Daisy, and my beloved son, Michael, who is the blood of my heart. They have patiently put up with my moods and temper during the writing. Daisy is more than patient, helpful and critical, and Michael's hands are all over the pages of this volume. They are my faithful supporters and without them nothing would ever be completed.

We have been as accurate as possible in the research and writing of this volume, but undoubtedly errors will turn up. Any that do are mine alone.

Kevin F. Kiley

▼ *Trumpeter, 4th Continental Light Dragoons.*

Picture Acknowledgements

Figure artworks are the property and copyright of Anness Publishing Ltd. Additional images were supplied by the following agencies.

BRIDGEMAN ART LIBRARY: 210021 p2; 214830 p6b; 183565 p6t; 37673 p8; 153760 p12t; 245652 p16t; 88459 p16b; 248866 p17bl; 181388 p19t; 245684 p20t; 70126 p21b; 30346 p25; 192106 p26t; 257139 p30; 223552 p31t; 154555 p32b; 183944 p33t; 205172 p33b; 184366 p37tl; 254746 p37b; 11651 p38b; 184822 p39; 223514 p40t; 254756 p40b; 120433 p41t; 254751 p41b; 183569 p43t; 86115 p43b; 38974 p44t; 19374 p45t; 269799 p48b; 108901 p48t; 75662 p109; 86910 p124; 153197 p126; 214830-1 p168; 185145 p170; 113090 p171; 162135 p171; 49860 p208; 2378 p210; 55369 p211; 2376 p215. NORTH WIND PICTURE ARCHIVE: USVA2A-00006 p10t; EVNT2A-00239 p11b; EXPL2A-00209 p12b; SOC13A-00054 p13tl; EVNT2A-00027 p13tr; USMA2A-00005 p13b; C PPREZ-00085 p14t; EVNT2A-00011 p14b; HSET2A-00002 p20b; PREV2A-00028, p23t; EVRV2A-00182 p25b; NATI2A-00119 p29t; EVRV2A-00188 p35t; EVRV2A-00164 p49; PREV2A-00013 p90; EVRV2A-00022 p91; EVRV2A-00043 p91 reuse p251; EVRV2A-00185 p170; EVRV2A-00244 p211; EVRV2A-00216 p212 ; EVRV2A-00138 p215; EVRV2A-00153 p250. PETER NEWARK LIBRARY: pp7, 10b, 11t, 15 both, 17br, 18, 19b, 21t, 22, 23b, 24t, 25t, 26b, 27 both, 28 both, 29b, 31b, 34t, 35b, 36b, 37tr, 42, 44b, 45b, 46, 127.